MW00785763

INTELLIGENCE ANALYSIS

INTELLIGENCE ANALYSIS

HOW TO THINK IN COMPLEX ENVIRONMENTS

Wayne Michael Hall, Brigadier General (Retired), U.S. Army
and Gary Citrenbaum, Ph.D.

Foreword by Patrick M. Hughes, Lieutenant General (Retired), U.S. Army

An AUSA Book

PRAEGER SECURITY INTERNATIONAL

An Imprint of ABC-CLIO, LLC

A B C ✦ C L I O

Santa Barbara, California • Denver, Colorado • Oxford, England

Library of Congress Cataloging-in-Publication Data

Hall, Wayne Michael.
  Intelligence analysis : how to think in complex environments / Wayne Michael Hall and Gary Citrenbaum ; foreword by Patrick M. Hughes.
      p. cm. — (An AUSA book)
  Includes bibliographical references and index.
  ISBN 978-0-313-38265-9 (alk. paper) — ISBN 978-0-313-38266-6 (ebook)
  1. Intelligence service—Methodology. I. Citrenbaum, Gary. II. Title.
  JF1525.I6H347 2010
  327.12—dc22   2009045757

14 13 12 11 10   1 2 3 4 5

This book is also available on the World Wide Web as an eBook.
Visit www.abc-clio.com for details.

ABC-CLIO, LLC
130 Cremona Drive, P.O. Box 1911
Santa Barbara, California 93116–1911

This book is printed on acid-free paper ∞
Manufactured in the United States of America

Copyright Acknowledgment

The authors and publisher gratefully acknowledge permission for use of the following material:

Peter Paret, On War. © 1976 Princeton University Press, 2004 renewed PUP. Reprinted by permission of Princeton University Press.

Contents

Foreword

Do not go where the path may lead, go instead where there is no path and
leave a trail.

Ralph Waldo Emerson

Brigadier General Wayne M. "Mike" Hall (U.S. Army, Retired) has followed the literal and spiritual advice of Emerson; this book represents
breadcrumbs and footprints, broken branches and turned rocks, and spots
of blood along a newly blazed trail of intelligence knowledge. All you, dear
reader, have to do is follow the signs and discern the portents.

Those of us who have engaged in the function of "analysis"—working
to determine the nature and imminence of threats to our nation and to our
forces and capabilities that go in harm's way—know that the quality of
thought and the application of sound reasoning applied to the complex and
dynamic conditions we encounter are the most important variables in the
work of describing, characterizing, anticipating, and forecasting what has
happened and will happen next. A quotation from an uncertain source
points up the challenge: "Forecasting is risky business, especially about the
future." To paraphrase this thought: Training people to think in the crucible
of contemporary warfare and the alleyways of terrorism is very demanding
indeed, especially when the enemy does not cooperate.

Brigadier General (U.S. Army, retired) Wayne M. "Mike" Hall, the
principal author, and Dr. Gary Citrenbaum, his collaborator, have met this
challenge head on, through the noble endeavor of communicating

knowledge borne of direct personal experience and vicarious study. Their work is a template for analytic action and cognitive success. Their effort provides a set of ideas and principles that any practitioner of analysis can apply in their own way. It also provides room for both immutable standards and freedom to conceive and imagine. In short, this is a handbook for understanding that which might otherwise seem incomprehensible. You can see and know the enemy through the intellectual and perceptive prism they have provided.

After reading this epic work on "advanced analysis," a deep and sweeping look at the disciplines of observing, thinking, interpreting, describing, and finding meaning and import—we can readily imagine the authors, each tormented by contemporary challenges and shortcomings, spilling their best thoughts and impressive experience onto the professional canvas of intelligence analysis in the hope of enhancing (and perhaps fundamentally changing) the work that analysts perform.

This book is filled with glittering gems of insight, like the fact that "links decay," and the idea that "anticipation is the essential aspect of initiative." One chapter is impressively titled "Solutions." Another chapter on "Critical Thinking" concludes with a most unusual admonition: "If done correctly, critical thinking is a powerful force. But, to engage in critical thinking fully, the intelligence analyst has to be humble and introspective. They must also see and take on constructive criticism and improve their cognitive performance." This is very human work.

What Mike Hall has done is something many others have aspired to do, but few have accomplished: he has set forth an impressive collection of ideas and concepts, and the mechanical detail of how to undertake the attendant functions—in a way that resembles the kind of enduring thought and wisdom that is the stuff of "principles," those dependable enduring precepts that guide us through our endeavors.

These fungible "principles of analysis" may not be perfect, but they are clearly better than anything else that currently exists in one accessible volume (or anywhere else for that matter). This is one of the important aspects of Mike Hall's effort. He has put the full scope of analysis in a single volume in a way that flows from beginning to end as an interconnected and synergistic set of innovative methods, procedures, and concepts. This work has no functional limit—it can be applied in part or in its entirety as a vital source of direct information and motivational ideas. It can be used to do the work—now and in the future—that analysts do, at any level: national, strategic, operational, tactical, and individual.

His work is encyclopedic—and provides both gritty detail and broad substance for the art and science that we call "analysis." He provides a framework for "critical thinking" that is brilliant. He deals with the idea of "complexity"—a construct that contemporary conditions and circumstances compel us to come to grips with—in a realistic and utilitarian way.

He discusses "analytic conditions" with rare candor and insight, and one immediately understands that he has "been there and done that."

He develops the elements of "risk management" and "uncertainty" in the context of decision-making in a way that will clearly assist the inexperienced and the expert. He speaks intimately to analysts . . . using the old but well-proven dictum to "know your enemy." He recognizes the fact that a single human mind cannot possibly deal adequately with all the information available now from our sensors, sources, and methods, advocating the need for a "virtual knowledge environment," to assist in the cognitive and collaborative challenges of the modern complex operational environment.

One of the best aspects of this book is the presentation and explanation of sometimes obscure, esoteric, and arcane terms—but terms every analyst must know and come to use nonetheless. This book is a dictionary and a lexicon, a thesaurus, a workbook, a glossary, and an intellectual map through the wasteland of failed thought and vapid misperception. It provides a cognitive toolkit of words that reflect meaning and ideas, which empower the reader to undertake insightful thought and deliberate reason, using a common set of terms. Without something like this book, we are collectively a tower of analytic Babel. With it we have something like a combination of the Rosetta stone, the compass, the flashlight, and the microscope, connected to the best minds (the analysts) to aid them in achieving the singular goal of coherence.

To what purpose will the "advanced analysts" of the future put these tools and this knowledge? This book is a learning (and teaching) journey— a wormhole—into the future culture and context of "military intelligence," and it is fundamentally about providing the information necessary to defeat the enemy. That's the right focus, but it is important to note, as the book does, that the "enemy" has changed and the application of intelligence, including that derived from and by military intelligence capabilities, can often be applied to other conditions and circumstances that threaten global stability, transnational security, and regional interests of the United States and our allies . . . and the domestic security of our nation.

The book moves from thinking, planning, and preparing, to gathering and amalgamation, to analysis, and finally to synthesis (the essence of analysis) and delivery in a way that gives every analyst a utility map of their discipline. In order to apply this imaginative cognitive pathway we must consider the context in which it occurs.

Technology has empowered much of the discipline and most of the functions of military intelligence; concurrently technology has become a dynamic component of threat and presents a challenge to our intelligence and operational efforts. Human terrain—the culture, society, and human condition in which we act—has become a critical component of our war fighting and our stabilizing functions. Signatures, reflections, emissions, anomalies against the ambient background, events outside the norm, and the speed, tempo, geo-location, area, and environmental composition are changing.

We are now forced by conditions extant to deal with all points of the compass, with all hazards and all threats, conventional,, unconventional, irregular, asymmetric or asynchronous, and to provide information that will assist in the effective and efficient application of military capabilities in response to domestic disasters and emergencies—not just the traditional organized enemies of the past, marching row on row.

The forces of emergence and convergence, which present amplified and compounded pressures against our goals,, besiege us. We are forced in many cases to deal with threats submerged in the sea of people—in a world in which shortly more than 7 billion will jostle and thrust for place and advantage.

We anticipate the likelihood of engaging in kinetic and non-kinetic military operations in complex urban environs (CUE) unlike any other context that we have ever operated in before. The prospect of entering, controlling, and containing cities with millions of people defies standard military approaches.

We are also anticipating the possibility of having to confront enemies that may employ weapons with mass and complex effects (WMCE). We will attempt to understand such conditions before such employment becomes an operational reality that demands a response.

We are deliberating on the meaning of dynamic environmental, biological, and chemical conditions and their impact on our stability.

We are concerned about our borders and the entry into our social order of people whose intent is inimical to our beliefs and values.

We are searching the far regions and the nooks and crannies of cyberspace to find the enemies that lurk in the digital domain, and we are watching the development of criminal subcultures that have impact on our nation's security. We are anticipating warfare in this same environment.

We are concerned with every dimension and every condition because in each and every aspect of what they represent—we can find threats to our nation and our people.

Things have changed . . .

It may seem that tradition has flown, the winds of change are strong, and the weave of our societal fabric is fraying. Mike Hall gives us the knowledge we need to work with modern information systems and to build upon unprecedented access to the many conditions and circumstances of the global and universal context—to meet the challenges of the coming age and to find solutions to the very real intelligence problems we face. This work is a modern handbook, a companion compendium, a reference, a treatise, and perhaps a blueprint for future forms . . . for the evolution of the function of analysis. It is a required volume for every serious analyst who values the work they do and the effort it takes to do it. No analytic library will be complete without this book.

For the analyst-reader: Mike Hall gets inside your head and roams through your thoughts, your concerns, and your own ideas, with a familiarity that you will recognize as being from "one of us." This is powerful stuff—if only the reader will take the time and gain the focus that this work demands. Easy—no! Worthwhile—yes! Even vital! A signal effort that standing alone provides a beacon for analysts to guide their work through the shoals and reefs of their particular roiling operational sea.

I wish I'd written this book. General Mike Hall and his collaborator, Dr. Gary Citrenbaum, have done it for us all. We owe them a debt of gratitude.

Patrick M. Hughes
Lieutenant General (Retired), U.S. Army
July 2009

Lieutenant General Patrick M. Hughes is a former Assistant Secretary of the Office of Information Analysis (Intelligence) at the Department of Homeland Security. He was a successful consultant to the U.S. Government and to many defense and security companies, and served as Director of the Defense Intelligence Agency, Director of Intelligence (J-2) of the Joint Staff, and Director of Intelligence (J-2) at U.S. Central Command. He also commanded several major U.S. military intelligence organizations, and worked as a collector and analyst for many years. He is currently the Vice President for Intelligence & Counterterrorism for a major defense, aerospace, and security company.

Acknowledgments

I started writing this book in my mind and on paper in 1984 when I attended the U.S. Army's School of Advanced Military Studies (SAMS). In particular, I thought about Hegel's synthesis of the dialectic, Clausewitz's synthesis of the battlefield in *On War*, and Sun Tzu's synthesis of leadership, planning, execution, and deception in his time and operational context in his treatise *The Art of War*. During our many "skull" sessions, my classmates and I (in particular my great friend Colonel [Retired] Mike Tanksley) debated and often argued long into the night about war, how intelligence plays in war, and in particular, how the opponent perceives, thinks, plans, decides, acts, and receives feedback, the importance of the initiative, and decision-making influence. It was a great year, and I'll always be indebted to Brigadier General (Retired) Huba Wass de Czege (the father of SAMS) and my small group seminar leader, Lieutenant Colonel (Retired) Dr. Doug Johnson. It was in SAMS that I experienced the thrill of learning and thinking about complex subject matter. It was in SAMS I learned that "how to think," is complementary to "what to think" and, in most cases, is the superior portion of the relationship.

I became the G2 (intelligence officer) of the 82 Airborne Division in 1987. To prepare for the work, I studied U.S. Army intelligence preparation of the battlefield (IPB) doctrine and realized it was a synthesis of many parts and pieces of the battlespace, including enemy, friendly, the populace, infrastructure, and friendly operations. It was in this difficult role that I started thinking that we should not call the essence of our intelligence work *analysis*, as the word means to break apart into increasingly smaller pieces. Instead, we should think about our intelligence thinking work as culminating in synthesis, which is a related but different thought than analysis.

Synthesis—bringing the parts we have broken into a whole whose value is greater than the sum of its parts when melding several combinations and relationships into a new whole—is a powerful concept and is one of the fundamentals of *Intelligence Analysis: How to Think in Complex Environments*. Three of my many great analysts included CW2 Roger Swinford, Major Mike Nifong, and then Captain Dave King. After experiencing many deployments to Honduras, Panama, Saudi Arabia, and Iraq with the 82d as the G2 and as commander of 313th Military Intelligence Battalion, I attended the National War College. There, with ample time to think, I wrote an article on synthesis in intelligence operations that was published in the *Military Intelligence Professional Bulletin* in the spring of 1992—"Intelligence Analysis in the 21st Century." I also wrote a paper for the War College on synthesis of planning—"Shaping the Future: A Holistic Approach to Planning," which the Association of the United States Army (AUSA) later turned into an essay with the title of "Holistic Thinking and Planning." In addition, I wrote about intelligence analysis in urban environments in a paper for AUSA called "The Janus Paradox," which I presented at the AUSA annual meeting in the fall of 2000. I also wrote about many aspects of intelligence analysis in my first book, *Stray Voltage: War in the Information Age*, which was published in the spring of 2003.

My thoughts about intelligence analysis continued to germinate as a brigade commander and J2 of U.S. Forces and Deputy C2 in Korea from 1994 to 1998. During these four years, my people and I worked hard to help others and ourselves learn how to think about analysis and synthesis, and even established a mystery program in which each intelligence analyst had a mystery to study about North Korea and would periodically brief me, my field grade officers, my staff officers, and when still in brigade command, my company and battalion commanders on their work to solve the mystery. During my brigade command, I was privileged to work on intelligence analysis with then Lieutenant Colonels Harry Bakken, Clyde Harthcock, Perry Hargrove, Tony Chaney, Jerry Proctor, Howard Baum, John O'Shaunessey, then Majors Mary Legere, Yvette Nonte, Scott Levin, Jerry Sharp, Mike Hall (no relation), CW3 Keith Hall (no relation), then Captains Matt Whitney, Ryan Whittington, Jenny Grisbeck, Lisa Price, and many other commissioned officers, warrant officers, and noncommissioned officers. As the USFK J2, I was blessed with great people—then Colonel Monte Montes, Mr. Steve Kinker, Mr. Frank Kleckner, and then Major John Anderson. All of these people contributed to my thoughts and helped me expand my thinking about intelligence analysis and push it further in both theory and training during sometimes eight-hour quarterly training briefings, mystery programs, and numerous sessions of questions and answers via Socratic interaction.

Upon returning to the United States, I was the director of a study about the future of Army Military Intelligence. I used a technique of dividing the task and vision into many panels and brought numerous very bright people together to enmesh their thoughts into the study and to make recommendations for the Chief of Staff of the Army. One of these groups involved intelligence analysis. The analytic panel labored mightily for weeks and came up with many terrific ideas. I learned much from this collective group, and undoubtedly have incorporated many of the thoughts that came forth as recommendations into my overall thinking about intelligence analysis. I remain indebted to these fine military soldiers and civilians for their contributions to my thinking about the advancement of intelligence analysis.

Following retirement, I gradually became a consultant in intelligence, knowledge operations, and information operations. I was able to work for Joint Forces Command for several years in experimentation ranging from huge experiments such as Millennium Challenge 02 to experiments such as Unified Resolve 04 and 05, where we worked at the BCT level of operation. I am indebted to General (Retired) Gary Luck for bringing me into the consulting business and mentoring me about "how to think," and encouraging me to think creatively and boldly about intelligence analysis to support current and future operations. He always inspired me to think deeply about many subjects, and he will always be a great friend and role model. I am also indebted to Mr. Duane Schattle, who was the Director of JFCOM's Joint Urban Operation Office (JUOO). Duane and his fine band of forward-thinking and hard-working people not only highlighted challenges with urban intelligence, surveillance, and reconnaissance (ISR), but also encouraged me to think about and pursue the subject of advanced analysis from which *Intelligence Analysis* emerged.

During my work for the JUOO, I had the opportunity to bring in some very smart and experienced people to think about some of the complicated aspects of advanced analysis and a virtual knowledge environment we called the Distributed Decision Support System (D2S2) Virtual Brain. During our ruminations at Suffolk and Fairfax, Virginia, odds and ends of people and groups talked, thought, and argued. I want to acknowledge some of the many people who contributed to and inspired my thinking about the subject of advanced analysis. Sometimes we didn't know much about particular aspects of advanced analysis other than to conclude there was something substantive there, but we batted around ideas and debated a host of subjects that certainly influenced my thinking and motivated me to think more and more about the subject that culminated in the book I wrote from December 2007 to June 2008. First and foremost, I want to acknowledge the contributions to my thinking of my friend and business partner Dr. Gary Citrenbaum. He has listened to my ruminations about intelligence analysis since 2001, when we first met at a JFCOM experiment. He and I have talked about intelligence analysis for years and I am indebted to him for helping me mature my thoughts, and of course for writing the excellent chapter on technology to support advanced analysis in *Intelligence Analysis*. In addition, among the people I want to acknowledge and recognize as participating in discussions and thereby contributing to my thinking about intelligence analysis in *Intelligence Analysis* are: Michael Scheuer, Dr. Bill Anderson, MD, Gene Poteat, Frank Anderson, Colonel (Retired) Carol Stewart, Martha Kessler, Colonel (Retired) Pat Lang, Colonel (Retired) Harry Bakken, Ed Levitt, Mark Finkelstein, Dr. Pauletta Otis, Dr. Russ Glenn, Andre Kesteloot, Hayder Alhamdani, and Kadhim Al Waeli.

I also need to thank Dr. Roger Cirillo. He encouraged me to write my first book, *Stray Voltage: War in the Information Age,* and he has helped me immensely in persevering with *Intelligence Analysis*. Roger is a very smart person and totally dedicated to excellence and doing what is right. He has just the personality and love of reading and thinking to keep pushing the Association of the U.S. Army's (AUSA) book program so the Army's soldiers can buy books at a reasonable price and enjoy a variety of military and security related books.

Last but not least, I need to acknowledge the thoughts and editing work of my wife, Colonel (Retired) Sandra Hall. She has inspired me over the years with a treasure trove of great thoughts, many of which I have woven into *Intelligence Analysis*. She has persevered in putting up with my moodiness and exhaustion while writing the book and in editing the manuscript many times, all the while still maintaining a lively discussion with me about the complexities and issues associated with intelligence analysis.

Wayne Michael Hall
Suffolk, Virginia

Introduction

> Intelligence analysts should be self-conscious about their reasoning process. They should think about *how they make* [emphasis added] judgments and reach conclusions, not just about the judgments and conclusions themselves.[1]

Arguably, intelligence analysis is among the most critical of human skills in conducting military operations against insurgent and irregular adversaries. One can peruse the annals of insurgencies and operations against irregular adversaries and an implication leaps forth: when engaging in urban operation environments (OEs), it is imperative to know and understand not only the enemy, the weather, and the terrain, but also the populace, culture, local customs, accepted social mores, and the supporting infrastructure. It is not enough to know the populace superficially. After all, it is within the populace that an insurgency blends, thrives, survives, and operates. To know the populace, one has to know and understand how people think, perceive, and view the world, as well as what they hold dear, how they view foreigners, and how they understand their desires, goals, and objectives. We must understand the culture well enough to use it to our advantage, not merely to cope and be aware.

Intelligence analysis helps us know and understand our insurgent enemy and his objectives, will, intent, and motives. At this time and far into the future, intelligence analysts must develop knowledge, find well-hidden targets, and satisfy vastly different information requirements than in the past. Through intelligence analysis we understand the fluidity of the OE. Through intelligence analysis we know where, how, and when to collect.

Through intelligence analysis we take collection-produced data and turn it into information, knowledge, and understanding for leaders' decision-making processes. But it is not through traditional intelligence analysis that we will come to know these things. It is through a different kind of intelligence analysis—*advanced analysis*—that we will come to know how to think about and subsequently use such knowledge to conduct intelligence operations to support decision-making in urban operational settings.

Why do we need a more specific kind of intelligence analysis? It is partially because traditional intelligence reference documents do not define intelligence analysis per se. Joint Publication 2.0, Intelligence, for example, defines intelligence as: The product resulting from the collection, processing, integration, evaluation, analysis, and interpretation of available information concerning foreign nations, hostile or potentially hostile forces or elements, or areas of actual or potential operations.[2] This publication also defines all-source intelligence as: Intelligence products and/or organizations and activities that incorporate all sources of information, most frequently including human resources intelligence, imagery intelligence, measurement and signature intelligence, signals intelligence, and open-source data in the production of finished intelligence.[3] But it does not define intelligence analysis. It is surprising that a guiding doctrinal document of this importance neither defines nor discusses intelligence analysis as a field of knowledge and a discipline of thought. This bland treatment of something as important as intelligence analysis, particularly in urban counterinsurgency and irregular warfare operations, prompted this book and its *raison d' être—advanced analysis*.

Advanced analysis is both a field of knowledge and a discipline of thought. It is appropriate for this day and age and is designed to help commanders make decisions in complex environments. It is also designed to help analysts be aggressive and to seek, find, and seize the initiative. Therefore, let us delve ever so briefly into advanced analysis with the promise of more discussion to come. Advanced analysis is: *the high-level cognitive processes producing specific, detailed thought and understanding of the OE, and knowledge superior to that possessed by the adversary.* Advanced analysis has 14 cognitive elements—decomposition; critical thinking; link; pattern; trend; anticipatory; technical; anomaly; tendency; cultural; semiotics; aggregation analysis; recomposition; and synthesis. This definition and the 14 elements of advanced analysis will be presented, discussed, and defended throughout this book.

Although it performed superbly in the past, traditional intelligence analysis is neither broad nor deep enough to provide sufficient cognitive support to planners, decision makers, and operators in a counterinsurgency and in operations against irregular adversaries. Let me briefly introduce what I am talking about. In a broad sense, intelligence analysis isn't specific enough to work on the nuance and subtleties involved with intelligence operations in urban settings and when working against embedded insurgents and terrorists. In addition, intelligence analysis isn't anticipatory enough to advise commanders how to outthink the enemy, seize the initiative, and use it for not just one, but a multitude of advantages—e.g., *freedom of maneuver, position, decision, knowledge, tempo, momentum,* and *technology.* Furthermore, intelligence analysts are not involved enough in collection—intelligence analysts need to develop very specific observables and direct collection efforts. Intelligence analysts must be involved with analytic condition-setting such as thinking about and designing knowledge, sensor, and data architectures to support the inputs and outputs of advanced analysis. In addition, the analyst must learn to engage in a thought process that is analytic wargaming to learn how to compete with adversaries for the initiative. Intelligence analysts are not sufficiently trained and educated in diverse subjects like anticipation, culture, semiotics, and technology (in a city) to be of maximum value in outwitting a capable enemy and understanding the culture in which they operate. Unfortunately, intelligence analysts do not receive sufficient training in some needed aspects of intelligence analysis to be effective, such as how to decompose and recompose, how to engage in and use tendency, aggregation, and anomaly analysis, how to think about and employ finer points of thought and more sophistication in link, pattern, and trend analysis, and finally how to engage in synthesis.

These shortfalls in analytic training, education, and operations are not the fault of the courageous and talented people who perform analytic work today. It is, sadly enough, the defense institution's fault, as it has not yet engaged in the hard thinking work to first understand what is needed to support intelligence operations in urban settings, and then to set about to change intelligence analysis to produce thinking sufficient to go after insurgent, irregular warrior, and terrorist threats in large urban settings no matter where the city might be located. Each of these subjects will be discussed in depth throughout the book.

Intelligence analysis to support urban operations against irregular adversaries and counterinsurgency operations must broaden in scope, significantly change the specificity of its focus, provide the cognitive capabilities for intellectually aggressive analysts to use, be underpinned by a philosophy, and employ a new system of thought. As such, it will include fourteen essential cognitive elements of advanced analysis, use five types of observables to guide collection, recompose and synthesize data to make sense of it, and aggressively and passionately engage the enemy in a war of wits to continuously win this struggle. Further, advanced analysis will be fungible in three respects:

First, its thought processes and "how to think" philosophy are appropriate for the full spectrum of future conflict.
Second, it provides "a way" to think that transcends locations or regional peculiarities. Advanced analysis can bore into immense detail at one location while

working as the cognitive means to develop strategic intelligence in another part of the world.

Third, it is applicable to a broader audience than the Department of Defense. That is, advanced analysis is applicable to homeland security analytic work as well as commercial corporation analysis. Regardless of location or its varieties of use, people using advanced analysis must perform against and defeat the minds of the modern threat not by happenstance, but purposefully.

This book does more than complain about a long-standing and well-known problem. It offers a detailed explanation of a new system of thought, ways to overcome analytic shortfalls, and a way to improve cognitive capabilities for using advanced analysis as a weapon system that can result in winning a constant war of wits around the world, all the time. This book, in its essence, advocates a way to overcome cognitive shortfalls that plague intelligence analysts today, offers ways to improve analytic cognition, and provides suggestions on how to proceed in awakening the intellects of advanced analysts.

Designing a different system of thought sufficient to outwit a capable adversary in every aspect of competition is a daunting task. Compounding the task at hand, many issues exist that must be dealt with to optimize advanced analysis, influence leaders' decisions, and survive over time. For example, there is a cognition understanding issue. There is a technology-assist issue. There are training and education issues. There are materiel issues such as modeling and simulation (M&S) to support advanced analysis. In addition, organizational process and procedure issues exist and influence outcomes. Further, policy issues abound, as intelligence analysis cuts across agencies, foreign countries, state and local governments, and private security organizations. Regardless of the difficulties, we must press on and make the case for advanced analysis. When the reader reaches the last page, we hope they will agree that we need advanced analysis and that America can do what is needed to bring it into being and to institutionalize it.

The following thoughts provide a brief glimpse of the main points you will read about throughout the book. It provides ideas about advanced intelligence analysis that:

- Provide a definition for *advanced analysis*, as the high-level cognitive processes producing specific, detailed thought and understanding of the OE, and knowledge superior to that possessed by the adversary.
- Work with individual or combinations of 14 cognitive elements of advanced analysis: *decomposition, critical thinking, link, trend, pattern, technical, anticipatory, anomaly, aggregation, tendency, cultural, semiotics analysis, recomposition,* and *synthesis.*
- Drive collection and make sense of resultant collection data, make sense of other data, develop information, and provide knowledge.

- Call for analysts to work as a team with collection specialists to optimize combinations of sensors, data, analysts, subject matter experts (SMEs), and data specialists.
- Advocate advanced analysts to partner with collection specialists to provide locations, times, expected outcomes, five kinds of observables, and analytic standards to focus collection.
- Help people learn to think like the enemy while minimizing their cultural biases.
- Advocate understanding and using the culture in question sufficiently well to do more than just being "aware," and instead to know the culture to actively seek, gain, and exploit advantages (e.g., freedom of maneuver, position, decision, knowledge, tempo, momentum, and technology).
- Develop and work with five kinds of observables: *cultural, technical, functional, situational,* and *biometric.*
- Provide aggressive, anticipatory thinking to engage and win in a war of wits with insurgents and irregular warriors around the world.
- Provide "a way" for analysts to set three types of conditions to succeed: *knowledge, sensor,* and *data* architectures.
- Require analysts to work in an organized and disciplined way with subject matter experts (SMEs) from a virtual knowledge environment (VKE).
- Depend on three kinds of up-to-date baseline databases—*technical, functional,* and *cultural.*
- Support two pillars of operational decision-making: lowering risk and reducing uncertainty.
- Explain in layman's terms the relationship of intelligence analysis with some aspects of complexity theory.
- Advocate the constant use of red teaming experts to help with precluding errors in thought and logic.
- Use technology to obtain advantages over adversaries and other competitors.
- Advocate seizing and holding the initiative and show how the advanced analyst plays an active role in this continuous struggle.
- Recompose and synthesize collected data into information and knowledge.

This introduction established the setting for reading and understanding the information that follows. It lists the most significant thoughts of advanced analysis with a promise to discuss them in more depth throughout the book. In addition, the introduction briefly identifies some of the shortfalls upon which advanced analysis improves. With these introductory thoughts in mind, we now turn to broadening our understanding of an urban OE. Gaining an understanding of the OE, complete with threat, provides the reader with an appreciation as to why any urban OE presents enormous challenges to all those who enter its domain, but in particular to the intelligence analyst. Although this book is not a primer on all OEs, it does discuss some common characteristics of urban OEs that intelligence analysts will always have to work with.

The OE in the context of this work is, "A composite of the conditions, circumstances, and influences that affect the employment of capabilities and bear on the decisions of the commander."[4] The OE is all-powerful and influences, as the definition states, commanders, their planning and decisions, and their organizations as well as the people, processes, activities, and organizations that exist in the space, processes, and influences of the OE.

Providing the means and explanation for improving intelligence analysts' thinking capabilities is the essence of the book. With this in mind, the book uses the following broad logic—discuss the OE, identify problems or shortfalls, identify and discuss ways to overcome the shortfalls, explain in depth the elements of advanced analysis, provide some technologies that will assist the analyst in this difficult endeavor, and tie all of the ideas in the book into a tapestry of meaning. This tapestry will close the book and provide a discussion of a system of thought, including the philosophy of advanced analysis, synthesis, and implications. It will also provide recommendations in the closing chapter.

Part I

The Continuous War of Wits

1

The Operational Environment

The urban OE is complex and fluid, primarily because of the nature of busy cities, the movement of people and machines, the invisible movement of data and RF energy, and the constant interaction of complex adaptive systems (CAS) as they intersect and collide. In addition, our enemies operate in the urban OE to accomplish their strategies and goals. They view it as a safe haven owing to the strangeness of the foreign, urban OE to American individuals and organizations. It is this notion of the criticality of the urban OE as a perceived safe haven that is so important to the embedded insurgent[1] and therefore must be of high importance to the advanced intelligence analyst. Quite simply, the insurgent cannot be allowed to view the urban OE as an unassailable base. Be that as it may, the insurgent will often use urban areas to set conditions for success, but he will pick and choose the times to venture into open terrain or engage in a pitched fight against U.S. military forces. Because cities are fluid with commerce, population activities, ethnic diversity and interaction, and fluctuating levels of activities, transactions, and behaviors, it is quite simple for an insurgent or terrorist to blend into the immensity of the city and remain mostly hidden. As an additional complication, globalization has arrived and enables information to flow rapidly to all corners of the earth in near real time. Thomas Friedman describes this phenomenon as the democratization of technology, and it

> is what is enabling more and more people, with more and more home computers, modems, cellular phones, cable systems, and Internet connections

to reach farther and farther, into more and more countries, faster and faster, deeper and deeper, cheaper and cheaper than ever before in history. The demise of distance has arrived, as people travel around the globe in a matter of hours, not days. People communicate around the world in an instant—information has been a main contributor to the term "global earth."[2]

When considering the OE and its enormous influence on intelligence analysis, we have to consider some characteristics that can intervene with commander's decisions, command and control, and intelligence analysis. One of these characteristics is a condition that surfaced earlier but was not discussed in depth. That is, the fluidity of a large, urban OE and its influence on all urban operations. Fluidity means everything is moving and constantly changing, even at night. People come and go, organizations conduct business, and the society in general is vibrant and dynamic. The fluidity also implies a connectedness among all people, all organizations, and all activities. In one way or another, when something happens in this fluid environment, its consequences ripple and create waves of energy and change not unlike throwing a pebble into a pond.

This environment is also complex. "Complex," in this situation, has several applications the intelligence analyst must consider. Although this work does not go into the scientific aspects of complexity theory, it does recognize the importance of complexity in urban settings and applies a few of its characteristics to advanced analysis. In brief, some of those thoughts follow now and will be discussed more at intervals throughout the book:

- *First,* what happens in a city is nonlinear. *Nonlinear* means "of or relating to a device whose behavior is described by a set of nonlinear equations and whose output is not proportional to its input."[3] A nonlinear problem has effects disproportional to its causes; therefore, it is difficult to solve and often impossible to predict with any degree of preciseness.
- *Second,* in a complex environment, small activities or events can cause enormous outcomes far greater in influence than the initiating event. This understanding is important in working with anticipating and understanding second- and third-order effects.
- *Third,* a complex environment appears chaotic because everything is moving and changing. Intermingling of people, machines, organizations, religion, and culture contribute to the turbulence and appearance of motion. But there is order in the chaos; however, people have to know much about the environment to be capable of finding the underlying order that could indicate, for example, the insurgents' condition-setting occurring amongst the normal hectic activities and bustle of a busy city.
- *Fourth,* a complex environment has sensitive variables. Variables involve change. Change comes with inducement or stimulation. Some change is stable and understandable. But when sensitive variables are at play, nothing is stable or understandable. It is the presence of volatile sensitive variables that are often the catalyst for exponential leaps in out-

comes, as in the just-discussed second- and third-order effects. In addition, along with sensitive variables influencing events in an urban OE, there will be windows of opportunity for influence—some with friendly forces, some with the enemy, and some with the host nation, neutrals, and host nation government.

- *Fifth*, in complex environments, one can find complex adaptive systems (CAS). CAS are

  a dynamic network of many agents (which may represent cells, species, individuals, firms, nations) acting in parallel, constantly acting and reacting to what the other agents are doing. The control of a CAS tends to be highly dispersed and decentralized. If there is to be any coherent behavior in the system, it has to arise from competition and cooperation among the agents themselves. The overall behavior of the system is the result of a huge number of decisions made every moment by many individual agents.[4]

- *Sixth*, in a complex environment, discerning causes from effects often proves difficult. Although important for our discussion in complex environments, this phenomenon has existed throughout the ages, as Clausewitz tells us in *On War*:

  in war, as in life generally, all parts of a whole are interconnected and thus the effects produced, however small their cause, must influence all subsequent military operations and modify their final outcome to some degree, however slight. In the same way, every means must influence even the ultimate purpose.[5]

CAS are important in the intelligence analyst's life for several reasons and will be discussed in several places throughout the book. Suffice it to say at this early point in our intellectual journey, CAS intersect, collide, and career off of one another sometimes by accident and sometimes in a purposeful way. They always compete with one another. As such, they learn from their activities and their environment, and adjust to out-compete their opponents. As a side effect, they constantly learn and adjust, thereby contributing to the dynamism and chaos of the OE. CAS always have niches of like-minded counterparts and gravitate toward them. In this way, suicide bombers gravitate to people who can employ them. CAS anticipate and attempt to predict to improve their odds of surviving and responding to perturbations in the environment. However, the outcomes of CAS activities are essentially unpredictable.

Often the OE will be populated with people who are xenophobic. This means having abnormal fear or hatred of the strange or foreign.[6] This state of being has a deleterious effect on intelligence analysis and collection, as one of the primary sources of information in an urban OE lies in individuals and human intelligence (HUMINT) they collect. If people possess this fear of foreigners, the flow of data coming from the populace will be slower than any aggressive analyst aspires to receive. A portion of the populace may often be in support of or at least sympathetic to the cause and activities of the insurgent. This support allows for a safe haven and places to perform both condition-setting and actual insurgent operations, all in the shadow of the occupying force or the hated foreign supporters of the government.

In all large urban OE, there is one underlying fact that affects everything else. It affects the thoughts of analysts and commanders who require valuable knowledge to make decisions. It comes from the complexity of the OE and the nature of the threat, and what is required to meet him, seize and retain the initiative, and defeat him soundly, not only in his own mind but also in the mind of the populace upon whom he depends. A city is always moving and changing. We have discussed how complex adaptive systems play a role in this fluidity. The many individuals who inhabit the city are each making decisions and carrying them out—each influences the whole. With a changing OE, missions will change, sometimes very rapidly. With rapid changes in mission come changes in decisions. With changes in decisions come changes in knowledge requirements to drive down risk and improve uncertainty. With pressure for such actionable and accurate knowledge comes stress on the intelligence surveillance and reconnaissance (ISR) system. With stress on the ISR system, the principal people under pressure to perform are intelligence analysts and collection specialists who are responsible for providing the actionable knowledge.

Now let us proceed to a brief and focused discussion about the threat portion of the OE. Our enemy is different than we faced in the past. We face a savvy, global, technologically capable, and adaptive threat whose intent is to kill Americans and impose a way of life that is antithetical to American values. Our intelligence services are in a constant war of wits against this formidable enemy. The object is, of course, to outthink the enemy, anticipate his moves, and thwart his attacks or break up his synchronization before any attacks occur. The insurgent has to be smart and adaptive because the conventional force outnumbers him—this is one of the most important reasons for beckoning the conventional force into the city in the first place. Author Dr. James Schneider tells us some of what he learned when reviewing T. E. Lawrence's original papers concerning what an insurgent must do to excel:

> In an insurgency, empathy plays an especially crucial role; it places the leader inside the hearts and minds of his men. He knows immediately and intuitively the physical and the psychological limits of his own troops. In guerrilla warfare the insurgent must always operate at the limits of normal human endurance—and often beyond—to maintain a moral advantage over his more powerful conventional enemy.[7]

The challenge begins because insurgents often look like locals, come from the same ethnic and religious backgrounds and speak the same language, have excellent security apparatuses, are paranoid, and avoid moving or doing things in broad daylight. Insurgents operate surreptitiously from their networks and have excellent security and secrecy. Their talents to hide and perform in secret have been handed down from generation to generation, and many of them have excellent skills of survival learned by surviving during the difficult times that come with living under repressive political regimes. These well-hidden nodes and links move, change, and morph, making them difficult to find and influence. Insurgent adversaries are often educated, creative, and smart. They learn well and share their learning quickly. U.S. intelligence analysts are in a race to seek, find, and sustain not only a learning advantage but an intellectual advantage over the threats in an urban OE as well. In essence, they have to outwit the adversary and anticipate where the adversary's thinking and actions are going. The insurgents' activities constantly change, owing to the enemy's proclivity to learn from their mistakes and from U.S. responses, and they quickly share their knowledge with their networked colleagues.

The networks the enemy uses are often invisible to America's sensors and analysts. These networks are the enemy's principal means to power. As one noted author explains, networks are extremely communicative and resilient:

> the typology of a small-world network is also able to adapt to changing circumstances and solve unforeseen obstacles in the execution of general plans . . . operations involve much uncertainty and many unanticipated obstacles. . . . network of information processors, where the network handles large volumes of information efficiently without overloading any individual processor. The self-organizing hubs and nodes topology of a small-world network or the dense topology of a clique performs this function very well. Communications are possible horizontally among multiple nodes, allowing them to solve their problems locally without having to refer them upward . . . This flexibility and local initiative of small-world networks and cliques contrast with the rigidity of hierarchies, which do not adapt well to ambiguity but are excellent at exerting control.[8]

Networks are difficult to describe, and they cannot be squeezed or manipulated into a mathematical formula or a program evaluation and review technique (PERT) chart to help people with engineering backgrounds understand their characteristics, purposes, and operations. What we can all agree to is that the enemy's networks contribute significantly to his success or failure. In addition, there are some commonalities among all networks, but in particular networks supporting an insurgency. The insurgent must receive support from the populace to exist and thrive. Insurgent networks represent a philosophy—of organization, learning, leadership, resilience, and of secrecy. The enemy's network is an organizational construct for accomplishing strategies and goals/objectives. The enemy's network depends on money, recruits, secrecy, security, and the movement of data, information, and knowledge. Further, the enemy's network is robust in that it can incur destruction of multiple cells and links but still survive.

The insurgent network's links are technical, human/social, organizational, functional, and thought/intent. These links are connections that come and go. The enemy's networks are for the most part flat and decentralized. In these networks, information sharing and movement occur quickly, allowing quick decisions, which in turn enable quick action and outcome assessments. A network adjusts rapidly to the changing environment and thrives on up-to-date valuable knowledge. The enemy's network is not a hierarchy; its leaders are empowered to make decisions without having to work through the layering of a traditional western organizational structure. These foes work with mission orders and their leaders' intent.

Insurgents and terrorists have excellent operational security, and they hide well. They present immense challenges to the anticipating and pursuing intelligence analyst as the insurgents cover their activities with cultural noise and culturally laden deceptive activities. One author provides reinforcement of this thought with the following excerpt from a *Military Review* article:

> The nature of the Afghan and Iraqi societies makes the populace expert at hiding, dissimulating, and deceiving. Loyalties are to family, close associates, fellow villagers, and clan or tribal members.[9]

These capabilities cause them to be very difficult to notice, let alone to find. Thus, the challenge for the advanced analyst is to understand the OE, understand the culture, and understand the enemy, and how all three relate. At the center of the struggle to outwit the enemy is learning how he thinks, plans, makes decisions, acts, receives feedback, and adjusts, by learning from his perspectives and thoughts. Find, fix, and finish–type of philosophy and decision-making cannot work without such cognition. To support commanders' decisions, analysts must think more broadly to gain depth of knowledge and find relationships leading to a well-hidden foe. They must find, track, and neutralize embedded terrorists and insurgents and do so without committing gross errors of logic, without creating undo negative outcomes through ill-conceived actions and a corollary increase in credibility problems with the populace, and without causing unwarranted collateral damage to the populace and personal and commercial property.

U.S. intelligence analysts have to look for and find links and relationships— the enemy insurgents', the populace's, neutral organizations', commercial corporations', and ours. The enemy's cellular connections or links are like gossamer in a flower garden. When we stand in a flower garden and the warm sun shines just right and the wind softly brushes across our faces, we sometimes see a single, fine, filmy, resilient strand of a cobweb—a gossamer. But in the twinkling of an eye, the gossamer disappears from our view. We know it is there but we cannot see it anymore. So it is with insurgents and terrorist's links: the mechanical connections, runners and couriers, logistical people bringing supplies, movement specialists, social relationships, intelligence collectors, organizational functions and processes, and direct action people are all mobile and, with that mobility, change and movement occur easily. Sometimes we can see the movement, links, and activities supporting the enemy's networks; at other times there are no visible indicants of such support. Hence, we face a persistent propensity to believe that the enemy's networks are invisible.

The enemy's networks give him the means to power. His network mimics some aspects of nature, as Dr. James Schneider tells us: "because insurgents have the physical characteristics of a fluid and the cybernetic structure of a hive, they are the most evolved of human networks."[10] In a general sense, an insurgency network has several characteristics:

1. It is difficult to kill but, if found, it can be stunned.
2. Any network has functions, physical and nonphysical characteristics, forms, connecting links, nodes, purposes, and dependencies.
3. Network activities in large urban settings most often are invisible to the western eye and mind owing to the people who make up the network. In addition, the enemy is buried within the culture in which they operate and, in fact, the enemy is often populated by people from the culture in question.
4. Because a small number of illicit activities occur within a large number of legitimate activities, the illicit is obscured.
5. The enemy and his network have absolute dependencies without which they could not successfully operate. Some of the more important dependencies include: secrecy, security, intelligence, movement of information, ability to learn and adapt, population support, purpose, intent, money, and recruiting, among others.
6. The network's links come and go—sometimes they are visible and sometimes they are seemingly invisible, but they are essential to the network's well-being and survival.
7. All insurgent networks have necessary functions (e.g., security, intelligence, planning, logistics, transportation, and so forth), as well as physical and intangible characteristics.

It is a given that insurgents could not survive without the support and at least passive complicity of the population in which they embed themselves. Some of the populace will actively support the network, but others will only provide intermittent support and often with a motivation of money and not ideology. These network supporters will vary in security proficiency and HUMINT tradecraft; however, even the best of them will make mistakes. These mistakes make visible that which seems invisible. The mistakes they make will often be cultural, technical, or personal/behavioral, and because of their nature, will be difficult for U.S. intelligence to purposefully look for, notice, or understand if they are even noticed. We will discuss the implications of this observation as the thoughts in the book progress.

What does it take to engage an enemy in an urban OE where the initiative lies waiting for those with the aggressiveness and moxie to seize it? It is through advanced thinking that we can learn to anticipate actions, develop specific observables, and understand the culture of the people we are working against. Advanced analysts will synthesize the results of collection, advise the decision maker, help design relevant effects, and assess outcomes. They must perform these cerebral activities faster than an enemy can either respond or choose an alternative course of action. Though it appears to be a daunting task, it is nevertheless fully implementable, particularly in light of U.S. capabilities in both the availability of educated people and technology at its disposal. One distinct advantage held by U.S. forces lies in their capability to leverage technology purposefully to help us think better and faster than the enemy. But to perform advanced analysis, U.S. analysts also need improved cognitive capabilities, occasional help from the experts of a virtual knowledge environment (VKE), which provides high-quality knowledge support from a distance, and synthetic environments to understand the enemy, the environment, and the cultural aspects of the population where the insurgent or terrorist is embedded.

This chapter has discussed the OE. It is extremely influential in determining the outcomes of military and nonmilitary actions in urban settings. It influences all thoughts, decisions, actions, and assessments in which U.S. commanders and their subordinates engage. It constantly evolves, indeed constantly morphs, into different shapes, forms, and characteristics. Within the OE, one can find the intersections and collisions of people, organizations, culture, beliefs, attitudes, motives, technology, and needs. The chapter also discussed the insurgent enemy and why this threat is so formidable. As such, the insurgent must receive support from the population to survive, let alone excel, and he must use a flat, constantly evolving network. This network is difficult to think about, seek, find, and influence. Yet it has characteristics (physical and nonphysical), functions, purposes, connecting links, nodes, and a variety of shapes and forms. It is the "means to power" of any insurgent organization planning and conducting missions in a large, complex, urban OE.

Along with the OE and the enemy, and his supporting network, the chapter introduced some of the notions of complexity and why these aspects of modernity are so influential on all outcomes in urban interactions. The chapter also introduced a layman's explanation of complex adaptive systems (CAS) and non-linearity—both essential to thinking about and operating in an urban setting.

Finally, the chapter discussed a logic that the advanced analyst must be aware of concerning the pressure a commander is under to make rapid decisions owing to the many missions he must complete. Now the reader is prepared to get into more specifics of advanced analysis. The next chapter will identify and discuss problems confronting the discipline of intelligence analysis in this type of environment against adversaries in conflicts that America will face over the next 100 years.

2

The Problem

With a discussion and heavy thinking about the urban OE and the insurgent and irregular warfare foes in mind, we can now begin to form some ideas about the problems and challenges awaiting any intelligence analyst venturing forth to perform his or her analytic duties. At the start of the chapter, a proposition sets the tenor of the conversation and discussion. That is, although intelligence analysis practices in the past have served the country well, they are inadequate to engage with insurgents or irregular warriors in urban settings and win the war of wits. To engage insurgents in urban OEs, a much broader perspective of intelligence analysis and the capability to delve into much more specificity and deeper knowledge is needed than what served so well in the past. Let us start the chapter by immediately delving into some of the important shortfalls in current analytic capabilities when considering intelligence analytic support to either counterinsurgency or operations against irregular forces.

- *First*, traditional intelligence analysis lacks specificity. In the past, we knew the basics of the forces arrayed against us and we could use a template to fill in the gaps with reasonable certainty. Fighting a war against global insurgents, who have neither organizational nor standard military structure and who are expert at blending with a host nation as well as in cover and deception, operational security (OPSEC), and security, creates the need for sufficiently specific and detailed knowledge to find insurgents' well-hidden network cells and to anticipate their deceptive activities. Quite simply, it is in the details where one discovers the hidden, nuanced, often fleeting observables that lead intelligence analysts to the enemy no matter how well he hides. But analysts must have sufficient knowledge to delve into such detail, which is extremely difficult to find or develop. This difficulty means that analysts do not habitually develop and advocate observables (to drive collection) that are specific enough. If analysts develop observables, most often they are functional in nature. But in an urban setting, along with functional observables, the analyst must learn to use technical, cultural, situational, and biometric observables. Without this breadth of observables to focus collection, the task of winning in a large urban environment becomes problematic. As a corollary activity, advanced analysts must employ these specific observables and drive specific sensor tasking. Optimum mixes of sensors, when using the previously discussed observables as their guide, seek indicants of the enemy at specific points, at specific times, with specific observables, even looking for signs, symbols, or indicants that are confoundingly abstruse, nuanced, or subtle. Through no fault of their own, intelligence analysts sometimes lack the training, expertise, and experience necessary to design such observables. Compounding the problem, they have no organized way to confer with VKE subject matter experts (SMEs) to seek help in designing this broad range of observables as well as to make sense of resultant collected data. Further, they have insufficient modeling and simulation (M&S) programs to wargame, decompose requirements, and anticipate the outcomes of faulty reasoning.

- *Second*, in a closely related problem, the existing U.S. military analytic/collection process inexplicably does not allow analysts to be involved in providing specific guidance to distributed collectors in direct support of their analytic efforts to the extent necessary for success in the difficult urban OE. Contrarily, detailed observables must drive very specific sensor tasking aimed at narrowly focused point targets to gain the data commanders need to transform into actionable knowledge. Sensors and their "handlers," particularly human sensors, need definite guidance about what to look for, when to look, where to look for it, and rationale for the effort. Purposeful direction gained from detailed observables puts rigor, positive energy, and directed purpose into the process and reduces a dependency on luck. When collection specialists don't receive specific analytic-driven guidance, they do the best they can; however, they do not usually possess the expertise to design collection to work against the types of observables required. What is the result? At times we find collectors performing area reconnaissance with unmanned aerial systems (UAS) with "soda straws," looking for generic things like "report anything unusual." Let us take a moment to explore this line of thought further.

In urban ISR, sensors, particularly human "sensors," need guidance about what to look for, and when and where to look. Analysts need to "arm" the sensors and HUMINT purposefully, with specific observables about where and when the analyst wants the sensors and HUMINT to observe and to provide data relative to the analyst's quest or vision. Arguably, people can accidentally come across unusual events and activities that urge them to investigate. But purposeful direction via detailed observables puts rigor and purpose into the process and reduces a disadvantageous dependency on chance.

Generally, intelligence analysts who should be developing the full range of observables and providing them and other guidance to collection experts and sensor operators are involved in other duties. Moreover, many intelligence analysts are not intellectually prepared in the military's training and education systems to perform sophisticated decomposition, to develop observables, to match up the observables with the right mix of HUMINT and sensors, and to make sense of masses of complicated data coming from collection. To be successful in the kind of war in which we currently find ourselves and to prepare for future conflicts, analysts must interact directly with all types of available sensors and their handlers. They also must make sense out of all kinds of collected data. The analyst must think hard and provide the observables, context, standards, and analytic intent to ensure the sensor operator knows precisely what to look for, where to look, and the rationale for looking. Human beings of all walks of life do well when they know the context of the request and specifically when, where, and what to look for.

Humans and machines must work together to collect and bring into being a symbiosis[1] to direct human intellectual and machine energies against something meaningful and relative to the enemy, and to focus energy on the friendly decision maker's intent. Working with observables in urban OEs takes copious amounts of timely knowledge, expertise, technical know-how, and cultural understanding. Analysts often will not have this kind of knowledge, mental capability, or experience, through no fault of their own.

As a related problem, analysts are often not adequately involved with collection, which leaves what should be a teaming process between the analyst and collection specialist to a collection manager ill-prepared to develop observables and specific orders and requests (SORs). Although the intelligence system can undoubtedly get away with such a bifurcation in a conventional conflict, it cannot do so in urban ISR when working against well-embedded insurgents and terrorists in urban OE. When observables are poor, collection-produced data is poor. Even if a process existed to turn this data into actionable knowledge, it is often the wrong data leading analysts to discern the wrong meaning and causing the wrong knowledge to come forth.

Once analysts develop specific observables, they face the challenge of working with their collection specialist counterpart to actually task human collectors, case officers, counterintelligence people, and collection managers explaining both observables and purpose to bring an optimum mix of technical sensors and humans to focus on the right activities, at the right places, at the right times, relying on the right observables to find the clues to analytic redemption. They must seek a synergy among analysis, collection, and knowledge subject matter experts (SMEs) to find and report on the subtle and nuanced observables one finds in urban environments. Good analysts, being knowledgeable of collection, and of course being knowledgeable about their observables, should request specific collection activities or sensors and be able to explain to source handlers and technical sensor programmers and observers the reason for the observables they want and why needed data is important in the larger OE perspective.

- *Third*, collected data often does not go through the rigorous mental activity that is synthesis. Synthesis will be discussed in depth later in the book, but suffice it to say it involves relating data to other data, building combinations, seeking and exploiting relationships (sometimes before the opponent even knows they are coming into existence), thinking about data and what it means, and transforming it into information and knowledge. Synthesis, one of the most intellectually arduous aspects of advanced analysis, is challenging to understand, learn, and teach. Regardless, it remains one of the most important mental skills for combating the insurgent and irregular. It is through synthesis that the enemy's network can be understood and seen. Synthesis also allows the intelligence analyst to understand aggregation and tendency analysis. Synthesis allows us to engage in anticipation and to fathom the enemy's goals, strategies, and tactics. However, owing to the challenges just addressed, synthesis remains perplexing to intelligence analysts. This is particularly true for analysts seeking to understand seemingly meaningless occurrences leading to other activities and the all-important relationships connecting people, nodes, network functions, and societal activities. The mystery is how to explain it, how to help people learn to use it, and how to employ it against the capable foe we face today. The solution to the mystery will come later in the book during the discussion of possible solutions and the in-depth discussion of synthesis in chapter nineteen.
- *Fourth*, today's analysts often lack sufficient knowledge of the culture in which they work to use it for gaining advantages over the insurgent adversary. What does this statement mean, specifically? Analysts sometimes experience difficulty in understanding the importance of social relationships inherent to a particular culture. Then Major General David Petraeus helps us understand the importance of the culture in

counterinsurgencies and operations against irregular warriors with the following thoughts:

> knowledge of the cultural "terrain" can be as important as, and sometimes even more important than, knowledge of the geographic terrain. This observation acknowledges that the people are, in many respects, the decisive terrain, and that we must study that terrain in the same way that we have always studied the geographical terrain.[2]

Analysts need extensive cultural training to understand that it isn't just the first degree of separation in human connections that is important, it is the sixth through the nth degree of separation that will yield the richest haul of relational "iron ore" mined from seemingly barren ground. Because cultural understanding is important but ever so challenging, analysts will often need help from cultural specialists or indigenous people to gain sufficient depth in understanding to pursue connectedness and seemingly disparate relationships to their logical, social, and functional conclusions. T. E. Lawrence provides an insurgent's perspective of his adversary, the powerful Turkish Army in Arabia in World War I, which helps us understand how important the culture and population are in counterinsurgency operations we face today and will continue to face in the future:

> Our rebellion has an unassailable base . . . It had a sophisticated alien enemy, disposed as an army of occupation in an area greater than could be dominated effectively from fortified posts. It had a friendly population, of which some two in the hundred were active, and the rest quietly sympathetic to the point of not betraying the movements of the minority. The active rebels had the virtues of secrecy and self-control, and the qualities of speed, endurance, and independence of arteries of supply. They had technical equipment enough to paralyze the enemy's communications . . . The presence of the enemy was secondary. Final victory seem[ed] certain, if the war lasted long enough for us to work it out.[3]

To help with understanding the culture, U.S. analysts face the challenge of learning to use vetted, properly cleared indigenous people (SMEs) to help conduct intelligence analysis, plan (including wargaming), execute, and understand the outcomes of intelligence collection operations, including engaging in decomposition and forming the observables previously discussed.

• Using indigenous SMEs presents challenges to the analyst. First, there is always a language barrier. Second, there is a trust issue, as the SME could be an enemy agent. Third, and related to the other two challenges, sometimes it will be difficult to locate the right SME with the right knowledge and the right clearances to help with operational planning and execution. This is a particularly acute issue for intelligence analysts who work with indigenous people for many aspects of advanced analysis. They need to learn to use these people to develop observables. They must learn to use indigenous, culturally and technically savvy sources to help plan intelligence collection operations to support their observables. Also, intelligence analysts must overcome the egregious mental error of mirror imaging; indigenous SMEs can be helpful in this endeavor. The intelligence analyst must learn to engage in complicated mental wargaming—indigenous SMEs can help, particularly serving as the thinking enemy in such activities. Advanced analysts are charged with turning data into information and knowledge—indigenous experts can be helpful in this effort. Moreover, the intelligence analyst faces the challenge of anticipating and identifying possible unexpected outcomes of direct action and judging outcomes of sensor or human collection— indigenous SMEs can help in this effort. Indigenous SMEs can also assist the analyst in identifying the times and places in which sensitive variables could come into play. With respect to detailed advanced analysis, advanced analysts must learn to use indigenous people to help with cultural and anomaly intelligence analysis work, which are fundamental to working against insurgents and terrorists. Analysts desiring to use advanced analysis also need to improve how they use properly cleared indigenous subject matter experts (SMEs) to help identify the ways that U.S.- and coalition-run HUMINT sources can penetrate enemy cells. As a final point, intelligence analysts must learn to work with their collection specialist teammates to use indigenous sources to observe stationary targets, follow people, and engage in mobile observation.

- *Fifth*, intelligence analysts must improve their capabilities to anticipate and deny enemy attacks in urban counterinsurgency and irregular operations. Anticipation is, at its core, about the struggle for *initiative*. U.S. intelligence analysts do not purposefully, intellectually, and aggressively pursue the initiative to the extent needed to win against an opponent who certainly understands the importance of the initiative. Let us review what some of the great insurgency theorists have to say about the importance of initiative. Counterinsurgency theorist David Galula tells us,

> If resolution is equally strong, then victory belongs to the camp that seizes and keeps the initiative . . . Since the insurgent alone can initiate the conflict . . . strategic initiative is his by definition. He is free to choose his hour, to wait safely for a favorable situation, unless external forces force him to accelerate his moves.[4]

Mao Tse-tung, one of the great guerrilla warfare theorists and practitioners of all time, tells us even more about the importance of the initiative:

What is meant by initiative in warfare? In all battles and wars, a struggle to gain and retain the initiative goes on between the opposing sides, for it is the side that holds the initiative that has liberty of action. When an army loses the initiative, it loses its liberty; its role becomes passive; it faces the danger of defeat and destruction.[5]

Even with the importance of the initiative being so obvious, the intelligence analyst is not prepared to enter this complex and intense competition with the enemy, who does a very good job in its recognition and exploration. This book discusses anticipatory analysis in depth; it is designed to compete for the initiative in urban OE against both insurgents and irregulars.

Without good, usable intelligence analysis of the kind this book addresses with respect to winning the struggle for the initiative, the enemy will focus and attack at will because he learns, adapts, and shares what was learned quickly, which enables him to hold the initiative. When the insurgent holds the initiative, other advantages accrue—freedom of maneuver, position, decision, knowledge, tempo, momentum, and technical advantages. If the enemy is allowed to hold the initiative, it puts U.S. forces and commanders at a serious and continuous disadvantage. Advanced analysis provides "a way" to anticipate and engage the enemy proactively and not reactively. In this way, the advanced analyst enters the struggle to win the initiative. With aggressive advanced analysis, the friendly commander can seek and find the foe, anticipate and preempt his activities, and sustain control of the initiative and its attendant advantages.

- *Sixth*, there is limited analyst overwatch. Owing to the complexity of urban settings, analysts need assistance from the intelligence enterprise and from a VKE (which will be discussed later). The deployed intelligence analyst needs dedicated analytic overwatch to help think about areas in which he or she lacks expertise and to pick up on necessary analytic functions the deployed analyst has no time to perform. Unfortunately, this type of analytic overwatch is often only provided on an ad hoc basis. It needs to be organized, disciplined, and continuous.

Also, analysts need to network with other analysts to be effective in volatile and knowledge-demanding urban OE. Analysts at the company, battalion, and Brigade Combat Team (BCT) and Regimental Combat Team (RCT) levels need analytic assistance from analysts at higher levels to perform the work they lack expertise in, or, owing to pressing activities of the moment, are too busy to perform. Continuing this thread of thought, the enemy in the city is so fluid that friendly decision authority must be at the lowest possible level where analysis, collection, and direct action work as teams. Speed and precision of thought and action are the quintessential aspects of counterinsurgency operations. To support the speed and precision required at the tactical edge, each intelligence operations/analysis center faces a challenge to network with all other operations/analysis centers so an analytic enterprise can exist and excel.

Along this same line of thought, analysts in a future intelligence enterprise, along with SMEs in a VKE, face the challenge to organize into an analytic unity of effort. This approach will help analysts with cognitive and knowledge chores they might not have time for. As an example, a unified conglomeration of analysts can lend a hand in working with machines and the mechanical function of data ingestion to gain some sense of meaning. Within the enterprise, people in the network must learn to operate in a virtual collaborative environment to assist each other, provide overwatch, offer thoughts, advice, and assistance, and engage in team solutions via virtual collaboration.

Although analytic overwatch is an obvious need, it is challenging to ensure it is organized and well understood by people with an overwatch responsibility. If on an overwatch mission, responsible people have to provide the support continuously and cannot drop what they are doing to do something else. Without a promulgated, demonstrated commitment of continuous support, the recipients of overwatch support will not trust the support and therefore could be more inclined to try to do everything themselves. Also, analysts in the intelligence enterprise must receive training to learn to "swarm" to engage analysts in need of help without taking the time to go up and down a hierarchy, seeking permission to act. This analytic "self-organization" is a learned skill and takes proficiency and training to perform at a high level. Unfortunately, it is not done well today, largely because of bureaucratic stratification of roles and missions, shortages of people, money, and time, and an inherent inability for the people in support to learn or know enough of the specific details about the deployed analysts' needs to make a meaningful contribution.

Make no mistake, with a few notable exceptions, intelligence analysis has served the country well. Nonetheless, in the future it will be inadequate for several reasons. The intelligence system needed by anybody performing advanced analysis is inadequately structured, trained, and equipped to meet the challenges discussed above. The intelligence system is now working against networks that lack discernable shape or form. Smart and creative people lead these networks and generally speaking, they either do or will operate from large urban areas. During the cold war, the U.S. military faced a large, conventional, and bureaucratic hierarchy in the former Soviet Union; in a significant departure from today and tomorrow, it must work against a global, transnational insurgent and irregular warrior possessing excellent mobility and having access to cutting-edge technology and the digital world (e.g., instant messages, communications from anywhere anytime, and a tremendous capability to move and communicate quickly). In the past our opponents were confined to geographical areas, except for their missiles and airplanes. Now, they can be anywhere in the world in less than 24 hours. In the past our opponents had nuclear weapons, but for the most part they were well-controlled. Today our enemies actively seek small, disguisable weapons of mass destruction (WMD) they can move and implant wherever they choose (that is, in the United States and in the cities of coalition partners). Whereas the military's intelligence preparation of the battlespace (IPB) proved effective against cold war opponents, without considerable adjustment, the same templates and thought processes will not serve well against the connected, mobile, global urban threat of today and tomorrow. It only follows that our thought processes, mental templates, and supporting machines must learn, adapt, and adjust to compete in today's urban OE against insurgent and terrorist threats that possess an increasing capability to use information technology for advantage. The challenge is of course how to take a very expensive intelligence system designed for a different time against a different enemy and superimpose it onto the OE and enemy discussed earlier in this book.

Information requirements continue to come from a variety of people and processes. People have, of course, discovered the potential power of information and knowledge, and want to use it for creating advantages over their adversaries. Thus, more and more people seek valuable information for use in their intellectual development, planning, decision-making, and assessments. In a military sense, priority intelligence requirements (PIR) and information requirements (IR) remain preeminent among these requirements. However, in this new age of reasoning, these two intelligence drivers are often too static and broad. Thus, PIR and IR must be dynamic and very specific, as the missions they support and the environment in which they drive intelligence requirements are both volatile and dynamic. Furthermore, along with PIR and IR, other inputs will also come to influence intelligence analysis and collection. Intelligence analysts and collection experts must learn to work as a united team to confirm or deny *hypotheses* coming from if–then drills and wargaming. In addition, intelligence analysts must learn to always develop and articulate *expectations* about the environment and discern what the enemy will or could be doing to further their goals or intentions, as well as considering their own responses to stimuli. Thus, expectations become important in identifying and defining intelligence analysis and collection requirements. Analysts will learn to develop and follow *hunches* about what the enemy will be doing or what outcomes could blossom into a bona fide problem of immense influence. As a final aspect of discerning what drives intelligence analysis and collection, good intelligence analysts must learn to define and work to solve *mysteries* about certain key elements of the OE—threats, neutrals, MNCs, host nation, indigenous forces, systems, processes, nodes, anomalies, links, patterns, behaviors, and odd activities. For analysts this means the aperture of requirements becomes much wider and infinitely more complex. For the decomposition and recomposition processes of advanced analysis, it means analysts need assistance from a variety of subject matter experts (SMEs), data/information/knowledge repositories, and centers of expertise to help meet the inherent thinking and knowledge challenges.

Let us think for a few minutes about conventional intelligence analysis and how incongruent it is with counterinsurgency and irregular warfare analysis in urban settings. Let us start the discussion with a question. What is wrong with the notion of attempting to overlay conventional intelligence analysis on the urban counterinsurgency and operations against irregular activities mosaic? The answer to this question is one of both philosophy and action.

Philosophically, to perform analytic work in a large, foreign urban setting, analysts' knowledge must be both wide and deep. What must they know? They must know the culture. In addition, they must know the infrastructure. They must know the visible world of the city as well as the invisible. They must know and understand technology and how it influences people, and the way they perceive, think, conduct business, and behave. They must know the threat, how he thinks, his modus operandi, and how he views the U.S. military and its intelligence system. In conventional intelligence, it is the opposing conventional military force that commands the analysts' thoughts and activities. In this respect, the analyst works on the enemy's disposition, composition, strengths and weaknesses, vulnerabilities, courses of action, and intent. The analyst works on intelligence preparation of the battlespace (IPB), which is open or at least non-urban terrain. He knows conventional forces have a command and control system, weapons to be maintained, voracious ammunition resupply activities, hungry and thirsty soldiers, medical care, organized units that face each other, reserves, reinforcements, airpower, strike forces, and naval forces. In an unconventional or irregular warfare situation, the analyst finds that IPB does not work in a city as it works in the open terrain against a conventional force. Instead of a hierarchical command and control system (C^2), the enemy uses the culture and a network to operate. There are no units or traditional military forms to work against, as the insurgent hides amongst the populace and performs his activities in the noise and movement of a busy city. Although the enemy's intent remains important to both types of warfare, the insurgent's intent is much different than that of a conventional military commander. To win, the insurgent often must simply not lose and must have the will to wait out the conventional force until the casualties and costs weary the supporting populace and governments. Although both the insurgent and the conventional force have objectives, the insurgents often attack key infrastructure, kill several of their opponent's soldiers, or set off a bomb to inflict maximum damage and casualties to the populace, simply to show them that there is no stability and security with the present government. With conventional forces, intelligence analysts can engage in successful prediction owing to the scientific nature of conventional forces (e.g., mean time between failure and automated resupply of relevant parts), time and distance, location and influence, and easy to understand cause and effect relationships. With a counterinsurgency in a large city, very little is predictable owing to the influence of complexity. Analysts then are faced with only being able to anticipate and to form and follow hypotheses concerning their opponent's behavior and activities. In a conventional war, the military forces most often avoid urban OE and operate in open terrain. In a counterinsurgency, the goal of the insurgent is to draw the conventional force into an urban setting where the conventional force's advantages atrophy in the face of constraints of physics as well as humanitarian concerns such as collateral damage. Finally, in a conventional force, the fighting involves military forces pitted against each other. Therefore, the center of gravity is often military related. In a counterinsurgency, the populace is the center of gravity; therefore, fighting in a military sense often becomes an adjunct to engaging in conflict via information, humanitarian relief, reconstruction, and police operations.

From an action perspective, to operate in a large foreign city effectively, intelligence analysts face a variety of challenges. They must learn to be intellectually aggressive. They must learn to anticipate the adversary and his thoughts, decisions, and actions. As such, they have to know and understand how the enemy leaders perceive, think, plan, decide, act, and seek and receive feedback on their actions. They must learn to drive collection with very specific observables. They must collaborate with other people in their headquarters, seek and use the support of an intelligence enterprise, and also seek the knowledge development support of subject matter experts (SMEs) from within their organization, external experts in theater (e.g., indigenous SMEs), as well as external SMEs in virtual knowledge environments (VKEs). Intelligence analysts must be able to think about, plan, and execute assessment of outcomes involving intangibles and human perception, as well as the destruction of enemy insurgents. These are immense challenges facing any aspiring intelligence analyst.

In conclusion, this chapter identifies problems, issues, and challenges associated with intelligence analysis. It identifies some of the more important problems and provides a segue into the next chapter, which provides solutions to these challenges.

The complex OE and networked, cellular threat pose immense challenges to any intelligence analyst. The OE is fluid and volatile; it changes rapidly and is enshrouded by a foreign culture, which is difficult for U.S. intelligence analysts to understand, let alone to manipulate for advantage. As discussed earlier, the threat is formidable too. It embeds itself in the OE, amongst the people who make up the culture, and hides its operations in the many everyday activities of a large, bustling city. The threat has an immense and amorphous network from which he operates and draws power. This network is largely invisible; moreover, its links and nodes appear and disappear with alacrity. Thus, it is very difficult to find and its functioning often seems to be invisible.

This discussion introduced formidable challenges facing the intelligence analyst of today and far into the future. This chapter's musings should have led the reader to conclude that to meet these challenges, U.S. intelligence analysts need significant intellectual development. They also need cognitive work to help them gain critical thinking skills, adequate depth of knowledge, an understanding of complex relationships, and specific technical and cultural knowledge to provide the focus and impetus for successful collection in urban insurgent situations. It is through advanced analysis that the intelligence analyst of today and tomorrow will master the cognitive capabilities to overcome the challenges and problems this chapter identifies and discusses.

Analysts must overcome these tough mental challenges and engage in advanced analysis in the war of wits, in which America is embroiled. This chapter suggests that analysts will have to aggressively engage in the knowledge intensive "front end" decomposition to develop observables that will intelligently drive the collection system. But the chapter also suggests the absolute need for a "back end" process too. In the back end process, analysts, with the help of subject matter experts (SMEs) and fast computers, face the challenge of recomposing collected data into information and using the challenging mental skill of synthesis to transform information into knowledge of sufficient value and timeliness to drive down risk and uncertainty in commanders' decision-making processes.

With these challenges in mind, the next chapter offers some solutions and "ways" in which improvements can be found. The improvements will be specific in the discussion. Then, the book will discuss some conditions that are vital enablers if advanced analysis is to take hold and drive intelligence analysis in support of operations against insurgents and irregular forces in urban settings. The book's logic continues—we have thought about the OE, we have discussed challenges and problems, and now we are ready to delve into possible solutions, many of which have been alluded to throughout the early portions of the book.

3

Solutions

This chapter offers some solutions to help overcome some of the problems and challenges identified in Chapter Two. These solutions are not comprehensive—other people will have very good additional solutions to the problems and ways to meet the challenges Chapter Two brought forth. Nonetheless, this chapter provides a starting point for how one can go about solving the problems facing intelligence analysts today and preparing for tomorrow's war of wits. This chapter also serves as a mental bridge for Chapter Four—"Setting the Stage for Advanced Analysis."

Intelligence analysts must engage in higher level thinking to be successful in urban OE. In this respect, intelligence analysts have to possess broad and deep intellectual skills and knowledge sufficient to outthink a continuously changing and learning enemy. These skills come with developing analysts' minds to engage in advanced analysis. For starters, intelligence analysts must set conditions for success. As such, they will anticipate a commander's future knowledge requirements. They will know how to use the military decision-making process (MDMP) and when and where to intervene to develop and implement analytic conditions for success. This condition planning involves establishing data, sensor, and knowledge architectures, and will be discussed in depth in Chapter Four. Suffice it to say, however, satisfying this triad of requirements will mean success or failure for advanced analysts, so it is a nontrivial aspect of advanced analysis.

A few aspects of advanced analysis are new. Some of the new aspects include the basic thinking about aggregation, tendency, cultural, semiotics, and anomaly analysis. Anticipatory analysis as well as new orientation of critical thinking also brings new aspects to analysis. Decomposition and recomposition are both old and new. That is, people have always engaged in some form of decomposition, but not as extensively as advocated in advanced analysis. In addition, people have always attempted to pull data together and turn it into information and knowledge, but not with the rigor of recomposition and synthesis presented in advanced analysis. The five types of observables are also new. Heretofore, it has principally been the collection manager who has developed observables. But they have been, at best, functional in nature. Advanced analysis relies on not only functional observables but also cultural, technical, situational, and biometric observables.

However, advanced analysis also takes many traditional elements of intelligence analysis and broadens their definitions, understanding, and uses, e.g., link, pattern, and trend analysis. For example, advanced analysis introduces five types of links, which are: *technical, social/human, organizational, functional,* and *thought.* Links have strength that can help analysts understand how they work, appear, and disappear. The strength of links includes *trust, time in operation, clarity, visibility* or the degree of being invisible, *proficiency,* and *improbability.* Links also have sources of power. These sources of power include functional, e.g., replenishment, performance, etc.; organizational, e.g., knowledge base; social, e.g., relationships; intent/thought, e.g., strength and clarity of thought; and technical, e.g., robustness, quality of service, etc. Links decay and regenerate. Links have a self-cleansing process that insurgents use to keep their links and critical centers and nodes vibrant, tense, flexible, and, as needed, disappearing. To understand this notion more fully, we can borrow the idea of cellular self-cleansing from science, in which cell cleansing is called *autophagy,* which is

> a cleanup process: the trash hauling that enables a cell whose cytoplasm [protoplasm exterior to a cell nucleus] is clotted with old bits of protein and other unwanted sludge to be cleaned out. Refurbishing the cytoplasm can give new life to any cell.[1]

Interestingly, one can search for, find, and use four kinds of patterns that advanced analysis identifies and discusses. These patterns include *technical, human/social, functional,* and *organizational.* Trends also have a broad scope and interpretation in advanced analysis. As such, advanced analysis works with four types of trends—*technical, human/social, functional,* and *organizational.* Link, pattern, and trend analysis will be discussed in later chapters explaining the cognitive elements of advanced analysis, but this short diversion helps us to understand the expanded scope of advanced analysis.

The concept of advanced analysis is the most important aspect of this book. Advanced analysis came about as a result of thinking about the problems America will face in the future at home and abroad, observing many experiments at the U.S. Joint Forces Command, writing a vision for the Office of the Under Secretary of Defense Intelligence (USDI) on the Joint Intelligence Operations Center After Next (JIOC-AN), and 38 years of experience working in intelligence operations at all levels of command. With all this thought came an understanding of the constantly changing OE, the determined and networked threat, and the growing realization that our intelligence analysis, while exceptional for conventional threats from the past and operating in an OE that was most often open terrain, is not adequate for today and tomorrow. What is needed is advanced analysis. It significantly broadens both scope and depth of intelligence analysis. It is fungible among problem sets in all OEs, is applicable to the full spectrum of conflict, and it is applicable to the company and battalion all the way to strategic levels. Although this book deals mostly with military issues in foreign lands, advanced analysis is totally feasible for homeland security and law enforcement analytic activities. It works against specific locations in urban OE aimed at neutralizing one cell of one network, ranging to its service as a guide in "how to think" about the strategic analysis of a nation.

As a review from the introduction, advanced analysis is "The high-level cognitive processes producing specific, detailed thought and understanding of OE, and knowledge superior to that possessed by the adversary." Advanced analysis has 14 cognitive functions. These 14 cognitive functions, briefly described below, are extraordinarily powerful to people who employ them as they think. They will be discussed in this order later in the book.

- *Decomposition.* Mentally breaking a thought or activity into its basic elements.
- *Critical thinking.* An intellectual process that "examines assumptions, discerns hidden values, evaluates evidence, and assesses conclusions."[2]
- *Link analysis.* Decomposing and gaining understanding and insight into behavioral and/or functional relationships, means of communicating, or being connected.
- *Pattern analysis.* Discerning a consistent series of related actions or events.
- *Trend analysis.* Discerning meaning from functionally oriented events or activities that occurred in the past to understand how functionally similar events or activities could happen in the future.
- *Anticipatory analysis.* Using thought, intuition, foreknowledge, knowledge, experience, or prescience to realize in advance what the adversary or competitor might do and testing, confirming, or denying the hypothesis or postulate.
- *Technical analysis.* Gaining knowledge and understanding about the technical aspects of particular events, situations, activities, and transactions.
- *Tendency analysis.* Discerning meaning through thought and study of the general proclivities of people, the behavioral and action inclinations

of organizations, mental snapshots of current environment or context situations, events, activities, and behaviors, the emanation dispersal of energy emissions, and what the interaction and enmeshing of all could portend for the future.

- *Cultural intelligence analysis.* Knowing a particular culture, its people, and their patterns of behavior as derived from traditional culturally induced attitudes, behaviors, social norms, and conditions.
- *Anomaly analysis.* Discerning a departure from the normal or common order, form, or rule; absence of what is expected.
- *Semiotics analysis.* Discerning meaning of cultural signs and symbols as reflected in drawings, paintings, photographs, syntax, words, sounds, body language, and graffiti.
- *Aggregation analysis.* Discerning meaning of several things, whether numbering from a few to millions, which are grouped, moving, working together, and considered as a whole.
- *Recomposition.* Cognition- and machine-driven recompilation of parts to understand the whole.
- *Synthesis.* Combining elements of substances to form a coherent whole.

Intelligence analysts must learn to anticipate enemy activities and lead the fight for the initiative. Although this may sound peculiar (to have intelligence analysts leading the fight for the initiative), it is necessary. After all, intelligence analysts have as their *raison d'être* to think like, about, and against the enemy. Within this thought process, it makes eminent sense for skilled intelligence analysts to engage in mental warfare against the insurgents for the initiative and thereby enable their commanders to take action—physical, informational, and intangible—to exploit what the analysts have thought up, while others engage in different, but related types of conflict. Dr. Jim Schneider, recently retired professor of theory at the Army's School of Advanced Military Studies, lends further insight to this theme with this thought about one of the great military theorists of all time, T. E. Lawrence: "Lawrence understood that in an insurgency, the real battle lay within the minds of the opponents."[3] As a corollary thought, schools for analysts, self-directed learning, and training and professional development sessions in units and organizations must provide them the means to constantly improve in the intense competition for advantages accruing to the antagonist holding the initiative. In the struggle for the initiative, advanced analysts must devise ways to achieve the initiative while denying enemy success, and in particular denying his control of the initiative. This denial involves a struggle, as the enemy will not willingly acquiesce to U.S. intelligence analysts' machinations to seek, find, and gain control over the initiative. Thus, the outcome of this struggle will often oscillate among competitors in the battlespace. Clausewitz helps us understand the duality of this struggle in the following passage:

War, however, is not the action of a living force upon a lifeless mass (total nonresistance would be no war at all) but always the collision of two living forces. The ultimate aim of waging war, as formulated here, must be taken as applying to both sides. Once again, there is interaction. So long as I have not overthrown my opponent I am bound to fear he may overthrow me. Thus I am not in control: he dictates to me as much as I dictate to him.[4]

Clausewitz' thoughts are necessarily true for entering the fight for the initiative. The enemy will contest control of the initiative and attempt to anticipate and deny efforts to achieve it. Our intelligence analysts must engage in anticipatory analysis to get ahead of the enemy's thinking and provide the commander with sufficient actionable knowledge to manage his definition of risk and reduce uncertainty so he can preempt or shape the enemy's thoughts sufficiently to deny him control of the initiative.

As a point of order, please note I did not constrain the connotation of competitors struggling over initiative to a binary problem. That is, this struggle involves more contestants than enemy and friendly. Other competitors in the OE will be seeking the initiative too, such as commercial companies, the host nation, nongovernment organizations, and peacekeeping forces. Each will pursue self-interests. Sometimes these interests will collide with those of U.S. military forces and thereby influence U.S. commanders' decisions. It follows that advanced analysts must work from at least four perspectives when considering the initiative—when the enemy has the initiative, when the United States has it, when the host nation possess the initiative, and when neutrals possess it.

To work with the initiative, advanced analysis provides the means to specific, detailed, and smart analysis. The cognitive rigor of advanced analysis provides the capability to do so. As such, its philosophy imbues analysts with an aggressive attitude, provides them with M&S capabilities to work multiple cuts of the act–react–counteract cycles, and an understanding of sensitive variables inherent to a complex urban OE that can influence this struggle. With such capabilities, advanced analysts can anticipate enemy action or their condition-setting activities they must engage in while preparing for action. With analytic hunches, expectations, and beliefs, advanced intelligence analysts focus collection on one, combinations, or all types of observables. It is very important, then, for the advanced analyst to think about, set conditions for, and steal the initiative from the enemy or other competitors whose goals are inimical or contradictory to those of the friendly force commander.

Priority intelligence requirement (PIR) and intelligence requirement (IR) are important words denoting concepts. They derive from the command decision-making process. Over the years, PIR have moved toward becoming static; however, they need to be dynamic. The commander, operations officer, and intelligence officer have to constantly reconsider changes in the OE, the enemy, mission, variables, infrastructure, and other intervening forces such as interaction with security companies and the host nation, and constantly update their intelligence requirements.

As mentioned earlier, along with PIR and IR to drive intelligence operations, there will be other drivers. Some of the most notable drivers include hypotheses, expectations, hunches, and mysteries. A *hypothesis* is a proposition, or set of propositions, set forth as an explanation for the occurrence of some specified group of phenomena, either asserted merely as a provisional conjecture to guide investigation (working hypothesis) or accepted as highly probable in the light of established facts.[5] A hypothesis or set of hypotheses often come from wargaming, which in the U.S. Army is part of its military decision-making process—Course of Action Feasibility and Wargaming. The hypothesis is important in that it must be decomposed and then drive collection for the purposes of testing the hypothesis and confirming or denying its validity. Working with hypotheses (e.g., coming from act, react, and counteract wargaming) is a broadened aspect of traditional intelligence analysis but is fundamental to advanced analysis.

Expectations are also important to advanced analysis. All analysts, as well as their commanders, will have expectations about themselves, the enemy, the OE, or impending actions or missions. An expectation is the act or state of looking forward or anticipating.[6] Effective analysts must develop and work with expectations and pursue them to a conclusion. This becomes increasingly difficult to perform at the tactical level; therefore, analysts at this level will often depend on an analytic overwatch team to perform this function of advanced analysis. In working with an expectation, the analyst will decompose it just as a hypothesis and resultant observables will drive collection. Each analyst will have several expectations they work on along with their other duties.

An analytic *hunch* is a premonition or suspicion.[7] Hunches are different than expectations in that sometimes a hunch is nothing more than a gnawing suspicion or a feeling of ill-ease coming from the subconscious. But hunches or gut feels are important in the OE we are discussing, and leaders must encourage analysts to pursue them to resolution. Sometimes this effort will result in nothing, but at other times working on a hunch will unravel an entire mystery.

A *mystery* is any affair, thing, or person that presents features or qualities so obscure as to arouse curiosity or speculation.[8] Mysteries are good for developing analysts' intellects. By nature, analysts should be inquisitive. This characteristic means they will have mysteries that they try to solve. For example, an analyst notices that a particular house has its rugs hanging out different windows at different times each day. With no apparent explanation, this observation can and should become a mystery. A mystery undergoes the same decomposition as a hypothesis, expectation, or hunch, and drives intelligence collection to solve the mystery.

As the reader can conclude, advanced analysis is indeed wider and deeper than traditional intelligence analysis. This expanded view of the drivers that influence intelligence analysis allows for a field of view and thought sufficiently wide and deep to operate in an analytic sense in urban settings against insurgents, irregulars, and their networks.

Urban advanced intelligence analysis must be extremely specific. With specificity, analysts' cognition and machine work enable them to understand the OE and the networked threat in sufficient depth to drive collection that finds specific observables and synthesizes incoming data into actionable knowledge. These observables enable analysts and sensor operators to spot and understand other nuanced, subtle, ambiguous, and often seemingly invisible observables. This type of observable can lead to enemy or their network supporters' interactions, activities, transactions, and behaviors. However, with the right instructions and guidance by way of observables, times, locations, and suspected activities, insurgents' and their supporters' activities become apparent and unambiguous in the observer's mind as enemy interactions, activities, transactions, and behaviors. Unfortunately, said observables will be fleeting, subtle, ambiguous, or opaque to the observer, therein causing the intellectual angst of knowing something is happening but not being able to say exactly what it is.

To be specific takes knowledge and its application to the problem at hand. Thus, an intelligence analyst has to either possess sufficient knowledge to be specific or find people who possess it and are available to help design collection and turn its results into actionable knowledge. The object is, of course, to turn data into information and synthesize it into knowledge, and understanding quickly and accurately. But what are some examples of what the advanced analyst has to know or find help to know?

As one example, intelligence analysts must know all aspects of the culture in which they operate. This knowledge has to be both broad and deep. Broad knowledge, in this context, means knowing a lot about a wide variety of subjects. Deep means along with knowing a lot about many subjects, analysts must know each subject in sufficient detail to use it for thinking. Knowing the culture also includes knowing cultural aspects of the infrastructure. An analyst's knowledge must be of sufficient quality, relevance, and depth to not just know the culture for the purposes of awareness but to exploit it for a positive purpose. Advanced analysts have to not only gain cultural awareness but also to use it to gain a friendly advantage. This is cultural intelligence, one of the fourteen elements of advanced analysis this work advocates as a requirement for intelligence analysts.

As another example of a knowledge capability, the advanced analyst has to know the OE's existing technologies. This means advanced analysts must know and understand the invisible world of infrastructure, communication, computer networks, radio frequency (RF) energy, television transmissions and energy, cellular phones, and encryption. Otherwise, they will be unable to use collection and analysis as aggressively as needed in a full range of operations to understand the difference between a "what is" baseline (normal) and anomalous activities that could be an indicant of enemy network activity.

Intelligence analysts must drive and purposefully commingle with all types of collection, including technical collection means, traditional human intelligence (HUMINT), and nontraditional sources and methods. Collection people and systems need this level of precision in thought and guidance from cognitively astute analysts all the time. Analysts and collection people work as a team and use combinations of collection means to watch for the flash or brief interlude in an OE in a specific neighborhood indicating either the absence or the presence of an activity of interest. Such activities will surface, albeit quickly, meaning U.S. intelligence collection must be watching for the right activity to come forth. Without advanced analysis and its close coupling with advanced collection, it will be difficult if not impossible to find an insurgent network, identify their nodes, see their connectedness, understand link and pattern decay, and anticipate their next activities. However, even though the validity of the aforementioned process for thinking about the enemy is obvious, we still face a contradiction. That is, U.S. analysis doesn't yield the requisite depth of thought and required knowledge of the culture sufficient to understand these culturally imbued perspectives, attitudes, and prejudices, nor how the neighborhood or community functions and who its leaders are. Unfortunately, all are essential in finding, understanding, and tracking activities in the insurgents' networks. It is through advanced analysis that the intelligence analyst learns to think deeply enough to engage in this kind of analytic work.

Advanced analysis recognizes three mental activities and outputs with which to pursue the insurgent or irregular warrior through collection. They are *signatures, observables,* and *indicators.* Some people use the words interchangeably; however, this book does not regard the words as interchangeable. Here are the working definitions of each of the three:

- *Indicator.* In intelligence usage, an item of information reflecting the intention or capability of an adversary to adopt or reject a course of action (DoD Dictionary of Military and Associated Terms). An indicator is a pointer, sign, instrument, etc., that indicates something of interest or provides information about an activity or lack thereof. The easiest to understand indicators provide statistical values that when taken together provide an indication of a condition or direction of interest to the analyst. An indicator involves collection activities that show the presence, absence, or concentration of a substance or the degree of reaction between or among entities by means of a characteristic change in properties, behavior, biometrics, patterns, or trends. An indicator is the broadest among indictor, observable, and signature.

- *Observable.* An observable is a physical, physiological, emotional property, or absence of one or all of the aforementioned that can be observed or measured directly.[9] It is the second most finite among the triad of indicator, observable, and signature.
- *Signature.* A signature is a distinguishing or identifying mark, feature, or quality. It is a feature in the appearance or qualities of a natural object or a distinctive mark, characteristic, or sound indicating identity. A signature is the most finite of terms among indicator, observable, and signature used to describe what the intelligence analyst and collection specialist look for when focusing collection on analytically anticipated outcomes.

This book uses only one of the three terms—*observables.* By way of explanation, it was impractical to try and use all three descriptive terms. In addition, the term indicator proved too broad, and signature is too specific. We settled on the term "observable," to provide the specificity that both analysts and collection people need to pursue deep and hardened targets, well-disguised WMD sites, mobile missiles, insurgents and terrorists embedded among the throngs of people in a large city, and extremely clever and well-financed drug runners as well as conventional forces using denial and deception such as Russia used against Georgia in the summer of 2008. Most assuredly there are even greater steps of specificity after one develops an observable; however, the term observable provides a suitable bridge to this domain of great specificity owing to its use of descriptors such as "observable" and "measurable." The essential element of information (EEI) is too broad and the Army's specific information requirement (SIR) is not described in enough detail, nor is it specific enough in a doctrinal sense to form the bridge from general to specific this book advocates. When considering how one might focus collection in this world of the subtle, fleeting, ambiguous, and micro, such mental travel involves events, actions, human activities, transactions, and behaviors that are indicative of enemy intent, perception, thoughts, decision-making, and his means of assessing outcomes of action or inaction.

By way of further explanation for this divergence from existing doctrine, Army intelligence doctrine discusses PIR that unknown people break into indicators and then into specific information requirements, which are used to drive collection. Naturally, the U.S. military's Joint system is broader and uses a thought taxonomy of PIR broken into essential elements of information (EEI).[10] EEI are: "The most critical information requirements regarding the adversary and the environment needed by the commander by a particular time to relate with other available information and intelligence to assist in reaching a logical conclusion."[11] This book postulates that intelligence analysts must have a systematic approach to breaking down, analyzing, or otherwise disassembling PIR and other requirements into something more specific than either PIR or SIR—that is, the term observ-able, as defined above. Once the analyst gets to the observable level of speci-ficity, he or she can work with specialists to form both technical and cultural signatures of great specificity to drive optimum mixes of sensors and HUMINT at the right time, right place, and using the right observables.

With respect to observables, as mentioned earlier, intelligence analysis and collection must look for, design, and incorporate more than one type of observable. The analyst's knowledge base must be wide to use these five kinds of observables, or they must have access to people or organizations with the right kind of in-depth knowledge for design, employment, and understanding of the resultant data. The five types of observables include: *cultural, technical, biometric, functional,* and *situational.* These observables drive collection; however, they are so specific and knowledge-driven that they must come from a highly skilled advanced analyst, as collection man-agers will not possess requisite cognitive and knowledge skills to design such specific observables. The definitions of the five kinds of observables are

- *Cultural observables*: Observed or measured, tangible or intangible properties deriving from the ways of living propagated by a particular ethnic group. Cultural observables have preeminence among the four types of observables owing to their importance in a society.
- *Situational observables*: Tangible or intangible properties observed or measured in the OE with or under a variety of circumstances and vari-ables indicating the presence or absence of activities or behaviors.
- *Technical observables*: Tangible or intangible properties observed or measured by identifying or recognizing technical aspects of an OE, the infrastructure supporting a culture, and visible and invisible electronic activities and energies so much a part of any OE.
- *Functional observables*: Observed or measured tangible or intangible properties belonging to categories or families of functions or activities. For example, a functional observable could be an insurgent moving the parts to make a bomb from one location to another.
- *Biometric observables*: Observed or measured tangible or intangible prop-erties belonging to unique human physiological emissions or emanations such as heart beat, blood pressure, retinal temperature, degree of aggres-sion, sweat, chemical emissions, gestures, REM, or lack of blinking, etc.

Improving intelligence analysis depends on useful training and education. The challenge is to help people learn to think and use individual and aggregate thoughts to fight the insurgents and irregulars in a seemingly invisible cognitive domain that is in a city whose citizens live in a culture dramatically different from American culture. Improving intelligence analysis so it can work with high standards in a variety of urban OEs will take a substantial influx of training and education resources, different approaches to learning, and long-term commitments to set conditions for improving how to think about insurgents who embed themselves and conduct operations from hidden networks in large urban settings.

As a first step, advanced analyst training and education must depend on a triad of interrelated activities. In its most fundamental version, this means the following thoughts. First, the individual analyst is responsible for their intellectual development as a person, not as part of a team. This means most of the time they have to learn on their own time. Next, intelligence analysts must have repeated but graduated access to schools and colleges for advanced individual and team training and education. Finally, they must have a vibrant, continuous, and organized training and education program in their unit or organization. This need is real and should not be obscured by the old saw that one hears about analyst training: "Don't worry about analytic training. They get all they need by working every day and through on-the-job training." This approach did not work to develop the human intellect in the past and will not work in the future, if we want to develop this underused aspect of future conflict.

Training and education programs must implant and nurture intellectual capabilities sufficient to innovate, imagine, and even create new ideas, organizations, ways to collect, perspectives, and understandings of the enemy and OEs. In intensive learning programs, people learn "how to think" along with "what to think." In this program, along with gaining technical and intellectual competence and proficiency, creative thinking, imagination, and innovation flourish.

Advanced analysis requires exceptional thinkers who understand the modern world, globalization, cultures, military theory, collection, technology, advanced analysis, and how to think about and operate in the information domain. Thus, the intellectual foundation for its training and education needs to be sound and supported by theory but also well grounded in reality. Advanced analysis training and education needs an advanced analysis philosophy, a solid intellectual foundation, support by an organized and disciplined VKE, and intelligence C^2 (for the M&S, replication of data environments, and intelligence processes such as analytic overwatch).

Interestingly, once we start thinking about how to train and educate people to use the culture factor—its significant influence on our operations and how to prepare intelligence analysts to know more than superficialities—we arrive at an immediate conclusion. If we are honest with ourselves, we must acknowledge that our thought processes are insufficient to understand the cultural, technical, biometric, situational, and even functional details necessary for conducting successful urban operations, let alone using these details for creating an advantage. Why is this so hard?

- *First*, although this might be an obvious statement, it needs to be said: People from other cultures do not think as we do. They have different values and outlooks. The United States is attempting to overlay its mindset, policies, and thought processes on urban OEs that are very different from what exists in the United States. Unfortunately, terrorists and insurgents are often much more aligned with how the contested population thinks, perceives, and views the world than U.S. forces, which are often viewed as interlopers from a foreign world that might as well be from another planet.

- *Second*, people from different cultures have different perspectives. These perspectives come from living in and being heavily influenced by cultural mores, traditions, language, history, myths, values, and religion, which enshroud their every breathing moment.
- *Third*, people form stereotypes of different cultures. Such stereotyping often lies directly at the center of disagreements and arguments; it also heavily influences individual and organizational behavior. These stereotypes form a cloud in which our views become veiled and distorted. They preclude us from both "seeing" and understanding what we see. They cause our conditioned minds to filter, twist, and manipulate reality into what we think to be truth or fact.
- *Fourth*, people from different cultures may not behave similarly. Sometimes what is normal for one culture is abnormal, even abhorrent, to another. For example, people from the Middle East use hand and arm gestures when they talk; western people usually have less demonstrative body language. People from the Middle East get physically close to people when they talk, which makes westerners uncomfortable. People from Middle East kiss when greeting each other, even among people of the same sex. This practice is unusual in the West and makes Americans uncomfortable. People from the Middle East often exaggerate when they talk; people who have lived in America for a long time are often more direct and less inclined to "stretch the truth."
- *Fifth*, to learn a culture, people must study it intensely for a long time, learning the language, immersing themselves in the culture, and experiencing its rhythms and vicissitudes. This takes time and effort—both are in short supply for skilled intelligence analysts.

This cultural discussion merely peeks behind the curtain of what intelligence analysts have to learn and know to perform good analysis of the ilk discussed in this work. Of course, the bottom line of all intelligence analysis remains—to provide commanders with actionable knowledge of sufficient value to enable them to make decisions and act. Layers of patterns and trends, masks of self-protection, and webs of relationships appear when one knows and understands culture. For any analyst to know and understand what causes behavior (a critical element in determining intent, motive, will, and morale) and to anticipate activities and transactions, they must know and understand that culture's influences on thought, perspectives, and behavior. These various aspects of being a culturally conditioned human being center on what we observe and conclude; the mental activities occurring in a person's hidden side; what might occur in a person's subconscious; and what is presented as a multilayered mask, deceptive looks, or self-protective, face-saving ploys. Under the smile or nod or clenched fist lies another world that differs considerably across cultures as well as among tribes, sects, or groupings within cultures.

Thus, it is safe to conclude that analysts must learn through training and education to think and perceive like the person or people they are attempting to know and understand. Combat-experienced author Stewart Herrington pondered what happens in his enemy's mind as he recalled the struggle against a formidable, elusive, embedded enemy in Viet Nam. He concluded it was important to answer the question "How many Viet Cong are there in a given village, and who are they? But it is equally important to know why they are out there and what goes through their minds as they hide."[12] In his book, Herrington does not go into depth on the importance of this statement. But he leads the reader to conclude that to fight insurgents one must know and understand the enemy's thoughts and the conditioners or shaping mechanisms influencing those thoughts.

However, other than devoting many years and dollars to the intense study of places around the world in which we may or may not become involved, how does one develop the depth and breadth of knowledge that advanced analysis requires? One answer lies in training and educating analysts about relationships. Relationships strengthen, indeed underpin, the inner person of any culture. People—family, friends, business acquaintances, school chums, and religious connections and relationships—make up the fabric of a person's life. These patterns connect with other patterns and groupings. Therefore, good analysts are trained and educated to intellectually understand social network analysis (SNA) not from the seductive power of their own perspectives, but from the cultural perspective of the country or neighborhood in question. Good analysts will also learn to use software tools or remote data scientists' expertise to help understand multiple connections and layers in human and organizational social and business fabrics, up to the "nth" degrees of connections. However, identifying relationships is not enough. Advanced analysts have to learn to understand connections among people, organizations, and infrastructures. These connections or links can be *physical*—wire or fiber-optic cable; *human*—a person or people; *functional*—activities, interactions, or transactions such as banking, bartering, security, or arranging for transportation; *familial*—individual or group of people tied by family roots; *thought*—association with or development of something observed, imagined, discussed, or connected by thought; and *intent*—movement and action in accordance with intent or earlier guidance that links only thorough purpose.

To understand the confoundingly complex aspects of a culture, intelligence analysts must learn, through training and education, how to engage in semiotics analysis, tendency analysis, anomaly analysis, and aggregation analysis—all essential cognitive elements of advanced analysis. All of these cognitive processes help us know and understand the culture in question and from that knowledge develop the subtle and nuanced observables that characterize, indeed define, activities within the context of a particular culture and recompose and synthesize data into information and information into knowledge.

Additionally, in all cases, effective advanced analysts seek the opinions of people who have significant expertise and cultural knowledge, or who might be a contrarian, as a double check on their thinking. As a further thought, effective advanced analysts are introspective. Thus, they examine their expectations and know their thinking well enough to look for mistakes in logic, assumptions, and how the culture in question influences their thoughts. However, as one acknowledged expert tells us,

> Expectations have many diverse sources, including past experience, professional training, and cultural and organizational norms. All these influences predispose analysts to pay particular attention to certain kinds of information and to organize and interpret this information in certain ways. Perception is also influenced by the context in which it occurs. Different circumstances evoke different sets of expectations.[13]

This is a provocative quote. It suggests the presence of an important issue: a human's intellectual proclivity and cultural shaping and influences cause the analyst to *expect* things to happen. Effective analysts, though, arm themselves with the foreknowledge that their cultural backgrounds and intellectual proclivities (i.e., how they think) heavily influence their expectations as well as what data they gather and how they choose to organize it. Thus, the analyst and his or her mentors must constantly inquire, "What if I am missing the correct expectation?" "What if my expectation is conditioned by *my cultural influencers* and *not the culture in question?*" Continuing on, the Heuer passage suggests the need for an analytic "sweeper" (perhaps a software tool) to search through discarded data relating to expectations for viable alternatives and to present them not only to the analyst doing the thinking on this particular problem but to a virtual Red Teaming board or individual that looks at the expectation chosen among those available and identifies either the reasonableness of it or the possible errors, dangers, and risks with the chosen expectation. A thought process of this nature does not suggest a bureaucratic entanglement slowing and tainting thoughts and analysis, but merely *the need to watch for false expectations in ones own mind.*

In addition, training and education must involve thinking about and understanding context. Context involves the circumstances in which an event occurs.[14] Context is important (in military terminology, context is the OE in which the analysis is occurring) for thinking about all activities, interactions, outcomes, and cause and effect relationships. Contextual influencers of thought include the enemy, the local populace, the neighborhood proper, neutrals present, the local infrastructure, culture, weather, religion, and its multitudinous influencers. These are some of the many interactions, transactions, and activities inherent to a particular social or cultural setting that is at best fluid and complex, all belonging to context.

Along another line of thought, training and education must help advanced analysts learn to explore contradictions—they are a rudimentary aspect of any intelligence analysis task. A contradiction is "a statement or proposition that contradicts or denies another or itself and is logically incongruous."[15] As previously discussed, an analyst working in urban counterinsurgencies or irregular warfare will have expectations and hypotheses; such an analyst will undoubtedly have many opinions and draw many conclusions in his or her mind as an expectation or hypothesis. But contradictions will cloud this analyst's perspective, critical thinking ability, and continuous search for the truth. Naturally, the analyst will feel compelled to resolve the contradiction(s). But to work with contradictions in urban counterinsurgency operations, analysts first have to know the inner workings of a society and its people well enough to recognize the multitudinous numbers of beckoning contradictions inherent to the problem at hand. Only then will the analyst be able to sift through the contradictions to find and select those most relevant for resolution.

If trained and educated to think this way, the analyst has the capability to engage in mental work to pursue the contradiction's antithesis. The antithesis and its inherent contradictions eventually lead to a culturally shaped synthesis. This cerebral process borrows heavily from Hegel's theory of dialectic. Frederick Copleston tells us about Hegel's dialectic in the following citation; the discussion has direct applicability to the higher-level thinking our modern advanced intelligence analysts energetically engage in. In this regard, Copleston tells us,

> In his account of dialectical thinking, Hegel makes a rather disconcerting use of the word "contradiction." Through what he calls the power of the negative, a concept of the understanding is said to give rise to a contradiction. That is to say, the contradiction implicit in the concept becomes explicit when the concept loses its rigidity and self-containedness and passes into its opposite . . . For the emergence of contradiction is the motive force, as it were, of the dialectical movement. The conflict of opposed concepts and the resolution of the conflict in a synthesis which itself gives rise to another contradiction is the feature which *drives the mind restlessly onwards towards an ideal term, an all-embracing synthesis, the complete system of truth* (emphasis added) . . . for Hegel it is precisely the impossibility of being satisfied with a sheer contradiction which forces the mind onwards to a synthesis in which the contradiction is overcome.[16]

Training and education has to help people learn how to think this way. As critical thinkers, we must consider some implications from Hegel's thoughts:

- Analysts need to be flexible in their thoughts, eliminate rigidity ("I know truth"), and actively search for contradictions, either obvious or as abstruse as a nagging concern. The first process isn't difficult, as all people comprehend obvious contradictions. Where the mental process becomes more difficult, though, is when contradictions lurk in the turmoil of our thoughts, when the contradictions are abstract or difficult to conceptualize, or when we don't understand what is causing the contradiction, only that one exists and is causing cognitive dissonance.
- The human mind is restless and constantly seeks either an existing or a new thesis. Eventually, through self-argumentation and criticism (perhaps even introspection), people find contradictions in the quest for truth in their theses (hypotheses). This drives us to search for, create, or borrow the antithesis. The antithesis and its inherent, implicit contradictions cause the restless mind to strive for a synthesis that, if found, is often innovative or creative.
- If the dialectic is used correctly with a cultural perspective, this style of thinking becomes a purveyor of innovation, imagination, and most importantly, creativity.

It is important and extraordinarily complex to engage in this type of thought. These cognitive activities require a constantly improving mind. This improvement comes with training, education, experience, mentoring, and continually challenging one's mind.

Complexity. Intelligence analysts must contemplate and learn how complex adaptive systems (CAS) interact in a large urban setting. In this respect, reflective people learn to understand how people, units, elements of networks, electrons, and organizations careen from contact, collide, or intersect in the crowded labyrinth that is a large urban setting. These interactions can be peaceful, unobtrusive, vigorous, invisible, or violent. Regardless of outcomes of the interactions, the collisions, intersections, and careening emit energy—some visible and some invisible. To be successful in advanced analysis takes aggressive work in purposefully looking for this energy in the observables designed to confirm or deny hypotheses, expectations, activities, mysteries, and even emergent behavior. They must know and understand each part of the infrastructure and culture enshrouding and inextricably entwining with every aspect of civil and government life. Discussion of complexity in the urban environment, unpredictability, CAS, sensitive variables, perturbation of the network, order in chaos, and potentially explosive second- and third-order effects—all aspects of complexity theory in practical form—will surface periodically throughout this work.

Urban infrastructure is the framework for the multifaceted life activities of the population—information, electricity, goods and services, transportation, and so forth. Our best thinkers form causal relationships among one or more areas such as crime, public moods, individual and group protests, the movement of information, support to insurgents, apathy, support to coalition/government, and general unhappiness or satisfaction of the population with individual and conglomerated segments and activities occurring in the infrastructure. However, to perform such intimate and detailed work with the infrastructure, people must have knowledge about its elements and characteristics. They must understand how the infrastructure influences society. In addition, they must understand how the populace and its leaders view the supporting infrastructure. Each aspect of infrastructure is technically complex and difficult to understand, particularly in how its elements fit within and influence the social fabric of the society in question. This complexity can be overcome through personal knowledge, or more likely through working with a dedicated, organized, and disciplined VKE.

The infrastructure is important to both populace and enemy. Insurgents must use portions of the infrastructure to operate their networks and influence the population as well as their opponents. Paradoxically, they must attack portions of the infrastructure to create the attitudinal influences they desire among the population, as well as to keep alive a perceived state of chaos in the society in which they embed themselves. This dichotomy provides excellent potential for analysts to exploit. To counteract insurgents' periodic capability to target and destroy portions of an infrastructure, advanced analysts must know the infrastructure from technical, cultural, and human perspectives, including those of the populace, the enemy, and the U.S. commanders.

This chapter has provided some solutions to several of the significant problems facing intelligence analysts, which preclude their entrée into advanced analysis. Many ideas come forth in this chapter as methods or thoughts in which analysts can meet analytic challenges and overcome attendant problems. However, the main thoughts to carry over into the next chapter on setting the stage for advanced analysis can be summed up as follows.

- Intelligence analysts must engage in higher level thinking to be successful in urban OE. Intelligence analysts have to possess broad and deep intellectual skills and knowledge sufficient to outthink a continuously changing and learning enemy. These skills, so essential to advanced analysis, come with organized and disciplined training and education.
- The chapter introduced and discussed advanced analysis. Advanced analysis is "The high-level cognitive processes producing specific, detailed thought and understanding of the OE and knowledge superior to that possessed by the adversary." Advanced analysis has 14 cognitive functions—decomposition, critical thinking, link, pattern, trend,

anticipatory, technical, anomaly, cultural, tendency, semiotics, and aggregation analysis, recomposition, and synthesis.

- The chapter brings forth the importance of the initiative in counterinsurgency and operations against irregular warfare operations. As such, when using advanced analysis, intelligence analysts anticipate enemy activities, and through the commander's direction lead the fight for the initiative. In fact, anticipatory analysis, as one of the cognitive elements of advanced analysis, centers on the initiative as its focus. Schools for analysts, self-directed learning, and training and professional development sessions in units and organizations must always provide analysts the means to constantly improve in the intense competition for advantage in the initiative.

- This chapter advocates a broadened perspective in how intelligence analysis motivates and guides collectors and influences overall collection. PIR and IR will retain their preeminence because they spring from the commander's decision-making process. Unfortunately, over the years PIR have become static; however, they need to be dynamic to meet the changing requirements certain to occur in a fluid urban setting. Therefore, along with PIR and IR, there will be other drivers of intelligence. Some of the most notable will include *hypotheses, expectations, hunches,* and *mysteries.* The chapter defined each and therefore will not restate them.

- The chapter also argues for advanced analysts to be specific in their thinking and actions. When specificity is the driving force in analytic work, understanding of the OE and the networked threat comes forth in sufficient depth to drive collection with specific observables and to synthesize resultant data into actionable knowledge. To be specific takes knowledge. Thus, the analyst has to either possess sufficient knowledge to be specific or find people who possess it and are available to help design collection and turn resultant data into knowledge.

- Intelligence analysts must drive, guide, and purposefully commingle with all types of collection, including traditional human intelligence (HUMINT) and nontraditional sources and methods. With respect to observables, as mentioned earlier, intelligence analysis and collection always look for, design, and incorporate more than one type of observable. In the past, people typically used only functional observables, but advanced analysts must work with and develop five types of observables: *cultural, technical, biometric, functional,* and *situational.* These observables drive collection; however, they are so specific and knowledge intensive that they must come from a highly skilled advanced analyst, as collection managers will typically not possess requisite cognitive and knowledge skills with which to design them.

- The chapter argues for a large effort in training and education to help people learn to perform advanced analysis. Improving intelligence analysis so it can work with high standards in a variety of urban OEs will take a substantial influx of training and education resources, different approaches to learning, and long-term resource commitments. These efforts are needed to set conditions for improving how analysts think about insurgents who embed themselves and conduct operations in large urban settings. As a first step, advanced analyst training and education must depend on and work with a triad of interrelated activities. The individual analyst is responsible for their intellectual development as a person, not as part of a team. This means they have to learn on their own time. Intelligence analysts must also have repeated but graduated access to schools and colleges for advanced individual and team training and education. Finally, they must have a vibrant, continuous, and organized training and education program in their unit or organization. Advanced training and education programs will implant and nurture intellectual capabilities sufficient to innovate, imagine, and even create new ideas, organizations, ways to collect, perspectives, and understanding of the enemy and OEs. In intensive advanced analysis learning programs, people learn "how to think" along with "what to think." Training and education will help advanced analysts learn to work with and use contradictions—they are a rudimentary aspect of any intelligence analysis task. These contradictions will cloud the analyst's perspective, critical thinking ability, and continuous search for the truth. Naturally, the analyst will feel compelled to resolve the contradiction(s). If trained and educated to think this way, the analyst will possess the capability to engage in mental work to pursue the contradiction's antithesis. The antithesis and its inherent contradictions eventually lead to a new approach, or synthesis. This is the dialectic, minus the laborious explanations of academia, but it is of extraordinary value to the advanced analyst.

With this summary in mind, the next chapter beckons. It discusses the activities and processes that must be in place to optimize advanced analysis.

4

Setting the Stage for Advanced Analysis

This chapter involves enablers for advanced analysis. In fact, the success or failure of intelligence analysts trained in the art of advanced analysis will often depend upon the successful contributions of each of the important enablers this chapter discusses. This chapter explains each of the enablers, but also implores the reader to recognize their importance and how they fit within the overall scheme of advanced analysis. Some of these enablers are not in existence now; however, this book strongly suggests the requirement for them to be brought into being as necessary enhancers for advanced analysis and for future intelligence operations writ large. The five enablers are: 1) analytic condition-setting, 2) VKE, 3) detailed guidance to collectors, 4) analytic wargaming, and 5) analytic strategy.

ANALYTIC CONDITION-SETTING

Intelligence analysts cannot be passive and wait for direction. Instead, they have to be anticipatory and aggressively active in setting the conditions that must be in place for them to succeed. To set conditions, the intelligence analyst must keep one foot in the present and one foot in the future. Because nobody will do the future planning for the intelligence analyst, he or she must develop, set, and initiate the conditions that provide the best opportunities for analytic success. This type of condition-setting does not exist today; however, it should. Unfortunately, this type of work is split among staff elements, if it is thought of at all, and certainly it does not appear within the current roles and missions of intelligence analysts. Although this condition-setting does not and will never advocate a singular approach only by intelligence analysts, it does advocate aggressive, anticipatory thinking and teaming with collection people and technologists for sensor and data condition-setting respectively. Analysts will have to coordinate for knowledge environment condition-setting with whoever is responsible for knowledge management operations on the staff or in the organization.

Without analytic condition-setting, the analysts' capabilities shrink proportionately. In a broad sense, without condition-setting, analysts will be, by definition, reactionary. Unfortunately, in urban operations, being reactionary is debilitating when related to the proactive activities inherent to insurgent or irregular operations. Intelligence is difficult precisely because it involves unknowns such as enemy intent, populace's perceptions, populace's reactions to friendly activities, politician's strategies, the influence of second- and third-order effects, the sudden appearance and influence of sensitive variables, and the influence of a constantly churning OE and its inhabitants. Regardless, the commander relies on the intelligence analyst to help him think through the enemy's intent, future courses of action, weak points,[1] and morphing of links and nodes of his supporting networks. Compounding these difficulties, intelligence analysts must cope with a logic that has been discussed, but is important enough to review once more. This logic provides the rationale for condition-setting of all three types. That is, the OE is fluid. This means people, organizations, and infrastructure conduct transactions, interactions, activities, and behave in ways to cause outcomes. Complex adaptive systems (CAS), which are discussed later, constantly collide, intersect, and career, creating the expenditure of energy and motion. Buildings go up and get torn down. The infrastructure works and performs in some areas of the city while not working in other parts. Complicating the logic, the enemy looks like the populace, sounds like them, lives in their midst, and hides his activities amongst the normal and legitimate activities of the populace. The enemy operates from an invisible, flat, amorphous (having no particular shape) network. Superimposed on this descriptive situation come constantly changing roles and missions for U.S. and coalition forces with corollary constraints and rules of engagement (ROEs) that differ from one situation to the next. These missions will differ, e.g., reconstruction, combat, health and welfare, etc., and all will have different tolerance levels for ambiguity, uncertainty, and risk tolerance. The changing decisions will cause immense pressure to produce knowledge that drives down uncertainty and assuages the negative impact of risk. This quest for quality knowledge (timely and usable) places immense pressure on the ISR system. The people on whom this pressure falls are the intelligence officer, the intelligence analyst, and the collection specialist.

This logic drives intelligence people to think ahead and set the analytic conditions for success. The prescient intelligence analyst must think through this logic and identify possible indirect approaches to vigorously going after the enemy given the constraints of the OE and the challenges presented by his network. Military theorist B. H. Liddell Hart helps us consider condition-setting in a slightly different but related all the same venue as an intent of condition-setting via indirect approaches and dislocation with these thoughts:

> In the psychological sphere, dislocation is the result of the impression on the commander's mind of the physical effects . . . The impression is strongly accentuated if his realization of his being at a disadvantage is sudden, and if he feels that he is unable to counter the enemy's moves. Psychological dislocation fundamentally springs from this sense of being trapped.[2]

Analytic condition-setting fits into three areas of thought and influence—data, sensor, and knowledge architectures. Each deserves some discussion.

Data condition-setting. Analysts depend upon data; therefore, they must think about and set up the data environment to provide the data they will need for the decision-making problem they will face in the next branch, sequel, or problem set. Nobody else will do this work for them. This is not to say they are alone in this endeavor. It simply says the analyst has to take matters into his or her hands and initiate and state the data requirements to the technologist, who is usually in the signal staff section, or at higher levels, the technologist in the JTF or COCOM J2 technical staff sections. Intelligence analysts have to set conditions to seek, find, and exploit data existing in data farms around the world. Why is this even an issue? Many of the databases housing the data that analysts require are closed to public consumption, are proprietary, or they cost money to access and use. Also, any database will have identification and password requirements, which take time to arrange. Many databases will be differently constructed than others. Veracity or truthfulness of data will be an issue, or better yet a lingering challenge for all analysts seeking data from either the open Internet or the closed portals of the military's classified networks. Analysts also have to work with both collection specialists and technologists to set up the data architecture for the type of collectors the analytic/collection team has developed to work against analytic-driven observables. Although this is a primary responsibility of the collection specialist, the analyst must be aggressive and drive the development of the data architecture to not only receive the data from his or her observables, but to receive it, process it, and develop it into information and knowledge in time to make a difference in command decision-making.

Sensor condition-setting. Advanced analysts have to work with sensor specialists to set conditions for access to the right kind of collection asset to meet the needs they prognosticate. This requirement cannot be left up to the collection specialist acting alone. Quite simply, the collection specialist does not understand the future as the analyst does, and does not understand corollary decisions and cascading data, information, and knowledge requirements. Analysts have to be involved with this kind of work. It is the analysts' observables coming from the decomposition that will drive what the sensor or HUMINT looks for, as well as when and where to look. This requirement becomes even more complicated when the analyst anticipates the future as to what the next mission will be, what the commander's intent and guidance will be, what decisions will have to be made, what knowledge will be required for making the best possible decisions, what observables will be driving the collection, and the specific kind, precise placement, and data flow of both technical sensors and HUMINT to satisfy analyst future information requirements.

Knowledge condition-setting. As mentioned earlier, analysts must set conditions for the development of knowledge they use while performing their work. To set this condition, it helps to understand what knowledge can provide. In a previous book, I wrote

> The underlying lesson for all human beings is the importance of striving to do something with knowledge that creates a lasting advantage. It follows that what is truly important in any conflict is what people or machines do with information to turn it into knowledge, to manage that knowledge so people can use it, think, plan, and make decisions faster and better than the competitor.[3]

Knowledge is critical to planning and execution—it is the means to power. It is a given that command decisions will be much more effective with high-grade, valuable knowledge than with data or even information. With knowledge, the commander can reduce risk and lower uncertainty to an acceptable (to his particular decision style) level. However, knowledge is not easy to develop, particularly in the changing, fluid urban OE we have been discussing. Thus, the intelligence analyst must establish a knowledge environment before the actual knowledge is required. Similar to sensor architecture work, the analyst must again use what they have prognosticated as the commander's future missions and decisions. They must anticipate what the knowledge requirements will be given the commander's predilections for decision-making with respect to both uncertainty and risk. As such, they have to anticipate their commander's knowledge requirements and set conditions to seek, find, and exploit knowledge to meet those future knowledge requirements. Sometimes, they will draw upon their own staffs for required knowledge—it could be sitting in a database, in need of only a slight "buffing" to add value. At other times, neither the analyst nor anybody on the staff will be capable of providing the "buffing" or developing new knowledge owing to an acute absence of relevant knowledge. At these times, the analyst will go outside his or her staff to acquire the right knowledge SME or the right knowledge database to find the required knowledge, to add value to existing knowledge, or even develop entirely new knowledge. The advanced analyst will have to line up this knowledge support early. In a reinforcing thought, two highly regarded authors advise people to contemplate and organize knowledge networks. Their thoughts provide some sage advice:

> Almost everyone who works in an organization is also a member of such cross-cutting networks. These join people in one organization to people in similar positions with similar practices in other organizations. For well-established practices, professions, and professional associations form the basis of such networks.[4]

Bottom line—as advanced analysts set conditions, they need to set up and establish knowledge environments for networking, sharing knowledge, and building knowledge to satisfy future command decision-making requirements.

The analyst, in this regard, will organize anticipated required knowledge experts for the type of planning, decisions, and interpretation of data and turning it into information and knowledge. As such, the analyst will have to turn to the intelligence enterprise, nongovernment organizations, commercial entities such as corporations, interagency people and organizations, indigenous SMEs, and of course a VKE (which we will shortly discuss in some depth). This knowledge work is challenging but essential to the success of the advanced analyst. No analyst can be expected to know everything that might come forward as an information requirement. It follows that the analyst will have to anticipate the expertise they will need, the thinking skills that working with some knowledge requires, and their own shortfalls (organizationally and personally). They must also set conditions to use a desired knowledge architecture before the crisis arrives. If they wait until the crisis arrives, obtaining sufficient knowledge would be clearly impossible owing to time constraints and complexity involved in finding, lining up, arranging for the contracts, doing the security clearance work, and finding a workable knowledge broker to help with such a task.

Analytic condition-setting is not something that can be hit or miss. It must be in place as part of every analyst's thinking skills. Their organizations must help them do this advanced thinking and planning, and line up the three architectures to give them the best opportunity to succeed.

VIRTUAL KNOWLEDGE ENVIRONMENT (VKE)

A VKE provides a conceptual and technical framework for standardizing current ideas and practices related to reach back. (*Reach back* is connectivity to and collaboration with assets and resources not locally available.) It congeals various parts and pieces of the information domain into an organized, virtual, next generation fusion process. The VKE has three distinct roles: 1) provide data, information, and knowledge support to commanders and intelligence analysts, planners, and military operations people; 2) provide specialized expertise to help work details of intelligence work; and 3) provide the cognitive and knowledge wherewithal to help commanders, operators, and intelligence analysts make decisions, seize the initiative, and stay ahead of enemy decision cycles. This capability does not exist today. It should. Instead, there are ad hoc arrangements based primarily on personal acquaintances, which are neither organized nor disciplined. In particular, units at all levels need to be capable of seeking, finding, and using world-class minds and cutting edge technology to help provide high-grade and valuable knowledge related to their complicated and difficult targets, which owing to timeliness, specificity, even clarity problems, the intelligence community cannot meet. A noted expert in decision theory provides us with the following highly related insight into the importance of using experts in problem solving:

> Military commanders also need to detect leverage points . . . Leverage points are just possibilities—pressure points that might lead to something useful, or might go nowhere. Expertise may be valuable in noticing these leverage points. Certainly in games like chess, the experts are more likely to see them. In interpreting situations, experts seem attuned to the leverage points—both the opportunities and the threats facing them.[5]

Unfortunately, the high-grade, current knowledge necessary to plan and make decisions in complex environments is difficult to find and make usable. It is difficult to find because the landscape, infrastructure, human interactions, and organizational activities occur and change so quickly. In addition, working with knowledge is challenging because of the constant change, motion, expulsion of energy, and cultural variables and dominants at play in all military activities in urban OE. In particular, knowledge concerning certain aspects of cities is difficult to use because it is often outdated; it sometimes isn't precise enough; or it doesn't take cultural, infrastructure, or neutral considerations and applications into account. Also, as we have discussed, working with advanced analysis takes very detailed and up-to-date knowledge not only to know but also to apply directly to intelligence problems and challenges. Thus, it is largely impossible for a traditional staff of any size to possess requisite expertise to develop sufficient, specific knowledge on a continuum to keep decision-making risk low and uncertainty at a manageable state. Advanced analysis uses a virtual knowledge environment (VKE) to overcome this shortfall.

Along with helping to understand urban challenges, knowledge also complicates urban operations. Finding and massaging knowledge so it is usable is no small feat, particularly in urban OE. Let us review some of the main reasons for this complicated status. Three types of knowledge exist, as discussed earlier. First, there is existing knowledge. Existing knowledge is often unusable. It could be interesting, but can be outdated, particularly in fast-moving situations. Second, there is value-added knowledge. This type of knowledge comes from subject matter experts (SMEs) adding their knowledge, experience, cultural background, and intuition to existing knowledge. Third, there is new knowledge. Sometimes no relevant knowledge exists. This circumstance necessitates an effort to build new knowledge.

What would a VKE appear as, from an organizational perspective? A VKE for reach back is organized and disciplined (meaning a VKE meets standards and does not veer off of a mission to place its attention elsewhere). Knowledge brokers lead elements of virtual and physical knowledge environments to provide knowledge support to deployed staffs and commanders. Elements of a VKE include knowledge brokers, problem managers, SMEs, centers of excellence (COEs), and highly skilled, world-class data scientists. These elements are for the most part virtual and are not a permanent part of any particular organization. When the requesting advanced analyst states his or her information or knowledge requirement, the knowledge broker and problem manager form virtual teams of the right SMEs, COEs, and data scientists to work on exceptionally difficult and specific problems brought via reach back to the VKE. Once the job is complete and the requestor is satisfied with the knowledge product, the virtual grouping disbands and another comes forth with a different slant, expertise base, and data, owing to working a different problem. These virtual groupings of great minds, highly proficient niche organizations, and data scientists working with the latest software tools are a great asymmetric advantage the United States has over any enemy.

Reach back for detailed knowledge support is too complicated and important to be left to ad hoc arrangements and happenstance. When any reach back system seeks SMEs or distributed data, decision makers need to know they are receiving the best SME support and the best (relative, precise, and trustworthy) and most up-to-date knowledge—this check for due diligence is left to happenstance with ad hoc systems. In addition, reach back must be timely. In any OE, commanders will use timeliness as one of

their standards for reach back operations. Meeting this standard is important and will fall on those organizations providing the reach back support.
The most difficult aspect of meeting this standard is ensuring the quality of
knowledge is good. Forward deployed commanders and staffs seeking to
use reach back must provide definitive guidance and standards that are reasonable. If commanders and staffs place unreasonable standards on reach
back operations, they must be willing to accept less-than-desired outcomes
caused by not having sufficient time to develop high-quality knowledge
products.

Interestingly, as an abstract but noteworthy characteristic of urban settings, large cities constantly change, causing usable knowledge to decay
with new knowledge gaining strength and ascending in importance only to
find itself in decay too. Thus, the process of setting conditions for seeking,
finding, adding value to existing knowledge, or building new knowledge is
in constant motion. In this regard, a large city is very much like an ecosys-
tem with very little remaining unchanged or unscathed second by second or
minute by minute during military combat, humanitarian relief, stability,
and reconstruction operations. Because people and organizations live and
interact in an urban environment, everything in a city forms a complex web
of interdependency and connectedness. An action taken at any level influences every other aspect of the system. A VKE provides the constantly shifting and adjusting knowledge to help decision makers understand these
cause and effect relationships and their consequences.

Let's work through a brief example. In a city in which an insurgency is
occurring, there will be enemy insurgent networks operating against U.S.
forces. These networks are challenging to find because elements of the population support them, they are masters at hiding and deceiving, and they
embed themselves in everyday activities of the city. One of the ways they
hide their activities is to use the façade of legitimate companies to perform
necessary activities. In such a case, the insurgents in question need vehicles.
They need them for transporting bombs, people, and ammunition. They
need vehicles for conducting reconnaissance. They need them to set conditions for attacks. Thus, they obscure illegitimate among legitimate vehicles
within an extant company's fleet, hiding them from the prying eyes of U.S.
intelligence analysts.

If deployed intelligence analysts believe this hypothetical front company is providing vehicles to the insurgents, they could very well want to
study the company's accounting books for tax irregularities and depreciation schedules that could possibly lead to evidence confirming the company
in question is "dirty." Although sounding simple, this is a difficult analytic
scenario. People on a U.S. staff won't know the country and city tax codes.
Intelligence analysts won't know the inner working of the company in question and how it uses depreciation for tax purposes in the host culture. What
they need is a native-born accountant, an expert in the current tax code and

inner workings of companies operating in particular business functional areas. In a normal situation, they would submit the request up the chain of command through the traditional RFI channels. They would probably receive nothing back, as the request is basically unrecognizable in the traditional intelligence system.

It is easy to see how difficult it would be for the traditional intelligence community to satisfy the requirement. First, if so inclined to act, they would look in their own organization for such expertise. Second, they would look in the intelligence community for the expertise. Third, they would start seeking help from informal communities of interest within and outside the government. This problem set would be tedious and undoubtedly too difficult to solve in a timely manner. So one can conclude this approach would be untenable. The analyst would grow frustrated and would undoubtedly choose to disengage from such an effort.

Now, let us examine the problem if we had an organized reach back capability connecting to VKE. The requesting analyst would go to a forward-deployed knowledge broker and ask for assistance to find an indigenous tax accountant to work on the books of the suspected company. The forward-deployed knowledge broker would go to a virtual knowledge broker with a VKE capability with the problem. The forward-deployed knowledge broker would work with a virtual knowledge broker to quickly search through a SME database to find people with expertise, current experience, and detailed knowledge capabilities necessary to support the request and ask them to participate in virtual teaming. The virtual knowledge broker would use data scientists to start the data mining process of searching for and pulling together data the indigenous tax SME would need. Knowledge discovery software would seek relationships, links, and patterns. Statisticians would perform statistical analyses, visualization, and knowledge discovery.

In short order, the knowledge broker finds the right people—three experts who will provide the best combination of expertise. One of the experts is indigenous and works in a tax firm in the city in question and has impeccable credentials. Another works in the U.S. Internal Revenue Service (IRS), and the other is a native-born retired tax accountant with dual citizenship from the country in question and the United States. Once the knowledge broker and problem manger find tax experts, they pull together a virtual team of experts, data scientists, and support people who work together in a virtual collaborative setting to solve the problem.

The advanced analyst must be an expert in using a VKE but also in perceiving a knowledge void to start with. Once identified, such a void can be overcome in one of two ways: by seeking assistance within the intelligence analytic overwatch enterprise or using a VKE for cognition support. The enterprise's ability to satisfy any given requirement is influenced by what is occurring elsewhere in the enterprise: the capabilities and experience levels of available analysts and how fast members of the enterprise can respond to requests for cognitive assistance. Furthermore, the forward-deployed or even sanctuary parts of the analytic enterprise may be unable to answer questions, develop knowledge, add value to existing knowledge, or be willing to engage in advanced wargaming. If this occurs, aggressive advanced analysts rapidly gravitate to using a VKE for support.

ANALYTIC GUIDANCE TO COLLECTORS

Advanced analysts provide specific guidance and instructions to collectors with no middle managers in between. Advanced analysts must provide specific guidance and advice to collectors about the operational context, where and when to collect, what to look for, a detailed description of observables with which to look, standards (the latest and earliest times information is of value), and expectations. The analyst should also alert the distributed collection community to think like the enemy and explain what their sensors could be seeing from the enemy's perspective. Author Orson Scott Card helps us to understand this idea in the following thoughts:

> He found that a great deal of what he had learned at Battle School transferred to the simulator. He would routinely reorient the simulator every few minutes, rotating it so that he didn't get trapped into an up-down orientation, constantly reviewing his position from the enemy point of view. It was exhilarating at last to have such control over the battle to be able to see every point of it.[6]

When resultant collection data flows back to decision-making nodes, usually via a Distributed Common Ground System (DCGS), advanced analysts, with the help of VKE SMEs and data scientists, rapidly recompose data into information and knowledge. Valuable knowledge provides commanders the wherewithal to make fast, effective decisions. This type of specific analytic guidance to collectors does not occur today to the extent necessary to maximize the capabilities of the ISR system. But it should. Author and warrior General Frank Kitson reinforces this requirement with the following thought from *Low-Intensity Operations*:

> The army has an important part to play in the business [counterinsurgency operations (author's emphasis)], firstly by ensuring that intelligence is directed in such a way that *its own requirements are met* [emphasis added], and secondly by making a direct contribution in terms of men and material as required, even if, as sometimes happens, the body operating the existing organization, e.g., the police, does not welcome the assistance.[7]

As Kitson suggests, intelligence in COIN and IW has to be directed and specific. To be specific requires deep and current knowledge. This knowledge comes from skilled advanced intelligence analysts, not collection people. It follows then, that intelligence analysts must direct intelligence collection with the results of their front-end analysis we call *decomposition*. Even in the chaos and tumult of urban operations, this guidance to intelligence collectors must occur. The analyst knows there is order in chaos[8] and directs collection to test hypotheses, to surveil a specific location, or to gather broad indicators in an area search. One author's explanation about the edge of chaos has specific application to what, where, and how the intelligence analyst directs intelligence collection by providing specific guidance to collectors:

> Instead, all these complex system have somehow acquired the ability to bring order and chaos into a special kind of balance. This balance point— often called the edge of chaos—is where the components of a system never quite lock into place, and yet never quite dissolve into turbulence, either. The edge of chaos is where life has enough stability to sustain itself and enough creativity to deserve the name of life. The edge of chaos is where new ideas and innovative genotypes are forever nibbling away at the edges of the status quo.[9]

This passage implies the analyst has to turn the seeming chaos into a vision of order, and this is where the functioning network can be disambiguated, located, found, and coherently worked. Unfortunately, this type of specific analytic guidance to collectors flies in the face of conventional wisdom accumulated over the years about what analysts do and should not do, rigid bureaucratic rules and procedures precluding a flattening (thus sharing and collaborating) of the analysts' and collectors' information networks, and inhibitions toward analysts who desire to pass specific guidance but who generally get into trouble when attempting to do so.

On the other hand, the advanced analyst communicates directly with collection specialists who actually perform or control discipline-specific collection operations, including HUMINT, counterintelligence (CI), technical collectors, infrastructure specialists, neighborhood specialists, functional specialists, e.g., Baghdad corporate tax codes, and open source specialists. Advanced intelligence analysts provide guidance to collection people in person, by telephone, through automation, through chat rooms, or via e-mail. Continuing with the means of dissemination, the analyst composes guidance and either transmits it via instant messaging (IM), online chatting with specific recipients, or posting to a Web site's electronic bulletin board, asking collection specialists (such as an imagery analyst working a Predator unmanned aerial vehicle (UAV)) to look for specific activities via observables or lack thereof. Of course, advanced intelligence analysts always make themselves available for discussion or interpretation. In addition, intelligence analysts always keep collection guidance up-to-date or inform collection people when the target identified earlier is no longer needed. Automation must help in this communication by: 1) reminding the advanced analyst of needed updates, 2) providing a partially filled-out update form or graphic, and 3) wrapping the message into a packet for fast, accurate, and secure dispatch over the Internet. As a final point, an analytic specialist provides specific guidance to collection specialists using the following framework:

- Operational context.
- Specific observables—*functional, biometric, situational, cultural, technical.*
- Locations and times of expected behaviors or other phenomena postulations.
- Reporting guidance and miscellaneous instructions, e.g., expectations of enemy counters to possible U.S. collection.
- Standards.
  - Timeliness (time constraints, willingness to take risk to meet the time constraints).
    - Latest time information of value (LTIOV) & earliest time information of value (ETIOV).
  - Specificity (specifics such as "watch at this intersection for a person standing on the corner with running shoes under his robe, a cell phone, no jewelry, with heavy sweat on the face").
  - Accuracy (coordinates, pinpoint locations with GPS).
  - Relevance (to the mission, PIR, IR, or other sources of intelligence requirements).
  - Clarity (concreteness, clear description, exact addresses, precise activity to watch for, National Imagery Interpretation Rating System [NIIRS] and the type and clarity of desired inputs from collectors).

ANALYTIC WARGAMING

Wargaming for the initiative—act–react–counteract—needs to permeate all ranks of intelligence analysts. Although some wargaming certainly occurs in some organizations, analytic wargaming does not occur with regularity in analytic organizations. A quote from *On War* helps to concentrate our efforts on the need to wargame:

> Once the antagonists have ceased to be mere figments of a theory . . . when war is no longer a theoretical affair but a series of actions obeying its own peculiar laws, reality supplies the data from which we can deduce the unknown that lies ahead. From the enemy's character, from his institutions, the state of his affairs, and his general situation, each side, using the laws of probability, *forms an estimate of its opponent's likely course* (emphasis added) and acts accordingly.[10]

This type of wargaming must be part of advanced analysis and taught as a highly sought cognitive skill to all joint and service intelligence analysts.

Intelligence analysts must use wargaming to arrive at "what could happen" as the result of interaction among friendly forces, the enemy, neutrals, and private citizens and businesses. To derive such conclusions implies, of course, development and implementation of a type of wargaming that is analytically and culturally driven. Without question, the analytic wargaming that will soon be described is cerebrally challenging and downright difficult. At least a majority of the difficulty lies in what we can call *pendulum thinking*: enemy's view of friendly, enemy's view of self, enemy's view of friendly's view of self and enemy, and the same for friendly, neutrals, and host nation. We need superb thinkers to use this kind of wargaming, and more importantly, the thought it calls for, and merge it with deep understanding of the enemy, environment, infrastructure, populace, neutrals, and commercial interests.

The goal of analytic wargaming is first of all to develop the wherewithal to *seek, find,* and *seize the initiative.* Thus, wargaming yields ways to work against the mind of the enemy, to know and understand how he thinks, to outwit him, and to anticipate and deny his moves. Wargaming in advanced analysis is different in several ways than the wargaming people conduct during military decision-making in the course-of-action feasibility step:

- *First*, wargaming in advanced analysis purposefully seeks the initiative. To find and sustain the initiative, advanced intelligence analysts work through friendly, enemy, neutral, and host nation activities. During this effort, each competitor will possess the initiative and thereby acts first in the act–react–counteract cycle. When people react instead of acting, there is a noticeable difference in outcomes and resulting hypotheses, which serve as an ISR engine.
- *Second*, advanced intelligence analysts go into great detail in the act–react–counteract cycle of wargaming. To gain a sufficient level of detail to understand both the environment and the competitors well enough to seek, find, and sustain the initiative, analysts must know a lot about the enemy, host, the culture enshrouding the host, and the OE.
- *Third*, advanced analysis wargamers work through the enemy, neutral, and host nation's plans, strategies, goals, intent, will, constraints, and resources.
- *Fourth*, advanced analysis wargamers seek to understand enemy, neutral, and host nation *condition-setting* for accomplishing their goals. Some of this condition-setting is tangible and easy to understand, but other aspects are largely invisible, hidden in the recesses of the human mind and difficult to extirpate and examine.
- *Fifth*, advanced analysis wargamers examine sensitive variables and windows of opportunity from a friendly perspective as well as from those of each competitor.
- *Sixth*, advanced analysis wargamers purposefully set out to anticipate the next steps and actions of competitors, and thereby provide the commander with the possibility of preempting the enemy, which causes him to react to the friendly commander's actions.

- *Seventh*, advanced analysis wargamers take resultant hypotheses coming from the act–react–counteract cycles, decompose them into observables, and work with collectors to seek these observables through purposeful, directed collection.

Advanced analysis wargaming is the essential aspect for understanding the enemy's decision cycle and the options and constraints at work. Although the need for sophisticated mental wargaming is intuitively obvious, writer T. E. Lawrence reinforces the need for this kind of thinking:

> It considered the capacity for mood of our men, their complexities and mutability, and the cultivation of whatever in them promised to profit our intention. We had to arrange their minds in order of battle just as carefully and as formally as other officers would arrange their bodies. And not only our own men's minds, though naturally they came first. We must also arrange the minds of the enemy, of people supporting us behind the firing line, since more than half of the battle passed there in the back; then the minds of the enemy nation waiting the verdict; and of the neutrals looking on; circle beyond circle.[11]

Analytic wargaming also helps analysts understand the enemy's strategic aim, his strategies, tactics, and how he could use his available resources to satisfy his strategies. It introduces the multiple levels of consideration the analyst must bring to any interpersonal cognitive effort. It also gives players some insight into abstract subjects such as the enemy's will, motives, intent, thought and planning processes, how he makes decisions, how he uses his intelligence collection (whatever that may be), and the sources of information he trusts most.

All of this is to say that activities, interactions, and transactions in any urban OE *involve people*—neutrals, the enemy, the people who support the enemy, the host nation, commercial companies, and innocent bystanders. All people have thoughts, perspectives, and differing attitudes toward that most elusive determinant—will—and how much hardship they will put up with, how much pain they will endure, or how much effort they will put forth to win or achieve their goals. Clausewitz helps us understand the importance of will with the following thoughts:

> If you want to overcome your enemy you must match your effort against his power of resistance, which can be expressed as the product of two inseparable factors, viz. the total means at his disposal and the strength of his will. The extent of the means at his disposal is a matter—though not exclusively—of figures, and should be measureable. But the strength of his will is much less easy to determine and can only be gauged approximately by the strength of the motive animating it.[12]

All of these people and organizations in some way, shape, or form compete among themselves and with the U.S. military and its interagency and coalition partners. All have their belief in and commitment to will. It follows that U.S. military and interagency people need to develop and use a methodical way to understand the desires, motivations, and elements of the will of the people colliding, intersecting, or careening off one another in the cauldron that is the city. It also follows that commanders should use this analytic wargaming process to preempt the behavior, shape it, or, if the choice is to let events unfold, to have contingencies in mind should the competitive activities and collisions come into being.

With the above rationale in mind, we can conclude that U.S. military and interagency people need to understand each of the competing elements in the OE and keep track of their motivations, goals, strategies, intent, will, and the tools and capabilities each has for accomplishing them. Interestingly, each competitor takes actions to create effects that they hope will lead to achieving their goals and their objectives. This effort is to create desired outcomes while neutralizing, surprising, or stunning their competitors with unexpected moves and actions. This is the initiative. Each uses their capabilities to accomplish goals when they think the timing is right. Owing to its proven importance, the initiative must be contested over, but its possession will fluctuate. Within that fluctuation lies the capability to reseize the initiative and prepare for the assaults certain to come from other competitors to seek, seize, and sustain it.

As one of the most important aspects of intelligence wargaming, advanced analysts understand competitors' decision cycles with the overall goal of preempting their effects and actions or simply being ahead of their activities to anticipate, seize, and sustain the most important advantage: *initiative*. Traditionally, the U.S. military uses the Colonel John Boyd model[13] of getting ahead of the enemy's decision cycle—the observe, orient, decide, and act, or OODA loop. Unfortunately, if people try to use this model against the competing elements in the fluid, large city OE, they will be behind their competitors' decisions and consistently find any quest for the initiative to be illusive, delusional, and unattainable. Why is this?

The observer in Boyd's model finds himself already in the fray in some way, shape, or form. Because this model came from a fighter pilot in the Korean War, it makes sense to observe while taking action. With skill and a healthy dose of luck, one can occasionally seize the initiative when already in the action. However, when working against embedded insurgents in a city, one can claim neither the tactical nor the operational initiative when constantly attempting to gain the initiative. Too many unexpected things can happen, because a city is full of unexpected chance events or activities—this is also known as instantiation of Clausewitzian friction. In addition, any of the four pairs—enemy, friendly, neutral, or host nation—may commence some new action and cause others to react and thereby lose the initiative. When starting in the "observe" mode, our forces can orient, decide, and act, but often it is the enemy, neutral, or host nation who will hold the initiative.

With advanced analysis wargaming, a slightly different model is at work. Instead of setting conditions for "reaction," this model provides a framework for being proactive. As such, advanced analysis wargamers anticipate other competitors' activities. They work through possible second- and third-order effects and endeavor to avoid mirror imaging. Advanced analysts also develop counters or preemptive moves and identify possible sensitive variables for use in seizing the initiative against other competitors (if they appear and are exploitable), all the while protecting themselves from variable manipulation. The advanced analysis wargaming model concept uses an addendum to John Boyd's model. This model, AWOODAM[2] [14] (anticipate, wargame, observe, orient, decide, act, measure outcomes, and modify activities) forces the intelligence analyst/planner and the operations planner to anticipate what a competitor's activities will be or what the competitor's reaction to friendly activities will be. It leads advanced analysts to understand how the enemy views the OE and how the enemy must attempt to set conditions for his activities. The AWOODAM[2] model motivates the advanced analyst to develop observables that will warn of impending enemy actions to seize the initiative.

In the wargaming part of the AWOODAM[2] model of thought, cultural experts represent the aims, strategies, planning processes, decisions, actions, and assessments of the enemy, of neutrals, and of host nation elements. With conditions set, intelligence and operations planners and the opposing experts go through the four pairs of wargaming to learn what potential activities the competitors will use to achieve their goals and objectives and, in particular, to seize the initiative. Four-pair wargaming also helps U.S. and interagency people identify and learn specific effects and actions that will serve the U.S. military and interagency operations the best or identify those to be avoided. This type of wargaming helps planners identify how competitors are thinking and perceiving, their range of options, how they anticipate what the U.S. is up to, their degree of commitment (will), and their decision cycle—that is, how they will react to certain actions.

As mentioned earlier and now deserving further discussion, as a measure to enhance Colonel Boyd's OODA theory, advanced analysis involves adding "anticipate and wargame" at the front of the model and "measure and modify" at the end. Anticipate and wargame means advanced analysts routinely use *deep think* cognitive techniques to anticipate what the enemy could be doing given the analysts' knowledge of the enemy, OE, and friendly situation. Analysts then run their anticipation hypotheses through a rigorous wargaming ritual complete with a synthetic environment and indigenous people working with US experts to provide an aggressive, thinking enemy to work against in the wargaming environment. Once this activity completes, analysts use Boyd's OODA to delve further into their theoretical construct of enemy activities and resultant counters or steps to take to be ahead of those actions. At the end of the wargaming cycle, analysts want to devise ways to *measure* the success of effects and actions when compared to intent, strategies, and aims, and *modify* their thoughts or actions as necessary. Once analysts have an idea how effective specific effects and actions have been, commanders possess the wherewithal to modify their plans, use more resources, or cease the activity in question. Analysts also work to measure from all relevant perspectives how other competitors are viewing the situation from their cultural position, their range of options, constraints, the necessary conditions to be set to instantiate options, the degree of will the competitor likely possesses, and their commander's intent. Analysts interpret and measure the competitor's capabilities and the limitations or constraints the local and regional OEs produce.

This topic's importance suggests a need for more discussion about traditional military decision-making wargaming in general. The existing wargaming methodology used by the U.S. military needs to change in several ways:

- Institute formality and regularity. Ad hoc, simplistic, mental wargaming that happens in one's mind and when in the mood is not what advanced analysis wargaming is about.
- Tie all wargaming to the political, military, economic, social, informational, and military functional areas. Include the multinational corporation and civilian operations one finds in nearly all counterinsurgencies as distinct and important considerations.
- Recognize that often the competitor/enemy will have the initiative and act first. In traditional wargaming, one often finds the U.S. or coalition forces acting first and holding a continuous grasp on the initiative; in counterinsurgency operations, the enemy or other competitors will often have the initiative, causing friendly forces to react. When one reacts in the act-react-counteract wargaming cycle, the forthcoming hypotheses are significantly different than when acting first. Pursuit of this hypothesis influences collection, which influences resultant cerebral activity to turn information into knowledge.
- Use indigenous people to act as enemies or competitors in intelligence wargaming. Traditional wargaming often uses U.S. people as the enemy and misses the culture factor and the importance it has on thinking, planning, decision-making, and resultant activities. It misses an understanding of how and what the enemy thinks and the opportunity to preempt his actions and deny the enactment of his strategies.
- As a continuing dialogue of an earlier discussion, incorporate at least four pairs of antagonists[15] in the wargaming. Wargaming is designed to be two-sided: friendly and enemy. Unfortunately, in the churning caldron of a fluid city, there are many competing elements constantly

colliding, intersecting, and careening. Because of the complex environment and the presence of many competing entities, advanced analysis wargaming postulates at least four pairs of antagonists: friendly, enemy, neutrals, and host nation. Each will possess the initiative at times, thereby causing the other antagonists to react to their activities and actions. Commanders therefore need to anticipate these positional changes and derive strategies to cope with reacting and for recapturing the initiative after losing it.

- Expect an enemy or other competitors to have a well-designed plan. Traditional wargaming often treats adversaries as if they had no goals and were incapable of planning, executing, and assessing outcomes. Quite the opposite is true. Our current and future adversaries will always have an aim, strategies, goals, objectives, resources, and degrees of will. These intangible aspects of modern conflict have to be represented in detailed intelligence wargaming.

- Anticipate the unknown. Unfortunately, acting as the red force or enemy in COA analysis is often a "pick-up game" at best, representing what U.S. intelligence analysts might do in similar circumstances. This pick-up game mentality leads to either rubber stamping a favorite course of action or mirror-imaging friendly value sets onto an enemy who thinks, perceives, and feels quite differently from friendly decision makers and staff officers.

- Use M&S. Although the U.S. military has excellent M&S for using kinetic energy in open terrain against conventional targets, it does not have the kind of initiative wargaming advocated here. Advanced analysts need to enter a synthetic environment and work their operations against all antagonists.

- Wargaming must drive intelligence analysis and collection. Today, wargaming for the initiative rarely drives ISR, mostly because ISR is primarily used for determining course of action feasibility, if involved in wargaming in the first place. The hypotheses coming from intelligence wargaming for the initiative must be decomposed and used to drive analytically focused intelligence collection. In this sense, wargaming and resultant hypotheses become *ISR engines*. This does not occur today, but it should as we prepare for tomorrow.

Another interesting aspect of analytic wargaming is that it must identify, in a high degree of detail, condition-setting required for success. These are good words, but what do they mean? In a continuation and direct application of analytic condition-setting we discussed previously, although ISR condition-setting is critically important, it is also difficult to contemplate, let alone initiate prior to future missions coming forth. As a reasonable standard, condition-setting for sensors relates to commanders' information requirements. However, if setting conditions for intelligence operations always occurs in the future and involves enormous unknowns, particularly in the volatile OE of a city, how do we know where and how to set those conditions? How do we know where and how to set conditions for data work? How do we know where and how to set conditions for congealing and instantiating a knowledge environment? How do we know what a commander's decisions—which will fuel his quest for valuable data, information, and knowledge—will be? How do we know the conditions under which the requirement will be satisfied? How will we know the antithesis represented by our competitors as they intersect with our interests, as they come to dominate our thoughts, as they careen from the collisions or intersections, or as our activities come to dominate and control our competitors?

The answer to these questions lies in *anticipation* that comes with analytic wargaming. Anticipation is necessary for creating both tangible and intangible counter-activities and actions. Anticipation leads to understanding how the future might evolve and thus the required intelligence data and condition-settings for collection. Anticipation provides commanders with the wherewithal to preempt the enemy's or other competitors' activities and to either deny, destroy, or shape their minds before they actually have the opportunity to act. To assist analysts in this knowledge-driven realm of analytic wargaming, intelligence and operations planners must use cultural experts and technical experts—supplemented by indigenous people who speak the language—to anticipate the competitor's moves, activities, or reactions, given particular problem sets and variance in the OE.

Optimum wargaming occurs in an M&S environment similar to what people experience when entering a (™)MYST-like synthetic environment or when watching battle scenes from the movies *Lord of the Rings*, *Gladiator*, and *Troy*. In such synthetic settings, analyst-planners and operations planners would encounter the physical and intangible OE realistically portrayed in three- or four-dimensional GIS (geospatial information systems), complete with the entities, buildings, infrastructure, and normal and abnormal activities people encounter in an insurgency (sometimes specifically where wargaming is focused). The software driving the simulation would not only portray reality, but it would provide options to the analyst conducting the wargaming and let those choices play out.

In this day of rapid media transmission, planners also must anticipate how competitors will attempt to seize the initiative in the invisible information domain. This domain, as abstract as it may be, has ascended to critical importance in the fight for the effects of holding the initiative in the physical and intangible domains.

To help the reader understand an even broader and deeper argument for analytic wargaming, more explanation follows:

- Wargaming helps people understand possible second- and third-order effects, coming from both tangible and intangible actions. Both effects and actions always have consequences, whether short-term or long-term, important or unimportant. In the city, with all its complexity, consequences can be tangible (such as an assassination) intangible (such as anger), or a combination of both. In the city, even very small actions done in good conscience with the best outcomes in mind can sometimes grow exponentially, influencing and exploding into enormous, negative outcomes. Commanders must have an organized, methodical way of anticipating such possible second- and third-order effects from their military, diplomatic, information, or economic effects and actions. Advanced wargaming can help anticipate the surfacing of such outcomes.

• Wargaming the act–react–counteract cycles of the principal actors or competitors can help analysts understand a wider range of possibilities, when they could happen, and, from the appearance or absence of observables or indicators, the most likely set of outcomes.

• Where cultural perspectives and knowledge of the city have such significant and chilling impacts on actions and effects, it makes perfect sense that the wargaming opponent or competitor has to be an indigenous person with an intimate knowledge of the peculiarities of the culture as well as the specific location where complex adaptive systems will interact. These indigenous wargamers impose a local and cultural perspective on potential outcomes or predicted actions. These indigenous wargamers could even be perpetrators locked away in a prison who are seeking benefits. They may provide insights that even an indigenous, well-meaning cultural expert could not bring because the perpetrator would represent ruthlessness a normal civilian would be hard-pressed to replicate.

• Expanded wargaming helps assess *assumptions* upon which the success of a specific plan rests. Poor assumptions, or even good assumptions that have decayed in truthfulness, can be the bane of all commanders and how they make decisions. In this regard, Clausewitz helps us consider the fickle nature of assumptions:

> Since all information and assumptions are open to doubt, and with chance at work everywhere, the commander continually finds that things are not as he expected. This is bound to influence his plans, or at least the assumptions underlying them.[16]

Commanders need a way to examine the *assumptions* that underpin their decisions and resulting plans, both continuously and methodically. Poor assumptions often result in plan or decision failure. They may come as a complete surprise because people didn't understand how faulty assumptions could influence subsidiary plans, tools used, and even ISR that could confirm or deny activity. Wargaming assumptions are an important aspect of modern planning in urban OEs.

Intelligence plays a major role in developing assumptions. It follows that intelligence should play an active role in discerning the validity of assumptions and their possible influences on the outcomes of certain courses of action or plans. People have to examine assumptions and play out various courses of action to logically anticipate the outcome of decisions, effects, and actions. In addition, assumptions evolve with a cultural perspective. Intelligence people must help operational planners view assumptions and potential outcomes through the prism of the culture in question.

Cultural specialists, supported by a smattering of indigenous people, will help to identify possible errors in thinking and the resulting judgment inherent in certain assumptions. In addition, cultural specialists can help discern potential outcomes if the developed assumptions are wrong, or how one might know if assumptions are faulty. Cultural specialists can assist intelligence planners in decomposing assumptions into constituent or essential elements and then mapping or tasking resultant observables into ISR collection, both traditional and nontraditional. Cultural specialists will help military analysts make sense of the data flowing to analytic centers as a result of ISR collection activities and therefore possess the wherewithal to advise commanders to adjust or discard assumptions that prove to be false.

- Wargaming helps operations and intelligence planners understand *sensitive variables* and *windows of opportunity.* Technically, a variable is a factor or condition that is subject to change.[17] A window of opportunity is a time, place, or circumstance in which one side or the other can strike to take advantage of the quick ascendancy of sensitive variables. Such a window is also a time in which one side or even all sides are susceptible to the exponential influence of variables or when such susceptibility is noticed by one side in a competition and used to gain advantage over an opponent. With such an understanding, people can know a friendly and adversary susceptibility to reaction when sensitive variables come into play, and the time, place, and circumstances under which such variable impacts—or windows of opportunity or vulnerability—can occur, and the importance of protecting one's self from the impact of a wise enemy using variables to their advantage.

As another interesting point, variables and wargaming have a close relationship. Why is this the case?

- As a starting point, variables possess intrinsic importance in a complex urban environment. Variables affect outcomes. For example, if commanders design effects and actions assuming unchanging important variables such as crowd attitudes, the original effect and action are flawed but only come to light with devastating force when that attitude does change.

- In an OE in which complex adaptive systems (CAS) constantly intersect, small perturbations can cause disproportionate outcomes. Commanders must anticipate this form of "friction" or the appearance and influence of unexpected chance events. The accidental killing of a small child darting across a street and being hit by the lead vehicle of a convoy can cause a disproportionate outcome such as a riot, a mass protest, and the world press decrying the presence of U.S. troops in the host country. The image of our three soldiers being dragged through the streets of Mogadishu in 1991 and the Blackwater security employees being hung from the bridge in Fallujah in 2004 serve as additional examples of how seemingly small (unfortunate), isolated situations can explode into events with huge consequences and second- and third-order effects. Such events have enormous impacts because of the unseen relationships among people, organizations, and activities whose presence on the days of the events happened to be the catalyst for the exponential growth in outcome and consequence.

- Urban settings are full of sensitive variables. Anticipating and understanding them through wargaming for the initiative becomes highly problematic without an understanding of the culture and the energy of a very fluid city and its relationships among people, religion, icons, weather, and customs. The challenge presented by sensitive variables becomes infinitely more complex when analysts and commanders acknowledge the difficulty in anticipating through wargaming both appearance and influence of these variables, oscillating degrees of importance, and their potential influence on mission accomplishment. That is, sometimes certain circumstances and variables cause nothing of consequence to happen; at other times, those same circumstances and sensitive variables will cause a situation to burst and influence far beyond its projected importance. The differences between the two sets of variables involve the invisible or "hidden" relationships among variables, people, and organizations, and the constantly moving and changing OE. Purposefully looking for and anticipating their potential presence and subsequent influence is one of the most important aspects of analytic wargaming for the initiative. All commanders need this type of work into what might be and how they can use this work to at least have a range of options if the situation so demands. What they do not want is to be completely caught by surprise, as denigration of decision-making always accompanies surprise.

- What then, is the preeminent danger inherent to sensitive variables and how does wargaming help to mitigate potential effects? It is, of course, *the surprise factor*, which often causes a form of decision and emotional paralysis. With such paralysis comes an extreme level of vulnerability for U.S. military forces and a great opportunity for an enterprising enemy. This type of surprise, however, can be assuaged if advanced intelligence analysts take adequate precautions such as identifying the possibility of surprise, its form, its domain (air, ground, cyberspace, cognitive, etc.), the time it could come forth to stalk the commander and his staff, the location of the act bringing about surprise, and through this anticipation, figuring out what might mitigate the effects of surprise.

- Any sensitive variable can be exploited or denied given good anticipatory wargaming has occurred and a range of operational contingency plans exists in which the commander or the staff can "audible" preemptive or anticipatory condition-setting actions. These openings, "gates," or "windows of opportunity," exist for all competitors operating in an urban OE. By anticipating the advent of sensitive variables and potential "gates" or "windows of opportunity" to exploit or defend against, competitors can realistically expect to obtain huge advantages in the full range of advantages, including initiative, momentum, tempo, position, knowledge, decision-making, and psyche influence. Thus, the advanced analyst must learn to anticipate the ascendency of sensitive variables and accompanying gates or windows of opportunity and can do so through analytic wargaming. The thinking skills needed for this level of intellectual sophistication lie in the cognitive process of advanced analysis.
- The influence of sensitive variables on operations is not without quirks and peculiarities. For one, variables are neutral and thus equally recognizable and exploitable by any party against any competitor. Another is the interplay involving internal recognition and exploitation of sensitive variables among competitors. That is, good analysts anticipate sensitive variables and associated gates or windows of opportunity for their enemies, neutrals, the host nation, and themselves. When armed with such knowledge and understanding, particularly the relationships causing variables to be or potentially become sensitive, concerned analysts, with the help of thought templates and automation, can decompose the variables for all four parties and develop observables to recognize when conditions are such that sensitive variables could come into play and indeed start their trip into reality and influence.

Advanced analysts recognize how danger and possibility entwine. Sensitive variables can be dangerous, or they can present possibilities to exploit for achieving advantages to any competitor. When armed with such knowledge, U.S. intelligence analysts can lobby aggressively for using ISR to monitor potential ascendency of sensitive variables and for protecting their force against enemy, neutral, or host nation attempts to exploit a particular situation and use the suddenly appearing variables to gain an advantage. Even when understanding their susceptibility to the influence of variables, advanced analysts watch for sensitive variables to arise in an adversary's activities and his degree of vulnerability. In this respect, commanders and their operations officers work closely with intelligence analysts and continuously take action to protect against variable manipulation. However, with the assistance of a highly attuned intelligence system, they also watch for and take advantage of the enemy's susceptibility to variables and windows of opportunity to manipulate them when most advantageous to the friendly force. Thus, to anticipate when the variables might become potent and when the window of opportunity for manipulation might be, they keep a close eye on the outcomes of both course of action (COA) and 4-pair wargaming. They attempt to gain insight into how an enemy or competitor probably views friendly force vulnerabilities to sensitive variables and how that same enemy views his own vulnerability to variable manipulation through intelligence wargaming. Or, in some cases, advanced analysts may determine the enemy lacks this level of thought, thereby making him all the more susceptible to the "hammer" of surprise associated with an unexpected assault induced by the sudden appearance of favorable (for friendly force manipulation) variables.

- Regardless how many red teams assess thoughts or how many double checks are made, people will make mistakes. Most mistakes are mental mistakes or misjudgments. Both people and machines conducting intelligence wargaming expose flaws in logic that cause mistakes. Some of the most common mistakes include false assumptions (and not changing when the assumption proves false), non sequiturs, errors of omission or commission, lack of knowledge or the use of distorted or outdated knowledge, mirror imaging, expert testimony, hasty generalizations, post hoc, ergo propter hoc, false dilemmas, over-generalization, circular reasoning, faulty analogy, and not recognizing contradictions. Once the potential for error comes forth, participants can change their behavior or proceed with caution, armed with more knowledge of the many forms of lurking danger.

ANALYTIC STRATEGIES[18]

Advanced analysts will have strategies for performing their work. To do otherwise is analytic chaos. Although all analytic organizations will have some system in place to assign work and to establish priorities for effort, the use of a dynamic analytic strategy is a necessary adjunct and enhancer for advanced analysis. Even though periodically a leader of vision and foresight will devise and use an analytic council and develop subsequent analytic strategies, this methodology needs to be fully explained and emplaced in joint and service doctrine to drive training and education, materiel development, leader development, and organizational design. An analytic strategy provides "a way" to think, plan, and execute analytic missions. A strategy in this regard means a plan, method, or series of maneuvers or stratagems for obtaining a specific goal or result.[19]

Analytic strategies will occur at all levels, from the four-star theater level to the company intelligence support team (IST) level. Analytic strategies will undergo constant change. Because analytic work must always be organized, an analytic strategy is necessary for identifying what is important and for being able to swing cerebral power and efforts to meet rapid change, to anticipate next moves for the United States and for the enemy, and to place special analytic emphasis on high-risk, high-potential outcome analytic efforts. Using an analytic strategy also helps to identify and implement leaders' priorities and to keep constant emphasis on satisfying the commander's PIR for making decisions. In the case of deployed analysts, the commander's PIRs and IRs will always sustain primacy among competing information requirements. However, as we have discussed previously in this work, advanced analysts will always have additional requirements involving hypotheses, expectations, hunches, and mysteries.

To avoid experiencing the debilitating effects of competing requirements, analysts will work with two types of analytic strategies. As one type, advanced analysts will work under the direction and mentoring of a master analyst. This person is the most senior and experienced analyst in whom the senior intelligence officer and the commander have the greatest trust. This analyst will lead the other analysts, implement the analytic strategy, which comes from the leadership in conjunction with analysts in analytic meetings, and provide mentoring to analysts by helping with their analytic challenges. The master analyst, who is responsible for implementing the senior intelligence officer's and commander's analytic strategies, plans work based on both magnitude of potential outcomes and talent available. The second type of analytic strategy comes from within individual advanced analysts' minds. All analysts will have strategies for working on their individual hypotheses, expectations, hunches, and mysteries, in addition to working on the PIR and IR. The analytic strategy will provide the means to pursue all analytic requirements. For all analytic work, the master analyst will serve as the initial interface with collection specialists and mangers, with VKE knowledge brokers, and with the larger intelligence enterprise. The master analyst and senior intelligence officer will distribute an intelligence analysis emphasis and priority message to the intelligence enterprise, distributed collection people, VKEs, and of course commanders and operations officers. This sharing of analytic strategies provides coherence to the expenditure of efforts to find sufficient data to turn into information and into knowledge to promote situational understanding and increased abilities to make good decisions, owing to the strategy's contribution to managing risk and lowering uncertainty.

Some of the elements of an analytic strategy will include

- Mission, priorities, and knowing what other analysts are doing for the purposes of analytic chat, cross talk, and sharing thoughts and ideas.
- Vision.

- OE/adversary.
- Goals.
- Mini-strategies.
- Condition-setting.
- Resources.
- Constraints.
- Use of a red team to check analytic assumptions, the presence of competing hypotheses, engagement in higher-level thinking (e.g., synthesis), and flawed thinking (e.g., mirror imaging, post hoc, ergo propter hoc).
- Analysis, collection activities, and focus.

In concluding this chapter, it is safe to postulate that advanced analysis depends on some important enhancements for its degree of quality. These enhancements come forth and receive both explanation and emphasis in this chapter. The chapter discussed several enhancements that will make advanced analysis even more powerful than it is. These enhancements include, in the order they appear: 1) analytic condition-setting (data, sensor, and knowledge architectures), 2) use of a VKE, 3) analysts providing intellectual catalysts to collection and forming partnerships with collection specialists, 4) analytic wargaming, and 5) analytic strategies. None of these five enhancements are easy to find or develop, but all are important for fully implementing advanced analysis. Although today's intelligence analysts undoubtedly do some of what the chapter discusses, many aspects of the discussion are not performed, or in many cases, even perceived as being important. This state of affairs can be attributed to a lack of doctrine, no recognition of the needs discussed in this chapter, traditional roles and missions, organizational cultures and structures (including money), inadequate training and education, and limited modeling and simulation for analytic mission rehearsal prior to deployment. This chapter, of course, suggests the absolute need to bring these enhancers to life and to resource their quick maturation for supporting advanced analysis.

With the end of this chapter, the reader is fully prepared to embark upon the next phase in this intellectual journey. As such, the next chapters provide the details and meaning of each of the fourteen elements of advanced analysis.

Part II

Advanced Analysis: In Detail

5

Decomposition

Definition: *Breaking a thought or activity into basic elements to discern meaning or facilitate a more complete understanding.*

Additional explanation: Decomposition is at the beginning of the intelligence process, preceded only by the mental act of thinking. It involves breaking a function, hypothesis, or activity into components or basic elements. Decomposition involves paring a concept, an idea, a requirement, or a tasking into its essential elements to gain insight, understanding, and wherewithal to search for and find relevant attributes, characteristics, parts and pieces of particular entities, activities, interactions, and behaviors by finding or observing its disassembled parts and pieces.

As an initial step in our inquiry about decomposition, we must address the question: Why do we engage in decomposition? The answer is quite simple. The first and foremost rationale for engaging in decomposition is to find the constituent or essential elements of activities, interactions, organizations, relationships, transactions, behaviors, and involvement between and among people and organizations that we are interested in as intelligence analysts. Second, intelligence analysts should have an organized method to look purposefully for parts, pieces, and aspects of "wholes" in the absence of full disclosure or actual truth. Third, analysts perform the front-end analytic work so collection can occur to confirm or deny their theories, hypotheses, hunches, expectations, and mysteries, and back-end analytic work can occur in a coherent way.

At the heart of the theory of decomposition lies its antithesis—that is, the ultimate requirement to recompose collected data and take resultant information and synthesize it into a whole that is knowledge. These two subjects—recomposition and synthesis—will be discussed later in the book.

Analysts use a variety of the essential cognitive elements of advanced analysis to perform decomposition. However, as they engage in decomposition, they always keep in mind that they are looking for more than the parts and pieces they have decomposed. Physicist David Bohm reinforces this notion with the following thoughts about wholeness:

> As has been seen, fragmentation originates in essence in the fixing of the insights forming our overall self-world view, which follows on our generally mechanical, routinized, and habitual modes of thought about these matters. Because the primary reality goes beyond anything that can be contained in such fixed forms of measure, these insights must eventually cease to be adequate, and will thus give rise to various forms of unclarity or confusion. However, when the whole field of measure is open to original and creative insight, without any fixed limits or barriers, then our overall world views will cease to be rigid, and the whole field of measure will come into harmony, as fragmentation within it comes to an end.[1]

The fourteen elements of advanced analysis are like a computer pick list in which the analyst chooses one, two, or several aspects of advanced analysis with which to guide his or her thoughts. Regardless of the elements of advanced analysis the advanced analyst chooses for use, the focus of analytic attention will remain on the output of decomposition—the five kinds of observables that will drive intelligence operations in urban settings—*cultural, technical, functional, situational,* and *biometric.* The focus also remains on designing observables to meet the analyst-induced standards of timeliness, specificity, accuracy, relevance, and clarity. The analyst's efforts remain firmly oriented on outthinking an elusive foe and developing observables of sufficient specificity to enable sensors and human collectors to pick up or notice subtle, nuanced, and ambiguous observables inherent to an urban OE.

When the advanced analyst starts decomposing a requirement into ever-smaller parts and elements so as to task the intelligence collection system intelligently, he or she must do so with the whole what they are looking for in their mind's eye. Why is this the case? In a world where everything is connected directly or indirectly and in a world comprised of wholes that enfold other wholes and unfold into larger wholes, the intelligence analyst must start with a vision of the whole he or she is looking for, what they think it will be doing, how it will act under a variety of circumstances, and what that whole might mean and imply once discovered. This theory of relatedness and wholes is amplified by the following thoughts about wholes, which are an important aspect of Eastern philosophy, from physicist Fritjof Capra:

> The most important characteristic of the Eastern world view—one could almost say the essence of it—is the awareness of the unity and mutual interrelation of things and events, the experience of all phenomena in the world as manifestations of a basic oneness. All things are seen as interdependent and inseparable parts of the same cosmic whole; as different manifestations of the same ultimate reality.[2]

This is a critical passage for the success of intelligence analysts. It compels advanced analysts to think about the wholes they seek even as they decompose PIR, IR, hypotheses, expectations, hunches, and mysteries. The analyst must have a vision in mind of what she or he thinks they are looking for and how it or its people are acting, interacting, transacting, and behaving. This work with wholes and their subsequent decomposition is crucial to tasking a variety of capable sensors and HUMINT, telling them to look, when to look, and the activity to look for.

Intelligence analysts cannot ask simple, broad questions of the collection system in urban counterinsurgency (COIN) operations and hope to receive answers in either the specificity or timeliness needed to produce actionable knowledge to meet their exact requirements. Unfortunately, intelligence analytic and collection systems were designed to do exactly the opposite of what is required for collecting valuable intelligence in urban settings. That is, the intelligence system is largely set up to work against conventional forces in open terrain. As such, it is a great performer in developing functional observables and using them to produce collection that provides moving target indicators (MTI), imagery, infrared (IR), geospatial, communications intelligence, and variants of human intelligence (HUMINT) when working against conventional military forces. Even in conventional warfare intelligence analysis and collection operations, the intelligence analyst must still decompose what he or she is looking for into observables for collectors to work against. The output of such decomposition though, provides functional observables—e.g., numbers of artillery tubes, numbers and formations of tanks, logistics support, communication support, and so forth. This singular approach to observables is inadequate for conducting intelligence operations in an urban setting.

In a large city, there is a paucity of conventional forces to use the ISR system against. Instead there are very smart and adaptive insurgents or irregulars well hidden among the people and the activities normally occurring in a complex urban environment and culture. The setting in which the insurgent and his networks operate is one that can only be described as fluid. This fluidity is the essence of the challenge of trying to understand what the insurgent is attempting to do, how he intends to do it, his motives, where he intends to execute his plans, and when. The result—the insurgent and his networks often appear invisible because they are obscured by the motion and energy of constant change inherent to the vibrancy of a large urban OE. Dr. Capra again helps us understand how timeless the notion of fluidity is with the following ideas:

> The Chinese . . . not only believed that flow and change were the essential features of nature, but also that there are constant patterns in these changes to be observed by men and women . . . The principal characteristic of the Tao is the cyclic nature of its ceaseless motion and change . . . The idea is that all developments in nature, those in the physical world as well as those of human situations, show cyclic patterns of coming and going, of expansion and contraction.[3]

Intelligence analysts working in urban OE must be much more knowledgeable and specific than their counterparts working in conventional situations in open terrain when they decompose information requirements from several respects. First, they must design and then aggressively work collection to look for observables. But what are the differences among an observable, indicator, and signature—the three standard bearers that historically drive intelligence collection? An *indicator* is an item of information that reflects the intention or capability of an adversary to adopt or reject a course of action.[4] A *signature* is a distinguishing or identifying mark, feature, or quality. An *observable* is a physical, physiological, emotional property or absence of one or all of the aforementioned that can be observed or measured directly. In this book, we narrow the problem set and work with observables only. The reason for this selection is due to the specificity of observables, to technical difficulties in understanding signatures, and over-generality issues with indicators. Along this line of thinking, signatures can become very technical—far beyond the nature of this book, and indicators are often too broad to be effective in city work—hence the selection of observables as the guiding focus of collection and the output of advanced analysis.

Let us take a moment and delve more deeply into observables. To operate in urban settings against either insurgents or irregular warriors, the intelligence analyst must use, as mentioned before, five kinds of observables—*cultural, technical, functional, situational,* and *biometric.* These observables were defined earlier in the book. These observables come from decomposing PIR, IR, hypotheses, expectations, hunches, and mysteries. It is with observables that the advanced analyst takes the outputs from decomposition and uses them to focus specific intelligence collection—right time, right place, and right activity. In this process, we find both the analyst's mental power and knowledge driving collection.

Unfortunately, in urban settings, it takes knowledge to first decompose requirements and to design the five types of observables. The pressure to know comes from the nature of the act of decomposing. Analysts have to know what they look for, e.g., the enemy, their condition-setting, their intent, their goals, their purposes, their weapons, and so forth. They will also understand that the enemy will always try to use what Sun Tzu calls the ordinary and extraordinary forces[5] because of the supreme advantages these forces bring by way of initiative and its corollary—freedom of maneuver. In addition, decomposition requires a vast array of knowledge and experience sufficient to know the elements and character of priority intelligence requirements (PIR), intelligence requirements (IR), hypotheses, hunches, expectations, and mysteries well enough to discern the essential elements of each into observables. In this regard, the advanced analyst must be able to understand, develop observables, and seek enemy leverage points and what seems invisible except to the expert mind of the analyst.[6] In addition, analysts performing decomposition have to know the OE and culture well enough to understand how its characteristics influence the enemy, the populace, organizations, and interactions, activities, transactions, and behaviors constantly changing within the environment.

The 14 cognitive elements of advanced analysis are imperative for proactively conducting intelligence operations in complex urban OE against embedded insurgents and irregulars. It is through use of one, two, or all of the elements of advanced analysis that the advanced analyst develops the observables to direct collection efforts. When an analyst who is using decomposition processes reaches the essential element of something that emanates characteristics, behaviors, manifestations, relationships, or energy, he has reached a sufficient level of knowledge and understanding to design observables fit to work against an embedded, elusive, cellular enemy. As we shall see, most analysts do not have the knowledge to decompose requirements to the extent necessary to design such observables. However, with the collaborative support of fellow analysts and a variety of subject matter experts (SME—indigenous and external), analysts can learn to decompose requirements and develop the type of observables required. In such an effort, the goal is for the observable's specificity to be of immediate and direct use to the commander as he attempts to reduce uncertainty, manage risk, and make effective decisions possible.

As another step in gaining understanding about this complicated effort, let us identify what gets decomposed in more depth than previously discussed. First and foremost come the commander's priority intelligence requirements (PIR). In addition, information requirements that come from the commander's staff must get decomposed. However, intelligence analysts working in an urban environment also have to pursue analytic requirements so essential in enacting the aggressive intelligence analysis required to maximize ISR in urban settings. These analytic requirements are expectations, hypotheses, hunches, and mysteries. The definitions for all of the intelligence requirements are as follows:

- *Priority Intelligence Requirement* (*PIR*): An intelligence requirement stated as a priority for intelligence support that the commander and staff need to understand the adversary or the OE—*DOD Dictionary of Military Terms*.
- *Information requirement* (*IR*): Those items of information regarding the adversary and other relevant aspects of the OE that need to be collected and processed to meet the intelligence requirements of a commander—*DOD Dictionary of Military Terms*.
- *Expectation*: The act or state of looking forward or anticipating.[7]
- *Hypothesis*: A tentative theory about the natural world; a concept that is not yet verified but that if true would explain certain facts or phenomena—*Wikipedia*
- *Hunch*: A premonition or suspicion.[8]
- *Mystery*: Any affair, thing, or person that presents features or qualities so obscure as to arouse curiosity or speculation.[9]

Now that we know and understand more about the theory of decomposition and what gets decomposed, let us venture into the realm of practicality. As a first step, let us discuss the analysts' role in driving collection. For the most part, today the analyst does not serve in a sufficiently active role in driving collection. This state of affairs is not the fault of intelligence analysts. They have not been trained in the intricacies of advanced analysis, which advocates a tight partnership between analyst and collector. In addition, per their leader's guidance and doctrine, they are busy with other functions.

The exclusion of intelligence analysts from the detailed work of the collection process leaves collection people short of knowledge about the very specific, analytically driven collection that must occur. Collection people are often left on their own to take broad intelligence requirements and derive observables. Of course, the collection specialist knows about his or her functional area, which is collection, but certainly does not possess the knowledge to use specific observables to drive collectors to drive collection at the right place and right time, against the right observables, and against the right activities. This decoupling of analysts from the collection process also leaves HUMINT and CI people to develop their own observables, and a distributed collection system to operate with a paucity of specific guidance or updates from deployed analysts—the necessary contextual knowledge and understanding to operate effectively.

So, can we identify some of the results of this "decoupling" of the analyst from collection in urban ISR operations? It results in a distinct lack of specificity in observables. It grooms people to think that there is only one type of observable to be used—*functional*. It can also result in collection people doing the best they can to design observables, but finding their efforts inadequate. Regardless of effort expended and well-meaning actions, the distributed analytic and collection system doesn't have specific knowledge about what the deployed analyst is looking for. In the absence of understanding what is needed and how to look for it, people will often perform area reconnaissance because it is easy to accomplish, when they need to be performing point persistent surveillance driven by very specific observables. In addition, guidance can become vague and confusing to the analytic and collection system; for example, guidance to report on "unusual sightings" with no time or location guidance rather than to watch for and report on detailed, specific observables complete with times, locations, and activities discussed above.

To complicate matters even further, the city is always moving and changing. This causes enormous strain on both analysts and collection specialists. This strain comes from changes in roles and missions, which cause changes in decision-making. Changes in decisions cause constantly changing knowledge requirements. Such changes for new and valuable knowledge place immense strain on analysts and collection specialists to produce the knowledge commanders require for lowering uncertainty and managing risk in their command and control (C^2) processes. Further, insurgents are embedded in and amongst the populace as they live their lives and perform daily activities and duties. In this cultural environment, the insurgent and his network supporters often look and speak like host nation people. Thus, they are almost invisible.

To locate these "invisible" interactions, transactions, activities, behaviors, and their networks, U.S. intelligence analysts have to look for and recognize or at least discern subtle, nuanced, and often fleeting observables. This is called *disambiguation,* meaning to make visible that which through ambiguity appears invisible; to remove the ambiguity from and make unambiguous.[10] *Disambiguation* refers to understanding what happens in a city with its multitudes of activities, interactions, transactions, interactions, and behaviors that constantly occur. Most of what happens in a city is legitimate, though some activities are illicit. The challenge lies in differentiating between two, particularly those supporting the insurgents' networks. When people interact, transact, act, and behave, certain outcomes and indicants of behavior occur. They have measurable properties people can notice, record, and comprehend to help understand what is happening or has happened. But these emergent properties are difficult to see, and if seen, to understand. They occur quickly and often don't happen again. Thus, they are often invisible or indistinguishable to the casual observer (for example, a cultural interaction between two people meeting on a busy thoroughfare).

This discussion is not to say that today's notion of fusion centers is doing poorly—quite the contrary. What the thought does postulate is that analysts must be involved in and actually drive collection, analysts must work as a team with collectors on a doctrinal continuum and not by exception, not all places performing intelligence operations will possess a fusion center, and the intelligence analysts' knowledge and mental acuity are what decompose the requirements into observables and eventually turn data into information and knowledge. It postulates that it is through good observables that usable collection will come forth. It is focused intelligence analysis and collection that will provide the data that the advanced analyst will turn into information and knowledge for the commander's use in decision-making.

Once analysts and SMEs decompose the information requirements into observables, the analysts team with collection specialists to design optimum collection to search for, find, and report on said observables. Through thought and machine work, analysts will transform data into information and knowledge, which will answer or satisfy PIR, IR, expectations, hunches, and mysteries.

Decomposition is a complex problem. Thus, the advanced analyst has some basic tools with which to help him or her perform the function. These aids include baselines, use of a VKE, use of indigenous SMEs, and intelligence wargaming. Each of these tools will be discussed during the remainder of this chapter. But first, let us briefly discuss baselines. So, what is a baseline? A baseline is a basic standard or level, or a specific value or values that can serve as a comparison or control.[11] What does a baseline do? It identifies what is normal so the intelligence analyst and his or her collection partners can identify anomalies. Are there different types of baselines? The answer is yes—there are technical, cultural, and functional baselines at work in any urban setting. Thus, we need to determine why baselines are important to an analyst attempting to decompose a requirement into observables.

A baseline is a fundamental line of departure for thought. If the analyst has a standard or starting point, he or she can measure change. In addition, baselines are essential to other aspects of advanced analysis other than decomposition, e.g., anomaly, aggregation, tendency, and cultural analysis. Even with their inherent usability, using baselines is challenging, owing to the time they take to either develop or update, the knowledge required, and the difficulty in even finding an up-to-date baseline that has uniform fields. In addition, the knowledge required to update baselines is often beyond the knowledge realm of the deployed analyst. Further, baselines change, so it is imperative to keep them up-to-date; otherwise, the commander and his staff could be thinking and making decisions from erroneous data. Regardless of the difficulty of the challenges, baselines are very important for advanced analysts who are contemplating decomposing requirements into observables through the use of anomaly, aggregation, tendency, and cultural analysis.

To decompose information requirements effectively, we have to make some considerations. We have to decide what to compose. We also have to use our minds to decompose the focus of our analysis. In addition, the analyst must decide which subject matter experts (SMEs) to go to for assistance in thinking and in knowledge and its application. In this respect, we push our minds into exertion:

> In particular, our minds have to conjure patterns of relationships and tapestries of linkages, networks, and the connectedness of the world. We also must consider a third context: the invisible context that affects us all. We cannot see the atoms or the cells that make up the universe. We cannot see or touch quarks or shadowy photons. We cannot see the digits that transform our world so dramatically. We cannot quantify our consciousness or our unconsciousness. Yet who can deny their existence?[12]

This passage suggests the importance of the invisible world surrounding and influencing all people, the connectedness of all things, and the importance of these invisible influences and connectedness on all activities. To do so requires deep introspection by the analyst and use of deep thinking, which will be discussed in the chapter on critical thinking.

As another consideration, the analyst must set conditions for success in three areas, as discussed earlier—the knowledge environment, sensors and HUMINT, and data architectures. This analytic condition-setting is forward-looking and anticipatory to the extreme, as the analyst engaging in condition-setting has to envision his or her requirements to meet a future state of affairs. As an example, the analyst must set conditions prior to the initiation of a point persistent surveillance operation of a suspected bomb factory in a residential sector of a large urban setting.

The analyst must consider the nature and influences of the OE. In particular, the analyst has to consider the infrastructure, cultural aspects and functions of the neighborhood surrounding a possible target, the technical environment, and even the structures of the possible target. In addition, the analyst must consider cultural influences on both people and baselines such as refuse, hygiene, religion, child's play, use of automobiles, and social visitation.

Friction is also an important consideration. As such, the analyst must anticipate to the extent possible the appearance and influence of friction (unexpected chance events) and how it might influence both analytic and collection operations.

The expert advanced analyst will specify analytic and collection standards as they undergo decomposition. These standards include timeliness, specificity, accuracy, relevance, and clarity. These standards have to go to the distributed collection system and its people, organizations, and machines.

Any effective advanced analyst who is involved with decomposition will also consider the influences of a complex environment, such as the quick ascendency of sensitive variables, windows of opportunity, and the possibility of second- and third-order effects. Some of them may grow out of control similar to the butterfly effect in complexity science. In addition, the analyst will have to understand that what appears to be chaotic may in reality be normal, and that within the chaos there will always be influential patterns of order. Often these patterns of order will involve the functioning and fluctuations of the enemy's network.

As three final considerations for engaging in decomposition, the analyst has to consider: 1) flaws in his or her thinking and to whom to turn for checks on thinking, 2) being aggressive and anticipating enemy activities, and 3) wargaming and defeating their own combined intelligence analysis and collection plan with the support of an organic or external red team that has indigenous experts. This method identifies to the analyst possible weaknesses and potential flaws in his or her thinking that could doom the impending intelligence operation.

Let's discuss a very broad practical example of decomposition. Let's put forth an illustrative hypothesis—there is a bomb factory operating in a house in a neighborhood in a large urban area in the Persian Gulf. To go beyond a broad approach to guide collection, how does one decompose this hypothesis into specific guidance to collectors regarding the time the analyst wants them to look and the activities the analyst expects to see? Decomposition, as you recall, is breaking something apart into its specific elements—the analyst reduces the hypothesis into greater and greater levels of specificity to find the elements making up the whole, but specific enough to search for in a distributed or fragmented way. We search our memories and remember the theory of wholes and relationships—anything and everything is in some way connected, has essential elements or constituent elements, and functions that must occur for it to be an entity. We also recall that enemy condition-setting is important and must be decomposed and watched for as well.

The analyst discovers he or she needs a mental model to work with. One aspect of the model is to consider what it will take to confirm or deny that the working hypothesis is correct or incorrect and what the enemy must think about, perceive, plan, decide, and enact to succeed in accomplishing his objective or goal. When working with our hypothesis, we can use the following adage as a part of the mental model assisting us—if my hypothesis is correct and if there is a bomb factory operating out of this home, I will see some activities, interactions, transactions, and behaviors occurring. The next few thoughts identify what the advanced analyst could very well be thinking as he or she ponders this analytic problem. The first person will be used in this narrative to promote understanding.

I will see some *functions* occurring. As one, countersurveillance will be in place to provide early warning to the bomb maker, if my bomb factory hypothesis is correct. I will see people bringing subsistence supplies. I will see deliveries being made to the house often under the cover of darkness. I will see some aspect of escape rehearsals. I will see increased use of indoor or outdoor privies.

I will see some *technical* activities. I will see increased heat emanating from the family's generator. I will see more cell phone transmissions. I will see more Internet usage. I will smell soldering—which is a burning metal smell. I may detect increased excrement and urine in indoor and outdoor privies. I will see heat emanating from the house itself at all hours of the day and night. I may see burning refuse and its smoldering in the back of the house. There will be the odor of burning refuse beyond what is normal. There will be increased consumption of electricity. The house in question will remain warm longer than other houses in the neighborhood during the hours of limited visibility.

I will also see *situational* activities that will help to confirm or deny my hypothesis. For example, I will see parked cars blocking entrée into the compound. I will see an absence of normal activities such as children playing. I will see more refuse in the back of the house. I will see more food and water being purchased than normal for the family in question.

I will also see or notice the absence of *cultural* activities. For example, I will not see people visiting the house as usual. I will not see the woman of the house staying when the owner goes to work. I will not see men and women using the same outdoor privy. I will see window shades staying down at all hours. I will not see people sleeping on the roof in the summertime. I will find no rumors about the house in the neighborhood.

I will also see *biometric* metrics and measurements that will be anomalous to normal. For example, the people who are residents of the house will appear more uptight and agitated than normal or more so than other people in the neighborhood. I will measure elevated blood pressure of people making deliveries to the house. I will also see more rapid eye movement of people making deliveries.

The outputs of this decomposition effort are observables—very specific observables with which to drive collection. However, once the analyst has the observables he or she desires, their work is not done. What else must he or she do to set up the best possible opportunities for success? The answer is that the analysts must work with the collection specialists to pick the right time, right place, and right circumstances to look or watch for the observables to appear. They must identify the times they think activities will be the highest and designate those times for when collection sampling rates and observations must maximize and surge. In addition, and a step away from current doctrine, the analysts must pass detailed guidance to elements (people, organizations, and machines) of a distributed collection system using an analytic collection guidance message, which was discussed earlier in the book. They will also work hard to think like the enemy. As such, they will think through the following questions from an enemy perspective:

- What is my perception of U.S. analysis & collection?
- How can I hide from his sensors and HUMINT?

- What will the Americans do that can cause my failure, and how might I surreptitiously counteract those activities?
- Where and how will American intelligence be watching or looking for me?
- Should I and my people be using cell phones?
- When, where, and how often should I move?
- How will I proceed with my functional planning and execution while the United States is looking for me?
- What is the best way to provide early warning of danger?
- How will I preclude the United States from finding indications of my countersurveillance?
- How will I become resupplied with material to make bombs?
- How will I recruit people to perform the many duties I need for sustaining my network and for performing tasks essential to my mission?
- Are there alternative ways to communicate so the U.S. intelligence people won't notice?

The insurgent will undoubtedly make some observations about the OE that would be of high interest to an advanced intelligence analyst. These enemy "thoughts" are conjecture, but they could be helpful in a generic way for analysts to think about decomposing information requirements in complex urban OE. Thinking about how the enemy thinks about the OE, when combined with thinking about the enemy's intent, goals, and strategies provides the advanced analyst with some powerful ways to operate against the insurgent. Some of the enemy's (the bomb maker we discussed earlier) thoughts could be

- The OE is fluid & constantly moving, which allows our nodes and links to morph and change without detection.
- The OE provides opportunities for our IED attacks, essential functions, and secrecy to allow IED attacks to occur without hindrance from the Americans.
- The OE enables us to mask our IED attacks.
- The OE allows us to attack multiple places to cause pressure on host nation and the Americans.
- The OE allows us to use the Internet and media to get our messages out after our IED attacks but before the Americans can respond after an IED detonates.
- The OE enables us to possess the initiative and use IEDs and vehicle-based improvised explosive devices (VBIEDs) to attack U.S. forces, host nation, and other sects/tribes at will at times, places, and intensity of our choosing.
- The OE enables us to collect intelligence pertinent to successful planning, emplacement, and execution without being noticed because we blend with the society and its constantly changing OE.
- The OE enables us to perform multiple critical functions necessary for our networks to exist and operate.

- The OE enables us to hide and execute our functional activities for successfully operating a bomb factory without fear of being discovered, as the American's ISR and communications advantages are negated in the city.
- The OE allows us to mask condition-setting activities.
- The OE is debilitating for American forces, as they cannot move, see, or use ISR to find our nodes and networks.
- The OE allows us to find the best IED sites, move improvised explosive devices (IEDs) to the sites, implant the IEDs, explode them upon the notification of our surveillance people, and create IO clips for the Internet.

Next, the advanced analyst has to understand why the mental effort involved with decomposition in a volatile, complex urban OE is so strenuous. The answer to this question revolves around the adversary. Why is this enemy so difficult to understand and find? The enemy is intelligent, well-schooled in the art of blending, camouflaging, and deceiving, and is adept at covering his physical and electronic tracks. In addition, portions of the populace are supporting the enemy and his network, but they do so by blending with normal activities or they do so passively by not reporting what they know to be occurring. Moreover, the enemy often blends with the population and talks, looks, and acts like the people in whose midst they reside and operate. The enemy's network functions and actions, even condition-setting, are buried within the activities, transactions, interactions, and behaviors already a normal part of daily life in the culture and its activities.

As yet another difficulty, the enemy's network is cellular and local, so clues about the nature of the enemy, his network, his activities, and his habits in one location don't always work in other locations. Also, the adversary's network links come and go. In this respect, they are like gossamer in a summer flower garden, just barely noticeable at times but totally invisible at other times, owing to just a slight shift of variables (like the wind or sunlight in a flower garden). The populace supporting the enemy's network instead of engaging in legitimate activities will not be easy to spot. Often, they will have years of practice in appearing innocuous, avoiding the appearance of suspicious activities, and they blend with the activities they know look normal.

However, some of these network supporters will make mistakes; these mistakes must be a target of decomposition, particularly when using anomaly, aggregation, tendency, semiotics, and cultural analysis. All people make mistakes. If they know they are involved with illegal activities that could cause them to go to prison, they will undoubtedly make more mistakes than normal. But even if U.S. intelligence has sensors and HUMINT watching, the activities of the enemy and his network supporters could remain largely invisible to the Western eye. The difficulty of the target also implies that the output of decomposition has the focus of collection. Further, understanding the nature of the target also implies that along with specific observables and optimum mixes of collection, analysts have to identify the right place, right time, and right activity to observe. How do we overcome these challenges, and how do we search for and find the types of activities, interactions, transactions, and behaviors that would indicate network activities that could lead to high-value targets? The next few thoughts identify some of the ways advanced analysts can approach and overcome these challenges.

When analysts and their SME supporters engage in decomposition, they have to use a framework of thought—cultural, technical, situational, biometric, and functional thought—focused specifically on what, why, and when they are involved in the act of decomposing. When analysts decompose requirements, from the start they must identify the SMEs or other analysts who possess the knowledge and thinking skills to assist them in developing cultural, technical, situational, biometric, and functional observables. They also have to identify the machine support they will need. In addition, they have to think about the sensors and HUMINT that have the potential to provide the required collection to find what the analyst is searching for and the data architectures with which to bring resultant collection data to the analyst.

In such a mental process, knowledge evolves from the simple to the complex—first knowing, then understanding, and then evaluating. Using such an approach, analysis and synthesis form an interactive, constantly changing whole. The idea is to keep breaking down constituent elements until arriving at the essence or core of what is sought. This is reductionism analysis—and something the U.S. military has done very well over the years. However, as soon to be discussed, there are dangers with pure reductionism, such as being intrigued with the process and working diligently to break down the requirement into the smallest feasible pieces, but failing to keep the reason for the effort in mind, being unable or unwilling to mentally connect the current effort with a larger meaning, and failing to synthesize the results of observable-driven collection into a larger and more meaningful whole.[13] A well-known historian helps us understand the danger of pure reductionism with these thoughts when pondering the air campaign in WWII against German cities:

> looking at the parts of the problem at the expense of the whole . . . lead-
> ing to a concentration on means rather than ends, running parallel with a
> tendency to confuse destruction with control, and at the same time reduc-
> ing strategy to a targeting problem.[14]

To avoid such reductionism problems when performing decomposition, analysts must first envision the end state of decomposition. Also, they must view decomposition as a process of machine and mental work with the goal of recomposing incoming collection data into information. As another outcome of decomposition, the analyst must prepare himself or herself to engage in the pure mental function of synthesis. It is synthesis that advanced analysts use routinely to transform data and information into knowledge and understanding. It is through this uniquely human mental function that the commander finds knowledge sufficient to develop situational understanding, make decisions, and take action. Finding these observables will not usually provide either truth or a complete picture. Instead, the intelligence analyst, with the assistance of machines and other analysts and SMEs, will weave "strands" of data into a "tapestry" of meaning. As such, analysts and supporting SMEs make sense of collected and gathered data, turn it into information, and synthesize it into knowledge. Often, owing to the limitations of time and knowledge, they will develop only partial knowledge for the commander to use in his decision-making. Thus, any modern commander working in an urban OE has to be comfortable with ambiguity, tolerant of fluctuations in risk, and willing to act with varying degrees of risk and uncertainty.

Through the process of decomposition, observables come forth as outputs: what we have deduced about the decomposed parts and pieces or how a particular system works as its elements function together. This deduction involves thinking about the requirement's inner workings and its sources of power, even those invisible to human thought processes and visualization. In addition, decomposers must think about how to find what they are decomposing to create a desired outcome. They should not quit the decomposition process just because they do not know how the resultant observables might be collected against. As mentioned earlier, it might be that the analyst/collection specialist team will have to seek help from other people in the intelligence enterprise as well as from a VKE to identify the "how to" of collecting observables.

In concluding this chapter, let us summarize what we have learned with respect to decomposition. First, we have learned to think about a very difficult problem. Second, we have learned "a way" to think about the commander's PIR and his staff's IR and to "tear apart" the requirements into their essential parts, and to use those parts to drive intelligence collection. During our ruminations in this chapter, we have discovered that analysts have their requirements too. These requirements relate to the advantages of knowledge and decision superiority as well as the importance of the initiative. Thus, along with PIR and IR, advanced analysts will engage in decomposition of *hypotheses, expectations, hunches,* and *mysteries.* Third, with the thoughts in this chapter, the analyst knows the outputs of the cognitive function of decomposition. The outputs are five types of observables unique to advanced analysis—*cultural, technical, functional, situational,* and *biometric.* Fourth, because of the complexity with advanced analysis and in particular decomposition, the analyst will often seek help in both the cognitive skills and the knowledge of other people and organizations. This thinking and knowledge support can come from within the analyst's organization, from the intelligence enterprise, from properly cleared indigenous subject matter experts (SMES), and from SMEs in a virtual knowledge environment (VKE). Fifth, as a final note, this chapter has emphasized the importance of analysts learning how to examine their thinking and knowledge capabilities, and seeking the assistance of red team people and other experts to critique their thought processes to ensure they understand the potential for committing mental errors and avoid pitfalls associated with cognition when working with the rigor of decomposition. They do not want to fall into the traps of logic and thinking that often befuddle analysts and decision makers alike when poor thinking takes primacy over the very best critical thinking possible. Thus, the next chapter discusses critical thinking.

6

Critical Thinking

Definition: An intellectual process that "examines assumptions, discerns hidden values, evaluates evidence, and assesses conclusions."[1]

THEORY BEHIND CRITICAL THINKING

Advanced analysis cannot work without critical thinking. People think; therefore, they err. All humans err; it is the burden of being human. With self-awareness of the specter of mental error, the advanced analyst remains wary of falling into traditional mental traps and errors of logic and thought. This analyst is aware that the mind can easily seduce itself into thinking that it neither has nor will make mental mistakes. Unfortunately, all human beings need to work on improving their critical thinking, as we all make mental mistakes and fall into traps. We become believers in our own brilliance and infallibility only to find, sadly, that even the brightest people make mistakes. But the advanced analyst, performing one of the most important analytic roles, methodically and continuously minimizes such errors and does the best he or she can to adjust before mistakes cause poor decisions and loss of lives.

To reduce the chance of error, or at least the impact of mental errors, advanced analysts need a purposeful mental process. Part of this process includes the need to take several steps to assuage the intensity and influence of mental errors. What might some of the more important steps be? For one, they need to engage in introspection and consider what mental errors they are likely to make. In addition, the advanced analyst using critical thinking could seek critiques from other people or organizations. For example, the analyst could form a hypothesis and seek the critical thoughts of a red team or a SME from a VKE. As another step, the analyst could search for similar problems that have occurred in the past from which the analyst can draw material and outcomes with which to judge his or her current work.

This approach sounds logical and practical. Yet we continue to err. Why does this happen even when we are aware of our proclivity to err? Several reasons exist:

- *First*, to admit to being wrong or to have made mental mistakes is extremely difficult for all people.
- *Second*, people are poor at introspection. It takes time, and more importantly, introspection is dangerous to our perspectives because, if people are honest, introspection will often prove us wrong.
- *Third*, when we engage in thought, we often don't want to take the time to check the validity of our thinking and the errors we might be making. It is too exciting to keep moving with our thoughts. Thus, though we might initially intend to come back to where we might have erred, eventually we are overtaken by events, and the potential for error identification and correction passes from our short-term memory. This problem becomes particularly ominous when we realize the thought we should have checked formed some of the basis of our follow-on thoughts.
- *Fourth*, both people and organizations can get in the way of seeking and using criticism of thought. We often don't have high opinions of the mental capabilities of individual people or, from a larger perspective, the bureaucratic perspective of groups of people. In this regard, even if the analyst receives good inputs identifying errors or potential errors, he or she will often reject what others have provided because the analyst suspects problems with their thinking.
- *Fifth*, if analysts seek out their own errors by reviewing the past and drawing historical analogies, the material from which they draw, or their own failure to look critically at the differences in circumstances between their own situation and the historical situation, could tempt them into false conclusions, particularly if they are seeking what happened in the past to confirm a hypothesis.[2]

These issues are serious challenges to good thinking. So, what is a good advanced analyst to do to engage in effective critical thinking? As one approach, the advanced analyst must have a useful theoretical foundation from which to draw. As another approach, the advanced analyst must have and use a critical-thinking thought template to help guide his or her *thinking about his or her own thinking*. Advanced analysts must understand its framework and underpinning thoughts for it to be useful. Furthermore, the analyst must know some of the challenges and problems inherent in critical thinking. Along with the problems, the analyst must know what to do to overcome the problems or meet the challenges inherent in critical thinking. Analysts also need to have the wherewithal to understand the nature and characteristics of a range of mental errors and how they might recognize them. In addition, they must know to whom they can turn to help them criticize their thoughts or the conclusions produced by their thought. There are both people and processes that can help in such a process.

As a first step of our journey, let us work with the theoretical foundations of critical thinking. There are some theoretical foundations that can help us understand what critical thinking means and how it can best be applied. Clausewitz in *On War* speaks of "critical analysis" (which is closely related to critical thinking). Clausewitz says that critical analysis is "the application of theoretical truths to actual events," and as such "it not only reduces the gap between the two but also accustoms the mind to these truths through their repeated application."[3] Clausewitz goes on to say that three activities are aspects of his approach to critical analysis—discovery and interpretation of equivocal facts, tracing of effects to their causes, and the investigation and evaluation of means employed in the action or battle.[4] Sun Tzu also indirectly talks about critical thinking. In this regard, Sun Tzu says,

> having paid heed to the advantages of my plans, the general must create situations which will contribute to their accomplishment. By situations I mean that he should act expediently in accordance with what is advantageous and so control the balance. All warfare is based on deception. Therefore, when capable, feign incapacity; when active, inactivity. When near, make it appear that you are far away; when far away, that you are near. Offer the enemy a bait to lure him; feign disorder and strike him . . . Anger his general and confuse him. Pretend inferiority and encourage his arrogance.[5]

Although it is easy to agree with both theorists, we have to disagree with Clausewitz ever so slightly in arguing that because of the importance of intelligence in modern conflict, we need to include the advanced analyst in critical thinking and not just the commander, for which Clausewitz so eloquently argues.

Mental errors in critical thinking do not occur on one side only—mental mistakes are common to all sides and to all people in an irregular warfare or insurgency situation. Just as common as making mental mistakes, people attempt to minimize their mistakes with backtracking after the fact to develop justifiable rationales for thinking the way they did. Because thinking is so important to the success or failure of critical thinking in advanced analysis, our next discussion centers on some of the most relevant and common cognitive errors people make, and some ways advanced analysts can work to either avoid or minimize the negative outcomes of such errors.

One of the most damaging mental errors involves *mirror imaging*. Mirror imaging is "filling gaps in the analyst's own knowledge by assuming that the other side is likely to act in a certain way because that is how the

U.S. would act under similar circumstances."[6] Mirror imaging is particularly egregious because it causes poor, shoddy, and superficial thinking. It also belies an undercurrent of arrogance inherent in the person who is doing the mirror imaging. Mirror imaging causes the intelligence analyst and commander to be surprised constantly and not know why. But we know why they find themselves in this continuing predicament—it is because they engaged in mirror imaging and did not engage in the difficult act of thinking from the true perspective of the enemy.

So how can the advanced analyst engaging in critical thinking know when mirror imaging is occurring either in her or his own mind or in the minds of others? The easiest answer to this question is to watch for key words and phrases such as: *I could never do what the enemy is going to do with my brigade at Ft. Hood. The enemy will do this because it makes sense to do so. The enemy is being totally irrational and needs to be treated irrationally. The enemy will not take this course of action because it makes no sense.* These are excellent triggering words that alert the analyst of an impending mirror-imaging judgment and should cause alarm in his or her mind.

Of interest too, the enemy will undoubtedly fall victim to this malaise of intellect. The wise analyst will use this common proclivity between competitors to seek advantages over the adversary's thinking. As such, the aggressive advanced analyst will use critical thinking about mirror imaging to gain intellectual advantage and thus freedom of maneuver, position, and intellectual ascendancy over the adversary.

To safeguard against mirror imaging, the advanced analyst must realize her or his proclivities to fall into such a trap. Once they know their own tendencies to engage in mirror imaging and have taken steps to be alert for such shortfalls, analysts can also take some other steps to avoid this cognitive scourge. For example, they can use U.S. and indigenous SMEs to critique their assumptions, conclusions, and reasoning. In addition, they can use a red team to provide critiques and to call into question the critical thinking the analyst engages in. Wargaming is a vulnerable place for the appearance of mirror imaging; it happens during this process repeatedly. Again, red team people and advanced analysts will be able to spot mirror imaging and need to bring it to the attention of the commander and staff. But identifying the issue is not sufficient. A good commander will thank the analyst for identifying the issue, but such a commander will also ask what he or she should do to overcome the problem. The advanced analyst needs to have a recommendation or several recommendations for resolving the issue, and they cannot be self-serving.

Another problem critical thinking brings forth involves *assumptions*. Poor assumptions often constitute the single point of failure in plans and execution of those plans. People generally make assumptions to bridge the gap between what they know and don't know. People need to make assumptions; otherwise, they would go nowhere in their planning or the execution of their plans because they have serious information and knowledge gaps during the planning phase of any activity. But they need to be wary of the potential for making mental mistakes through their assumptions. According to the DOD *Dictionary of Military and Associated Terms,* an *assumption* is

> A supposition on the current situation or a presumption on the future course of events, either or both assumed to be true in the absence of positive proof, necessary to enable the commander in the process of planning to complete an estimate of the situation and make a decision on the course of action.[7]

Making poor assumptions can lead to poor intelligence analysis as well as poor planning and decision-making. As one author tells us,

> Experience tells us that when analytical judgments turn out to be wrong, it usually was not because the information was wrong. It was because an analyst made one or more faulty assumptions that went unchallenged.[8]

With bad assumptions underpinning their thinking, people often make bad decisions, which can result in flawed execution and assessment of outcomes. Clausewitz also recognized the potential problem with assumptions in his treatise *On War* by saying:

> he will draft the plan of the war, and the aim will determine the series of actions intended to achieve it: he will, in fact, shape the individual campaigns and, within these, decide on the individual engagements. Since most of these matters have to be based on assumptions that may not prove correct, while other, more detailed orders cannot be determined in advance at all, it follows that the strategist must go on campaign himself.[9]

Given that the intelligence analyst cannot go on all the operations to see if his or her assumptions are true and given that he or she works with several assumptions each and every day, how does the intelligence analyst overcome, or at least minimize, the potential for developing and following erroneous assumptions? This is the essential question, and we will answer it in just a few paragraphs.

As we work our way through this line of thought, it is safe to conclude that in intelligence work, assumptions are always at play. The advanced intelligence analyst needs assumptions because she or he works with unknowns. In particular, the analyst faces many unknowns when dealing with the enemy and many aspects of the OE. The analyst faces unknowns when thinking about how to search for and find a well-hidden enemy and his network supporters. Thus, the intelligence analyst must make assumptions about the enemy's strategies, goals, objectives, targets, techniques, and weapons. The intelligence analyst has to make assumptions about future enemy attacks and methods for executing these attacks. Going into even more specificity, the analyst must always make assumptions about the enemy's condition for setting up his attacks or his activities, such as operating a safe house. Assumptions drive how the analyst thinks and considers the unknown or the future. Assumptions underpin how the analyst and collection expert decide upon and implement a collection strategy. Assumptions underpin how the analyst recomposes and synthesizes data into information and knowledge. Thus, it follows that analysts must continue to make assumptions—assumptions are an essential aspect of critical thinking. But the problem comes when analysts develop and use assumptions that are wrong, thereby having an adverse influence on their critical thinking. Thus, the next portion of the discussion identifies ways the advanced analyst can make the best possible assumptions and how to check for the presence and subsequent influence of poor assumptions.

How might the advanced analyst check on the validity of her or his assumptions and attempt to improve them? One way is for the analyst to be cognizant of the importance and power of assumptions. In this regard, the analyst must know what an assumption is and what potential errors could come forth from a poor assumption. The analyst must be aware of her or his assumptions and constantly worry about their validity. This seems obvious, but it isn't, because often people make assumptions or believe them as facts but tend to forget about them as their minds become occupied with other activities. As another way to check the validity of assumptions, the intelligence analyst must ask for other people to examine and critique her or his assumptions. They can do so by seeking the assistance of other analysts on the staff, within the intelligence enterprise, and even with SMEs in an external VKE. Within the staff, if a red team is present and working, the red team members would be an excellent group of people to help the intelligence analyst examine the validity of his or her assumptions. As another approach, analysts identify their assumptions and do not forget they used the assumptions. Instead, they approach the assumption as they would a hypothesis and they test it for its validity. As a final approach, the analyst can decompose her or his significant assumptions into observables and watch for appearance of events, activities, transactions, interactions, or behaviors that provide the analyst with insights as to the validity or invalidity of the assumption in question.

A cognitive phenomenon we can call *deep think* is another aspect of critical thinking. It is so important that this book postulates it as fundamental to advanced analysis. Despite its importance, deep think is often neither thought about nor understood. *Deep think* is defined as taking the time and expending the mental effort to think critically and deeply about a particular subject.

Who can deny the importance and requirement for deep think in the business of intelligence analysis? Yet, even though not many people would argue against its importance, events, activities, and organizational settings trap the intelligence analyst in a working environment that makes deep think impossible. What are we talking about? As a straightforward proposition, deep think is often impossible to perform. Sometimes analysts are neither trained nor educated to engage in deep think. Sometimes the noise and energy of operations and activities of a deployed military force preclude the analyst from engaging in deep think. Sometimes the pressure to design briefings and develop products takes all of the available time in an analyst's life. Thus, deep think, as defined, becomes an aching contradiction in the lives of busy intelligence analysts who know they should be engaging in deeper thought but also know they are caught up in a maelstrom of activities and energy to provide analytic output, to surf the Internet, to work with data, to build slides, and to engage in the myriad daily activities in the lives of busy intelligence analysts.

Intelligence analysts are constantly working with the computer and adhering to business rules and security requirements while being bombarded with a stream of data, missions, activities, production schedules, and briefings. Quite simply, they don't have the time to engage in deep think. Thus, analytic products are sometimes shallow and filled with errors of logic and thought. In addition, many intelligence analysts have not been afforded the opportunity to learn how to engage in deep think. They are trained to use automation but not to learn "how to think." Dealing with the complex environment, the wily embedded insurgent, the technical demands of the infrastructure, and the complicated culture, and still engaging in the higher-level thinking of advanced analysis requires time, effort, and a suitable environment. How might we rectify this contradiction, indeed the dilemma, analysts face?

This is clearly a leadership challenge. The senior intelligence officer must set the standards for her or his analysts' capability to engage in deep think, and other leaders in the intelligence organizations must help provide the advanced analysts the wherewithal to engage in deep think. Perhaps only the very best of advanced analysts should be provided the environment and the time to engage in deep think, because it would probably be impractical to try to organize and provide the time for all analysts to engage in deep think. Regardless, it is the senior intelligence officer who must recognize the need, provide the environment for deep think, and then work with the advanced analysts in one-on-one encounter sessions to probe into the minds of those charged with the mission of conducting deep think about the environment, the enemy, the culture, the populace, the infrastructure, and so forth.

Deep think is, of course, about thinking. But what thinking? Engaging in deep think takes thinking with a variety of techniques. It takes exploration. Deep think also involves being inquisitive about unknowns or mysteries. Deep think involves reductionism with the firm understanding that what is reduced gets reassembled into a higher order of thought through synthesis. Otherwise, reductionism can lead to emphasizing the process of thinking rather than the results of deep think. Russian author Fyodor Dostoevsky explains a danger of reductionism when it is devoid of the intent to synthesize its results into a higher level of meaning:

> man is a frivolous and incongruous creature, and perhaps, like a chess player, loves the process of the game, not the end of it. And who knows . . . perhaps the only goal on earth to which mankind is striving lies in this incessant process of attaining, in other words, in life itself, and not in the thing to be attained.[10]

But to take what is reduced to smaller and smaller parts and put it into a higher level of meaning gives purpose to reductionism. It becomes more than just the act of decomposing it into smaller and smaller parts or pieces. In this respect, when engaging in reduction or decomposition, the analyst who engages in deep think has synthesis in mind as she or he goes through the process. Thus, the analyst who decomposes has what she or he thinks will be the observable and even what the outcomes of collection against the observable might be. This generally comes into the analyst's mind as a vision and is expressed as a hypothesis or expectation.

Along with synthesis, which helps to overcome the negative effect of one aspect of deep think, the advanced analyst has some other methods of engaging in deep think at her or his disposal. For example, as advanced analysts engage in deep think, they purposefully engage in *cause and effect analysis*. Using improper causes and effects can be one of the shortfalls of critical thinking. But if done correctly, cause and effect analysis can be a tremendous boon to analytic thought. Clausewitz helps us understand why cause and effect relationships are important in critical thinking. In this respect, Clausewitz states:

> The critic's task of investigating the relation of cause and effect and the appropriateness of means to ends will be easy when cause and effect, means and ends are closely linked . . . But in war, as in life generally, all parts of a whole are interconnected and thus the effects produced, however small their cause, must influence all subsequent military operations and modify their final outcome to some degree.[11]

When using cause and effect relationship analysis, the advanced analyst must first understand the actual (in the case of the output of effect and action) effects and trace what caused the effect to its origin or originator. Unfortunately, in the complexity of the urban OE, there are often multiple causes of effects. But usually there will be a primacy among causes of the effects in question. Even in Clausewitz's time, military theorists had difficulty finding single causes linking to single effects. In this respect, Clausewitz tells us there are usually many causes that can be traced to effects or outcomes:

> effects in war seldom result from a single cause: there are usually several concurrent causes. It is therefore not enough to trace, however honestly and objectively, a sequence of events back to their origin: each identifiable cause still has to be correctly assessed. This leads to a closer analysis of the nature of these causes.[12]

As another aspect of critical thinking, the analyst will also consider and think about constraints. Some constraints are self-imposed, such as U.S. military rules of engagement. Other constraints are unique to the enemy. Shortages of bomb parts or explosives could be an enemy insurgent bomb maker's constraint. Or a third kind of constraint involves inhibitors to action and activities of strength and relevance to all sides in a competition between the United States and its coalition partners and the insurgent operating in an urban setting. Of further interest to the advanced analyst engaging in deep think, thinking about the rise and influence of sensitive variables and windows of opportunity should be in the intellectual repertoire of the advanced analyst. Sensitive variables could be the mood of people, a sudden dust storm, and an errant bomb that sets off a chain of events leading to aggregations of people and energy that sometimes cannot be controlled. So it is best to anticipate the possible arrival and influence of sensitive variables with windows of opportunity and how they might influence all sides in a conflict.

In any urban setting, complexity will be preeminent. Though this isn't the time or place to go into detail about complexity theory, any large city will involve complex adaptive systems (CAS) interacting, acting, colliding, intersecting, and careening, with outcomes being unpredictable. Everything is connected, and when there is a perturbation in one cell or node or with one person or with an organization, other parts of the fabric of the city will change too. Author Mitch Waldrop explains this phenomenon:

> In example after example, the message was the same: everything is connected, and often with incredible sensitivity. Tiny perturbations won't always remain tiny. Under the right circumstances, the slightest uncertainty can grow until the system's future becomes utterly unpredictable—or, in a word, chaotic.[13]

Through deep think, the analyst can comprehend the incredible connectedness of all things. This understanding will help the analyst to understand causes and effects, perturbation of relationships, sensitive variables, and windows of opportunity for their manipulation or for defense against their power. This understanding will cause the analyst engaging in deep think to always look for the apparent and hidden connections. There will be second- and third-order effects that could go from a small, seemingly insignificant action to a huge international scandal. Sensitive variables will appear for brief periods of time and cause enormous outcomes. The time for the ascendancy of these variables and their enormous influence can best be described as a window of opportunity. As a final point of complexity in urban settings, everything is constantly moving and changing in an urban setting, including people. Thus, the city is fluid and appears chaotic with no order and no discipline. The analyst must learn to engage in deep think about an arena that is ever moving, always changing, always surprising, and seemingly falling into the abyss of chaos but in reality only teetering on the edge of chaos.[14] But with complexity theory, one realizes that there is order even in the chaos.[15] The advanced analyst, through the deep think aspect of critical thinking, thinks about and searches for the hidden order because it often will yield clues about what the enemy is doing in the noise of the chaos.

As another aspect of critical thinking, the analyst must search for facts and evidence. Finding undeniable facts and using them as evidence is difficult in non–life threatening situations. But it is extraordinarily difficult for advanced analysts involved in situations moving and changing quickly to find and use facts for argumentation. Sometimes facts and evidence are not available to the analyst because they are buried in the noise of an OE, because the enemy is securing them, because the populace won't provide facts contributing to evidence, because the analyst does not have the resources to search for and find facts and evidence, or because it takes too long to produce the required evidence. So what is an analyst to do? The answer has three parts:

- *First*, the analyst must discern what facts he or she has available and if more can be found or if more will eventually surface.
- *Second*, the advanced analyst will make a claim, state a proposition, or put forth a hypothesis about the situation.
- *Third*, he or she will have to prove the claim or test and prove or disprove the hypothesis.

To prove the claim or prove or disprove the hypothesis takes evidence and facts. Therefore, the analyst sets out to gather evidence and facts and often actually seeks to disprove his or her hypothesis or proposition rather than confirm it, because confirming causes a mind-set that is more interested in proving a claim than finding the truth,. The analyst works with the collection specialist to help find evidence for the claim and seeks SME support from a VKE and intelligence enterprise to help confirm or deny the claim with evidence. This too is part of critical thinking and using the intelligence system through analysis and collection to find the evidence.

As a next step in our journey into the depths of critical thinking, we will discuss some of the common errors in thinking and logic the analyst can make. This discussion, however, is not only about the errors advanced analysts can make but also thinking about and developing the capability to spot errors other people are engaging in. This discussion will not go into great depth on any of these aspects of critical thinking but will simply introduce the errors to the reader and provide an example or two of each to help with comprehension and application in the daily work of an intelligence analyst.

- EXPERT TESTIMONY is an argument that relies not on facts but on opinions, beliefs, or theories of experts or on testimonials of people with rank. Expert testimony presents a classic rank problem in the military. Sometimes, people are inclined to believe and agree because another person has a higher rank, and they think that the rank makes his or her thinking or conclusions superior to anybody else's thoughts or conclusions. As we can say in the safety of this paper, that is not true, and without equivocation we can say that rank does not equal brains. This is, however, an insidious problem in that people with higher rank hold an enormous amount of power over subordinates. Thus, there is a real tendency for lower-ranking people to defer to the conclusions of higher-ranking people. This is a dangerous proposition, because the higher-ranking person can be wrong. Thus, the lower-ranking person has to have his or her day in court, so to speak, and has to be able to present the case not to appease the higher-ranking person, but to provide the analyst's best thinking about a problem. If this thinking is at odds with higher-ranking people, so be it. The good leader will always hold these in-depth sessions with people of all ranks and will listen and often accept the ideas and thoughts of subordinates. These enlightened leaders will understand that rank does not equal brains.
- AD HOMINEM is a fallacy people commit most often in politics. Instead of answering the question or building a logical argument, they choose to attack the person they are arguing with. Ad hominem means: (1) appealing to one's prejudices, emotions, or special interests rather than to one's intellect or reason; (2) attacking an opponent's character rather than answering his argument.[16] For example, rather than discuss the errors or points of disagreement in a briefing, intelligence analyst Sergeant Smith tunes out his mind because he believes Sergeant Jones is a fool and always gives poor presentations because he isn't smart.
- CIRCULAR REASONING is a use of reason in which the premises depend on or are equivalent to the conclusion, a method of false logic by which "this is used to prove that, and that is used to prove this"; also called circular logic.[17] An example of this would be, "I believe Salafi Arabs are

evil and behind the suicide bombings because their fundamentalism justifies the permissibility of suicide for the fundamentalist cause; Salifism condones suicides for the fundamentalist cause, therefore the Salafi Arabs are behind the suicide bombings." The analyst must watch for falling into this logic trap; it is easy to commit. The conclusion should follow the premises, but the conclusion should not be the same as the premises no matter how artfully a person cloaks the premises to hide their direct linkage with the conclusion of an argument.

- OVERSIMPLIFICATION is to simplify to the point of error, distortion, or misrepresentation.[18] As an example, we can think for a moment about America's entrée into WWII. A mental error would involve the oversimplification that postulates that the bombing of Pearl Harbor in December of 1941 caused America's entrée into WWII. Of course we know this was just one of the causes for America's entrée into WWII. If the analyst becomes mentally entangled with oversimplified logic, he or she will ultimately make other errors such as non sequiturs and errors in cause and effect reasoning.

- HASTY GENERALIZATION is a generalization postulated with too little evidence or a sample that is too small with which to draw conclusions. Stereotyping is a type of hasty generalization. Another type of hasty generalization could be the intelligence analyst forming a conclusion about the extent of an enemy network in one neighborhood because an automobile driving through it was found to have several garage door openers. The analyst must be careful not to fall victim to forming hasty generalizations. He or she must take the time to verify with facts a growing suspicion or generalization. In a fast-moving situation, this can be difficult, because the analyst has neither the time nor the resources to engage in a deliberate, painstaking effort to build a case for a hypothesis that comes from generalizing and extrapolating to a larger whole with very little evidence. But the analyst can and should use these generalizations to turn into *mysteries*, because not everything will be clear at the start of an analytic episode. Thus, the analyst must have the wherewithal to form generalizations and to pursue some of them in analytic mystery work. Enough evidence must be gathered to warrant generalizing, and the evidence must not be exceptional or unusual.

- POST HOC, ERGO PROPTER HOC, meaning "After this, therefore because of this,"[19] is the mistake of assuming that because one event followed another, the first must be the cause of the second. Analyzing the sequence of events can lead to the corollary conclusion that because one event followed another, the one that followed is linked or caused by the first event or activity. Analysts with scanty evidence, such as those working in urban areas, can sometimes fall victim to this fallacy. Let us consider an example. People who believe in the infallibility of forensics without other sources of information to fuel their thinking could be susceptible to this kind of error in logic. Consider this sequence of events and the conclusion. A convoy was driving down a road and was attacked by an IED. Upon the arrival of security and subsequent sweep of the area, a young male was found with a video camera. The sergeant in charge concluded that because the man was found with the video after the IED exploded that the person was a perpetrator whose mission was to take video to use in the insurgents' information operations campaign. Unfortunately, the male was an innocent bystander who happened to get swept up in an event at the wrong time and place. But it will take a lot of time to figure out the error in logic. As another example, consider the analyst performing trend analysis. This analyst delves into the past and reviews significant activities reports. He concludes that because attack B followed attack A, attack C will occur in the same place at roughly the same time. When attack C occurs in a different place at a different time, the analyst knows that his or her logic was wrong somewhere, but he or she does not know exactly where his or her thinking failed.

- FALSE DILEMMA involves a situation in which two alternative statements are held to be the only possible options, when in reality one or more other options exist that have not been considered.[20] A false dilemma is an effort to eliminate the middle ground by drawing a sharp distinction between parts of a complex whole when the facts show a gradation or shades of gray between and among the parts. For example, an advanced analyst performing cultural baseline duties of a particular neighborhood in Baghdad is thinking about how the enemy exists in a society if the people are not actually insurgents. He can go along two pathways of thought. He can believe that people are either friendly or insurgent. With this thought, he would be committing the fallacy of false dilemma, because he has not thought about people who might be "fence sitters" or people who are afraid and therefore passive. People's motivations are often much more complex than simple yes and no or black and white. Thus, the analyst should have considered the second pathway of thinking. That is, he or she should have recognized that there is no situation involving human beings in which simple yes or no, black or white, or unequivocal positions or slants exist. Instead, complexity is always at work, and people have an infinitely complex rationale for their decisions and subsequent behaviors.

- HISTORICAL ANALOGY is often used to buttress arguments. Historical analogies are useful to the advanced analyst as long as she or he doesn't become a victim to fallacious reasoning that can be associated with historical analogy. So, what is the problem with using historical analogies as a means of thinking and arguing? Richards Heuer tells us that using analogies is good from one perspective, owing to its use of comparison. But he says there are some dangers the analyst needs to be cognizant of. As one, Heuer says,

The difficulty, of course, is in being certain that two situations are truly comparable. Because they are equivalent in some respects, there is a tendency to reason as though they were equivalent in all respects and to assume that the current situation will have the same or similar outcome as the historical situation.[21]

It follows that in order to use historical comparisons or analogies, the analyst needs to not only identify comparisons, but also to think through the differences that may make drawing conclusions from a historical analogy inappropriate. If the analyst starts drawing conclusions from the comparison that are not applicable or inappropriate, he or she runs the risk of making errors in logic and thought.

- NON SEQUITUR is an inference or a conclusion that does not follow from the premises.[22] This is an interesting fallacy. It involves thought processes in which people argue about something that is not linked to their position or premise. It involves discussions that have nothing to do with the original premise or proposition. An example might involve an analyst discussing Sunni insurgents. His or her logic might go as follows—the Sunni insurgents mostly come from Saudi Arabia; therefore, Kurdish fighters will never commit acts of terrorism in Iraq. Or when working with an indigenous SME on suicide bombing, the SME says Iraqis will not commit suicide bombings because in Islam, they will go to hell if they commit suicide; therefore, the only people using suicide bombs will be Saudi fundamentalists.

As discussed earlier, critical thinking is one of the most challenging subjects in advanced analysis. Although thinking is fun and produces stupendous outcomes, it also causes us to err and to commit mental mistakes. Critical thinking involves the mental travail of thinking about how we think, how other friends and enemies think, and how people and leaders in the culture in which we operate think. This thinking is not a simple consideration of how we or our competitors might think. No, it goes much beyond such a simple equation. As such, all analysts have to be capable of *thinking how the enemy thinks the friendly leader and his intelligence team think about his thinking and subsequent actions and activities.* In turn, friendly commanders and their intelligence team have to think about how the enemy thinks not only about himself, but *how he thinks the friendly commander and his intelligence staff think about the enemy and how he thinks about himself, the friendly commander, and his intelligence staff.* This line of thought identifies the complexity of the world in which the advanced analyst lives and operates.

We must be truthful when considering our own thinking. As mentioned earlier, all people err and do so continuously. Therefore, it follows that advanced intelligence analysts have to be aware of their cognitive shortfalls and the errors they habitually make and do something about overcoming these problems or at least mitigating their influence. In addition, analysts must recognize the importance of thinking about how their opponent thinks about himself and friendly force capabilities and how he thinks about how friendly leaders think. All of these challenges make for a brew of complexity. But without entering into this world of "others' thinking," intelligence analysts will never succeed.

So, what are some of the potential errors in thought that will have an adverse affect on the analytic mission and what are some ways to overcome the potential errors? (For ease of understanding, the following rhetorical questions are phrased in the first person.) Have I neglected to find the right expertise to help with my particular problem or challenge? Have I failed to ask for support from other analysts? Have I not stated my requirement correctly? Have I, in the interest of saving time, oversimplified the situation? Have I presented poor assumptions or presented no assumptions behind my thinking at all? Have I engaged in mirror imaging and therefore neglected to identify the correct tactics the enemy might use, and therefore failed to identify the potential condition-setting the enemy will have to put into place? Have I seized upon expert opinion (my commander's or another authority figure's) and thereby failed to explore alternatives through the eyes, minds, and perceptions of the enemy? Have I used faulty cause and effect logic in exploring anomalies in relationship to baselines?

To be more specific, I must ask what are some of the errors analysts can make with the technical environment. In this kind of probing for mental error in analysis, several possible problems can exist. As one, the analyst, in a self-critiquing role, may worry that he or she may have oversimplified the technical environment enshrouding the problem set. Oversimplification could be serious and cause the pursuit of the subtle and invisible technical world to be cast away as neither pertinent nor knowable. With such an attitude and attendant errors of omission, the advanced analyst could be missing valuable observables. This could be because he or she fails to identify, explain, and ask for coverage of said technical observables or fails to seek the right technical assistance to understand the technical environment and to disambiguate that environment to make it knowable and "seeable." The analyst might fail to think through how the enemy will be using technology. Similarly, the analyst might fail to consider how the populace thinks about and uses technology and how they think about U.S. technological prowess. He or she may have oversimplified the technical baseline or failed to seek assistance from technical experts on the staff, indigenous technical experts, and experts from the VKE to design the technical baseline and then to identify anomalies that could occur if the enemy was performing his technical condition-setting activities, and what these activities might look like or appear to be in the invisible world of technology.

What are additional cognitive problems analysts may experience when dealing with critical thinking? As one pitfall, the analyst might neither seek nor find the right SME or analytic support in the intelligence enterprise to help with the specific problem or challenge he or she is working with. But on a positive note, when using critical thinking, these analysts should conclude that they need to find the right SMEs to help engage in critical thinking and in developing knowledge sufficient to support decision-making. In this regard, the advanced analyst needs to understand precisely how SMEs or the able assistance of other analysts in the intelligence enterprise can contribute to his or her effort.

Some of these people will be from the society in which the analysts' organization works. As such, the advanced analyst will engage in an inner dialogue that might go as follows: "I need to find and use indigenous people to help me develop the three kinds of baselines required for using advanced analysis in urban COIN settings—technical, cultural, and functional." Continuing along this line of thought, analysts must answer the following questions: Where can I find the right SMEs? How can I elicit their support? What should I ask them to do by way of solving requirements? How do I ensure they understand what I am asking them to do? How do I explain my standards? How do I critique the knowledge products I have requested?

These are good questions but unfortunately they are never easily answered. Often, a knowledge broker can help. Or the analyst can work with the right community of interest in the intelligence enterprise or the right leadership in the hierarchical portion of the larger intelligence enterprise (including analytic overwatch people and organizations) to find the right people to help in answering these questions and to hone the analyst's focused requirements and requests for information and knowledge. For example, let us consider cultural SME support to an analytic effort in a large city while conducting counterinsurgency and counter–irregular war operations. Deployed analysts will clearly require cultural support to perform the basic roles and duties of advanced analysis. Some of these SMEs will be from the United States and its coalition, but some of the SMEs will be indigenous people familiar with the city in question and knowledgeable about the neighborhood where intelligence operations will occur. Some of the required SMEs will need to know the neighborhood in which the analyst will work to the point of not only understanding subtle, ambiguous, and often fleeting observables, but also having enough knowledge to know how to look or watch, where to look, and when the best time might be to look for the analyst's requirements, voiced by way of operational context, observables, constraints, and standards. This process sounds easy, but in reality, with the current state of affairs in intelligence operations, this type of support is difficult to seek and difficult to use. What are the causes of some of these difficulties?

Supporting the commander's decisions is the raison d'être of advanced analysis. But in a hierarchical intelligence enterprise, this particular situation is one of several hundred. Thus, owing to reasons out of the analyst's control, there may be neither capability nor priority to request SME support in the intelligence system. Or, as a related problem, the intelligence community might not be able to find the right kind of SME to support the analyst with his or her particular requirement. On an individual level, the analyst may have failed to use cultural SMEs familiar with the neighborhoods in question to work on wargaming, identifying points of friction, and pursuing expectations, mysteries, and hunches from a detailed cultural perspective. In addition, the analyst may have asked for the wrong SME support from the VKE knowledge broker. Also, the analyst may have stated his or her knowledge requirements incorrectly, which could cause duplication of effort and confusion among the SMEs of the VKE, among the intelligence enterprise, and even with the knowledge broker in direct support of the relevant intelligence operation.

The advanced analyst must have a close relationship with collection specialists. Unfortunately, this has not always been the case in the past, because of stovepipe thinking, organizational hierarchies, and, most egregious, a clear failure of senior intelligence leaders to understand the need for such a relationship between analysts and collection specialists. Organizations have built walls around each function (analysis and collection) and have kept each function strictly thinking about and performing its specialty. Thus, analysts do not habitually develop and provide observables to collection people. In addition, analysts do not generally provide detailed guidance to the many parts and pieces of the distributed intelligence collection enterprise. Thus, although they mean well, people in a distributed node in the United States might not know the specific context, observables, and standards the deployed analyst requires support on. Stuck in his or her analytic "lane," the advanced analyst might have forgone developing a relationship with collection specialists. This error in critical thinking leaves the collection specialist to focus collection, even though he or she does not have the expertise to develop the five types of observables we have been discussing throughout this book. Additionally, perhaps the analyst does not know either the capability or availability of sensors and HUMINT. Therefore, analysts do not have the wherewithal to work with observables, collection, and a time/space continuum. In a related error, even if by chance an analyst might have developed observables for collection, perhaps they are not good enough. Going into further detail, the introspective advanced analyst may have failed to anticipate friction from three perspectives: (1) his or her perspectives, (2) the perspectives of the collector, and (3) those of the enemy. The advanced analyst also may have oversimplified and failed to ask for collection to work against his or her hypotheses, expectations, hunches, mysteries, and assumptions, and failed to provide the distinct means to lower uncertainty and reduce risk, thereby making an often complex and ambiguous situation more manageable to the commander. Now let us delve into some more-specific kinds of errors in critical thinking about collection.

- *Designing and ensuring data flows.* The analyst may have failed to discuss and help design data and sensor architectures with collection specialists and technologists. The analyst may have failed to identify standards for data—latency, latest time information of value (LTIOV), and earliest time information of value (ETIOV). The analyst may have forgotten to think about how nontraditional and low-level sources will provide data for use in time to make a difference. This takes working on data architectures with technical specialists and collection specialists with whom the analyst has bonded and made part of the collection and analyst team.
- *Keeping collectors informed of analytic guidance.* As briefly mentioned before, the analyst might be thinking that he or she has failed to understand the holistic nature of the intelligence collection and analytic enterprise and therefore failed to contact and explain the rationale for his or her needs to each collector. As such, the analyst may have failed to think through when he or she needs the collection and analytic systems to surge and to have the highest sampling rate (tied to when the analyst believes enemy activities will be the strongest). The analyst may have failed to be specific enough—right time, right place, right observable, and right activity. Or the analyst may have failed to think about keeping the various collectors he or she is working with informed of changes and a new emphasis based on up-to-date knowledge. Our hypothetical analyst may have failed to articulate his or her standards—timeliness, specificity, accuracy, relevance, and clarity. The antipode of these possible failures is, of course, what the analyst needs to do to succeed in the complex OE against the wily insurgent we are discussing.
- *Access to and use of incorrect or outdated data.* It is quite possible to believe that this error in critical thought might not be appropriate for discussion. After all, some people certainly believe in the supremacy of data. As a corollary thought, these same people believe that all one has to do is provide access to data and the analyst will figure out what to do with it. Unfortunately, if somebody makes these assertions, he or she is wrong. Upon what do I base this proposition? Often, the analyst will have a difficult time swimming in the vast pool of available data and being able to seek and find just the right kind of data at the right time with a proven state of veracity and usefulness. To think well, the analyst must have access to what we can call useful or valuable data. But unfortunately, not all data is of value, because some is outdated, erroneous, and wrong by way of facts, figures, and

conclusions. Thus, ensuring analysts are working with good data, information, and knowledge comes to light in our consciousness as an important, if not critical, aspect of critical thinking. Let us briefly examine some of the errors in critical thinking the advanced analyst might fall victim to when considering data.

The analyst needs data. But what kind of data will suffice? As all of us know, masses of data are available in open sources through the Internet. In addition, the analyst will also have access to massive amounts of data though the close intelligence and operations systems. Thus, the analyst could easily fall victim to working with the wrong data, not being able to find the most relevant data, or working with out-of-date data, all of which means the analyst's thinking could be erroneous from two perspectives—thinking poorly with correct data and thinking well but using wrong, corrupted, erroneous, or outdated data.

- *Errors in acquiring knowledge.* With the short discussion of some of the thinking errors associated with data, it is time to turn our attention to knowledge. What are some of the challenges and problems the advanced analyst might have when searching for usable knowledge, knowledge that adds value, or when the analyst must build new knowledge? For the sake of discussion, if the reader will be so kind as to indulge this brief trip into an analyst's mind to present some of the rhetorical questions he or she might pose, it will be helpful for understanding how knowledge relates to critical thinking. Let us consider some troubling postulations about the knowledge that the analyst seeks.

  - As one, I might seize upon the first knowledge I come across. This is a natural tendency, particularly for an inexperienced analyst who suffers from stress and a shortage of time. Or I might be using outdated knowledge with which to think. This is an issue because I will be using knowledge as the basis for my thinking. My thinking, of course, provides knowledge to the commander as actionable intelligence. Thus, I must have a way that is not time-consuming to verify the accuracy of my knowledge.

  - As another critical-thinking problem, I might confuse data with knowledge. Data, for the purpose of discussion, is "a single piece of information, as a fact, statistic, or code."[23] Knowledge is "familiarity, awareness, or comprehension acquired by experience or study."[24] Knowledge, of course, is difficult to develop and to use—it takes synthesis and analytic judgment that comes with training, education, intuition, experience, and, of course, access to other knowledge. Data is different. It is often singular and presents a single fact or statistic, or a series of facts and statistics. In intelligence work, data can be blips on a screen, a single report, an image, or computer language streaming into a processor. But generally speaking, data does not provide conclusions or meaning—it takes machine and human cognitive work to turn the data into information and knowledge of the kind commanders need for decision-making. Meaning involves the higher-level thinking skills of synthesis and evaluation. The data "is what it is," as it arrives, whereas knowledge is what one makes it after machine and cognitive work.

• As another issue in critical thinking, I sometimes do not take the time or expend the intellectual energy to check acquired knowledge for veracity (truthfulness). Thus, the material could be wrong, outdated, or even duplicitous, thereby signaling the potential for possible deception.

• As a final possible issue with knowledge, the person, people, or organizations responsible for developing knowledge the analyst requires might have erred and developed inappropriate knowledge that is chock-full of mistakes and errors in logic.

What can the advanced analyst do to overcome these problems? Several broad aspects of thinking come to mind.

• ORGANIZATION. As a fundamental step, advanced analysts must organize their thinking to be effective. This might seem like a trivial conclusion; however, in the busy world of stress, fear, fatigue, heat or cold, and constant pressure to produce, organization is not a trivial matter. Thus, it is wise to work with an advanced analysts' critical-thinking thought template. This template should not be a rigid step A, step B, step C, and so forth. The wrong use of a template can result in the use of and dependence upon a checklist. A checklist mentality may cause the advanced analyst to conclude: "If I just check off every item in the checklist, all will be OK." Instead, the template should serve as a guide for how to think about difficult problems and challenges. It should be a stimulus for thinking about the important aspects of analytic requirements. It should encourage thinking about how others perceive and think.

> A critical-thinking thought template should lead the user to consider how the enemy might choose to surprise the friendly force and how the friendly commander might choose to surprise the enemy. A critical-thinking thought template should help the analyst determine what is important and critical. It should encourage the analyst to consider difficult problems, which require extensive knowledge and thought, such as knowing and using the culture for gaining an advantage and not just to seek and gain cultural awareness. An effective critical-thinking thought template should encourage creative and higher levels of thinking by causing the analyst to pull together various strands of data, information, or knowledge and weave them into conclusions, into a series of implications, or into a

whole to answer questions such as: What does this outcome mean? If we do this, what will the outcomes be? What are the variables and why might they be sensitive? What can make the variables inherent to my situation suddenly become sensitive and cause effects to achieve vast influences?

- CULTURE. Inevitably, intelligence analysts will make mistakes when trying to understand and use the culture of the OE in which they are operating. Advanced analysts are no exception unless they recognize the problem and do something to eliminate their mistakes or at least mitigate their impact. Some of the mistakes advanced analysts might make with respect to the culture could include the following types of difficulties:
  - I may have failed to consider and thwart my penchant to engage in cultural mirror imaging.
  - I may have failed to design cultural observables using cultural intelligence, anomaly analysis, aggregation analysis, synthesis, and tendency analysis.
  - I may have failed to seek and use the expertise of red team people.
  - I may have failed to seek and use the expertise of indigenous SMEs.
  - I may have failed to seek and use the expertise of the VKE's cultural SMEs, engineers, and scientists.
- INTROSPECTION. If the advanced analyst is introspective, he or she will know whether he or she has a proclivity to engage in mirror imaging. If the analyst knows that he or she commits the mental error of mirror imaging, he or she can do his or her best to avoid it by projecting his or her mind into the minds of the people whose thoughts he or she is attempting to emulate. To do so, analysts will need the help of U.S. and indigenous cultural SMEs who can help them think similarly to the people they are trying to emulate. These SMEs can also criticize their thoughts and help analysts to maintain the best possible semblance of intellectual purity by helping to come up with feasible alternative conclusions or approaches to thinking, ultimately gaining the right knowledge to support commanders' planning and decisions.

DIALECTIC

Now that we have discussed some of the errors associated with critical thinking, let us turn to thinking about some ways the advanced analyst can engage in aspects of critical thinking to support his or her analytic efforts. One of the elements of critical thinking involves use of the dialectic. In this work, dialectic does not involve the pure application of the Hegelian dialectic, nor does it involve the dialectic of Marx, Engels, or the former Soviet Union. Instead, it presents a dialectic variant as an exquisite way to engage in creative thinking by understanding the elements of issues, problems, or arguments sufficiently well to search for and find contradictions that lead to further thought and a search for new or different answers.

This kind of dialectic is an aid to higher-level thinking. It is defined as

> The process especially associated with Hegel of arriving at the truth by stating a thesis, developing a contradictory antithesis, and combining and resolving them into a coherent synthesis.[25]

As mentioned, the dialectic consists of a thesis, antithesis, and synthesis. The dialectic has, at its core, the notion of contradiction. An interpreter of Hegel, Frederick Copleston, provides us with Hegel's idea of contradiction, which has great value to advanced analysts:

> But contradiction is for Hegel a positive force, which reveals both thesis and antithesis as abstract moments in a higher unity or synthesis. And this unity of the concepts of being and not-being is the concept of becoming. But the unity gives rise in turn to a 'contradiction,' so that the mind is driven onwards in its search for the meaning of being, for the nature or essence of the Absolute in itself.[26]

The dialectic depends on the presentation of a thought, proposition, or hypothesis that is the *thesis*. When people examine the thesis in detail, they find contradictions, which are logical incongruities with the thesis. The contradictions lead to discussion, thought, debate, and argumentation. Soon, an *antithesis* comes forth as a solution to the contradiction. The antithesis is an equally assertible and apparently contradictory proposition. Soon, through still more discussion and argumentation, contradictions about the antithesis come forth. Through more discussion and argumentation, both sides in the argument seek and reach a higher plane of solution or reason. It is often new or different and is the *synthesis*. The synthesis in the context of the dialectic is the mutual contradiction being reconciled on a higher level of truth by a third proposition, which is the synthesis.[27] Soon, people find contradictions in the synthesis and the process starts again in the constant search for truth that is never found. In this respect, the dialectic is an intellectual process for higher-level thinking and is a catalyst for creative thinking and fomenting change.

KNOWING THE TECHNICAL ENVIRONMENT

Workarounds exist for overcoming problems in the technical environment. As one workaround, analysts must remind themselves to engage in thinking about the technical environment. This jog of memory can and should come when using a critical-thinking thought template. Advanced analysts must be introspective about their technical skills and understand what they are capable of doing. Analysts can also realize the presence of at least two dimensions in all technical analysis problems—the visible, physical world (e.g., power station generator), and the invisible, nonphysical world (e.g., RF energy). They must seek the help of people who have the right technical expertise and credentials on their organic staff; within the interagency with which their unit or organization works; with the indigenous engineering and scientific community; within the coalition; and finally, with the use of a VKE and its access to technical SMEs, engineers, and scientists. As another aid to technical analysis, the advanced analyst must have a systematic way of using technical observables for all situations in which he or she plans to collect. As such, the analyst must seek the technical support of scientists and engineers as discussed above to perform three basic functions. *First,* they must decompose their requirement (PIR, IR, hypothesis, expectation, hunch, and mystery) into technical observables (along with cultural, situational, biometric, and functional) to give the right and specific guidance to all types of collectors. *Second,* they must use technical experts to help wargame enemy act/react/counteract activities in the technical range and understand how these activities relate to cultural, functional, biometric, and situational aspects of any OE. *Third,* advanced analysts must seek and use technical experts to help them recompose data into information and then synthesize the information into knowledge. Advanced analysts must make this effort purposeful, because if they are not technically inclined, they might choose to avoid dealing with this important aspect of advanced analysis altogether.

RED TEAMING, WARGAMING, AND CRITICAL THINKING

Once the advanced analyst recognizes his or her need for cognitive and knowledge assistance, he or she has to learn when to seek it and from whom. Analysts will not need assistance all the time. This statement is particularly applicable to analysts who have served in a particular city in a particular culture for an extensive period of time and have subsequently learned a lot about the threat, OE, and the culture. But with the enormity of any city and its fluid environment, there will always be information and knowledge requirements that even the most experienced U.S. intelligence analyst will need help with.

DATA AND DATA FLOWS

What is an analyst to do by way of searching for usable data that is the fuel for the engine of critical thinking?

> *First,* the analyst must realize the most serious challenges with seeking relevant data. These challenges include seeking the right data, finding and using corrupted data, using filters to sift the good data from irrelevant data, finding good data but failing to recognize its problems with latency, and sorting the right data from the large amounts of available data.

Second, the analyst must use guiding standards for data work, such as timeliness, specificity, accuracy, relevance, veracity, source bona fides, and tracing the data to its originator. For the most part, at this time, these capabilities are not available for the critical thinker's use; regardless, the analyst has to understand what they mean and seek to satisfy and judge each of the elements. *Third*, the analyst must search for the right data in the right places. This requires knowing what data can be found where or using a smart tool to help find the right data and secure its access. Searching for and extracting data requires analysts to think about access, links, passwords, identification entrée, and data pathways with which to search for, find, extract, and then be able to use the data they desire.

Fourth, the analyst depends on data; therefore, he or she must think critically about his or her data requirements and never leave their correct flow to others who do not know what the analyst requires.

KNOWLEDGE

I have to think critically about the value of knowledge and the possibility of it being wrong. I have to think critically about how to check for possible errors or deception. One of the ways I might do such a check would be to check the origination of the knowledge, the people or organizations who developed the knowledge, and even use SMEs from the intelligence enterprise or a VKE who might have authenticated the knowledge. Such a critique is part of the thought process the analyst needs to go through in critical thinking.

THINK LIKE THE ENEMY

As another pillar of critical thinking, the advanced analyst must learn to *think like the enemy*. To do this, the analyst must see the world through the eyes of his or her enemy and the enemy's cultural prism. Analysts must experience the inputs of the senses, think and perceive, and act and assess in the way that the enemy goes through these mental activities. Such an effort is difficult for anybody to consider, let alone accomplish, because each of us are closely tethered to our perceptions and backgrounds. Thus, *apperception* becomes an important consideration for critical thinking in advanced analysis. *Apperception* is "the education, culture, upbringing, religion, history, myths, and customs that condition a person's mental outlook and identity, and generally influence how that person thinks, views the world, and solves problems—it is the essence of one's perceptions that guides one's thoughts about truth and worldview."[28] To understand apperception, the advanced analyst has to work with cultural SMEs. If they are fortunate, analysts will have an experienced Foreign Area Officer (FAO) to help them. But even a FAO will not have the cultural moxie to get into the nuance, subtlety, and ambiguity that an indigenous SME will bring to the effort. In addition, the analyst, in a perfect world at least, will want to balance the views of indigenous sects, such as by obtaining the views of both Sunni and Shia, for instance, and balancing their inputs with a U.S. cultural anthropologist who speaks the language and has recent ground time in the city in question. Again, this is the ideal, and it will usually be unavailable in its entirety to the analyst. Thus, the advanced analyst will take what help she or he can find and use it to the best of her or his ability. Importantly, however, the mere act of being aware of the need to think like the enemy in detail will contribute to the avoidance of making errors in thinking and at least suggest to the analyst to be wary, to understand that his or her hypotheses and hunches could be wrong, and to hedge uncertainty with antipodal efforts such as using ISR to watch for observables indicating what "could be" by way of the unexpected occurring.

Even with our own innermost perceptions, it is difficult to think about why we perceive the way we do, why we associate causes with effects, how we decide what is most important, how we see what has heretofore been invisible, and why we are comfortable with inductive reasoning when others are more comfortable with deductive reasoning. Most people do not have time to engage in such mental gymnastics. But the consequence of not doing this for ourselves—that is, to think about thinking and how we think— leaves us vulnerable to the ravages of naivety, perpetual surprise, and a lack of understanding about how our enemy thinks and perceives when things turn out differently than we had expected. So for the sake of argument, let us assume that as advanced analysts, we have examined how we think and we have sufficient expertise available to help us overcome cultural hurdles and to go deeply into the enemy's apperception and thinking processes. Let us examine how we can learn to think like the enemy and the potential pitfalls we should avoid. To start with, we need to undergo some questions and answers from what we think the enemy's thoughts and perceptions are.

- As a first question, we ask *What is my perception of U.S. analytic capabilities, HUMINT, and technical collection?* To answer this question from a U.S. analyst's perspective, we need to use cultural and indigenous experts. We also need to use interrogation reports and discussions with people who have been insurgents but who have been working with the government to peek inside the minds of perpetrators to learn how they think and perceive. In addition, the analyst would pose related questions to analytic overwatch people, interrogators, and even HUMINT and CI people who work with indigenous agents to learn how the enemy engages in such thinking. But always we have to ask of ourselves, *What could be wrong with my thinking and how might I know if I am wrong?*
- A second question that could be important from the enemy's thinking and perception is *How can I hide from American sensors and HUMINT?* U.S. analysts need to understand the strengths and

weaknesses of both sensors and HUMINT. To do so, they need to use technical and HUMINT collection specialists to identify shortfalls and weaknesses with each type of collector and to assume the enemy has figured out the same and will be taking appropriate countermeasures from their point of view. Advanced analysts could also systematically look for dead space the enemy might perceive and supplement it with ground, air, or HUMINT coverage, given that the target set (such as the enemy planning an attack on a key oil pipeline generator) is of value to the friendly side. They could also use 3D/GIS models to identify how the enemy might attempt to counter U.S. surveillance and use dead space. As with the first question, analysts should always go through self-examination and find out what could be wrong with their thinking.

- As a third question, analysts put their mind into the mind of the enemy and ask, *What will the Americans do that can cause my failure, and how might I surreptitiously counteract?* In this regard, the enemy will surely know and understand what aspects of condition-setting, planning, and execution are critical to his success. For certain, the enemy will worry about interruption of necessary condition-setting. He will worry about the Americans preempting his planning, condition-setting, and actual attack activities. He will worry that the Americans will find his network nodes and cause early evacuation and end up thwarting his attempts to synchronize his plans and activities. Again, however, analysts must examine their thinking to look for mirror imaging and other errors in thinking and logic.
- As a fourth question, the enemy will be asking, *Where and how will the Americans be watching for me or actively looking for my activities?* The smart insurgent will be wary about using his cell phone unless it is for purposes of deception. But it will be impossible to control cell phone usage for all of the people supporting the insurgents' networks. The insurgent will also be thinking about U.S. and coalition HUMINT operations. Thus, he will always be worried about insiders and people in the neighborhood providing adverse information to the Americans. Of course, this implies that U.S. HUMINT cover stories must be solid and make cultural sense. It also implies careful selection of the means to communicate collected data to the U.S. intelligence services. In addition, the enemy will be worried about being spotted by unmanned aerial sensors (UAS). He will consider taking appropriate actions to move late at night and then only in the shadows of streets and alleyways lacing the labyrinth of complex city dwelling. After going through this type of critical thinking, as when working with other questions dealing with critical thinking, analysts must look within and check their thinking, *Am I right? Am I engaging in mirror imaging? Am I looking at how the enemy thinks from a cultural perspective? Do I understand what is important to the enemy? Do I understand the enemy's perspective of will and how he views my perspective of will?*

- As a fifth question, the analyst must ask from an enemy's perspective, *How will I proceed with my functional planning and execution while the United States is looking for me?* The enemy will think about, plan, and execute what from his perspective is an effective countersurveillance plan that uses the culture and often will be low-tech in order to avoid the U.S. version of high-tech sensors. The enemy will have well-rehearsed escape routes. In addition, for very smart insurgents, baselines and anomalies will be an issue. That is, the insurgent will think through how the U.S. analysts and collectors will look for him and will determine the importance of baselines with which U.S. analysts will search for and find anomalies—cultural, technical, functional, situational (neighborhood peculiarities), and biometric anomalies. Continuing with this line of reasoning, the U.S. analysts will anticipate that the enemy is thinking about the best way for his early-warning network to warn him or her of impending danger. Owing to the enemy's belief that U.S. technical collection is the best in the world, he will undoubtedly attempt to use semiotics, couriers, children playing and being couriers, watchers, and movers for his HUMINT early-warning and countersurveillance. Analysts will check and double-check their thinking about this issue via red teams, cultural specialists, and properly cleared indigenous people.
- As a sixth question, the analyst must think like the enemy thinks and ask, *How will I recruit people to perform the many duties I need for sustaining my network and for performing tasks essential to my mission?* Analysts will anticipate enemy use of local leaders to recruit people for the network and provide necessary money for this task. To the greatest extent possible, insurgents will not provide the people supporting the network with any information about the network and will focus their effort on single missions. This means advanced analysts will have to weave multiple inputs that seem isolated and disparate into a whole of meaning much as the insurgent does as he weaves the single activities of a multitude of people to form the activities of his whole—his supporting network. In the insurgent's thinking, he will consider using people who won't be suspected as readily as young, eager males. As such, he will consider using old people, beggars, derelicts, mentally deficient people, women, and children to accomplish network support tasks. Again, advanced analysts will engage in analytic introspection and think about what could be wrong with their thinking when considering how the enemy is thinking.

CONCLUSION

In concluding this important chapter, critical thinking is something in which the analyst must continuously engage and improve upon. Arguably, engaging in self-criticism is much more difficult than criticizing others. Nonetheless, it is something that must be done not just once but continuously. Critical thinking is important for bringing forth the best in thinking, because it asks the analyst to think in three spheres:

> *First*, the analyst must internalize critical thinking and consider how he or she is thinking as an individual.
>
> *Second*, the analyst must seek help from outsiders to help with thinking, as is the case with indigenous people and technical experts, and to examine his or her thoughts critically.
>
> *Third*, the analyst must be critical of the way other people are thinking and learn to spot errors. They are obliged to challenge what appears to be erroneous assumptions and poor thinking.

In this chapter, the reader learned about how some of the great theorists thought about critical thinking. The author borrowed the thoughts of both Clausewitz and Sun Tzu to help illustrate and explain some of the important aspects of critical thinking. In addition, the reader learned about *deep think* and how important it is to critical thinking. The chapter also listed and discussed the multiple types of thinking and logic errors the analyst is susceptible to, such as mirror imaging; ad hominem attacks; oversimplification; post hoc, ergo propter hoc; false dilemma; historical analogy; and non sequitur errors. In the latter portion of the chapter, the reader was introduced to some of the challenges associated with critical thinking and ways and methods with which to meet and overcome these difficult challenges and succeed in the important work of good thinking. In closing the chapter, the author leads the reader through a series of questions relating to how the enemy thinks about U.S. intelligence analysis and collection. This is an important but often forgotten aspect of critical thinking. It is important to consider critical thinking from the perspective of not only the friendly force—and in particular the individual analyst performing the act of critical thinking—but also the enemy, as well as how the enemy engages in critical thinking about himself and the U.S. military.

If done correctly, critical thinking is a powerful force. But to engage in critical thinking fully, the intelligence analyst has to be humble and introspective. Analysts must also seek and take on constructive criticism and improve their cognitive performance. In addition, because of the complexity of the modern OE, to engage in successful and effective critical thinking, the analyst needs help from other analysts, from internal or external red-teaming experts, from people in the intelligence enterprise, and from SMEs in a virtual knowledge environment. The chapter on critical thinking flowed logically from the intense work required of people engaging in decomposition. Now, again in a logical flow, the thoughts on critical thinking flow into link analysis.

7

Link Analysis

Definition: Gaining understanding and insights into behavioral or functional relationships, means of communicating and being connected, and how connections and relationships work between and among people, organizations, internal network nodes, and among networks.

THEORY BEHIND LINK ANALYSIS

A link is any element of a system that represents a behavioral, physical, or functional tie between or among nodes. A link is also a unit in a series of connected units, such as any element of transportation or communications systems, an association or bond, a causal, parallel, or reciprocal relationship, or a correlation. Link analysis closely relates to the other 14 elements of advanced analysis. It is different enough, however, to discuss in some depth to understand what it means.

Link analysis relies on in-depth knowledge of connections and the connectedness between and among people and organizations. It involves knowledge of the links of friendly and coalition forces, as well as of enemy links and connections. Link analysis is particularly important for planning and making decisions in urban environments. Densely populated urban settings are chock-full of relationships and connections constantly activating, deactivating, appearing, and disappearing. Link analysis is also important for understanding the connectedness among elements of the environment, such as infrastructure, people, organizations, and cultural processes like religion. Because people are the most important aspect of urban operations,

U.S. planners must exert an immense amount of time and effort to correctly understand and focus on the connectedness of people and organizations. Thus, links, along with nodes or cells, become important in day-to-day analysis, planning, decision-making, execution, and outcomes.

Oddly enough, the links connecting wholes, such as the enemy's numerous networks, form an interacting whole of both strengths and vulnerabilities. Strong links make a strong network; weak links, just the opposite. Often cells and nodes cannot be found or, even if found, influenced. Links, on the other hand, can offer a way to influence a cell or node and can provide a treasure trove of information for the astute planner and decision maker to use in influencing cells and nodes and generally affecting the attitudes of people and organizations. Links, in a theoretical sense, relate to the Clausewitzian notion of friction. It seems that good commanders can actually sense friction arising from links with the past and the present. In this regard, Clausewitz tells us,

> Moreover, every war is rich in unique episodes. Each is an uncharted sea, full of reefs. The commander may suspect the reefs' existence without ever having seen them; now he has to steer past them in the dark. If a contrary wind springs up, if some major mischance appears, he will need the greatest skill and personal exertion, and the utmost presence of mind . . . An understanding of friction is a large part of that much-admired sense of warfare, which a good general is supposed to possess.[1]

Why should advanced analysts care about links? Links connect people, things, organizations, processes, transactions, interactions, and activities. At the same time, they are reliable conduits of information. They provide a vast array of power and energy to nodes and activities, which might include chemicals, money, thoughts, data, information, and knowledge. Links are the lifeblood of relationships between people, from people to organizations, and between organizations.

With high-grade knowledge and an intimate understanding of the influence that can be gained through effects, U.S. elements of power can attempt to influence targets both directly and indirectly. Often, the indirect approach involves attacking, manipulating, stimulating, or perturbing the links connecting people, organizations, functions, machinery, and processes. Naturally, the antithesis holds true: opponents can attack friendly nodes or important points or functions by attacking related links. Furthermore, various types of links (among the five types discussed in this chapter), while serving to connect wholes with other wholes or aggregates with other aggregates (to be discussed later in the book), also serve as conduits for creating surprise, the variables to attack or manipulate, or the purposeful inducements of friction (chance events). The object here is to do the antipode of what Sun Tzu offers as advice:

The ultimate in disposing one's troops is to be without ascertainable shape. The most penetrating spies cannot pry in nor can the wise lay plans against you. It is according to the shapes that I lay plans for victory, but the multitude does not comprehend this. Although everyone can see the outward aspects, none understands the way in which I have created victory.[2]

That is, through link analysis, expose what the enemy is trying to hide and find his shapes as he connives, moves, and buries himself in the hustle and bustle of a busy city.

Relationships count, because we are and will be in people-oriented conflicts. Conflicts of the future will be struggles between and among people in large metropolitan areas. Struggles among people will always involve relationships. People are social animals. Thus they have person-to-person needs. People must form and use relationships with other people and organizations to exist. Human links, therefore, are essential to the functioning of any society and, in particular, to the successful functioning of an insurgency. This point is reinforced in the best-selling book *Freakonomics*. In this book, the author recounts a study of a drug enterprise. In the enterprise, an enormous number of links were in evidence. In this case, they were primarily human links that bonded with purpose and rewards:

> So the top 120 men on the Black Disciples' pyramid were paid very well. But the pyramid they sat atop was gigantic. Using J. T.'s franchise as a yardstick—3 officers and roughly 50 foot soldiers—there were some 5,300 other men working for those 120 bosses. Then there were another 20,000 unpaid rank-and-file members, many of whom wanted nothing more than an opportunity to become a foot soldier. They were even willing to pay gang dues to have their chance.[3]

This passage suggests, of course, the enormity of challenges advanced analysts face as they attempt to use link analysis. Virtually everything and everybody is connected in some way. Through the thoughts contained in this chapter, advanced analysts will have the intellectual wherewithal to narrow the problem set and learn to think through the use of link analysis.

Links are critical in conducting successful counterinsurgency warfare. The insurgent or terrorist operates in cells or nodes embedded in cities. These cells or nodes connect with many other cells and nodes through links; all these links are, in one form or another, highly relational. But connectedness is neither continuous nor easy to find or recognize. Links provide the means of making the mental connections that will lead to comprehending or "seeing" the relationships these nodes or cells enjoy. If intelligence analysts are able to discover links, they will find and fix cells or nodes. For example, if U.S. intelligence operations cannot locate an insurgent's cell or node that performs a certain function, they would look for and find the links connecting any related cells or nodes and their functions. People are often the links connecting the hidden enemy who is operating in cells and nodes with people in other cells and nodes. Even the "lone wolf" will require some type of connection for support.

Obscure links that seem to be invisible can be discovered with a partnership between the human mind and the machine. Human cognition and machines, when working as a team, can find the obvious and yet seemingly disparate links connecting elements of a society and the insurgents' networks, as well as the human connections among their communities of friends and relatives. By thinking this way, an analyst using the cognitive elements of advanced analysis can start viewing the cells and links as cobwebs and gossamers with cells and links that come and go and connect and disconnect with other cells and links.

Unfortunately, as can be easily surmised, many kinds of unrelated links connecting cells and nodes already exist, which compounds the difficulty of searching for and finding the particular cells and nodes analysts might be looking for. This complexity and multiplicity places an exponentially higher premium on high-grade knowledge of, awareness of, and anticipation of link and cell morphing.

As a related thought, links enable aggregation. It is through links that information spreads rapidly, often causing exponential leaps and significant outcomes in aggregates (which will be discussed later). A combination of human and mechanical links contributes to the appearance of the phenomenon of aggregation. Links can be in place, operating, and obvious one day, but the next day they may become invisible, inoperative, or dormant. Through decomposing aggregates, the advanced analyst can start to surmise, indeed understand, the multitude of links connecting the many cells and nodes that make up the insurgents' networks of networks. In addition, the astute analyst realizes the ephemeral nature of links even in the ultimate state of aggregation with other links, cells, and nodes. Links can be apparent and serving as conduits one minute and then disappear from view only to return to view, or be visible one minute and then disappear forever, perhaps morphing elsewhere or appearing in a totally different domain. Good thought and cutting-edge machines can consider, visualize, and work through cause and effect relationships as commanders ponder what to do about the links, which provide the lifeblood of the network.

What is the nature of a link? Links can be strong and weak. A network is only as strong as its links. A link's strength can be thought of as *trust* between a bomb maker and his couriers; *length of time* a link is operating; *clarity* of transmission, such as in the case of fiber-optic cables or a radio link; *visibility or invisibility*; *proficiency*, such as in the case of an insurgent female who is a HUMINT agent; and *improbability*, such as in the case of mentally handicapped people being used as suicide bombers or a beggar being used as a courier. A weak link degrades the overall strength of a network and its connection to other links and cells. Links are the Achilles' heel of any network, because they can be made transparent, they can be manipulated, and they can be weakened. In addition, links can be made to "fibrillate."[4] Link fibrillation involves movement and change. This movement and change can be ever so slight or it can be obvious. With link fibrillation, however, the advanced analyst can cause links to change and therefore show connections, purposes, character, and strength. Links can be mechanical, such as the fiber-optic cable that connects people and organizations via communications. Links can be transitory, such as people coming and going from a large airport, or permanent, such as the communications and power cables leading into the airport.

The analyst must consider links and their sources of power. The source of power for a human link might be trust or frequency of use. The source of power for a mechanical link could be its source of power generation and ability to return to action after a devastating blow such as a breakage coming from construction. The source of power for an electronic link could be the speed with which packets move through cyberspace or the bandwidth available for the packets to move. The source of power for a thought link could be the strength and character of the thought and intent and the recipient's ability to understand and implement it without direct guidance. The source of power for a functional link could be the capability to replenish a commodity expended in a function, the availability of a vehicle for transporting network leaders, or money that is the catalyst for the function to occur. Finally, the source of power for an organization could be its relationships with other organizations or its combined knowledge base.

Links can portend the future. In this line of thought, links connect the present with the future. As we imagine what could be changes in the enemy's operations and his network, we can also imagine what the links connecting the present with the future might be and watch for their ascendancy. As an example, the enemy could be planning an assassination. To plan, rehearse, and execute such a mission, the enemy must set conditions for success. Part of the condition-setting process involves establishing links and nodes in the network. As each or all of the types of links come into being, there are observables associated. These observables come forth in the analyst's mind during decomposition or normal interludes of analytic deep think.

There are five kinds of links the analyst must be familiar with. This discussion of links will range from highly concrete links to those that are abstract and largely invisible.

- TECHNICAL LINK—such as wire or fiber-optic cable between two or more points in a telecommunications system, packets, bandwidth, Internet, cell phones, electrons or radio frequency energy, heat emissions, energy emissions (e.g., computer clocks).

- HUMAN OR SOCIAL LINK—a person, especially one of influence or importance, with whom one is associated; connectedness; relationships; friendships; religion.
- ORGANIZATIONAL LINK—a single organization or groups of organizations that work together and communicate.
- THOUGHT LINK—association with or development of something observed, imagined, discussed, or connected by thought.
- FUNCTIONAL LINK—movement and action in accordance with a particular functional area such as intelligence collection, infrastructure maintenance, etc.

Sensitive variables can affect the strength of links. A *sensitive variable* is something that is potentially reactive to stimuli, perturbation, or influence and has the potential to quickly affect one's mission or condition-setting activities, given that the right environmental or situational conditions are present in particular settings and circumstances. When variables become sensitive to change or exponential growth, they can increase or decrease in strength, and they have the potential to increase or decrease the strength of links or make invisible links visible. Often, there will be very short windows of opportunity that signify the opportunity for peak influence of sensitive variables. We can call these periods of time sensitive-variable windows of opportunity. Strength and weakness in such processes show as intangibles, such as trust in human links; longevity of a link, such as in a physical link; strength of a link, such as in a familial association; clarity of intent, purpose, and mission-type orders, such as in an intent link; and associations, relationships, and perpetual connectedness by thought, such as in a thought link.

In our analysis, we should not forget about the connectedness of all things. In this regard, with some effort, we can see webs of relationships. Within each web, we can find relationships and linkages connecting with other relationships and links. In many ways, the connecting tissues of the webs of relationships, which are links, are similar. As author Frances Cook tells us in his description of the pearls of the Hindu god Indra,

> In accordance with the extravagant tastes of deities, the artificer has hung a single glittering jewel in each "eye" of the net, and since the net itself is infinite in dimension, the jewels are infinite in number. There hang the jewels, glittering like stars in the first magnitude . . . If we now arbitrarily select one of these jewels for inspection and look closely at it, we will discover that in its polished surface there are reflected *all* the other jewels in the net, infinite in number.[5]

Similar to the mythical "network" of the pearls of Indra, links can be physical and visible or they can be physical yet out of sight (such as buried cable connecting two buildings). Links can also be invisible, such as the relationships and connections between and among human beings, which involve behavior, emotions, thoughts, and perspectives. Human links, which connect people's thoughts, predilections, emotions, and involvement with activities, are culturally dependent and can be difficult to find. The easiest links to find are the physical links, such as telephone lines or electrical power lines. The hardest links are the on-again, off-again human links actually connecting people and organizations, and serving as invisible conduits of data, information, and knowledge. The most difficult of all are intent and thought links, which bond elements of the network with its leader's intent and mission-type orders. An example of this type of link involves loosely connected al Qaeda thought links such as those shared by small groups of terrorists in Spain, Germany, and Indonesia linked by intent and thought with Osama bin Laden and his band of terrorists hiding somewhere.

Link analysis strongly relates to several other cognitive elements of advanced analysis—tendency, culture, aggregation, anomaly analysis, and synthesis. It will be useful to explore ever so briefly some of these relationships in our effort to understand link analysis.

- LINK ANALYSIS AND TENDENCY ANALYSIS. *Tendency analysis* is the discerning of meaning through thought and study of the general proclivities of people; the behavioral and action inclinations of organizations; mental snapshots of current environment or contextual situations, events, activities, and behaviors; the emanation dispersal of energy emissions; and what the interaction and enmeshing of all could portend for the future. Links help the analyst recognize the slightest changes in current situations sufficient to enable him or her to anticipate and watch for actions to unfold. The links that connect everything in a neighborhood are often imperceptible to the human eye, hence the difficulty in using tendency analysis. But with forethought, analysts can purposefully cause link fibrillation, discussed earlier, to show the now active links and what they connect to, how often they are active, and their characteristics and functions. Analysts can target links to cause change and therefore cause change in the enemy's network. These changes can enable the advanced analyst to understand tendencies and the movement that tendencies portend, and therefore enable the analyst to wisely use one or all of the five kinds of observables to watch for this movement into an altered network state or position.
- LINK ANALYSIS AND CULTURAL ANALYSIS. *Cultural analysis* is defined as knowing a particular culture, its people, and their patterns of behavior deriving from traditional, culturally induced attitudes, behaviors, social norms, and conditions. Links connect people who have relationships. These relationships vary in intensity, visibility, frequency of use, method of activation, and their strength and decay. How links work depends on

the culture they perform in. Thus the advanced analyst must know and understand the culture and how it influences human links to use links for the purposes of intelligence analysis and collection. In addition, links connect people with organizations. These organizations can be businesses, religious organizations, or recreational organizations. The purpose of link activation is varied, such as a person purchasing food from the market, buying a television, visiting an Internet café, or even meeting for coffee or tea. Insurgents and terrorists may hide their activities under the guise of seemingly legitimate organizations. Thus, the advanced analyst must identify, track, and connect people with organizational links. Advanced analysts need to think about enemy activities or non-activities not as U.S. intelligence analysts, but as people and organizations of the culture in question. This leap into the minds of people from a culture different than that of the United States is a prodigious feat, but essential all the same. To understand links at work in a culture means one must understand the culture. Then and only then can U.S. intelligence analysts understand the links, their connectedness, their strengths and weaknesses, and their periodicity (tendency to recur at regular intervals).[6]

- LINK ANALYSIS AND AGGREGATION ANALYSIS. *Aggregation analysis* is defined as discerning meaning of several things, numbering from a few to millions, that are grouped, moving, working together, and considered as a whole. Aggregates connect; links provide the connections. Aggregates have "glue" that binds them internally to make an aggregate and externally to make up a macro-aggregate. To understand the glue that binds aggregates (such as an angry crowd in which the glue is the emotion coming from the loss of a child to an errant bomb), one has to understand the links that connect aggregates. Aggregates have a propellant (which in our case would be the degree of pent-up emotion that has grown and solidified over time sufficient to allow emotion to overrule rational behavior) that causes them to move and change, ranging from the smallest of changes or the death of the aggregate all the way to the aggregates of the butterfly effect, in which the smallest, seemingly innocuous aggregate can grow into a huge outcome, disproportionate to the input. To understand these types of aggregate second- and third-order effects, one must understand the links that connect the aggregates.

- LINK ANALYSIS AND ANOMALY ANALYSIS. *Anomaly analysis* is defined as discerning meaning in departures from the normal or common order, form, or rule—absence of that which is expected. Anomalies involve comparisons between what is considered normal and deviations from normalcy. Links help the advanced analyst understand anomalies. As links move and change, the analyst can surmise that the potential for anomalies to appear is greater than before. In this respect, because of the relationship between links and anomalies, often the advanced analyst will disturb or disrupt established links in order to induce anomaly or speed current anomalies coming into maturity for earlier exploitation. Anomaly analysis depends on finding or developing and using three types of baselines—technical, cultural, and functional. Links are prevalent in the baselines and thus help us comprehend anomalies. This is true for all six types of links.

- LINK ANALYSIS AND SYNTHESIS. *Synthesis* is the human cognitive activity that combines elements of substances, events, activities, or energy to form a coherent whole. Synthesis involves combinations. That is, our minds search for, find, and combine thoughts and activities to bring forth a different or new whole. Synthesis, though related to analysis, brings the multiple thoughts from analysis into a higher, more meaningful and usable level of thought. Synthesis also relates to anomalies, aggregates, and recomposition. To synthesize, we often need assistance from both obvious and seemingly disparate links that help bind, "glue," or hold aggregates together in larger wholes. To use links to help us synthesize means we have to possess extensive knowledge about the six types of links and how each serves to bring other thoughts, activities, and interactions into a different combination or higher level of thought.

We can also help ourselves by answering internally developed rhetorical questions about links. These questions include the following:

- *What is a link?* The answer to this question could include anything serving to connect one part or thing with another; to join, connect, or unite; a unit in a connected series of similar items;[7] a unit in a transportation system; an association or connection; a causal or reciprocal relationship.
- *What kinds of links exist?* The answer to this question includes technical, human, organizational, functional, and thought.
- *What do links do?* One answer to this question is—given that we recall the five kinds of links—connect people, organizations, things, activities, transactions, interactions, and behaviors; bridge relationships; enable nodes to combine; move information; help people learn; move money; move supplies; move people; provide a facsimile of structure and regulation in an unstructured network.
- *What relationship does a link, or several links, have with the network writ large?* The answer to this question includes many things, but here are a few examples. Links can provide functions; they can be a vulnerability; they can be a window into the network's inner workings; their decay can weaken the network writ large; they make the network strong when working correctly; and they serve as a conduit for passing information, for people moving and exchanging thoughts, for causing action to come into being, and for following up on earlier actions.

- *Do links decay?* The answer is yes. Link strength can vary but sometimes dissipates almost from the moment of inception. Some links take longer to decay, such as well-protected fiber-optic cable, whereas other links are sensitive to perturbation and decay quickly and constantly, such as a courier to a bomb maker. When the bomb maker has high trust in the courier, this link is strong. When the bomb maker starts doubting the courier's intentions and veracity, the link starts a decay process and is difficult to make strong again. The signs of decay will be present, so during decomposition, the advanced analyst must design observables to deal with link decay, because this condition could certainly lead to the soft underbelly of the network.
- *Do links engage in self-cleansing?* The answer to this question is unknown. But it makes sense that links, nodes, and a network writ large would have a process of cleansing the unwanted, undesirable, or unneeded parts and functions and thereby cleanse itself to prolong the life, vibrancy, and proficiency of the links. Thus, we can postulate that links have a self-cleansing process that insurgents use to keep their links vibrant, tense, flexible, and, as needed, disappearing. To understand this notion, we can borrow the idea of cellular self-cleansing from science, which calls cell cleansing *autophagy*, defined as

  > a cleanup process: the trash hauling that enables a cell whose cytoplasm [protoplasm exterior to a cell nucleus] is clotted with old bits of protein and other unwanted sludge to be cleaned out. Refurbishing the cytoplasm can give new life to any cell.[8]

- *How might the enemy view his links?* The enemy will view his links as a critical part of his network. They contribute to the network's strength; they can contribute to its weakness; they can contribute to its decay; and they can contribute to the demise of the network. To our advantage, the enemy can also be guilty of mirror imaging and may believe U.S. intelligence analysts and sensors will have a difficult time picking up on-again, off-again links. A very smart enemy will undoubtedly run false links and networks and will attempt to use links to deceive. With good countersurveillance and early-warning security setups, the adversary will undoubtedly know when there is perturbation in any of his links that support his nodes and networks writ large.

Interestingly, the advanced analyst can anticipate the kinds of links the insurgent will have in place and operating to perform insurgent missions satisfactorily. These links will vary among insurgent missions—safe house, bomb factory, attacking infrastructure, kidnapping, suicide bombings, and the like. Regardless of the mission, however, links must be present. With this understanding in mind, there are challenges for the analyst.

First, the advanced analyst must know what to look for by way of link types, characteristics, degree of strength, what gives the link strength, stages of decay, and the cause of such decay.

Second, the advanced analyst will have to recognize all five types of links when they appear, regardless of their vagueness or attempts to obscure them.

Third, the advanced analyst will have to track the links and attempt to find the source of power for each link, e.g., money paid for services rendered, receiving instructions, receiving training, rehearsing, etc.

Fourth, the advanced analyst will have to know how to perturb or stimulate each kind of link to gain insights into the aggregates that comprise the network.

How do links work? All links serve some purpose or function; otherwise, they would not be links. Functionality describes their purpose: links connect nodes and cells; they provide information and communications; they serve as conduits for transportation. Consider, for instance, a node we are all familiar with: a large airport. An airport connects with other airports over well-defined routes of travel for each airline. These can be called air links. An airport has communications links to local businesses and other airports, receiving food, fuel, and parts logistics support from a variety of vendors and businesses. These are links. Mechanics travel to and from the airport to repair aircraft. The airport receives security support from the federal government via the Transportation Security Administration (TSA) and local police. Taxi companies and drivers provide transportation. Custodial people come to work and clean the landing and departing aircraft. All these workers have other personal links to friends, families, banks, hairdressers, churches, and, of course, the company they work for. People come to the airport to travel—these, too, are links, albeit transitory links. Thus, one single airport has an untold number of working links with any number of social and commercial enterprises. Together they constitute a complex endeavor to observe, but what else does this complexity mean for the analyst?

- When an analyst attempts to find an insurgent or terrorist cell or node, he or she must understand the notion of *multiplicity of links* supporting the cells and nodes. Many variations of links go in and out of the cell or node. Advanced analysts must have a frame of mind that encourages searching for not only the obvious links going to and from cells and nodes but also the subtle, often invisible links. They must consider not only functional links but also the technical, cultural, situational, and biometric nature of links.
- Analysts must understand the differing characteristics of links connecting to cells and nodes. Links coming to and going from cells and nodes

have many different characteristics. The analyst pondering the links must be capable of considering all of them to the deepest extent possible. The object here is, of course, to know enough about the links to decompose and use the resultant observables to task a variety of collectors to find, fix, and track these links. This will be easy if the link is permanent, such as a fiber-optic cable, but difficult if the link is highly mobile and fluid, such as a courier. The analyst must recognize the predominant links and either know or learn about them to be able to successfully recommend the right effects and actions that will influence either the cell and node in question or the links connecting them.

- Analysts must consider the element of time when thinking about links. Some links will endure, some will be short-lived, some will be transitory, and some will be a one-time linkage.

- Analysts have to understand that links are relational by nature. Links relate to cells and nodes, and they relate among themselves. Going back to the airport analogy, a person going into and out of an airport relates to the airport itself but also to transportation and the people providing the transportation in the use of taxis or commuter trains to arrive at and depart from the airport.

- Analysts must consider the element of link decay. If links are seen at all, they can appear strong and vibrant, slowly moving and acting, or they can disappear in the blink of an eye. Links can be strong but over time they can decay in strength because of lack of use, human distrust, interruption, or natural outages or breakdowns in human relationships. Once decay sets in, the link will weaken, morph, or even die.

  - Link decay deserves more discussion. Some of the relationships or links that become active will be initially strong but will decay over time. Let us continue our thinking by once again delving into the example of a courier bringing information to a cell that houses a bomb maker, several days in a row. The bomb maker considers this a strong link in that the same person repeatedly makes the delivery—his arrival, recognition, trust, and contributions make this link strong. But if that same courier does not appear again for several days, or his behavior is erratic when he does arrive, the link is called into question. This is an example of a link that has incurred decay: decay in power, trust, and observability. Some decay will be natural and accepted by the bomb maker or cell leader. Other decay features will cause the cell leader to grow suspicious and take steps to increase security, deny the courier access, or eliminate the courier all together. The analyst thinking about links has to consider decay as the observables associated with decaying energy levels in links will be of less and less value with each decrement or decay in the link. In addition, if the courier is a HUMINT source, the analyst has to consider normal and abnormal decay and the observables that can be gleaned from both (from the adversary's perspective), and then design conditioning and shaping operations to ensure the source remains as a nondecaying and strong link.

- The people who perform many of the essential functions of a network, such as operational security, logistics, communications, sustenance, etc., are links that come and go. These links (people) are totally enmeshed in a given culture; they manifest the cultural characteristics of their location (dress, speech, gestures, behaviors, and social norms). They lead to other links, which lead to still other links. They constitute webs of relationships and together make up networks of networks (human and mechanical). If one person provides functional logistics support to an insurgent or terrorist cell, that person is a link. But, in addition, that individual has links with his cousin, brother, friend, spouse, daughter, or son. In other words, there is always more to a link than meets the eye or registers within our cognitive faculties. Social network analysis (SNA), then, because of its ability to identify even the most subtle relationship, is an important corollary activity of link analysis.
- Links move various forms of energy to and from cells and nodes. Energy comes forth in disparate ways: as thought, as the medium's energy, as a conduit in itself, as accomplishment, as service, or as enactment of function. Some links are conduits of electrons; an electricity link could be an example of this type of link. Some links are conduits of information that provide the catalyst for an expulsion of energy; e-mail is one example.

A network cell's strength lies in its interconnectedness with other cells and with the whole. If a cell breaks or weakens, the network loses proportionate strength. If cells remain united through strong links, the network has strength—stronger together as a whole than a single cell or the sum of multiple cells. This idea suggests a viable way to think about and work against a network and its cells, nodes, and links: the cognitively intense method of finding and fixing enemy networks involves searching for, finding, and understanding links. The well-trained analyst must learn about links, nodes, and cells in order to be able to see such links even when buried in the noise of the busy human interactions characteristic of a large urban OE. Interestingly, at the right time, the analyst and commander must perturb links to disturb, influence, or eradicate cells and nodes in order to spot their energy or movement and, most importantly, to learn about the nature of the link and its relationship with one or more nodes.

As mentioned before, the enemy will inevitably grow wiser; therefore, he will surely develop sham cells and nodes and run decoy links to deceive and confuse U.S. intelligence. Thus, intelligence analysts remain ever wary when working with links, because they could be counterfeit and created only to deceive. In the chess game of move and counter-move, if intelligence analysts are smart enough, they can use the links connecting the enemy's cells and nodes and performing necessary functions as the medium for intelligence collection, deception, and double-agent operations.

There is an interesting duality of thought that comes into play when working with links. One part of the duality involves friendly links being vulnerable to attack and manipulation. The other involves enemy links, which also are vulnerable to attack and manipulation. It is an intense competition between two intellectually endowed competitors; the United States has to win these struggles to control both the initiative and the enemy's mental and emotional faculties. Thus, advanced analysts have to know and understand the links from the enemy's perspective: not only functionally (how they work) but also how the enemy leader and subordinates think about their own links and how they anticipate attacks on them. Using the precepts of advanced analysis, analysts identify vulnerabilities by watching for the enemy's efforts to overcome his self-analyzed link vulnerabilities and to prepare for what he assumes will be future assaults on those link vulnerabilities. On the other hand, friendly forces have to mask and deceive their own efforts to harden or strengthen links, because the enemy will surely be observing, looking for critical vulnerabilities to attack, manipulate, or deceive.

To perform link analysis, analysts will find it beneficial to understand how complex adaptive systems (CAS) interact in the OE. When complex adaptive systems collide, intersect, or career, there is expenditure of energy. Each CAS will try to continue on with its mission, retreat or change its posture, and/or assume a different shape, which allows for activities of its choice. These activities leave energy trails we can compare to pheromones and wisps. As pheromones, the links that collide, intersect, and career will leave indelible imprints as they move toward the location or domain of collision. They will backtrack using the pheromones much as an ant uses them to return safely back to his anthill. A *wisp* is, in this case, a thin streak or a slender trace. The colliding complex adaptive systems will leave these traces of activity as they interact with other such systems and attempt to move along or go back to their respective bases. We can seek and find links to help us understand their modus operandi and their point of origin and route of movement. In this respect, the links leave a wisp. This line of inquiry brings our thinking to the CAS links, whose on-again, off-again nature is similar to *ignis fatuus*, which is a "flitting phosphorescent light seen at night, chiefly over marshy ground, and believed to be due to spontaneous combustion of gas from decomposed organic matter."[9] Analysts must think about and design observables to watch for links appearing and disappearing, not unlike the *ignis fatuus*.

As a final aspect of link analysis, we must identify the challenges associated with link analysis and how the advanced analyst can overcome them.

- Extensive, up-to-date, and relevant knowledge is required to perform link analysis.
- The advanced analyst must drive collection to work against links.

- The advanced analyst must ensure the right data, sensor, and knowledge architectures are planned for and in place.
- The advanced analyst must think about and anticipate possible second- and third-order effects involved with pursuing link analysis.
- The advanced analyst must consider and plan for the surfacing of sensitive variables and windows of opportunity that he or she can find and exploit and, from a friendly perspective, vulnerabilities by way of the appearance of possible sensitive variables and windows of opportunity.
- The advanced analyst must understand relationships to understand links. These relationships are perplexing because many are cultural, technical, and behavioral—all difficult for a U.S., non-engineer intelligence analyst.
- The advanced analyst must know how the enemy thinks about his network and links and how he thinks about how "we think" about his networks and links.

How can the advanced analyst overcome these challenges and use link analysis? The following list provides a way to proceed in thinking about these challenges.

- WORK WITH A TEMPLATE. The advanced analyst must work with a mental template for link analysis. This template is a guide for how to think about these difficult challenges.
- SEEK THE SUPPORT OF EXPERTS. Use them for advanced analytic support, for the necessary functions for performing link analysis, and for support with related aspects of advanced analysis, e.g., aggregation, anomaly, cultural and tendency analysis, and synthesis. These experts will assist with the detailed cultural, technical, and human behavioral challenges inherent to link analysis.
- FORM A PARTNERSHIP. The analyst must drive collection by providing the observables and informing the distributed collection system of the operational context, observables, rationale, earliest time information of value (ETIOV), latest time information of value (LTIOV), and standards, and keep them up-to-date via automated tools.
- MANIPULATE LINK DECAY. Consider causing link decay to occur more quickly or more slowly than the norm. With link decay, we can gain insights into the network writ large and its functions and characteristics, and we can narrow the hunt for finding the key nodes of the network.
- WATCH FOR WISPS AND *IGNIS FATUUS*. Links will be periodic. As such, they will appear and disappear. They will always leave a residue, such as pheromones, or we will seek quickly appearing and disappearing wisps. But we must know when, where, and why to look; what to look for; and prepare observables for all. Then, we must be able to recognize a link

wisp or pheromone when it appears as raw data coming to the DCGS as a result of specific collection activities.

- USE RED-TEAMING AND WARGAMING. Engage in red-teaming, wargaming, and critical thinking to help consider networks—the links that connect the parts, pieces, and functions of the network in question; how the links move, form, disappear, reduce in strength, and decay; and the observables associated with each. Use red-team people to check the analysts' thinking, assumptions, and conclusions, and to avoid typical and atypical errors and traps in thinking.

- THINK LIKE THE ENEMY. In reentering the familiar thought pattern of thinking like the enemy, the analyst must work through a template of possible enemy activities. Some of the questions the enemy leader might be asking himself about links include the following:
  - How can I make my necessary activities appear normal?
  - How can I thwart the U.S. intelligence system's attempts to disambiguate and therefore find signs of my network and its links and their presence or activities?
  - How can I attempt to anticipate how the United States will think about my networks and supporting links?
  - How can I make network functions and links in the neighborhood appear normal?
  - What is my perception of U.S. analysis and collection and their capability to understand and search for and find my network links?
  - How can I hide my network and links from U.S. sensors and HUMINT?
  - What will the Americans do that can cause the failure of my network and supporting links, and how might I surreptitiously counteract?
  - Where and how will the Americans be watching or looking for my network and its supporting links?
  - During what part of the day should I use my network and its links to perform my necessary functions?
  - What is the best way to provide early warning of danger to my network and its links?

In closing this chapter, a summary of the main ideas is in order. In a broad sense, it is obvious how important links are to the insurgent and irregular warrior's networks—links are their great source of power and strength. Thus, it is incumbent upon the advanced analyst to study the nature of links, in order to perform detailed analyses. This difficult mental work is to not only know and understand the links in question but to learn from them and influence their activities, appearances, and morphing. Throughout the chapter several important ideas were introduced:

- Human, organizational, and functional connections and connectedness are important. Connections are the essence of links and networks. U.S.

intelligence analysts have become quite good at link analysis, in no small measure because of learning and honing the skill through interaction with law enforcement officers who have engaged in human link analysis for years.

- The main "actors" of link analysis are people, organizations, and infrastructure and the activities, interactions, transactions, and behaviors each engages in (human as well as mechanical).
- Links light up, dim, disappear, and reappear. This is why they can often be extremely difficult to search for and find.
- Links can lead to the adversary's critical centers and nodes. In fact, the adversary's network will wither and move toward a state of entropy without well-functioning links and the functions and activities they perform.
- Links decay. They start decaying from the moment of their inception. This decay process is natural in all links and therefore, it serves the intelligence analyst well to understand the process of link decay and to watch for such indicants to appear and disappear.
- Links have some interesting but seemingly disparate characteristics, including trust, clarity of transmission (if a mechanical link), visibility or invisibility, proficiency, and even improbability. *Trust* involves trust between two or more people. This is in play when the link is human or can even involve the trust a human can have for the efficacy of a mechanical link. *Clarity* involves the purity of data, the clarity of a phone transmission, and even the semiotic meaning of a cultural code or symbol. *Visibility* comes with both human and mechanical links. Sometimes a link will be active and appear in a variety of ways, such as RF transmissions or a person carrying a report from a surveillance operation to a bomb maker. At other times, a link can turn inactive. In some cases, even when active, a link can be *invisible* to the human eye and mind. A *proficient* link is one that can do what it is intended to do. A human courier charged with delivering money to the leader of a safe house comes to mind as an example. An *improbable* link is one in which its performing a link function is highly improbable. Recently, in Iraq, the insurgents used a mentally handicapped person to act as a suicide bomber. To many people, this act was barbarous and totally improbable, but it was still a link with the function of death.
- The chapter discussed *link fibrillation*. This term comes from the medical profession and describes a tingling or vibration of an important organ or muscle (in the case of medicine, the heart is often defibrillated when it goes into fibrillation or stops). In our case, the intelligence analyst perturbs or vibrates links, which can cause the entire network to move and fibrillate, thereby exposing parts, elements, and functions of links and even the overall network, which would have been much more stationary, even invisible, if it hadn't been for the intentional perturbation.

- The chapter also discussed the presence of five types of links—*technical* (fiber-optic cable, RF energy, electrons), *human/social* (couriers, relationships, religious activities, medical workers), *thought* (I know what the bomb maker is thinking right now and will act accordingly), *organizational* (individual or groups of organizations that work together and communicate), and *functional* (intelligence collection, security).
- Finally, the chapter identified in some depth how link analysis relates with other aspects of advanced analysis. As such, it strongly relates with tendency, cultural, aggregation, anomaly, and pattern analysis and synthesis. In fact, the elements of advanced analysis perform sub-optimally when people try to use the components in isolation. Advanced analysis works best when its cognitive elements work in optimum mixes to produce the best possible thought.

With the completion of this chapter, the reader is ready to proceed to the next chapter, which discusses pattern analysis. Just as link analysis had to wait until the completion of critical thinking to be introduced and discussed, pattern analysis follows link analysis, because it is with links that patterns connect and appear.

8

Pattern Analysis

Definition: Discerning a consistent series of related actions or events.

THEORY BEHIND PATTERN ANALYSIS

Patterns involve the composite of traits or features that are characteristic of an individual, a group, or a recognizably consistent series of related acts. Patterns are built upon relationships that drive human behavior, such as everyday activities, interactions, and transactions (in a very low-level sense), and strategy, will, and decision-making (on a higher plane of thought and action). There is a philosophical approach to patterns that can help us comprehend their power and their meaning well beyond what traditional pattern analysis yields to intelligence analysts. In this regard, physicist and philosopher Fritjof Capra explains,

> The Chinese on the other hand, not only believed that flow and change were the essential features of nature, but also that there are constant patterns in these changes, to be observed by men and women. The sage recognizes these patterns and directs his actions according to them.[1]

This passage implies the need for intelligence analysts to understand the constant actuation and change in the universe all the way to the subatomic level, but analysts should also be aware that there are understandable, visible patterns that always accompany this actuation and change. This is what pattern analysis strives to search for, find, understand, and turn into actionable knowledge to support commanders' decisions.

To understand pattern analysis, we have to delve deeply into what *patterns* and *pattern analysis* mean. As a first step, analysts must understand that there are four kinds of patterns. There are *technical*, *human/social*, *functional*, and *organizational* patterns. Analysts must realize that pattern analysis is one of the essential aspects of anticipating the next moves of enemies or competitors. Patterns among the human species occur because human beings are comfortable with habitual activities, thoughts, and movements; people rarely change their patterns even in light of evidence suggesting a need for change. Both people and organizations fall into activity ruts and patterns even if they try to avoid setting the patterns. People are creatures of habit and almost subconsciously exhibit patterns of behavior. When they break (or are caused to break) from their patterns of behavior and activity, they become uncomfortable. Being uncomfortable causes very specific observables to come forth; therefore, the wise advanced analyst sometimes causes patterns to change. Along with ordinary, innocent people being caught up in a pattern change, conspirators and network supports or even perpetrators themselves using the patterns for masking ulterior motives will be caught up in the change and subsequently change their behavior and their patterns of activity. As another example, the enemy might use the fact that people always queue to cross a busy bridge after going through a security checkpoint. If friendly forces change the pattern of the crowd and the way the crowd goes through the checkpoint, the use of the pattern by the insurgents for advantage could be taken away. Consider some other common examples that represent many human beings. People travel the same way to work every day. They follow rituals with their morning newspaper and coffee. They sit in the same place in the conference room. They dress the same way. They socially intermingle with the same groups. They do business following patterns of personal connections that stem from family and school classmate relationships. People like to establish and get good at routines; there is a degree of comfort in patterns (routines) for all of us.

Next, the advanced analyst considers how to use pattern analysis in his or her thinking. Patterns enable us to see relationships between and among aggregates. Patterns enable the advanced analyst to understand and visualize relationships between and among links—technical, social/human, organizational, functional, and thought. Patterns could come forth as mental images or messages. As an example, cultural and functional messages could occur as a result of enemy condition-setting before an attack on key and critical infrastructure. Patterns could also come forth as semiotics. Semiotics analysis—which is defined as discerning meaning of cultural signs and symbols reflected in drawings, paintings, signs, symbols, photographs, syntax, words, sounds, body language, and graffiti—often uncovers patterns. Semiotics analysis could yield patterns that experts with cultural and language expertise could help us understand. Specifically, advanced analysts would want to find and understand hidden cultural meanings and indicants of future behavior in semiotic patterns. This requires the analyst to know a lot to first search for the right patterns by way of observables and then to make sense of incoming data, eventually synthesizing data and information into knowledge and situational understanding. Sometimes, analysts won't recognize patterns, but with the pulse of obscure meaning inherent to all patterns, the analyst could have an insight about the appearance and meaning of a pattern.

Patterns could involve deviant behavior and criminal activities. If criminals robbed homes in a particular neighborhood at particular times, stealing the same things over time, we would want to use pattern analysis to break the case. If a raucous crowd gathers in a well-known roadhouse at the same time, at the same place, on the same day, and with the results always being a brawl, we would have a pattern in place. Sometimes, authorities have to engage in preemptive action on burgeoning patterns. The pattern of the gathering raucous crowd might be a good pattern to stop with a preemptive action such as parking a patrol car in the parking lot of the roadhouse in question. As a final example that might be of some use to advanced analysts, how, when, and where people attend religious events and services are definitely patterns. An example would be the people who attend the mosque at the same place, same time, and same day, moving along the same street each week. Such a pattern is helpful for finding and exploiting a pattern, and also helpful when spotting a deviation for the purpose of establishing an analytic mystery or establishing the need for an urban, point-persistent surveillance operation. The null would be important too. That is, if we were tracking patterns and all of a sudden there was no pattern or only a partial pattern, we would have cause for delving deeper into the situation as an analytic mystery or hypothesis.

Are there patterns we should be looking for as we perform advanced analysis against insurgents in urban OE? The answer is, of course, yes. As an example, insurgents have to engage in condition-setting whether they plan to attack a key bridge, occupy a safe house, or operate a bomb factory. With each of the network activities, there will be patterns even if the enemy is very security conscious. For example, the populace would have to provide sustenance. The populace delivering the sustenance would have to carry away refuse. There will always be security, countersurveillance, and early-warning operations occurring in and around the house we suspect of being either a bomb factory or safe house. How the insurgents perform these functions will vary some, but there will always be sensors, human watchers, alerts, escape activities, sustenance, health care, and in the case of the bomb factory, possession of explosives and the delivery of detonation and packaging parts for the bombs. Each, if we observe and interpret correctly, will exhibit patterns. Unfortunately, these patterns will most of the time be invisible and will yield only the smallest wisp of telltale signs of being in operation. Thus, patterns often take very patient and detailed intelligence analysis and collection, empowered by high-grade cultural, technical, biometric, situational, and functional knowledge that comes from the advanced analyst's mind or from the minds of SMEs.

Patterns include organizational behavior and the activities, interactions, and transactions individuals engage in. When many individuals engage in activities unified by a mission or a vision, the aggregate of individuals levied to accomplish the mission forms an organizational pattern. Bureaucracies are laden with patterns. They strive to establish routines in their processes, procedures, and activities. These routines become patterns of organizational and individual behavior. When employees rigidly interpret and follow these bureaucratic rules, over time patterns come forth and come to dominate human thought processes. Good advanced analysis can anticipate these outcomes simply because aggregated behavior becomes a recognizable, predictable pattern. As an example, the FEMA response to Hurricane Katrina followed set procedures even in the face of overwhelming evidence that the procedures were inadequate. Even in the face of a national emergency, FEMA employees left trucks of ice and water alongside roads while people needing the ice and water were only miles away. The FEMA workers operated in a large, government bureaucracy in which volumes of rules and regulations dictated patterns of behavior and usurped common sense and delegation of authority. The inaction, inertia, and seeming paralysis of the FEMA workers was the result of patterns of organizational behavior that had accrued over time into embedded rules and regulations. This pattern could have been anticipated; however, for a variety of reasons, patterns were neither anticipated nor thought about in sufficient depth.

It is also useful to think about how pattern analysis relates to trend, link, tendency, cultural, anomaly, and aggregation analysis as well as synthesis—all essential elements of advanced analysis.

- TREND AND PATTERN ANALYSIS. *Trend analysis* is defined as discerning meaning from functional-oriented events or activities that occurred in the past to understand how functionally similar events or activities could happen in the future. Pattern analysis is different in that it involves discerning a consistent series of related actions or events. Patterns enshroud trends and sometimes obscure trend clarity. Patterns enable people to seek, find, and understand trends and their connections and influences once they appear. Patterns help us understand the meaning and, more importantly, the implications of trends. Patterns are often the harbingers of trends, and trends can be the harbingers of patterns. In this sense, we find patterns and trends inextricably entwined, albeit subtly. This is a subtle cognitive requirement for the advanced analyst who works with trend and pattern analysis—they are closely related, and those who fail to remember this relationship shall reap the consequences.

- LINK AND PATTERN ANALYSIS. *Link analysis* is defined as behaviors, functions, relationships, means of communicating, and means of being connected, and how connections and relationships work between and among human, organizational, electron, mechanical, and thought links. Link analysis relates to pattern analysis too. For example, links connect patterns. Links connect the aggregates that can become patterns. In addition, links identify patterns and indicate the ascendancy of patterns as they either come into being or become dormant through decay and affect the pattern's clarity, motion, and energy emanations. Links between and among people and organizations will often show patterns. Why? Quite simply, people use links routinely. Links provide the means for individuals and organizations to connect and communicate. The connections (how, when, and where) result in patterns, particularly if the behavior and activity occur over extended periods of time. But, of course, the analyst must understand how the links enable connections, how connections bring forth aggregates, and how aggregates eventually evolve into patterns to be of specific analytic use.

- TENDENCY AND PATTERN ANALYSIS. *Tendency analysis* is defined as discerning meaning through thought and study of the general proclivities of people; the behavioral and action inclinations of organizations; mental snapshots of current environmental factors, contextual situations, events, activities, or behaviors; the emanation and dispersal of energy emissions; and what the interaction and enmeshing of all could portend for the future. Patterns can indicate the start of a tendency or the presence of dormant tendency potentialities. Patterns relate to people, and people initiate or bring tendencies into being. Furthermore, patterns show individual and organizational inclinations that blossom into tendencies, build up, or develop over time. Patterns can house or enfold tendencies and therefore obscure analysts' knowledge and understanding of tendencies and their implications. In addition, pattern analysis, as we recall, identifies a consistent series of related actions or events; these related actions or events often involve aggregates of individuals and could involve aggregates of organizations. Along this line of thought, patterns are the consistent ways that aggregates of people or organizations move, gain power, lose power, or decay. Such movements, stasis, or decay portend tendencies, but they are maddeningly difficult to search for, find, recognize, and use to take advantage of knowing about a tendency and what it means. If we find these patterns, delve into their basis and inner workings, and provide clues into tendency analysis, we have the potential to seize an advantage, such as freedom of maneuver and position, which will cause the enemy to become reactive.

- CULTURAL AND PATTERN ANALYSIS. *Cultural analysis* is defined as knowing a particular culture, its people, and their patterns of behavior deriving from traditional, culturally induced attitudes, behaviors, social norms, and conditions. Cultural and pattern analysis relate. Patterns can be people, organizations, and functions, all of which are strongly affected by cultural influences. People exude patterns in what they do, how they interact, how they conduct transactions, and how they behave. The culture strongly, indeed indelibly, influences patterns. People think in patterns that manifest as behaviors or nonbehaviors, but a person's cultural background influences not only how the person thinks but also how he engages in patterns—social, behavioral, functional, technical, and organizational. The culture can obscure or illuminate each of the different kinds of patterns. The problem is that the subtleties of the patterns will be nearly impossible to notice, because they are enshrouded by many aspects of the culture in question. How people prepare for weddings, births, and death can be social patterns. Because perpetrators sometimes take advantage of such events to attack, move weapons, or move money, it would behoove the analyst to understand such patterns. But unfortunately the culture can obscure the anomalies that would have to be present to enable recognition of the enemy's network and its patterns of nefarious activities. Thus, to understand most of the patterns in a strange land in an even stranger city, advanced analysts have to know how to use the culture to make visible that which appears invisible—that is, to use cultural disambiguation to look for, find or notice, and know how to take advantage of discovered patterns. To gain this depth of knowledge about culture and its patterns, the analyst will work with cultural SMEs. Usually the most valuable SMEs will be indigenous and in particular from the neighborhood in question. These SMEs will help decompose what the analysts are looking for (in this case the patterns) and use cultural analysis to do so. The SMEs will help the advanced analyst and collection specialist map or task the forthcoming observables to collectors, and then help make rapid sense of relevant incoming data. Cultural baselines relate to patterns because they help identify anomalies within cultural activity. Anomalies are excellent indicants of changes of behavior and often show the aberrations within established patterns, which could foreshadow future events. Activities in the culture can obscure the patterns for which analysts look. If the advanced analyst doesn't know the

culture he or she is working with in depth, or if he or she does
not use a SME, the pattern could be so abstruse that the analyst
will miss it altogether.

- ANOMALY AND PATTERN ANALYSIS. *Anomaly analysis* is defined as
  discerning meaning in departures from the normal or common
  order, form, or rule; absence of that which is expected. Anomaly
  and pattern analysis strongly relate. As one contribution to
  evidence supporting this proposition, baselines are necessary to
  discern anomalies. Patterns are part of cultural, functional, and
  technical baselines. In addition, anomalies involve differences
  from or the absence of what is expected to be normal, as baselines help to indicate. Patterns are part of this thought process
  because their presence or absence can indicate the presence or
  absence of anomalies. To search for and find anomalies means
  the searcher must have patterns in mind with which to direct the
  physical and mental work. These patterns can be part of the
  baselines we have mentioned. Or the patterns can be the absence
  of expected patterns. Even the slightest changes in patterns can
  indicate anomalies. Thus, advanced analysts need to conclude
  first that they need to consider this relationship, and second, that
  the surfacing of anomalies strongly suggests that the analyst
  needs to look for changed patterns. Thus, it is viable to conclude
  that patterns and anomalies are inextricably entwined.
- AGGREGATION AND PATTERN ANALYSIS. *Aggregation analysis* is
  defined as groups, clusters, and conglomerates numbering from a
  few to a million moving as one and exerting power with the
  strength of more than the power of single entities. Aggregation
  analysis identifies the capabilities of subtle activities, interactions,
  transactions, behaviors, and emotions to grow from seemingly
  innocuous and separate things into aggregates of enormous and
  unpredictable power. Patterns often portend the arrival of aggregates. Aggregates enfold many different patterns. Patterns show
  how aggregates could act either in the present or in the future.
- SYNTHESIS AND PATTERN ANALYSIS. *Synthesis* is the human
  cognitive activity that combines elements of substances, events,
  activities, or energy to form a coherent whole. People synthesize
  the activities, interactions, transactions, and behaviors of people
  and organizations to recognize and understand patterns. People
  synthesize what happens with the interaction of people and technology. The result is the ascendancy of a pattern. People need
  functions to live. Analysts synthesize functions to recognize
  patterns. As an example, people need food to eat. Thus, people
  purchase food from vendors and markets. What and how much
  they buy often forms patterns. The advanced analyst uses such

patterns but has to synthesize what one person or one family purchases and compare it to others in the same neighborhood to find if there are aberrations within the functional pattern for sustenance.

Let us take a few moments and discuss how patterns can be used and why they are important. Patterns are essential for planning, executing, and assessing operational security (OPSEC). Risk managers in charge of the OPSEC aspects of a commander's critical information requirements constantly warn against setting and following patterns, because of the advantage it gives to an enemy attempting to collect intelligence and discern U.S. intentions.

Patterns are also essential for planning, executing, and assessing the outcomes of deception operations. Analysts have to know how the enemy views friendly force and activity patterns and set conditions conducive to perpetuation of his beliefs about those patterns, to the point that they will sufficiently serve as a conduit for duplicitous data, information, and actions. To deny the enemy the opportunity to deceive, friendly commanders and planners have to know their own patterns, the enemy's perceptions of friendly patterns, how he thinks about his patterns, and what the enemy believes and trusts by way of intelligence or open source collection. In addition, patterns are critical to wargaming because friendly intelligence and deception planners must discern how the enemy views patterns and what he collects in his effort to find patterns and draw conclusions about intent and courses of actions.

Now, let us narrow the thinking about patterns to the specifics of intelligence analysis and collection. Patterns are important for thinking about how to collect intelligence against the enemy. Often the leaders or key people of an enemy network will establish patterns of movement and security. If U.S. analysts and collection specialists have designed observables in order to watch for patterns and nuanced observables and have assigned various collectors to watch for them, they will have the capability to see the enemy's actions, which comprise patterns that up to that point in time have appeared invisible.

Just as often, however, the wise enemy leader will be cautious about establishing patterns and will constantly change routines and activities to reduce the chance that people or sensors watching will discern these patterns and be able to locate or track them. People supporting the enemy's network, however, are not so acutely aware of others watching their activities, transactions, interactions, and behaviors. Supporters usually will not be sufficiently skilled in tradecraft to avoid following human patterns, nor will they be capable of dispelling or confusing efforts to find and track them back to their "anthill." These network supporters will form patterns of support that can lead to nodes, links, and network decisive points.

Analysts anticipate and find patterns and track them to help learn about a network, how people support it, and how those supporters' activities provide the network with energy and functionality. This is the indirect approach to fighting the enemy's network. It is doubly powerful in that not only can the enemy's network be found and observed but also, when action against it occurs, the enemy will suffer from cognitive dissonance perpetrated by the discovery of something he thought was invisible to the American eye.

From the aforementioned discussion of pattern analysis in advanced analysis, the reader will undoubtedly grasp the complexities in thinking about patterns when working against insurgents in a large urban setting. That said, how does one proceed to think successfully using pattern analysis when looking for and trying to know and understand patterns?

- *First*, the analyst must know the subject matter. As we have discussed, patterns come forth in several types. They include *technical*, *human/social*, *functional*, and *organizational* patterns. These are a good representation of the types of patterns; however, there can certainly be more, which analysts will identify and codify with experience and the help of SMEs. Because analysts won't know and can't know all that needs to be known about patterns, they must seek help from people who do know enough to advise the analyst how to find, understand, anticipate, meld with other elements of advanced analysis, and engage in sense making. Both indigenous and U.S., coalition, or other SMEs who are fluent in the language, have been on the ground in the country concerned, and are truly knowledgeable about the current problem, including the neighborhood in question, are the SMEs of the most value.
- *Second*, the decomposition part of advanced analysis is critical in searching for and finding patterns. Of course the enemy does not want his patterns to be found. If found, patterns can lead to understanding intent and operational weaknesses of his supporting and operating networks. Thus, he will hide and obscure his patterns and he will put forth false patterns, providing U.S. analysts with red herrings to pursue. Therefore, advanced analysts must decompose what they are looking for into many specific aspects of patterns, understanding that the wise enemy will be trying to confuse and deceive with false patterns. The advanced analyst will anticipate and deny the enemy's efforts to deceive with patterns, but this is only possible with a thorough, knowledge-driven, front-end analysis discussed earlier called decomposition.
- *Third*, pattern analysis helps people search through current data, information, and knowledge to first recognize patterns and then to understand their importance and the implications for the U.S. operation at hand.
- *Fourth*, the analyst using pattern analysis looks for new patterns or to find and understand patterns in existing data. To do so, he or she must understand how patterns relate to aggregates, anomalies, semiotics, cultural

analysis, and synthesis. Pattern analysis works best when analysts enter the higher domain of thought and cognitively link the fundamentals of all of these facets of advanced analysis.

As the previous discussion mentions, patterns have a strong relationship with deception. As a precursor to this part of the discussion, let's think about deception. What is deception? According to the *DOD Dictionary of Military and Associated Terms*, deception is

> Those measures designed to mislead the enemy by manipulation, distortion, or falsification of evidence to induce the enemy to react in a manner prejudicial to the enemy's interests.[2]

The measure most helpful in creating deceptive moments lies in patterns. Patterns in relationship to deception, however, have two sides—friendly and enemy. In addition, there can be the host nation; neutrals; multinational corporations; security companies; and local, regional, international, and U.S. domestic media that figure into the equation involving patterns and deception. Sun Tzu helps us think more deeply about the relationship between patterns and deception. Sun Tzu writes,

> The ultimate in disposing one's troops is to be without ascertainable shape . . . Then the most penetrating spies cannot pry in nor can the wise lay plans against you. It is according to the shapes that I lay the plans for victory, but the multitude does not comprehend this. Although everyone can see the outward aspects, no one understands the way in which I have created victory.[3]

Sun Tzu is advising us, as good old friends should, to avoid presenting shapes and patterns to the enemy unless we want to use them to confuse or deceive him. He is also advising us to understand that the enemy will be watching and collecting. Thus, as an implication, we need to understand what patterns the enemy could be looking for or what we should be watching for by way of the enemy's patterns. He also advises us to concentrate on the mind of the enemy commander as we attempt to find his patterns and to recognize his use of purposefully manipulated patterns to deceive us and vice versa.

Now, let's become even more specific and discuss in depth the many complex relationships between deception and patterns. As a first step, the advanced analyst must consider both or all sides in a conflict and how each side thinks about its patterns and ours. In this respect, the analyst has to enter the enemy leader's mind and realize he undoubtedly is attempting to get into ours. Deception at its basic level is a mental contest and is chockfull of anticipation and deceptive, duplicitous thoughts and activities. This war of wits is described in the following thoughts:

challenges advanced analysts face when using pattern analysis include the following:

- Knowledge support is required to perform pattern analysis. Performing pattern analysis takes a high degree of knowledge in the culture and in the four types of patterns—technical, human/social, functional, and organizational.
- Advanced analysts design observables through the use of pattern analysis, but they always keep their end state in mind. That is, when resultant collected data comes in, advanced analysts use pattern analysis to help make sense of the data and turn it into information and knowledge. This knowledge helps to test hypotheses, to validate expectations and hunches, or to solve mysteries.
- The advanced analyst must know how to perturb the enemy's network and elicit associated patterns from it. Such perturbation induces action, provides insights into sensitive variables, and creates windows of opportunity in which to identify patterns that will become exposed during such turbulence.
- The advanced analyst must understand complex relationships to understand pattern analysis. The advanced analyst has to know how the enemy thinks, perceives, and visualizes his patterns and friendly patterns. He or she also has to know how friendly leaders think about their own and the enemy's patterns. This is the acme of complex thought.

Advanced analysts do have some options to help them meet the challenges associated with pattern analysis. These options include the following suggestions:

- Advanced analysts must use a thought template to help keep their thoughts focused and to serve as a trigger for thoughts they might forget in their busy lives.
- Advanced analysts must seek the support of experts. These SMEs can be local and indigenous or they can be distributed U.S. or coalition SMEs. Regardless, to use pattern analysis, advanced analysts will inevitably need to employ the services of a variety of SMEs who have current expertise in a wide range of subject matter pertinent to the problems at hand.
- The advanced analyst must have as his or her closest partner the collection specialist. As such, the advanced analyst has to do the front-end decomposition work to design workable observables and then work with the collection specialist to drive collection to find the observables that relate to enemy and local populace patterns.

The cerebral struggles of deception are, for the most part, invisible. They involve a contest of wits rather than of might. Though physical things certainly still have a place in deception, the wise deceiver hypothesizes how physical effects will influence the mind of the adversary, how to manipulate these physical things, and, of course, how to pick the right times to deceive.[4]

In addition, we have to consider what the enemy is purposefully showing us by way of patterns for deceptive purposes. They will not want to show patterns, because of the danger in doing so. A passage from the book *Ender's Game* helps explains this effort by the enemy and how difficult it is to discern well-hidden patterns:

> It was subtle. Ender couldn't see it for a long time. The bugger ships kept moving, all of them. There was no obvious flagship, no apparent nerve center. But gradually, as Mazer played the videos over and over again, Ender began to see the way that all the movements focused on, radiated from a center point. The center point shifted, but it was obvious, after he looked long enough, that the eyes of the fleet, the I of the fleet, the perspective from which all decisions were being made, was one particular ship.[5]

Could it be that the enemy's networks emanate similar patterns—difficult to see, almost invisible to the naked eye, but there, pulsating, performing all the time, right in front of our watchful eyes?

In this regard, we have to anticipate that the enemy is also anticipating. That is, he is anticipating how we view our patterns in relationship to how we attempt to deceive him. Thus the quest for both sides is discerning "real" from "unreal" patterns with our analysis and collection activities. We can, however, conclude that the enemy will be wary of the patterns we present unless they make sense from his background and perspective; they are true from a historical incident perspective; and they fit with what should or could be true from the enemy's mindset, perceptions, and cultural biases.

As an additional thought about patterns and deception, advanced analysts must realize how prone they are to mirror image their own value sets about patterns to the enemy's individual and collective mindsets. This is extremely dangerous if we are dealing with a smart adversary. Thus, we have to work with indigenous people and U.S. cultural experts to realize what might be real from an enemy's perspective and what he might view as being bogus or culturally crude attempts to manipulate his mind. Friendly forces always attempt to find the enemy's patterns because they tell us much about his intent, decision-making, degree of training, and discipline in security and OPSEC. The wise commander anticipates through the cerebral deliberations of advanced analysis what the enemy will "want" to see by way of friendly patterns and show him what he wants to see to set conditions for deceiving his mind and perturbing his decision cycle. In the meantime, the commander well schooled in the intricacies of modern deception will work aggressively to preclude the enemy from finding the patterns we don't want him to find.

As a final point in this discussion of deception and patterns, we must remember that patterns relate to aggregates. The aggregates I'm identifying are formed by the "conjunction or collection of particulars into a whole mass or sum."[6] These aggregates can be organizations, people, activities, and in some cases patterns within aggregates themselves. These patterns within aggregates can help discern possible future potentialities that could be coming into being and if so, they will surely influence the mind of the person we are trying to deceive.

Another aspect of patterns we will think about at this time involves *pattern decay*. Decay in this context involves a loss of strength or influence. Patterns have varying degrees of strength or influence. Fluctuations in strength or influence are caused by recency of the pattern formulation, degree of human motivation in a behavioral pattern, importance of the purpose that a pattern serves, links with other patterns, influence on other aggregates or patterns, and the accuracy of a pattern to anticipate similar patterns or activities of other patterns.

It is important for advanced analysts participating in pattern analysis to understand the phenomenon of pattern decay in order to understand why patterns appear, disappear, and sometimes reappear. What should we consider as we work with pattern decay?

- Patterns decay with the passage of time, with disuse, and with no inputs into the shape or purpose of the pattern.
- Patterns decay over time if people forming the pattern become increasingly aware that they are or could be forming patterns and take counteractions to improve their operational security (OPSEC).
- Patterns often decay when one side or the other in a conflict is purposefully manipulating the appearance and disappearance as well as the strength and weakness of the pattern in question.
- Finally, patterns decay if the links that connect them with human consciousness (enemy, friendly, neutral, and host nation) weaken or become less than obvious.

In our work with advanced analysis, we have to ask ourselves if we can use pattern analysis against an organized, functioning enemy network. After all, an enemy network in an urban setting is flat, changing, moving, and often invisible to the Western eye and mind. Does this network emit patterns? If so, can we seek, find, and exploit the enemy's network pattern? The answer to both hypothetical questions is an unequivocal yes! But to do

so we have to understand the enemy's network and how it works, [ ] enemy uses it, and how the populace supports it, and we must also stand the network's functions and characteristics.

All people and organizations, even a network such as I have de will emit one or more patterns. Please recall that at the start of the sion on pattern analysis, we talked about four kinds of patterns—*te social/behavioral*, *functional*, and *organizational*. If we approach th and his network with these patterns in mind; if we understand, help of indigenous SMEs, how the enemy's mind works; if we und how the populace supports his network; and if we understand the fu and characteristics of the network, *we will understand and start r ing the patterns his network emits*. Carrying the thought further, to identify the types of patterns for which we look and whether or will be visible or invisible. We have to understand normalcy and a in baselines of the neighborhood we are working in and the three I baselines of interest—*technical*, *cultural*, and *functional*.

We also have to understand the enemy's condition-setting to plish missions. These condition-setting activities present a var patterns (again visible, invisible, and the four types). We have to und the types of patterns that would show and accrue as the populace s the network. As an example, if the enemy leader thinks U.S. and c people and machines might see his activities at night, he will have ies of food, water, parts, medicine, and so forth made at night. Th will see a pattern emerging as *delivery activity* at night. In addition, undoubtedly see a pattern emerging as to a *window of time* these d are made. We will see patterns involved with the enemy's *counter lance* and how a legitimate (from the enemy's view) supporter can d e.g., use of semiotic codes and use of technical codes (text m flashlights with red filters, etc.)—and we will see a *pattern of reco* and *duration of time* it takes for the *supporter to be recognized* perpetrator or owner of a house and even a *pattern of physiq* emerging, if the supporter carries trash away under his or her openly carries a trash bag.

None of this work with pattern analysis is easy—quite the c Challenges abound. Of course we would need watchers and ground alert and watching for these activities to emerge. But if they know wh are looking for by way of observables, and if advanced analysts use analysis to make sense of collected data, even the best and most se enemy network becomes more visible and hence more vulnerable t manders' actions.

By way of ending this chapter, we need to first identify and discus of the significant challenges advanced analysts face when attempting pattern analysis. Then, the conversation will address what analysts to improve their capabilities to overcome these challenges. Some challenges advanced analysts face when using pattern analysis include the following:

- Knowledge support is required to perform pattern analysis. Performing pattern analysis takes a high degree of knowledge in the culture and in the four types of patterns—technical, human/social, functional, and organizational.
- Advanced analysts design observables through the use of pattern analysis, but they always keep their end state in mind. That is, when resultant collected data comes in, advanced analysts use pattern analysis to help make sense of the data and turn it into information and knowledge. This knowledge helps to test hypotheses, to validate expectations and hunches, or to solve mysteries.
- The advanced analyst must know how to perturb the enemy's network and elicit associated patterns from it. Such perturbation induces action, provides insights into sensitive variables, and creates windows of opportunity in which to identify patterns that will become exposed during such turbulence.
- The advanced analyst must understand complex relationships to understand pattern analysis. The advanced analyst has to know how the enemy thinks, perceives, and visualizes his patterns and friendly patterns. He or she also has to know how friendly leaders think about their own and the enemy's patterns. This is the acme of complex thought.

Advanced analysts do have some options to help them meet the challenges associated with pattern analysis. These options include the following suggestions:

- Advanced analysts must use a thought template to help keep their thoughts focused and to serve as a trigger for thoughts they might forget in their busy lives.
- Advanced analysts must seek the support of experts. These SMEs can be local and indigenous or they can be distributed U.S. or coalition SMEs. Regardless, to use pattern analysis, advanced analysts will inevitably need to employ the services of a variety of SMEs who have current expertise in a wide range of subject matter pertinent to the problems at hand.
- The advanced analyst must have as his or her closest partner the collection specialist. As such, the advanced analyst has to do the front-end decomposition work to design workable observables and then work with the collection specialist to drive collection to find the observables that relate to enemy and local populace patterns.

so we have to understand the enemy's network and how it works, how the enemy uses it, and how the populace supports it, and we must also understand the network's functions and characteristics.

All people and organizations, even a network such as I have described, will emit one or more patterns. Please recall that at the start of the discussion on pattern analysis, we talked about four kinds of patterns—*technical, social/behavioral, functional*, and *organizational*. If we approach the enemy and his network with these patterns in mind; if we understand, with the help of indigenous SMEs, how the enemy's mind works; if we understand how the populace supports his network; and if we understand the functions and characteristics of the network, *we will understand and start recognizing the patterns his network emits*. Carrying the thought further, we have to identify the types of patterns for which we look and whether or not they will be visible or invisible. We have to understand normalcy and anomaly in baselines of the neighborhood we are working in and the three kinds of baselines of interest—*technical, cultural*, and *functional*.

We also have to understand the enemy's condition-setting to accomplish missions. These condition-setting activities present a variety of patterns (again visible, invisible, and the four types). We have to understand the types of patterns that would show and accrue as the populace supports the network. As an example, if the enemy leader thinks U.S. and coalition people and machines might see his activities at night, he will have deliveries of food, water, parts, medicine, and so forth made at night. Thus, we will see a pattern emerging as *delivery activity* at night. In addition, we will undoubtedly see a pattern emerging as to a *window of time* these deliveries are made. We will see patterns involved with the enemy's *countersurveillance* and how a legitimate (from the enemy's view) supporter can deliver—e.g., use of semiotic codes and use of technical codes (text messages, flashlights with red filters, etc.)—and we will see a *pattern of recognition* and *duration of time* it takes for the *supporter to be recognized* by the perpetrator or owner of a house and even a *pattern of physique bulk* emerging, if the supporter carries trash away under his or her robe or openly carries a trash bag.

None of this work with pattern analysis is easy—quite the contrary. Challenges abound. Of course we would need watchers and ground sensors alert and watching for these activities to emerge. But if they know what they are looking for by way of observables, and if advanced analysts use pattern analysis to make sense of collected data, even the best and most secretive enemy network becomes more visible and hence more vulnerable to commanders' actions.

By way of ending this chapter, we need to first identify and discuss some of the significant challenges advanced analysts face when attempting to use pattern analysis. Then, the conversation will address what analysts can do to improve their capabilities to overcome these challenges. Some of the conditions for deceiving his mind and perturbing his decision cycle. In the meantime, the commander well schooled in the intricacies of modern deception will work aggressively to preclude the enemy from finding the patterns we don't want him to find.

As a final point in this discussion of deception and patterns, we must remember that patterns relate to aggregates. The aggregates I'm identifying are formed by the "conjunction or collection of particulars into a whole mass or sum."[6] These aggregates can be organizations, people, activities, and in some cases patterns within aggregates themselves. These patterns within aggregates can help discern possible future potentialities that could be coming into being and if so, they will surely influence the mind of the person we are trying to deceive.

Another aspect of patterns we will think about at this time involves *pattern decay*. Decay in this context involves a loss of strength or influence. Patterns have varying degrees of strength or influence. Fluctuations in strength or influence are caused by recency of the pattern formulation, degree of human motivation in a behavioral pattern, importance of the purpose that a pattern serves, links with other patterns, influence on other aggregates or patterns, and the accuracy of a pattern to anticipate similar patterns or activities of other patterns.

It is important for advanced analysts participating in pattern analysis to understand the phenomenon of pattern decay in order to understand why patterns appear, disappear, and sometimes reappear. What should we consider as we work with pattern decay?

- Patterns decay with the passage of time, with disuse, and with no inputs into the shape or purpose of the pattern.
- Patterns decay over time if people forming the pattern become increasingly aware that they are or could be forming patterns and take counteractions to improve their operational security (OPSEC).
- Patterns often decay when one side or the other in a conflict is purposefully manipulating the appearance and disappearance as well as the strength and weakness of the pattern in question.
- Finally, patterns decay if the links that connect them with human consciousness (enemy, friendly, neutral, and host nation) weaken or become less than obvious.

In our work with advanced analysis, we have to ask ourselves if we can use pattern analysis against an organized, functioning enemy network. After all, an enemy network in an urban setting is flat, changing, moving, and often invisible to the Western eye and mind. Does this network emit patterns? If so, can we seek, find, and exploit the enemy's network pattern? The answer to both hypothetical questions is an unequivocal yes! But to do

The cerebral struggles of deception are, for the most part, invisible. They involve a contest of wits rather than of might. Though physical things certainly still have a place in deception, the wise deceiver hypothesizes how physical effects will influence the mind of the adversary, how to manipulate these physical things, and, of course, how to pick the right times to deceive.[4]

In addition, we have to consider what the enemy is purposefully showing us by way of patterns for deceptive purposes. They will not want to show patterns, because of the danger in doing so. A passage from the book *Ender's Game* helps explains this effort by the enemy and how difficult it is to discern well-hidden patterns:

> It was subtle. Ender couldn't see it for a long time. The bugger ships kept moving, all of them. There was no obvious flagship, no apparent nerve center. But gradually, as Mazer played the videos over and over again, Ender began to see the way that all the movements focused on, radiated from a center point. The center point shifted, but it was obvious, after he looked long enough, that the eyes of the fleet, the I of the fleet, the perspective from which all decisions were being made, was one particular ship.[5]

Could it be that the enemy's networks emanate similar patterns—difficult to see, almost invisible to the naked eye, but there, pulsating, performing all the time, right in front of our watchful eyes?

In this regard, we have to anticipate that the enemy is also anticipating. That is, he is anticipating how we view our patterns in relationship to how we attempt to deceive him. Thus the quest for both sides is discerning "real" from "unreal" patterns with our analysis and collection activities. We can, however, conclude that the enemy will be wary of the patterns we present unless they make sense from his background and perspective; they are true from a historical incident perspective; and they fit with what should or could be true from the enemy's mindset, perceptions, and cultural biases.

As an additional thought about patterns and deception, advanced analysts must realize how prone they are to mirror image their own value sets about patterns to the enemy's individual and collective mindsets. This is extremely dangerous if we are dealing with a smart adversary. Thus, we have to work with indigenous people and U.S. cultural experts to realize what might be real from an enemy's perspective and what he might view as being bogus or culturally crude attempts to manipulate his mind. Friendly forces always attempt to find the enemy's patterns because they tell us much about his intent, decision-making, degree of training, and discipline in security and OPSEC. The wise commander anticipates through the cerebral deliberations of advanced analysis what the enemy will "want" to see by way of friendly patterns and show him what he wants to see to set

- The advanced analyst must work within his or her headquarters, the intelligence enterprise, and with a VKE to understand, anticipate, watch for, and comprehend pattern decay. With such knowledge, the advanced analyst can accelerate the decay, delay its advances, or draw implications from its presence.
- The advanced analyst should always tie patterns with aggregates. When looking for aggregates, often the advanced analyst can look not at the whole but at portions of the whole of aggregates that we call the "glue" that holds elements of the aggregate together and the "propellant" that fuels the speed of the aggregate as it enfolds other aggregates. These aggregates will often display patterns, particularly as the aggregate grows in size, power, speed, and influence.
- The advanced analyst must seek the help of red-teamers and ask them to check his or her thinking, assumptions, and logic. The advanced analyst must be aware, in an introspective sense, of his or her penchant toward making mental mistakes when working with patterns and ask the red team person or persons to double-check their thinking.
- The advanced analyst must always seek the help of a VKE. In particular, a VKE can perform many of the duties the advanced analyst needs help with or doesn't have time for. As such, the advanced analyst can use a VKE for SME support, wargaming, designing observables specifically designed to look for and find patterns, and to recompose data using pattern analysis and turn it very quickly into information and usable knowledge.

As this chapter comes to a close, we see that patterns have been important for all sides in a conflict for centuries. In urban operations, in a modern OE, patterns are more plentiful and more complex. The multitude of patterns and their complexity make pattern analysis extremely challenging if done correctly. Unfortunately, it is easy to slip into a self-deceiving mode and convince ourselves we are engaging in pattern analysis when we are simply working with one simple aspect of patterns. Given this situation, what is an advanced analyst to do? As one tactic, the advanced analyst uses a thought template to help think through the issues of pattern analysis. As another tack, the advanced analyst understands how pattern analysis relates with other elements of advanced analysis and tries to use them in combinations—e.g., link, trend, aggregation, anomaly, and tendency analysis as well as synthesis.

As we have discussed, patterns are important from several perspectives.

- *First*, patterns are important to both sides in a conflict—in protecting their own and thereby confusing the enemy's attempts to discern intent in patterns, in vigorously seeking and discerning deceptive patterns, and in aggressively attacking or manipulating the enemy's patterns.

- *Second*, though seemingly invisible, the enemy's condition-setting patterns are multitudinous and susceptible to pattern analysis and exploitation.
- *Third*, the analyst performing pattern analysis must know the enemy, the culture, the enemy's network, his condition-setting, and how he perceives, thinks, decides, acts, and assesses in detail.

With the setup of these previous discussions of link and pattern analysis, the reader is ready to venture forth into a discussion of trend analysis. The reader will find this discussion interesting for discerning what trends can and cannot do, how trends differ from tendencies, and applications of the five kinds of trends advanced analysis draws our attention to.

9

Trend Analysis

Definition: Discerning meaning from technical, cultural, and function-oriented events, interactions, transactions, behaviors, or activities that occurred in the past to understand how similar events or activities could happen in the future.

THEORY BEHIND TREND ANALYSIS

Intelligence analysts recognize trends with good thinking, statistical analysis, visualization, high-speed data fusion, and thoughtful observation of events that have transpired in the past. Trends can also be adjuncts to good decision-making in that decision makers and their staffs can purposefully watch for the appearance of trends that might sabotage their well-knit plans. There are four types of trends and each is important to our overarching subject of trend analysis.

- HUMAN/SOCIAL TRENDS show how people talk to relatives, engage in recreation, work, marry, bury their dead, and exchange information. Social trends are critical for understanding the potential outcomes of trends as they unfold, gain influence, decay, or die. Human/social trends show how people act out their lives. People behave and exhibit manifestations of behavior that occurred in isolation or in and around events that have occurred in the past. Trends show when people are most likely to be stressed when acting or thinking in isolation and when they aggregate into ever-larger aggregates. People exhibit behaviors indicating the presence of trends by how they engage in functional activities. As an example, how people prepare for and go to work and what they do along the way can be aggregated and trended out. Deviation from the trend can flag our attention because it will be an anomaly.

- FUNCTIONAL TRENDS can come from simple leisure activities to those activities as complicated as caring for one's dead. Functional activities of the insurgent are of paramount importance. The insurgent has to set conditions to attack or to execute a suicide bombing. The conditions are, for the most part, functions. All functions, however, are part of trends that stretch back to a beginning, that show cause and effect relationships, and that can help us anticipate what the insurgent will do next.

- TECHNICAL TRENDS show up in the way people use technology. Technical trends appear as people make phone calls; access and use the Internet; use electricity, water, and sewage; use automobiles and other forms of transportation; and even use the medical infrastructure.

- ORGANIZATIONAL TRENDS are influential too. Organizational transactions, intersections, activities, and behaviors exhibit trends if one looks hard enough and knows enough about what composes the trend(s) we are looking for. Also, many organizations are bureaucracies. Bureaucracies always try to do things in an organized way and therefore are essential in watching for and identifying trends. Organizations receive inputs from a variety of means and provide outputs stretching across many different potential areas of influence. The inputs into organizations, such as corporations or even networks, and their outputs, whether organized or accidental, show the potentialities for trends and can lead to the identification and understanding of obvious or hidden trends.

One of the ways trends are important involves how the insurgents set conditions for their nefarious activities. The insurgents must set things in place to accomplish their mission. For example, if planning to attack a bridge, they must conduct reconnaissance and intelligence collection. They must recruit people to work in their network. They must find and occupy a safe house. They must have food and water. They must have weapons, ammunition, and explosives. They must have communications and so forth. Trends from the past tell us how the enemy might go about performing these functions and give us some ideas about how they might occur in the future.

Interestingly, there will be a heavy dose of trends such as intelligence collection at the start of any planning cycle. The leader responsible for successful execution of the mission must gain information about the target. Thus, trends tell us that there will be an initial surge of intelligence collection activities that become visible during trend analysis. Then, this particular trend will decrease significantly as active collection becomes passive collection just watching for changes. Shortly before the attack, active intelligence collection will pick up again from many different angles and sources far above and beyond the mere observation of the bridge. Thus, the trends display visually in what we can call a "bathtub" curve. If analysts are not aware of this curve, they might quit looking for condition-setting activities, when in reality the activities are simply dormant and preparing to surface again right before the attack.

When working with such a curve, analysts may see that early activities involving intelligence collection suddenly decrease, and then they seem to disappear. In reality, this is the bottom part of the curve. This part of the operation will find dormant intelligence collection that is occasionally monitored to ensure nothing dramatic has changed. Then, as the attack draws near, there will be a connected upside of the trend that is the far side of the bathtub curve, indicating intensified collection. Studying former attacks on infrastructure can yield such trends and, if our analysts are on their toes, they can notice trends unfolding with current data that transforms through analysis into current trend information as it unfolds before their eyes and minds.

Trends are closely associated with three kinds of baselines—*technical*, *functional*, and *cultural*. Let's quickly review what these baselines mean.

- TECHNICAL BASELINE—a mental template that serves as a normal technical standard with which to look for and find anomalies relating to technical processes, emanations, and emissions coming from a house, a portion of the infrastructure, activities, conveyances, a neighborhood, an aggregate of neighborhoods, and, in the macro, from a city writ large.
- FUNCTIONAL BASELINE—a mental template that serves as a normal functional standard with which to look for and find anomalies relating to functions or the assigned actions, duties, and activities required or expected of a person or of group processes.
- CULTURAL BASELINE—a mental template that serves as a standard relating to the shared knowledge and values of an element of a society by which things in a particular neighborhood are measured or compared, denoting, deriving from, or distinctive with regard to the ways of living of a particular group of people.

These baselines are so important to trend analysis that it cannot be done well without them. But baselines also have to be current and accurate—no small feat in the swirl of a vibrant urban OE. In addition, the analyst must understand that trends relate to anomaly and tendency analysis because they depend upon the same kind of baselines. Thus, an advanced analyst cannot use trend analysis in isolation. The analyst has to use anomaly, trend, and tendency analysis as well as know how to think about and use the three kinds of baselines for each type of analysis. Why are baselines so important for trends? Several reasons exist:

- Changes in trends mean a departure from the norm depicted by baselines. Something causes the changes—this is a distinct cause and effect relationship.
- Without these three baselines, we won't understand what has happened in the past when compared with the present. Without such understanding, there is no chance that the analyst can anticipate the future.
- Intelligence analysts have to understand baselines in order to recognize and understand anomalies. It takes an understanding of anomalies to perform excellent trend analysis.

What is the nature of what I'm trying to locate or notice? This is a key analytic question that trend analysis can help the advanced analyst with. For one thing, the analyst is trying to discover or notice *technical aspects* of an activity, nonactivity, interaction, behavior, or transaction. The technical aspect of what we are looking for is often invisible. Thus, the analyst must delve into the technical baseline to find what is happening in the invisible world of technology. In addition, the analyst must seek and use the knowledge of technical specialists to help understand the environment, the technical baseline, and how technical anomalies would look if they appeared, as well as to help design observables that would assist the analyst in understanding trends in order to better anticipate the future.

In addition, the analyst must understand the cultural aspects of what he or she is looking for. The *cultural aspects* of what the analyst is looking for involve how the people who are part of the culture act, interact, go about their activities and businesses, transact, and behave. It also involves how the people who make up a culture think, perceive, feel, communicate, engage in nonverbal communication, make decisions, view socially imposed constraints, and view and use technology. Cultural trends are therefore of great importance in the accomplishment of intelligence analysis missions.

Analysts must also be interested in *appearances* to perform trend analysis. Appearances can be permanent, fleeting, visible, or invisible. Analysts have to identify and understand appearances so they can begin to understand trends whose manifestation often registers no recognition in our minds. We will rarely find one aspect of the culture acting by itself. Instead, we will almost always find cultural aspects of what we are looking for entwined with other aspects, such as technology or societal or personal functions.

Another angle that can help us recognize and comprehend trends is *periodicity*. Periodicity is the appearance or occurrence of something at regular intervals. We need to determine if our hypothesis about the trends forthcoming from societal and enemy activities is recurring, appearing as part of a cycle, or appearing randomly—here one minute and gone the next.

The seemingly invisible nature of trends also can be caused by degrees of *vagueness, subtlety,* or *ambiguity* in trends themselves. These descriptors are often culturally and technically laden words; therefore, one must know the details of the culture and the technology it uses to understand the degrees of vagueness, subtlety, or ambiguity that obscures or identifies trends.

As a final point, when attempting to understand the nature of what we are looking for, we have to pay attention to *relationships.* Advanced analysts have to set out purposefully to identify relationships that indicate the presence and perhaps even the meaning of trends. Unfortunately, often relationships of the kind we are considering aren't immediately apparent. They are seemingly invisible except to the experienced eye of a thoughtful indigenous person or a person with a technical background who understands not only the technical particulars of relationships but also how they influence the culture and become entwined with cultural relationships.

Understanding relationships often can lead to understanding causes and effects and how they might foreshadow the future. But we have to know and understand the culture, functions, and technology in a significant degree of depth to understand relationships well enough to use in trend analysis. Furthermore, we can find relationships among technical, cultural, and functional baselines—everything is connected. Thus, when one relationship moves because of some sort of perturbation, the other relationships hooked to that relationship change too. To complicate matters more, we also find relationships between and among interactions, behaviors, transactions, and activities. In addition, we find many relationships among people and organizations that constitute the sinews of trends as they unfold or enshroud the trend in question. We can surmise that active trends always move, and they always emanate energies and signatures in varying degrees of magnitude that can become observables.

At this point we need to talk about what makes trends challenging. As a starting point, we need to identify some of the challenges analysts will have with trend analysis. Then, we will identify some of the ways advanced analysts can overcome the challenges of trend analysis.

- Trend analysis is arduous because sometimes trends appear and disappear rapidly. This here-again, gone-again nature of trends makes their tracking and intellectual continuity challenging to commence, let alone sustain. The movement of the city and the multitude of interactions, activities, transactions, and individual and organizational behaviors cause this oscillation. Trend oscillation comes from breakdowns or attack-induced damages caused by direct/indirect and tangible/intangible attacks on the infrastructure supporting the city.
- Trends decay. That is, they show as nascent trends and gain strength because of related activities or transactions composing the trend, only to lose strength because of lack of inputs or actual breaking of relationships.

- Trends can be buried in the noise of a busy city. Along this line of thought, the real trend or trends can be obscured by misguided thinking about what the analyst is seeing and misguided conclusions about or formed from what he or she is reading. This confusion can come from a variety of causes, such as the overwhelming motion of a busy city, the multimedia noise characterizing all cities, and the analyst's lack of cultural, technical, and functional knowledge required to identify and track both obvious and obscure trends.
- Trends deal with what has happened in the past. Trend analysis tries to take what has happened in the past to form a straight line into the future. Unfortunately, life does not usually occur along highly predictable, straight lines. Thus, we have to consider exponential leaps, epiphanies, and creative leaps of logic as well as a straight line from the past to the future.
- Trends are highly influenced by mirror imaging. As a reminder, *mirror imaging* is defined as superimposing one's own thoughts, experiences, and values to another person of a different culture and/or background in order to understand how they think and will act. Let's review just a few very basic examples of mirror imaging:
  - EXAMPLE 1. The enemy is going to attack a mosque because from my perspective it is the smart thing to do.
  - EXAMPLE 2. The enemy won't attack in the night, because they don't have night observation devices (NODs), and no military person would attack without being able to see well during periods of visibility.
  - EXAMPLE 3. The enemy won't conduct a suicide bombing against gathered women and children, because no civilized person would attack nonbelligerents.

Keeping these challenges associated with trend analysis in mind, we need to consider some of the ways to overcome their influences on our thinking.

- *First*, and probably most important, analysts need to use a trend analysis thought template to help them think deeply and accurately while under the direct influence of stress, fatigue, and apprehension.
- *Second*, analysts must learn to think about, confirm or deny, and test their hypotheses concerning what they have identified as trends. Trends are so important in bringing forth accurate situational understanding that their surfacing and interpretation cannot be left to happenstance. Trends are an important aspect of situational understanding: the commander's capability to synthesize information and knowledge and use resultant understanding to make decisions. *Army Field Manual 3.0* defines situational understanding as "the product of applying analysis and judgment to the Common Operational Picture (COP) to determine relationships among factors of mission, enemy, terrain, time, troops available, and civilians (METT-TC)."[1]

- *Third*, analysts must learn how to think about trends. That is, analysts must learn to think about the many pieces that make up trends and weave them into a whole (trend) using the loom of their intellect, experience, and intuition, as well as using the help of either indigenous or U.S. SMEs to assist when needed. This mental travail will enable analysts to find both obvious and hidden meaning in trends.
- *Fourth*, analysts should seek help from the intelligence enterprise, a VKE, a red team, and wargaming compatriots to help develop trends and ensure that mental errors are not at play. As such, analysts need to check their thinking and purposefully set out to murder board their assumptions, conclusions, and hypotheses about trends. They need to use current and helpful baselines, as we have discussed earlier, and use developing and developed trends to anticipate future enemy activity, paying particular attention to being on the lookout for observables indicating exponential leaps in logic in relationship to the straight-line movement of the trend from the past to the future.
- *Fifth*, the analyst needs to work with collection specialists to look for and locate activities, interactions, transactions, and behaviors that indicate the presence of current trends, the decay of trends, or their demise. This process starts in the advanced analysis function of decomposition, in which the analyst designs observables.
- *Sixth*, the analyst needs to learn to think like the enemy to first know what to look for by way of trends and then to understand collection well enough to work with collection specialists to look for observables relative to trends or their influence. The advanced analyst has to be intellectually savvy enough to understand resultant data and blend it into a whole of meaning. Part of this work includes gaining entrée into the enemy's mind and understanding his perspectives relative to U.S. commanders' actions and the capabilities of his supporting intelligence system. A smart enemy, for example, will understand trends and will plant indicators of false trends in his deception plan. Advanced analysts must anticipate such sophisticated thinking, which links to actions and leads to effects—mental effects or outcomes in the minds of U.S. commanders and their supporting intelligence people.
- *Seventh*, advanced analysts must consider friction in their search for and understanding of trends. What do we mean by *friction*? Friction, according to Clausewitz, involves unexpected, chance events and is described as follows:

> Countless minor incidents—the kind you can never really foresee—combine to lower the general level of performance, so that one always falls far short of the intended goal . . . This tremendous friction, which cannot, as in mechanics, be reduced to a few points, is everywhere in contact with chance, and brings about effects that

cannot be measured, just because they are largely due to chance . . .
Friction, as we choose to call it, is the force that makes the apparently easy so difficult.[2]

Friction influences how we review and think about incoming data and
how we weave data into trends. But let's examine why friction is so
prevalent and why it has such a powerful influence on trend analysis. As a
starting point, it is a truism that friction will always be a factor in urban
counterinsurgencies. The city is constantly moving and shifting. People are
always active and thereby cause change. With change comes friction almost
exactly as Clausewitz describes it. What Clausewitz doesn't explain, however, is that friction occurs for both or all sides in a competition, which
means we are in a race of sorts to identify and exploit friction as it affects
the adversary. We can see indications of the potential for friction in the
trend analysis we perform, but only if we understand the kinds of trends
and phenomena such as trend decay, trend death, trend relationships, and
the bathtub curve of trends.

Examples of friction in counterinsurgency operations include the unexpected arrival of NGOs in a neighborhood in which U.S. intelligence forces are
conducting point-persistent surveillance operations; police randomly inter-
cepting a runner whom we wanted to cause change or perturbation in the
enemy's network; a beggar appearing at the doorstep of a suspect house when
we don't want any interruptions; a utility worker unexpectedly showing while
our "fake" utility workers are installing small sensors on a telephone pole; and
a refuse truck breaking down right next to the house we are watching and
causing inadvertent perturbation that we were not expecting, leaving us
unable to capture what the perturbation yielded from the enemy's network. In
addition, complex adaptive systems (CAS), which are insurgent people, their
supporters, and U.S. forces and their coalition partners, will always *collide*,
intersect, and *careen*, thereby causing blips in *energy emanations* and creating
wisps of energy as they collide, intersect, and careen. From these interactions,
complex adaptive systems will pull back, bypass, and attempt to continue with
their business or abort their missions. Although we cannot plan for friction (if
we could, there would be no friction), we can anticipate unexpected variables
coming into play. We can develop agile organizations and mindsets able to see
how friction influences trends. Sometimes we must conclude that friction was
the cause of the effect we believed to be a trend or something that contributed
to a trend's disappearance or decay.

Trends surface into consciousness as occurrences and happenings over
time; they trigger cognition that inquires and seeks further explanation.
Trends always come forth from the past. But trends can be formed with a
current report or discovery and blended with what has transpired in the past.
Sometimes analysts believe trends almost always continue along the same
avenue or path along with similar events as they project into the future. But

this isn't always the case. The smart analyst recognizes the potential fallacy of such assumptive reasoning.

What kind of thought would be more helpful? Trends should not be based on a single functional aspect of a significant activity, e.g., an IED exploding and its direct implanting and detonation. Instead, we might choose to look for or develop trends involving the enemy's network, his condition-setting, his strategies, and his various network functions and characteristics and their associated trends. Trends often appear when undergoing a cause and effect analysis. This type of analysis can occur before the action, during planning, or after execution of a plan in the postmortem. Clausewitz gives us cause to ponder whether use of cause and effect analysis would work in a relationship with trend analysis. As such, he tells us the following in *On War*:

> But in war, as in life generally, all parts of a whole are interconnected and thus the effects produced, however small their cause, must influence all subsequent military operations and modify their final outcome to some degree, however slight. In the same way, every means must influence even the ultimate purpose.[3]

This passage suggests that people using trends can often become confused about causes and effects. But when people attempt to use cause and effect analysis, it can become confused with trend analysis. The best analyst works with both, understands their relationship with one another, and is always wary about the cloud of confusion that hovers in the distance, waiting to pounce on an unsuspecting intelligence analyst.

Much of forensic analysis (hence the stuff trends are made from) is built on assessing a situation after the event and sifting through old reports, reviewing imagery, and backtracking from the event to try and find important information about insertion, movement of people and munitions, and other elements of IED condition-setting. This type of analysis is required and helpful. But it is not the only cognitive work required. Trends must include a broadened perspective cued by a wide swath of inputs—cultural, technical, situational, biometric, and functional. The data inputs people use in trend analysis should come from more than one specific location in which a past IED event occurred. People engaging in trend analysis must realize its relationships with other activities, transactions, interactions, and behaviors, and how all come together to produce the kind of trends one needs for decision-making.

As a final point, as alluded to earlier, trend analysis works best when it partners with other elements of advanced analysis. Trend analysis works hand in hand with anomaly, aggregation, tendency, semiotic, and pattern analyses as well as synthesis. The intellectual power of an advanced analyst using all or a combination of these cognitive tools not only produces specific observables to help with anticipation of future events or activities, but also helps to very quickly make sense of incoming data useful for command decision-making. When such incoming data has several cognitive elements of advanced analysis, and when analysts run them through a rigorous gauntlet of mental deliberations, the analytic output is knowledge and situational understanding of sufficient quality to help commanders to make fast, effective decisions.

Trends can be misleading. This is not to say that they have no value, but simply that analysts need to be wary of trends as their sole source of intelligence analysis. Analysts shouldn't devote all their time on vigorously tracking trends; they must also actively search for conditions, variables, and human interactions that could cause the enemy or competitor to break with the trend; use different techniques, tactics, and procedures; or vary his method, as well as what we can call "hidden" or "invisible" nascent trends and trends that have been in being for some time.

Trend analysis relates to tendency analysis in that both involve movement, projections about the future, intense cognition, and assistance from automation. Trend analysis, however, differs from tendency analysis in that it involves projections about the future coming from forensics and collection of events and data that have happened in the past. From such analyses, analysts form conclusions about the future. Tendency analysis, on the other hand, involves a snapshot of a *current street, neighborhood,* or *activity* and either consciously or subconsciously ingests small fluctuations or differences in the situation, or anticipates dangerous activities right now or in the future. Trend analysis deals with significant activities and past events and uses mathematical modeling to move along a straight line toward the future; e.g., if a significant IED attack occurred in this location with these observables, then it will happen again in an area in close proximity to the original event. Tendency analysis is holistic and involves bringing subtle and nuanced observables into one's consciousness, synthesizing them into a whole, and anticipating not only similar activities *but dissimilar activities* in the neighborhood or area in question and even possibly in other areas. When engaging in tendency analysis, the analyst seeks what people have neither noticed nor thought about. People notice seemingly obscure indicants of events, activities, interactions, transactions, and behaviors, but they don't articulate meaning because what they see seems vague, abstract, ambiguous, or meaningless. Thus, what they see goes to their subconsciousness, lingers, and eventually fades into nothingness unless analysts pull the data, reflections, observations, and thoughts from where it lingers. Tendencies often come with experience and familiarity with a subject, road, neighborhood, block, activity, or building. When a tendency is occurring, people intuitively realize something will happen, is happening, or is not happening as expected and take action or change what they are doing.

Advanced analysis recognizes the importance of trends in any operation. In fact, we can conclude that trend analysis is vital. But it needs to be more specific and more in-depth of thought than ever before. Why? The answer involves an adaptive enemy who learns about trends and takes counteractions with deception or other forms of minimizing the impact of his trends, which cannot entirely disappear. With that in mind, let us review the important points of this chapter:

- The chapter discussed four kinds of trends—human/social, functional, technical, and organizational.
- The chapter introduced a "bathtub curve," which is at play when the enemy is setting conditions and subsequent trends start appearing. That is, when the enemy first starts his condition-setting, such as intelligence collection of a particular target singled out for later attack, there will be enough data to form a trend concerning intelligence collection. The trend line will be climbing and will reach a plateau. When the enemy has enough data to plan, rehearse, and wargame, the intelligence collection activity will fall off to periodic monitoring and reporting. Thus, the plateau we just spoke of will fall dramatically. Then, when the enemy is ready to attack, the trend will rise again because the insurgent commander will need lots of data to confirm his plan, to prepare for execution, and to engage in aftermath activities.
- The chapter emphasized how much trend analysis depends on the three types of baselines—technical, cultural, and functional. Analysts will not do well in working against trends if they do not possess current baselines.
- The chapter provided a short discussion of some important ideas when working with trends. These important ideas are appearances of trends; periodicity (their rate of showing or surfacing); degrees of vagueness, ambiguity, and subtlety; and relationships within and among trends.
- The chapter provided thoughts on the challenges analysts face when working against trends. Some of the major challenges include the following: trends come and go; trends appear and disappear; trends decay with the passage of time and changes in both threat activities and OE; trends can be invisible or so obscure as to convince the analyst that nothing is occurring that could be construed as a trend, when in reality a trend has been born and is thriving; trends always involve the past; and trends are influenced by mirror imaging.

The chapter also provided some thoughts about overcoming shortfalls in working with trends. Analysts must form hypotheses or expectations concerning trends, decompose them, and use ISR to confirm or deny the validity of the expectation. Analysts need to learn how to think about trends—they are wholes with interrelated parts and functions, beginnings and ends, and causes and effects. Analysts must be aware of and aggressively look for enemy trends to exploit. One of the best techniques for working against trends is to think like the enemy, who is trying to hide his trends or at least to sow obfuscation sufficient to confuse American intelligence analysts regarding the location, nature, degree of decay, and bathtub curve of the trend in question. Finally, the chapter discussed how the intelligence analyst needs to anticipate friction (unexpected chance events) in the pursuit of trends and to be undeterred from discovering the meaning of the trend in question, even when confronted with the confusion and chaos associated with friction-laden events and activities.

10

Anticipatory Analysis

Definition: Using thought, intuition, foreknowledge, knowledge, experience, or prescience to realize in advance what the adversary or competitor might do and testing, confirming, or denying that hypothesis or postulate.

Anticipation is an essential outcome of advanced analysis. The thought processes and machine work needed to perform the mental activities on which anticipation is founded do not come naturally—people have to learn how to think about and employ anticipation. That being said, anticipation is an excellent way to seek, find, and seize the initiative from an adversary who does not want to give it up. Anticipation focuses on an adversary's thinking, perceptions, energy fields, moves, and activities. It also involves developing hypotheses concerning an adversary's intent, will, aims, strategies, motivation, decision-making, capabilities, condition-setting necessities, and associated activities and actions to accomplish his or her desired effects. Yet, I ask, do we approach the subject of thinking about, planning, making decisions, and acting in a methodical way to seize and retain the initiative? Do we understand that the enemy will attempt to take it back? Do we realize the struggle is always ongoing and stretches across all active domains of conflict—air, ground, cyber, and information? Surprise, a key component of the initiative (hence of anticipatory analysis) is difficult to achieve. French counterinsurgency theorist Roger Trinquier helps us understand what happens when a regular force attempts to conduct operations against a guerrilla force with respect to the all-important aspect of conflict—surprise:

> Despite the ingenuity, even mastery, which some commanders have demonstrated in moving their units about, these operations are always the same. Surprise, that essential factor of success, is practically never realized. As we have seen, the people among whom our troops live and move have as their mission the informing of the guerrillas, and no movement of troops can escape them. The noose is never completely tightened.[1]

As we venture into the important subject of anticipatory analysis, there will be a lingering question that will tug at the thoughts of readers if it is not dealt with now. They will ask: what is the difference between anticipation and prediction? This is an excellent question and certainly deserves an answer before we delve into the specifics of anticipatory analysis. The meaning of *predict* is to foretell with precision of calculation, knowledge, or shrewd inference from facts or experience.[2] Joint Publication 2.0, Joint Intelligence, uses the term *prediction*,[3] but advanced analysis does not use the term. The reason for this departure from doctrine is that urban OE is in constant motion, the collisions, intersections, and careening of complex adaptive systems are extraordinarily difficult to forecast, and sensitive variables are too susceptible to rapid change and growth to predict with any degree of accuracy and therefore are unpredictable. But, the Joint Publication 2.0 does say, "Although intelligence must identify and access the full range of adversary capabilities, it is most useful when it focuses on the future and adversary intentions."[4] Advanced analysis certainly agrees with the Joint doctrine in the meaning and implications behinds these words. The telling words for our consideration in this discussion include the meaning of *prediction*, which is "precision of calculation, knowledge, or shrewd inference." On the other hand, the meaning of *anticipate* is to realize beforehand; to expect; look forward to; to nullify, prevent, or forestall by taking countermeasures in advance.[5] To anticipate is much less precise than to predict; therefore, it is a much more appropriate descriptor for the kind of urban setting conflict the U.S. military is involved in now and will be involved with over the next 100 years.

In the urban OE in which U.S. military forces will be conducting counterinsurgency and irregular warfare operations, both the OE and its elements as well as occupants of the city will be changing, moving, morphing, and adapting—a far cry from a seemingly orderly, linear, and predictable system of conventional settings. Instead, the OE will border on being chaotic, further contributing to the rejection of any precision when people and organizations are interacting with one another as well as their living and work environments.

At the heart of the issue lie complex adaptive systems (CAS). CAS represent people and organizations as they interact, act, transact, and behave. CAS interact as exemplified by how they intersect, collide, and career after colliding with one another. CAS are special cases of complex systems. They are complex in that they are diverse and made up of multiple interconnected elements and adaptive in that they have the capacity to change and learn from experience.[6] In addition, with complex environments, we find a plethora of potential second- and third-order effects, with some being capable of exploding into strategic significance thanks to the presence of sensitive variables and windows of opportunity. With complex environments, Clausewitzian friction will be at its apex, as the CAS we are dealing with will rarely act as we either want or anticipate.

It follows that in the OE we are discussing, in which people and organizations compete, military operations will be fraught with error and risk. The best that intelligence analysts can do is aggressively anticipate but with the certainty that they will be wrong some of the time. To compete in a complex OE for the initiative, commanders must understand this high risk of error. But, without anticipation and aggressively fighting for the initiative, they will always be reacting—anathema to all professional soldiers over centuries of recorded military history.

When U.S. military forces are conducting COIN operations in a large urban setting, everything is constantly changing and moving. It is complexity that describes this environment. It is not a static, clean, linear experiment in which variables are tightly controlled so that quantifiable metrics can be designed and outcomes predicted. Complexity is best described as

> complex, in the sense that a great many independent agents are interacting with each other in a great many ways . . . In every case, moreover, the very richness of these interactions allows the system as a whole to undergo spontaneous self-organization . . . Furthermore, these complex, self-organizing systems are adaptive, in that they don't just passively respond to events the way a rock might roll around in an earthquake. They actively try to turn whatever happens to their advantages. Thus, the human brain constantly organizes and reorganizes its billions of neural connections so as to learn from experience . . . Finally, every one of these complex, self-organizing, adaptive systems possesses a kind of dynamism that makes them qualitatively different from static objects such as computer chips or snowflakes, which are merely complicated. Complex systems are more spontaneous, more disorderly, more alive than that.[7]

Anticipation is the essential aspect of initiative. Initiative is "The setting or dictating of terms of action throughout an operation."[8] This is a good high-level definition. But, what does it really mean and why are we interested in it? The simple answer boils down to the meaning of initiative. Let me explain why initiative is so important to anybody conducting military operations in a large urban setting. Whoever holds the initiative has several advantages:

- *First*, holding the initiative results in a positive expenditure of energy toward a goal. The holder of initiative is acting and not reacting, thereby infusing himself with positive energy, which fuels movement toward his goal.
- *Second*, the holder of initiative has the advantage of deciding when and where to conduct actions or activities to accomplish goals.
- *Third*, the holder of initiative has positional advantage. Position can be physical, such as a unit holding a key building in a city, or nonphysical, such as a cyberbot moving faster and ahead of an enemy cyberbot to find a position of ambush or deceptive maneuver in cyberspace. Position can also be intellectual in dominating the enemy commander's thoughts and decisions.
- *Fourth*, the holder of initiative holds the advantage of freedom of maneuver, which brings forth advantages in both tempo and momentum. Military philosopher Sun Tzu helps us comprehend the importance of thinking about, seeking, and holding the initiative with the following thoughts:

> Thus, those skilled at making the enemy move do so by creating a situation to which he must conform; they entice him with something he is certain to take, and with lures of ostensible profit they await him in strength. Therefore a skilled commander seeks victory from the situation and does not demand it of his subordinates.[9]

The initiative is so important that all sides in a competitive endeavor seek it. In this regard, the great guerilla warfare theorist, Mao Tse-tung, tells us:

> In all battles and wars, a struggle to gain and retain the initiative goes on between the opposing sides, for it is the side that holds the initiative that has liberty of action. When an army loses the initiative, it loses its liberty; its role becomes passive; it faces the danger of defeat and destruction.[10]

Thus, in all competition, initiative comes and goes, and all sides strive to obtain and hold it to gain an advantage over the others. Initiative is not just a physical event such as attacking first. It is also intellectual in that the commander and his staff should know how the enemy and the populace (particularly important in a COIN environment) think and perceive. The commander is obliged to work with his staff to seize the initiative by acting first and then having a good idea how the enemy will react. Sir William Slim, a famous World War II British general, provides the following insight into how important the initiative is:

> I usually discussed with the intelligence officer whom I had selected to represent the Japanese command at my headquarters . . . what the enemy's reactions to this plan were likely to be. I was, of course, kept daily in the

picture of the Japanese actions, intentions, and dispositions, as far as we knew or could surmise them, but I intentionally waited until I had selected my plan before considering the enemy response to it as I intended him to conform to me, not me to him.[11]

Along this line of thought, the commander and his staff must realize that they will not always have the initiative. Thus, they will sometimes be reacting, but they must understand how the enemy thinks about their own attempts to re-seize the initiative. In this respect the commander and his staff are interlocked with the enemy in a never-ending circle of struggles across all domains of conflict and competition for the initiative.

So, who is the most important participant in this struggle for initiative? Given that the commander is always the most important person in any struggle, the next most important people are intelligence analysts. They help the commander to know how the enemy and populace think and perceive, how the friendly commander can confirm or deny his hypotheses coming from wargaming for the initiative, and the possible second-and third-order effects emanating from the endless struggle for the initiative.

In an urban insurgency, the struggle for initiative takes many forms and occurs across all domains of conflict. It can occur by providing the populace with goods and services such as security, water, sewage disposal, and lights. It can occur by providing true information over multiple means of communications. It can occur by talking with people and listening to their concerns and doing something to ameliorate their anguish. With respect to the embedded enemy who is well hidden, the commander is faced with a dilemma. On one hand, he needs to take the fight to the insurgent because if he does not, the insurgent will take the fight to him with all the attendant advantages inherent to people who hold the initiative. On the other hand, the commander cannot undo what has been done by way of gaining the initiative with nonviolent actions and activities just to seek and kill the insurgent. The commander must resolve this dilemma. But the question is, how?

It is through anticipatory analysis that the commander can resolve this dilemma. Anticipation involves knowing the opponent's goals, motivations, and intent, knowing how he intends to accomplish his goals, and knowing what he must do to execute his planned activities by way of *condition-setting* and *shaping*. More specifically, the commander and his staff can use anticipatory analysis to postulate the enemy's intentions, tactics, and resources. They can use anticipatory analysis to understand what the enemy wants to do, when he could attempt to do so, and what he might hope to accomplish with the action—*this is discerning his intent*. Most importantly, the commander and his staff can anticipate what the enemy and his network must set up to conduct the attacks and other activities for accomplishing his goals and strategies. It follows that the friendly commander and his staff must anticipate these many activities and actions and, in particular, know and understand the *condition-setting activities* that the enemy needs to accomplish his mission. The commander's advanced analysts will design observables to identify condition-setting activities, understand the relationships among the condition-setting activities, and conduct analysis on possible outcomes of those activities. The commander's advanced analysts and collection specialists will collect data relating to the condition-setting activities and recompose and synthesize resultant data into knowledge that is actionable and sufficient to reduce uncertainty and manage risk. This process has the potential to enable the commander to *preempt the enemy's actions* or to "be there waiting" when the enemy attempts to conduct his attacks.

When armed with inklings or thoughts about what the enemy might do next or how he might respond to a friendly parry, the advanced analyst considers how he will know if the enemy is doing what is expected or, conversely, how he will discern deception from truth. Intelligence analysts must also discern between friendly-induced enemy activities and independent enemy activities. An analyst does this by understanding and differentiating between U.S.- or coalition-induced cause/effect phenomena and the phenomena induced by non-U.S. or noncoalition-induced actions. Analysts must not only know that a friendly action is occurring but have a very good idea how that action will play out. Along this line of thought, the analyst must rely on ISR to receive data and information to anticipate what the enemy might do next and how the effects and outcomes of future action outcomes will appear from the enemy's perspective.

Anticipation-driven operations can be wrong. After all, when people engage in anticipatory analysis, they have to be aggressive, and, as mentioned earlier, they are working against an intelligent, adaptive, and aggressive foe who will not do what the analyst wants. Thus, the advanced analyst must take chances to get ahead of the adversary's decision cycle with sufficient foresight and energy to cause entropy in the enemy's planning and decision-making. After all, advanced analysts are pitted against human beings who adapt, try to outthink them, and most assuredly work hard to avoid exploitable patterns and trends. Thus this foe will not always be susceptible to anticipatory analysis. With that variance in mind, however, it must be acknowledged that if intelligence analysts understand the enemy's intent, will, strategies, and resources to accomplish strategy-driven goals, they can narrow the enemy's options sufficiently to form hypotheses and pursue the many benefits of anticipating the opponent's actions or behaviors.

There is a duality involved with anticipation. This duality means for everything we do by way of perception, thought, and action, there is at least one other grouping of pertinent perceptions, thoughts, and actions. This other half of the duality occurs in the minds of adversaries (or competitors in noncombat situations). As intelligence analysts attempt to engage in anticipatory analysis with the intent of getting ahead of the enemy's decisions and attendant actions, they can be and should be certain that the enemy and other competitors will be doing likewise. Thus, as the friendly commander and his analysts think about the adversary and how he thinks, they can rest assured that the adversary is thinking about the U.S. commander and his supporting staff and how they think and perceive. As the friendly commander and staff anticipate the enemy's goals, objectives, strategies, and condition-setting, the enemy or other competitors will be doing likewise. This notion of duality in anticipatory analysis is put forward in a book titled *Ender's Game*:

> He kept his mind on the game, trying to learn from the battles. And not just the particular lessons of that battle, but what the buggers might have done if they had been more clever, and how Ender would react if they did it in the future. He lived with past battles and future battles both waking and sleeping. . .He would use the time while the others rested to pore over the replays of past games, trying to spot his own weaknesses, trying to guess what would happen next. Sometimes he was fully prepared for the enemy's innovations; sometimes he was not.[12]

These invisible struggles, although seemingly abstract, are in reality quite normal. They are common to any competitor who wants to win. Thus, any competitor will always strive to anticipate his opponent's thoughts and resultant activities and reap attendant advantages for anticipating his opponent's moves or actions. But this kind of mental work takes people who know the OE, enemy, and populace in depth. Then, these people must be willing to anticipate, attempt to confirm the anticipated outcomes, and use valuable ISR assets to confirm or deny resultant hypotheses or expectations. Thus, to work with anticipatory analysis, the commander and his staff must possess two other advantages relevant to this type of intellectual combat— knowledge and intellectual advantages.

In expanding this line of thought just slightly, the reader must agree that anticipatory analysis and its risk-taking modus operandi is neither for the faint of heart nor for the perfectionist. It is for people who recognize the importance of the initiative and who want to outthink the enemy because they realize the immense benefits of the outcomes and corollary advantages awaiting those who engage in anticipatory analysis and preemption. It follows that ISR is crucial to anticipation and the struggle for initiative. To reiterate what was discussed previously, the friendly commander and his staff must use ISR to confirm or deny what they are anticipating. In addition, they must use ISR to watch for the enemy's efforts to anticipate friendly actions and reactions to his actions. As a final note, the friendly commander must use ISR to watch for the enemy's attempts to exploit the situation when he perceives that he possesses the initiative and to watch what the enemy is doing to ensure that he does not lose the initiative.

Let us now venture even further into the world of anticipatory analysis. Anticipation requires intelligence analysts willing to lead efforts to outthink the enemy. This involves getting in the enemy's mind and thinking like he thinks in order to identify what he is considering, to know what his capabilities are (from his perspective), to comprehend how he views the OE and its influences on all sides, to realize how he thinks about the initiative, and to understand how he intends to accomplish his objectives. It also involves thinking about what the adversary must do from his perspective to set conditions for achieving success and for achieving both positional and knowledge advantages to execute an intended effect. This work to understand the adversary's mind, of course, must avoid the scourge of mirror imaging, which was introduced and discussed in Chapter Six. Thus, analysts using anticipatory analysis must watch for its appearance and use a variety of techniques, such as red teaming, indigenous SMEs, and U.S. cultural SMEs to help ward off this potential issue that can become a malevolent influence on analysts' minds.

Anticipation requires analysts (and their leaders) to work with hypotheses, expectations, mysteries, and hunches. It also requires analysts who, along with knowing a lot about their opponent's thought processes and capabilities, know U.S. and coalition traditional and nontraditional intelligence collection activities. It requires analysts to work in a close relationship with collection managers and actual collection execution people, such as HUMINT case officers and people operating UAV systems. Because counterinsurgency people must work quickly to outmaneuver a nimble enemy who operates in a fast-changing, fluid network, a tight nexus must always exist among analyst, collector, and operators for anticipatory analysis to work well.

Unfortunately, anticipation sometimes receives short shrift, owing to the difficulty of the task and more than average risk of adverse outcomes. But, when friendly forces do not engage in anticipation, the antithesis can occur: reaction. Reaction condemns leaders to a loss of positive individual and organizational energy, an inability to experience freedom of action, and a loss of positional (physical, intellectual, cyber) advantage. Commanders and their intelligence analysts must lead the effort in understanding and using anticipation in this aggressive way of thinking and employing ISR, as its advantages far outweigh negative consequences.

One of the most influential impediments to analytic anticipation is caused by analysts' preoccupation with intelligence production. This comment is not a condemnation of all intelligence production. Intelligence production is and will remain an important aspect of intelligence operations. It is an argument, however, for a better balance between intelligence production, which is the preparation of reports or products to meet the needs of intelligence users, and the purposeful employment of analytic work to outthink the enemy. Owing to the inherent complexity of anticipatory analysis, dedicated people must work on a team to anticipate the enemy's thoughts and moves and thereby, with the right actions, advise the commander on how best to thwart those moves, seize the initiative, and create entropy (slowing or breakdown) in the enemy's decisions. Intelligence production will remain necessary, but it is time consuming, and if people are not careful, intelligence production—such as writing summaries and developing briefings—can become the underlying purpose for the presence of intelligence analysts at the expense of many other roles they must perform in urban COIN.

Continuing with this thread of thought, unfortunately, intelligence production often involves thinking about what has already happened. For example, trend, pattern, and link analysis, though important and necessary for the conduct of good intelligence analysis, primarily involve the forensics of past events. When analysts use trend, pattern, or link analysis in isolation or as a preferential method of performing analysis, they will sometimes not do well in accounting for thinking about human creativity, experiencing exponential cognitive leaps or epiphanies, or even anticipating future actions. Trend, pattern, and link analysis are important, but only if people balance them with anticipatory thought and aggressive analysis.

As mentioned earlier, anticipation involves *understanding* the enemy's aims, strategies, tactics, techniques, and supporting activities. Understanding is more than knowing. Understanding involves both knowledge and the relationships that comprise the knowledge. Unfortunately, this type of understanding is culturally and technically intensive and sometimes remains elusive and far beyond what analysts can know, unless they are cultural anthropologists or a variety of engineers who understand the specifics of technologies and in particular their use by people and organizations in the society in question. Thus, to engage in these types of analyses, analysts must often find and use SMEs, including properly cleared indigenous people, to assist them in working with advanced analysis to overcome knowledge or thinking shortfalls.

Now, this inquiry must delve further into another key aspect of anticipatory analysis—condition-setting. As a first step into more depth of understanding, we have to ask ourselves, how does condition-setting relate to anticipatory thinking? The answers are really quite simple. If the enemy is going to launch an attack against a guarded part of the infrastructure, we must assume he will have to set conditions for success. Given this assumption is true, and given we have identified the steps he must take to successfully establish conditions for an attack, we must decompose those steps into observables. To engage in this decomposition to the depth required, undoubtedly we will have to seek the help of the intelligence enterprise and the VKE to find and exploit the knowledge and experience of SMEs to help develop the five kinds of observables relevant to the enemy's conditions setting. Once the analyst and SMEs have decomposed the steps in condition-setting leading to the anticipated action and have the observables in hand, they work with collection specialists and task/ask sensors and HUMINT to collect information about when, where, and why they anticipate the condition-setting activities to occur. If the anticipatory analyst and their SME assistants are able to weave resultant data into a pattern or trend, they will be able to provide their commander with enough situational under-standing to act. His action will be to disrupt or preempt the enemy's efforts to set conditions and to synchronize his activities. If the anticipatory analy-sis and corollary preemptive effects and actions are successful, at worst the friendly commander will have caused the enemy some amount of delay and desynchronization and at best the commander will have preempted the enemy's activities or attack plans. With such a sequence of events, the friendly commander will seize the initiative, albeit in a subtle way.

Anticipatory analysis will undoubtedly seem easy to the reader; how-ever, it is very challenging. Why? First, the friendly commander and his advanced analysts are working against other human beings whose motiva-tion is strong and who have a corollary strength of will to accomplish their mission. Second, the enemy is embedded in the culture and hidden within the society's activities. Thus, his activities and condition-setting will be very well concealed and masked. Third, the people doing various parts of the condition-setting will often be ignorant of anything else pertaining to an attack other than their own task.

How do advanced analysts get their heads into the details of anticipa-tory analysis? For starters, they must think aggressively. As such, they must continuously pursue the enemy, and not just his physical characteristics and behaviors but how he perceives, thinks, plans, makes decisions, acts/executes, and receives feedback on the execution. The analysts must also consider the enemy's tasks and his perspectives of constraints, obstacles, the OE, U.S. capabilities, and how he will define success. The advanced analysts must also set their own conditions and establish a knowl-edge environment to help find and line up the right people with the right knowledge and expertise to help with identifying the enemy's condition-setting necessary for problem sets that in a cumulative sense constitute what the enemy must go through to accomplish his mission. These problem sets and condition-setting will vary with the mission; e.g., a bomb factory and IED condition-setting will differ from an attack on a portion of key infrastructure he wants to destroy. As an additional tack, the analyst can engage in intelligence wargaming to discern what the enemy could be doing and the signs he would show when he is conducting his activities when he has the initiative and when he is reacting. The advanced analyst would have to wargame his attack scenarios and attendant condition-setting for each to enable each scenario to succeed (again, from his perspective). The patterns and observables will be in some ways similar but in many ways quite different. The analyst has to identify the similarities and differences. As part of the intellectual work, the advanced analyst can start thinking by using anticipatory analysis. To this end, the advanced analyst engages in thinking that goes something like the following:

- What is the enemy trying to do?
- How can I anticipate his actions and disrupt his condition-setting or attack preparation plans?
- How and what elements of the culture would influence the enemy if he is considering a nefarious action?
- Where would the enemy's people be located for each step in condition-setting and how would they interact, behave, conduct transactions, and engage in their condition-setting activities?
- What are the cultural signs or symbols that would be present or not present in each type of condition-setting activity?
- How would I would look for and see people performing surveillance from windows, street corners, or even children playing in the street?
- What would the technical elements or emanations be if my expectations about his condition-setting are true?
- Would I see increased cell phone calls from a variety of places along approaches to the potential target?
- Are there patterns among these cell phone calls?
- Would I see refraction from camera lenses his watchers are using?
- Would I see increased Internet communications in houses near potential targets?
- What are the biometric elements or physiological changes or manifestations of bodily activities exhibited by the people performing condition-setting for an action?
- What are the functional elements or activities, transactions, interactions, or behaviors involved with condition-setting if my expectation is true or false?
- Are there are any strange noises, smells, or signs of anomaly that could indicate enemy condition-setting?

One of the intriguing aspects of advanced analysis is how many of its cognitive elements relate to other elements. In this case in particular, anticipatory analysis relates to tendency analysis. Let us discuss how this is so. To start the discussion, let us briefly define tendency analysis (it will be covered in more depth later in the book). *Tendency analysis* is "Discerning meaning through thought and study of the general proclivities of people, the behavioral and action inclinations of organizations, mental snapshots of current environment or contextual situations, events, activities, behaviors, the emanation dispersal of energy emissions, and what the interaction and enmeshing of all could portend for the future." This discussion provides more explanation of tendency analysis and how it relates to anticipation as well as lending some practical insights to a difficult subject.

To avoid cognitive regression while going from one state of tendencies to the next, when something of interest or importance occurs, or when something a little out of the ordinary surfaces into consciousness, our stimulated subconscious starts giving our conscious intellect a special "feeling." At this stage, the person trained and educated in advanced analysis experiences a sense, a hunch, or gut feeling. As analyst George Friedman says,

> There is nothing absurd about a gut call in intelligence . . . Analysts live in a world of incomplete and shifting intelligence, compelled to reach conclusions under the pressure of time and events. Intuition of experienced and gifted analysts is the bridge between leaving decision-makers without an analysis and providing the best guess available.[13]

The "feeling" or "sense" starts forming as a perception in the analyst's mind. With research, consultation with fellow analysts in the enterprise, with his or her own creativity and ability to synthesize data into knowledge, and with SMEs in a VKE, the analyst develops concrete thoughts from the unimaginable feeling or sense. But, even when this process occurs somewhat automatically for some experienced analysts, sometimes it helps to stimulate the environment and the variables intrinsic to a particular situation to bring forth subtle micro-changes so necessary for tendency analysis. Through stimulation or perturbation, the advanced analyst can mature or clarify the sense or feeling that is causing cognitive dissonance in his or her mind. A short example will help the reader understand the closely related phenomena of anticipation and tendencies. The anticipation comes in when the analyst takes the results of tendency analysis and turns those senses into action via anticipation and its attendant ISR activities.

If an advanced analyst has a sense from tendency analysis that something untoward is going to occur in a particular business in a particular neighborhood in a large urban OE, he or she would engage in data collection and manipulation in the buildings and the businesses located within its confines. The analyst would engage in the mental function that is analytic *Fingerspitzengefuhl,* which helps stimulate intuition or a status of "intrinsic actuality." In military history, *Fingerspitzengefuhl* is the sense or touch a great commander has when presented with a battlefield or situation in which he has multiple inputs that allows him to instantly draw conclusions from his mind, experience, intuition, and the context of the situation. Clausewitz calls this sense *coup d'oeil,* which is comprehending a situation or an occurrence quickly, perhaps with just a glance; it, in Clausewitz's thoughts, provides the spiritual underpinning for anticipation. In this regard Clausewitz says in his treatise *On War*:

> If the mind is to emerge unscathed from this relentless struggle with the unforeseen, two qualities are indispensable: first, an intellect that, even in the darkest hour, retains some glimmerings of the inner light which leads to truth; and second, the courage to follow this faint light wherever it may lead. The first of these qualities is described by the French term, coup d'oeil; the second is determination.[14]

The advanced analyst uses a derivation of the commander's *Finger-spitzengefuhl* and *coup d'oeil,* but it is the sense of the analyst who has, through experience and intuition, formed a particular expectation, antici-pation, or hunch about the enemy or state of the OE. It is this sense that connects tendency and anticipatory analysis. With this sense that something is going to occur, the analyst then engages in anticipatory analysis to make understandable that which is only a premonition with tendency analysis.

The analyst, with the help of SMEs and the intelligence enterprise, decomposes the expectation or hunch coming from tendency analysis into observables in order to anticipate the enemy's activities. The analyst works with the collection manager and collection specialists to not only task HUMINT and sensors, but to explain to collection specialists the following elements of effective, analytic driven collection: (1) operational context; (2) observables; (3) location; (4) time; (5) suspected activities, and (6) standards (timeliness, specificity, accuracy, relevance, and clarity). This list is a thought template for analytic guidance to collectors in the overall concept of advanced analysis. This guidance is quite neces-sary when eliciting the collection system's machines and people to watch for observables in a large city, when dealing with a network, and when trying to find signs of the enemy's condition-setting for attacks and other activities. Quite simply, the brain of an alert human observer must receive stimuli to comprehend what to search for or find. Such stimula-tion is relevant to many sources and machines, whether a HUMINT source watching for activity, a linguist sitting a SIGINT position listen-ing for a key word, a computer programmed to skim through data look-ing for a relevant image, or a sensor operator watching a UAV full-motion video screen to see if an expectation is unfolding at a named area of interest (NAI). Advanced analysts must provide guidance and focus to both people and machines to watch for the right observable at the right time and place to be able to successfully perform anticipatory analysis. In the case of the human being, the alert human observer is similar in an important way to a quantum detection device; it can amplify small signals to begin to comprehend larger macroscopic activi-ties or transactions part of a larger, evolving whole. But, these brains need priming, prompting, and stimulating.

Back to the example: the analyst performs research and tries to find existing knowledge on the suspect business. The analyst consults with fel-low analysts in the intelligence enterprise and SMEs in a VKE. With the compilation of data and knowledge, the analyst progresses from a simple sense to a substantial degree of depth in anticipatory analysis. But, since the business is in a highly sensitive and volatile neighborhood, the analyst must be right that the business is "dirty" before advocating a direct action. So, he advocates a persistent surveillance operation of a specific point to confirm or deny his premonition.

Once the persistent surveillance operation starts, the analyst recommends that the commander create perturbation of the insurgents' network in the neighborhood but not directly on the business. So, the commander sends a slowly moving U.S. and Iraqi patrol into the neighborhood three blocks away from the business. The persistent surveillance operation, armed with a bevy of cultural, biometric, technical, situational, and functional observables, watches the business to learn what happens during the attempt to perturb the enemy's network with the slowly moving patrol. This type of "cat and mouse" activity is essential in countering the insurgents' advantages in being hidden and secretive while the analyst is engaging in anticipation and trying to find signs or hints that can either confirm or deny his expectation, hunch, or hypothesis.

In this case, the advanced analyst anticipates the observables he or she wants to follow and learn from. In particular, the advanced analyst knows he or she must discern cultural influences on enemy perceptions, plans, decisions, assessments, and adjustments from feedback. Thus, the analyst will use SMEs and properly cleared indigenous people to identify the right observables to engage in anticipatory and tendency analysis. The analyst will also use analytic experts, as a part of organized analytic overwatch, to watch for the appearance of observables and indications of windows of opportunity to influence variables that could impact the enemy's capability to act or react to friendly activities.

The analyst then works with the collection manager and collection specialists to use HUMINT and optimal combinations of sensors to find/notice nuance and tendencies—mechanical/human, traditional, and nontraditional. In this case, the patrol will undoubtedly cause perturbation in the enemy's network, if in fact there is illicit activity occurring in the business. But, the activity could be imperceptible to the noncultural observer. Thus, the analyst will work with his indigenous people and SMEs before the event occurs to wargame how the enemy could respond with his network. The analyst and his enterprise supporters anticipate functioning of the network that could emit projected observables to confirm or deny the analyst's hypotheses. In this respect, the analyst casts a wide net of expertise to help him think like the enemy, as they bring forth their activities with and without perturbation. The analyst considers the enemy's assessment of what the perturbation means, the means to confirm or deny his assessments, his thoughts, intellectual predilections, and the way culture influences his ability to think. This process is the essence of anticipation.

Technology helps advanced analysts work with anticipation. This occurs in several important ways that will have distinct meaning to advanced analysts:

- Through M&S, identifying possible physical and mental alternatives the opponent might have in any given circumstances, thereby assisting the analyst in anticipating activities, interactions, transactions, and behaviors.

- Using software and hardware power to help decompose and prioritize alternatives for collection specifically to help the analyst anticipate the enemy's next actions or behaviors and impose friendly action to shape, deny, desynchronize, or thwart the best of enemy plans. In this respect, anticipation can have a devastating influence on the enemy leader's decision speed, perceptions, and morale.
- Using nonphysics-based complexity models to watch an opponent's network perform roles and missions in a particular situation and see emergent behaviors and postulate how real people from a particular culture might act or react. This behavior drives intelligence collection to help confirm or deny anticipatory hypotheses.
- Using GIS and three-dimensional modeling to see what an opponent sees, smells, feels, and hears using his network of sensors, alarms, personal vision, and the vision of others as well as his *proprioception,* which is the unconscious perception of movement and spatial orientation arising from stimuli within the body itself to anticipate possible behaviors and latency of thought to action.[15] High-fidelity imagery, GIS products, current three-dimensional terrain data, and thematic layering all contribute to cases in which this aspect of anticipation is useful to decision-making.

Other important technically driven analytic functions exist that contribute to anticipatory analysis—including searching for data; manipulating data; guiding intelligence collection with analytic-derived, specific observables; engaging in wargaming; anticipating the enemy's activities; and designing collection to confirm or deny an enemy's anticipated moves. Each requires time and effort.

Anticipation, which requires understanding the enemy's aims, strategies, tactics, techniques, and supporting activities, is culturally and technically sensitive and sometimes remains elusive and far beyond what our analysts can know unless they are cultural anthropologists, experienced foreign area officers (FAOs), or engineers. Thus, to engage in these types of analyses, analysts must find and use SMEs, including properly cleared, indigenous people, to assist them in working with advanced analysis to overcome knowledge or thinking shortfalls.

As a final part of the discussion, we shall identify some of the particular challenges associated with anticipatory analysis and what the advanced analyst can do to meet these challenges.

- As a first challenge, the advanced analyst must know "how to think" about anticipatory analysis. As an essential aspect of this challenge, the analyst must know and understand how the enemy thinks. Since the enemy does not come forth and tell us how he thinks about initiative, T. E. Lawrence in *Seven Pillars of Wisdom* helps us understand some of the essential aspects of the initiative from the enemy's perspective:

> The corollary of such a rule was perfect intelligence so that we could plan in certainty . . . It [the insurgency] had a friendly population, of which some two in the hundred were active, and the rest quietly sympathetic to the point of not betraying the movements of the minority. The active rebels had the virtues of secrecy and self-control, and the qualities of speed, endurance, and independence of arteries of supply.[16]

These qualities—perfect intelligence, support of the population, speed, endurance, and independence—are critical to the initiative, and the advanced analyst must think hard about taking each and every one away so as to set conditions for seizing the initiative. Using the anticipation analysis thought template will help the advanced analyst use pertinent elements of advanced analysis and the right observables to anticipate the enemy's condition-setting and actual attacks.

- As a second challenge, the advanced analyst using anticipatory analysis must find the right knowledge to assist his or her anticipatory analysis. This aspect of struggling for the initiative is essential but problematic. One author helps us to understand that part of this challenge is knowing the enemy is seeking advantages with knowledge too:

An invisible competitive dynamic is at work here—a struggle or duel of sorts for achieving advantage . . . over an adversary. Both sides in the competition know they face a formidable foe. Each also knows that the side that is able to develop the best knowledge and use it more quickly and ably than the other stands a superb chance of achieving intellectual advantage, perhaps even a decision advantage.[17]

The advanced analyst can use a VKE and knowledge broker to help with anticipation if they are available. This same line of thought holds true when the analyst seeks support from within his or her own headquarters as well as seeking support in the intelligence enterprise. The advanced analyst must use indigenous experts who have the right security credentials. The analyst must use these SMEs to help with anticipation in decomposition, matching anticipatory observables with the right collectors, making sense of resultant data, and wargaming. In addition, the analyst must be certain to design the request for SME and knowledge support early in the planning process during analytic condition-setting to put everything possible into place to satisfy the anticipatory analysis requirements.

- As a third challenge, the advanced analyst must anticipate the enemy activity in question. In the case of an impending attack, the analyst must anticipate not only the attack in itself, but how, when, why, and exactly where the attack will occur. This is an intelligence wargaming issue that can only be done with intelligence people, red team people, and indigenous and U.S. cultural SMEs. It is one of the most important aspects of anticipatory analysis. As such, the wargaming activities will attempt to anticipate how the enemy will set conditions to conduct his attack and merge that understanding with the vagaries of the OE and, in particular, the neighborhood where the attack or the preparatory activities are going to occur. In addition, the advanced analyst will go through an act, react, and counteract wargaming sequence with indigenous people playing the part of the enemy. This same sequence has to occur when the network is operating and its attendant condition-setting activities are occurring. In intelligence wargaming, the analyst must work through many variations of the ways the enemy could act, how they might achieve surprise, the ways they could mask their activities when engaging in condition setting, and how they would anticipate what the U.S. analyst might be thinking and what collection capabilities he or she is using to anticipate and thwart his condition-setting, attack, or other activities. The analyst must do this mental work with both day and night scenarios. As a final point, the advanced analyst using anticipatory analysis must use red teamers to criticize his or her thoughts and assumptions to look for errors in logic such as using poor assumptions, falling into the trap of mirror imaging, and oversimplifying the complexity of the culture.
- As a fourth challenge, the advanced analyst will form a tight partnership with collection specialists and work with them to design the right combinations of collection. This relationship must be close to enable the team to be sufficiently aggressive to engage in anticipatory analysis. As such, the advanced analyst must let collection people know several things such as what he or she is thinking, what the analyst believes the enemy will do under certain operational circumstances, the analyst's explanations of detailed observables, and rationale for analytically developed standards enshrouding the analytic/collection operation. The advanced analyst must work with the collection people to design collection that will meet analytic requirements. The advanced analyst and collection specialist must also work as a team to pass original and subsequent analytic guidance to distributed collectors and ensure they remain up-to-date as the situation changes. Further, the advanced analyst must let the collection specialist know what collection is most important and the observables that need to be watched for—right time, right place, and right observables.

- As a fifth challenge when using anticipatory analysis, the advanced analyst must know the culture he or she is working in. This is an extraordinarily difficult task when the culture is as different as, say, Iraq's is from
America's. So, how does the advanced analyst meet this challenge? As
one technique, the analyst can strive to gain a working knowledge of the
culture and recognize the uniqueness of the cultural. In this respect, the
analyst will come to realize that he or she will never have the in-depth
knowledge and understanding that a person born in the culture will possess. But, with determined study, working with SMEs, and repetitive
tours of duty, the analyst can become knowledgeable of the culture in
which they work. The cognitive requirement does not stop with a working knowledge. They also must move their knowledge and apply it to the
neighborhoods in which their unit is working, as the specifics of culture
are always neighborhood-specific, varying from neighborhood to neighborhood. Thus, the analyst must always seek help from indigenous
SMEs as well as from external cultural SMEs with extensive, recent, on-
the-ground experience and a fluent language capability. As another way
to work with the culture, the analyst must seek ways to use the culture
for advantage, e.g., using beggars along a busy street as a source or
informant. Along this line of thinking, the analyst, HUMINT and counterintelligence specialists, and technical collection specialists must
develop sources and contacts to serve as an indication and warning net
of sorts to identify when cultural anomalies and nascent tendencies
occur. As another way to help understand the culture, the advanced analyst must learn the basics of how the society in question thinks about
and uses technology. In this regard, the analyst must understand the
invisible world of technical emanations, but to do so they need the help
of indigenous and U.S. or coalition electrical engineers and other scientists. This work with engineers and scientists is particularly important in
the task of finding, updating, and using technical baselines to help design
technical observables. The wise advanced analyst will also use both U.S.
and indigenous scientific SMEs to help design collection to work against
the relative technical observables as well as to help make sense of collected data. As a final point, the advanced analyst must understand and
use how the enemy thinks about the U.S. dependency on technology and
collection capabilities to find them in both day and night situations
among all types of activities. The object is, of course, to outthink the
enemy and to negate or manipulate how he uses available technology to
carry out his network activities.

This marks the end of the chapter on anticipation. The chapter contains a fascinating subject—that being, anticipation and its close relationship with initiative. The chapter made a strong case for the close
relationship between anticipatory analysis and initiative and, of course, the

importance of holding the initiative. Although it seems difficult to seek, seize, and hold the initiative in urban operations, purposefully attaining the initiative can be done, and must be done, according to military theorists whose thoughts military thinkers have revered throughout the ages. This struggle for initiative is never ending. But it can swing to the United States and largely remain as a great advantage, given that U.S. intelligence people and their commanders learn to think and act through anticipatory analysis. To engage in the thought and action of anticipatory analysis, however, commanders must underwrite, protect, and encourage their analysts and operators to be bold and aggressive. The execution of anticipatory analysis will sometimes result in "dry holes" and mistakes, as U.S. forces will always be operating in a friction-laden environment against unpredictable people or organizations whose intelligence, adaptability, and creativity defy stereotyping into simple, lethargic entities. But, U.S. intelligence analysts, with the help of SMEs and indigenous people, can learn to think like the enemy, the populace, and other competitors and anticipate what they need to do to accomplish their goals, objectives, and strategies— this is called condition-setting. These two words—*condition-setting*—are important words for our deliberation on anticipation.

Anticipatory analysis is how one (1) understands condition-setting, (2) anticipates its subactions and activities, and (3) when the time is right, preempts or desynchronizes it. But, the chapter also identifies how perplexing it is to see the actions and activities comprising condition-setting, when people performing the steps blend with and hide in the motion and noise of a busy city. As such, the chapter discussed the definition of prediction and why it is largely an inappropriate term for thinking about complex urban OEs.

Complex adaptive systems (CAS) interactions were introduced, discussed, and described as constantly intersecting, colliding, and careening, making it impossible to predict the outcomes of these actions. But, it is possible to anticipate and follow that analytic hunch, theory, or hypothesis and follow it toward the first glimmer of light, which is meaning, and eventually comprehending the identity of all-important relationships that comprise a whole (e.g., a pending insurgent attack on a bridge). For, as always, the goal of anticipatory analysis is, through good thinking, to be waiting when the enemy comes to perform his condition-setting and network activities, to preempt or desynchronize his plans, decision-making, and actions, and to seize the initiative.

Now it is time to move to the next chapter, which is technical analysis. Technical analysis will take the reader into a world that is both visible and invisible but whose importance is critically important to planning and conducting COIN and IW operations in urban OE.

11

Technical Analysis

Definition: Gaining knowledge, understanding, and insight about the technical aspects of particular events, situations, activities, and transactions.

THEORY BEHIND TECHNICAL ANALYSIS

Technical analysis involves the mechanical inner workings of all types of machines, tools, and infrastructures. Scientist Ray Kurzweil helps us understand what technology is with the following thoughts:

> Thus one interpretation of technology is the study of crafting, in which crafting refers to the shaping of resources for a practical purpose . . . What is uniquely human is the application of knowledge-recorded knowledge—to the fashioning of tools . . . But when materials—and in the case of modern technology, information—are assembled in just the right way, transcendence occurs. The assembled object becomes far greater than the sum of its parts.[1]

Technical analysis involves understanding how electrons and radio frequencies and other sources emanate energy and thereby can provide invaluable signatures and observables. Technology and its associated presence, in a visible sense and energy emanation in an invisible sense, affect OEs and how enemies, competitors, and the populace think. All people have some thoughts about technology, how they use it, and how it contributes to their goals. In this sense, insurgents are no different than ordinary human beings going about their daily lives and businesses, highly dependent on technology.

Technology is critically important to people performing advanced analysis. This is a particularly important statement when considering the difficulty of the intelligence analysts' charge to conduct intelligence analysis against insurgents in an urban OE. In this environment, insurgents hide by blending with the population and its everyday movement and activity. But, the insurgents and their network supporters must use technology. Unfortunately technology is, for the most part, invisible to the naked eye. But all is not lost. With the help of technology, such as visualization, modeling, and high-speed computing, intelligence analysts can start understanding what they are up against when working against an enemy insurgent's network. While complicated, the enemy's network can be found and dealt with. As a first step, we need to learn "how to think" about the enemy's network. Author and scientist Kevin Kelly helps us understand the enemy's network:

> [W]e find many systems ordered as a patchwork of parallel operations, very much as in the neural network of a brain or in a colony of ants. Action in these systems proceeds in a messy cascade of interdependent events. Instead of the discrete ticks of cause and effect that run a clock, a thousand clock springs try to simultaneously run a parallel system. Since there is no chain of command, the particular action of any single spring diffuses into the whole, making it easier for the sum of the whole to overwhelm the parts of the whole. What emerges from the collective is not a series of critical individual actions but a multitude of simultaneous actions whose collective pattern is far more important. This is the swarm model.[2]

Thus, even if we cannot see the technology at work, we know it is there, operating and emitting different kinds of observables and signatures, as Kelly describes. Thus, it is incumbent upon advanced analysts to turn what appears to be invisible into something visible.

Technical activity is challenging to search for and find even if the analyst knows what to look for and tasks the collection system to provide data related to technology accordingly. The resultant collection-derived data is often obscure, and its meaning remains elusive even to the most technically gifted analyst. What the advanced analyst does to cope with this problem is the purpose of this chapter.

As a first step in this inquiry, let us think about some of the insurgent enemy's advantages and disadvantages when using technology to operate a subversive and violence-prone network in an urban setting. Let us discuss some of the advantages that might accrue to him with respect to the use of technology. He must first of all blend in with technical noise inherent to the culture. The insurgent and his supporters must use technology like the indigenous population, and they must ambiguate their use of technology. That is, they must blend their use of technology to the point that ambiguation—is it the enemy or is it the normal populace?—is the predominant dilemma facing U.S. intelligence analysts. As another technical advantage, the insurgent can rely on an arrogance, inherent to the technologically strong such as America, which causes a large conventional force to use technology for everything and depend on it for solving every problem. Such arrogance and associated thought proclivities open possibilities for the enemy in the human dimension. As an example, the insurgent can use low-tech communications and semiotics for communicating signs and symbols—it blends in nicely with cultural activities and will appear baffling to most U.S. intelligence analysts. They can also limit use of technology by supporters of the enemy's network in order to remain hidden from the prying eyes of U.S. technical intelligence. This backing away from the constant use of technology to avoid detection does not mean the functions of the insurgency will not occur. The insurgent will still conduct condition-setting activities, such as intelligence collection, but he might not be so ready to transmit what his observers see by cell phone. To assist in his efforts to deny detection, he will attempt to understand what differences his activities could make in a technical sense to people using technical collection and determine a counter.

As a second step, let us consider what the phrase "how to think" means. Technical analysis will always involve what to think as technology is chock full of technical capabilities and specifications. Thus, we will always conclude that with technical analysis, intelligence analysts need to know the technical specifications and characteristics that cause or enable the technical world to occur. But, knowing what to think is insufficient when operating against the insurgent opponent. What is the nature of this insufficiency? The answer to this question lies in subtleties and relationships as well as envisioning the largely invisible world of technical activities. When we consider how to think, we have to consider the opposite of what we see and concentrate on what we do not see. We do not see the RF energy moving around a given space. We do not see electrons bouncing from one place to the next. We do not see emanations of heat coming from a house. We do not see smells, and we do not see sounds. Yet, all are vitally important to technical analysis. Thus, we have to envision what we do not see, but we also need to visualize the "hidden" relationships among these technologies as they work and interact. As another "way to think," we have to consider how both populace and enemy use technology as they *interact, act, transact,* and *behave.* These four terms provide a nice template for analysts to use as they start taking their thoughts into sufficient detail for actual use in analysis and collection. As another point, technical baselines provide the wherewithal to think about normal technical activities as well as the anomalous activities. With technical baseline work, we can think about "what is" vis á vis technical analysis and "what should be" and try to explain reasons for "what is not" but "what should be." We will discuss the importance of technical baselines in greater depth as this chapter unfolds.

This enemy will also have some disadvantages with respect to using technology in a large urban setting. For example, neighborhood people will know about insurgent activities occurring in their neighborhoods—they could very well gossip about these activities in person and electronically, and they will make small technical changes in their normal routines. What are some examples of what local people could do when insurgents are in their midst? They could limit or increase cell phone calls and be obviously careful in what they say, which could be a departure from the norm. They could depart from the norm as they turn lights on and off in their homes. They could limit use of texting and the use of televisions and Internet during the night. They could show extreme caution in using home generators to conserve fuel when operations are pending. In addition, all people make mistakes—they will be like pheromones if we know what to look for and track them. Some of the mistakes and "tracks" will be technical. Further, local people will know outsiders are in the neighborhood, whether they are people occupying a safe house, people bringing supplies to the safe house, or people disposing of trash. People supporting the network will leave an electronic trail, and the neighbors will know it and possibly talk about it or change their electronic habits. In this regard, outsiders' use of technology will be different than the norm or baseline. Since people will know of enemy activity, they will ultimately change their technical behavior. Such change could be very subtle, nuanced, or barely perceptible, but the norm will be disturbed and the advanced analyst must be ready when their observable-driven collection picks it up.

Technology affects just about everything human beings do, even how they engage in their most intimate thought processes. How humans think about, respond to, proactively use, and strive to achieve advantage over competitors has been, is now, and always will be a pillar of conflict. This pillar, however, assumes a Janus-like quality. At first glance, advanced intelligence analysts have as one of their principal roles and missions to understand what has happened in the past and presage the future. Rotating this same pillar 90 degrees, one can deduce another consideration for how to think about technology and technical analysis. That is, understanding what has happened in the past and what will happen in the future from several different perspectives: from the enemy's, from the host nation's, from a neutral's, and so forth. Continuing with the pillar rotation, intelligence analysts must rely on external expertise to help with technical intelligence to gain the technical knowledge they need to supplement their thinking because no staff or organization can hope to answer all questions and provide all knowledge that pertains to all technological issues. On the final rotation of the pillar of future conflict, the advanced analyst must be aggressive in thought and derive ways, through knowledge and specific detail, for friendly forces to seek, attain, and sustain a *technological advantage* over an opponent and other competitors.

The technology issue becomes more complicated when we think about it from a functional perspective, e.g., how an electrical grid works or what are the essential technical pieces of a suicide bomb. Analysts must consider how the enemy thinks about technology and how he plans to use it as a generic weapon system. Unfortunately, a wide and ever-expanding range of technologies exists that have profound influences on military and civil operations. As mentioned earlier, in and of itself, this range of technology suggests the absolute inability of any staff—military or civilian—to have all the requisite technical expertise a decision maker needs to make fast decisions while keeping risk at a manageable level and uncertainty low. This range of technology cannot be ignored. Therefore, modern intelligence analysts must learn to use a VKE or the intelligence enterprise to find and use knowledge and application possibilities and to provide technical expertise the decision maker requires.

The Department of Defense needs intelligence analysts well trained in the basics of physics, engineering, and other sciences *and* in thinking about the use of technology and its implications. What will not work for the future, however, are intelligence analysts considered to be experts but who possess a very narrow range of knowledge pertinent to only one technology in one location. Such people certainly are valuable, but they cannot hope to help intelligence analysts meet the wide range of technical challenges they will constantly face. Arguably, intelligence analysts must understand the basics of technology, physics, and electrical engineering. But, even more important, intelligence analysts must learn to find, use, and lead true technical experts from a wide variety of fields in collaborative work sessions to bring the right technical knowledge to bear on the decision maker's problems. Perhaps a few technically minded individuals can be true technical generalists, particularly when their background and training can help analysts with less technical skills perform the heavy lifting involved in advanced analysis. But when advanced analysts and the technical generalists just mentioned need specific scientific and technical background, there needs to be a way to access such capabilities.

Since technology is neither location- nor nation-dependent, people engaged in advanced intelligence analysis have to consider global technology trends, patterns, and events. Thus, people engaging in advanced analysis have to constantly search for, locate, understand, and take advantage of technology-driven situational awareness. With this awareness, the advanced analyst can remain abreast of developing technologies or the advent of new technologies that might be brought to bear against U.S. interests or those that U.S. intelligence analysts might use to help gain informational superiority over any competitor.

It is instructive to give some thought to the importance of technology in conflict situations. Why is technical analysis invariably important in all we do? The answer, while appearing complicated, is quite simple. We are in a technical age. Many, in fact, most activities in which friendly and enemy forces participate involve technology. In fact, all sides in a conflict will compete to gain advantages through technology. Sometimes in such competition the enemy will use asymmetric technologies, which may happen to be low technology in design; at other times they will use the latest in high technology that they can easily procure off of the Internet or on the open commercial market. These adversaries will use their thoughts and technology to attempt to negate any technical advantage the United States possesses. They can best assuage such advantages by engaging the United States and its strong elements of national power in urban OEs.

The OE in which military forces plan, decide, act, assess, and adjust will always have technical implications. Thus, working with technical analysis cannot be left to happenstance; it must be purposeful, thoughtful, and designed to give friendly forces a sustained advantage. The urban terrain in which an insurgent or terrorist operates and which can influence military operations depends on technology. Often, particularly in a large city, technology has a breadth and depth breathtaking in scope. It ranges from transportation and electricity to communications, sanitation, and healthcare to individual means of accessing and sharing information.

Insurgents use technology to compete and fight with U.S. military forces. They use a variety of low-tech devices: homemade bombs, including improvised explosive devices (IEDs), which have improved exponentially in Iraq and Afghanistan; crude weapons lacking a fire direction system, such as 60 mm mortars; surface-to-surface missiles; and an endless supply of AK-47s, rocket-propelled grenades (RPGs), and machine guns, all of which are crude in comparison with the U.S. military's weapons but effective in an urban setting all the same. Although low-tech in comparison with the U.S. government's array of high technology, the insurgents' use of technology has proven effective. As insurgents become more aware of U.S. technical capabilities, they counteract with improvements in their own technologies. They learn quickly and distribute what they have learned among the fighting forces as only a flat, cellular network armed with modern communications and Internet connections can do. Furthermore, insurgents can descend into even lower rungs of low technology and still remain effective in offsetting U.S. technical prowess and advantages. Unfortunately, high technology may not overpower or even create advantages over opponents using low technology.

As an example, insurgents use the Internet to plan, learn, rehearse, coordinate, deconflict, and communicate. The insurgents also use cell phones to communicate, send instant messages, and take and transmit digital images. It follows that intelligence analysts must anticipate how the enemy uses technology to perform functions such as intelligence collection, security operations, the reporting of information (e.g., during the condition-setting operation of surveillance and intelligence collection), and the conveyance of his decisions and plans. Analysts also have to consider how the civilian populace in a particular culture uses technology to engage, perform, transact, interact, and behave, as in this information one can find clues about the enemy and his supporting network.

So, how does the advanced analyst cope with a situation in which he or she might not have requisite technical knowledge to work with technical analysis? As a starting point, the analyst works with and answers the following rhetorical questions:

- What are the technical implications of what the enemy is doing?
- Is there a technical baseline available and is it up-to-date?
- Are there technical aspects of situational, functional, biometric, and cultural observables?
- What are the technical aspects of cultural interactions, activities, transactions, and behaviors of the people who live and work in the neighborhood where insurgent activities are occurring?
- What are the technical characteristics of potential high-value or surveillance targets?

As one of the most important aspects of technical analysis, the advanced analyst must have a technical baseline. A *baseline* is a database that is, by way of a working definition, a departure point of a setting or situation in which we can measure or judge change. A *technical baseline* is a mental template with elements that serve as a normal technical standard with which to look for and find anomalies relating to technical processes, emanations, and emissions coming from a house, a portion of the infrastructure, activities, conveyances, a neighborhood, an aggregate of neighborhoods, and, in the macro, a city writ large.

There is no template that suffices for a technical baseline. Thus, until scientists and technologists develop a framework for technical baselines that analysts can use in deliberating technical intelligence in counterinsurgency operations in urban settings, analysts are left on their own to figure out what is technically important. The following list provides an example of the starting point for a technical baseline:

- Cell phone frequencies
- Heat expenditures of houses and businesses and cultural buildings
- Amperes being expended from buildings
- Water consumption
- Generator use
- Fuel sales

- Phone line usage
- TV/radio station broadcasts
- Light generation
- Electrons flowing over landlines
- Heat and cooling differentials, e.g., of a house with and without people
- Temperature of target
- Ground temperature
- Air temperature
- Refuse pile temperature
- RF energy from computers and even their clocks
- Fumes from latrines
- Fumes and smoke from refuse piles
- Smoke from cigarettes
- Sounds—metal, wood, carrying, lifting, digging, automobiles starting
- Animal excrement
- Human waste
- Music
- Cooking smells
- Energy from movement

The analyst needs a technical baseline database to understand both normalcy of technology and how technology works (visibly and invisibly) in the various interpersonal, business, and individual functions and activities in specific locations such as a neighborhood or a business. Unfortunately, any technical baseline is highly relational. That is, while some technology is generic and widespread, most technology and how people use it or receive its benefits are highly locational. This means, of course, analysts must either have a baseline of the specific area they are interested in or they must have the analytic wherewithal (time, expertise, current knowledge) to update any available technical baselines.

A usable technical baseline must be up-to-date and easily accessible. If the analysts does not have a technical baseline, they have two choices—they can build a baseline, if they have the time and expertise, or they can seek help from a VKE or the intelligence enterprise to update or build a new baseline.

Advanced intelligence analysts must always delve into specifics to use technical analysis. These specifics influence how intelligence analysts think and use technical analysis and the level of detail they are prepared to go into. As advanced analysts decompose PIR/IR, hypotheses, expectations, hunches, and mysteries into observables, they engage in specific technical parameters and statistics and consider and develop technical observables. As a reminder from earlier discussions, technical observables are observed or measured tangible or intangible properties observed or measured from identifying or recognizing technical aspects of an OE, the infrastructure

supporting a culture, and visible and invisible electronic activities and energies so much a part of any OE. Technical observables come by combining
knowledge of technologies available to U.S. military forces and interagency
organizations with knowledge of the host nation's technology and the specific use of technology among specific age groups in specific functional areas
in specific neighborhoods. This is important for tracking perpetrators but
also for providing intelligence support to information operations.

Any urban area has an infrastructure with technical particulars, characteristics, and properties. Each part of that infrastructure—including the
electrical grid, the telephone wiring, the sewage and water systems, the
healthcare network, the fire support, and the transportation framework—
relies on its own particular type of complicated technology. These technologies, by default, must enter into a decision maker's consciousness as either
something he can influence or something that can influence him. In either
situation, intelligence analysts must know and understand in depth the
engineering and technical specifics of the technologies underpinning the
infrastructure. Without such knowledge, decision makers cannot hope to
enact their desired effects and actions with consistence and anticipation of
outcome. Without technical knowledge, they could very well be the witless
victims of technologies that power the infrastructure.

Such cerebral work takes technical experts to assist advanced analysts.
As mentioned earlier, this type of expertise traditionally will not be located
on military staffs. If analysts need help, they will have to seek it outside
their headquarters. For example, how many nuclear physicists, electrical
engineers, mechanical engineers, or psychologists does a typical staff have?
The answer is, of course, none. Yet the paucity of expertise does not obviate the need for it. Therefore, commanders must access technical expertise
through their analysts and through their subsequent entrée into the world
of virtual expertise.

Preparing advanced analysts to use technical analysis should be one
aspect of intelligence mission rehearsal and rock drill system at Combat
Training Centers (CTCs). Scenarios should address technical intelligence
problems. At the forefront of helping prepare advanced analysts to employ
technical analysis, virtual SMEs should be role-playing experts from
national labs, S&T organizations, and academia emulating how technical
SMEs will help them meet the challenges of technical analysis. In addition,
technical SMEs should serve as virtual mentors to deployed analysts during
mission rehearsal preparations at home stations, before they go to any of
the CTCs, and prior to deployment to a combat zone. This mentoring relationship could continue even after the analyst deploys. If advanced analysts
cannot find a suitable expert or center of excellence to help, they do the best
they can with the machines and knowledge in their possession.

To use technical analysis in a coherent way, analysts need a conceptual
framework. This framework will help them develop sufficient technical

knowledge to support all decision-making. Some of this framework will include a working knowledge of technical functional expertise resident on their military staffs, a working knowledge of technical functional expertise that lies with interagency organizations as well as host nation and coalition country organizations in the vicinity of the deployed unit, a process for finding and integrating these needed SMEs and data scientists, and a thought process for designing and asking them to provide specific knowledge for specific questions. In this regard, intelligence analysts must rapidly find relevant knowledge expertise/support to help them understand the inner workings of technical systems and devices. This support will help in decomposing the activity under scrutiny; therefore, it has to be in sufficient depth to not only find and understand the inner workings of the technical focus of effort but to influence it. In addition, this support must identify technical observables and help analysts and machines recompose the collected data into information and knowledge for use in developing situational understanding and ultimately decision-making.

Analysts need a working knowledge of important technologies that have considerable influence at a specific location. They will, out of necessity, be most interested in the technical aspects of infrastructure. They will also be interested in the technical aspects of weapons, communications, computers, telephones, television, explosives, cameras, robots, and unmanned aerial sensors (UAS) and the technical means of tracking, moving, and distributing goods and transportation, to name just a few. Analysts will also need a perspective of how people from a particular culture and neighborhood actually use technology: how they think about technology from their own use and perspectives as well as their perception of how Americans use technology. As an important cognitive variant, the analyst must always consider the use of technical knowledge as an indirect means of influencing both populace and enemy.

TECHNOLOGY IN URBAN SETTINGS

The modern analyst must know how to think about the role of technology and the technical implications of plans, decisions, actions, outcomes, assessments, and adjustments. They must also know how to set conditions for technical analysis to occur. That is, in any situation the intelligence analyst must learn the technical, system, and information architectures at work early in any in-depth analysis. Advanced analysts must anticipate what kind of technical knowledge commanders need in different problem sets and set the stage for technical SME support. They also set up a knowledge environment to support the previously discussed organized reach back—fast, streamlined, and transparent to the user. This reach-back capability to connect with technical SMEs in an organized, robust, and disciplined way must be a part of any deployment. Advanced analysts need this capability to have a mechanism in place to search for and find technical knowledge. Analysts also need a knowledge broker to link them with the right kind of technical SMEs who posses valid bona fides, up-to-date knowledge and experience, and the credentials sufficient to truly help the deployed intelligence analyst with the intricacies of their cognitive work. This is part of technical condition-setting that all advanced analysts must learn to perform.

The analyst must think about the technological implications of what he or she is trying to find or conclude. To do so, the analyst must know the influences that technologies currently exert or those that may influence a decision maker's efforts to accomplish missions or impose effects upon an opponent, on other competitors, on a host nation, and on neutrals. The analyst must ponder how the enemy thinks about and leverages technology to achieve technical advantages and engage the enemy in his quest to achieve technical superiority. The analyst must also consider the enemy's creative use of technologies in the race for decision advantage and initiative. In this effort, the skilled analyst will use pattern, link, and trend analysis to help portend what might be the next step in an enemy's use of technology and how a friendly force might influence that step.

The engaged advanced intelligence analyst will consider how a host nation populace uses technology in their personal daily lives (at their homes) as well as in their political, social, economic, legal, educational, religious, infrastructure, and information interactions, transactions, and situations. In particular, it is imperative for the intelligence analyst to understand the basic technologies supporting a host nation's infrastructure, since the functionality of infrastructure is a key variable in the struggle for the hearts and minds of the populace. The infrastructure, though, even in the most primitive of societies, can be frightfully complicated and well beyond the knowledge capabilities of intelligence analysts (and perhaps even beyond the technical staff such as communications people and engineers).

The intelligence analyst must know the basic physics and technologies of weapons the enemy is using, particularly the parts of homemade explosive devices, whether they are IEDs, land mines, or suicide bombers' explosives vests. The analyst must understand the technology the enemy puts to use in building explosive devices, the technology he uses in implanting or placing such devices and detonating them, and the information and sensor technologies used by the enemy's support network. Such understanding is important not only to negate the effects of the insurgents' technology, but also to anticipate how he will set conditions to use it.

Technology also plays a large role in insurgent missions, such as in conducting reconnaissance and HUMINT operations, long before direct action missions. This technical knowledge supports anticipation by helping the advanced analyst understand technical support the enemy must use to *set conditions for future attacks*. With such detailed and specific knowledge and understanding, the advanced intelligence analyst possesses an important way of anticipating and denying future enemy attacks. Thus, part of the detailed decomposition work involves the specifications of the technologies the enemy might be using or planning to use.

The advanced intelligence analyst knows a lot about technology in planning, executing, assessing, and adjusting effects and conjoined actions on the enemy, populace, neutrals, and competitors. Such knowledge has two perspectives. It helps to understand how the enemy uses technology. In addition, it helps the analyst to understand how knowing technology helps him or her design friendly uses of technology to create effects and actions. Understanding technical knowledge has several additional perspectives:

- *First,* if the decision maker wants to influence mechanical network nodes, someone on the staff has to know the mechanical aspects of the node in question to a significant level of detail sufficient to design the activities to create the desired influence. This knowledge must extend to how the node works, where the node draws its sources of energy, and how the node and its parts relate to possible second- and third-order effects if destroyed or perturbed.
- *Second,* the intelligence analyst must know and understand the technology of the intended target well enough to design actions—tangible and intangible—that will create desired effects.
- *Third,* the intelligence analyst must know the technology that makes the target function, its influences on the target, and its relationships with other, transitory, or peripheral mechanical devices well enough to design outcome-assessment operations.
- *Fourth,* the intelligence analyst must understand the technology of the target well enough to understand what outcomes—tangible and intangible—will be observable.
- *Fifth,* the intelligence analyst must know the technology in question well enough to understand how influencing pieces of the whole could lead to undesirable outcomes and what actions could mitigate the force and influence of those outcomes.
- *Sixth,* the intelligence analyst has to know target technology well enough to identify indirect approaches to those targets.

As an example, if an advanced intelligence analyst is working against a nuclear production site, that analyst would have to understand the technology of the site well enough to comprehend each functioning part of the system. This breadth of understanding would require knowledge of software, hardware, and safety equipment maintenance requirements; mean time between failure; key or decisive points in the system; how one might overtly or covertly influence the system; and maintenance, logistics, human services (food, water, shelter, medical care, communications) and custodian requirements essential to successful operation of the nuclear node. The details of the intelligence analysis would even include identifying and locating the living areas of all workers, from the engineers to the janitors and cooks required for maintenance and services.

The intelligence analyst using advanced analysis must keep several things in mind when pondering the best use of technical analysis. Analysts cannot become mentally lazy and put aside technical problems owing to the complexity of the situation or their own basic ignorance. Analysts have to be both humble and confident to the extent of admitting a need for assistance and persevering to find the right knowledge and the right subject matter expert to help gain advantages in technology. Intelligence analysts have to realize they are in a race to the future against people who want to use technology to gain advantage and do harm to U.S. forces and coalition partners. Advanced analysts have to gain access to higher skilled, more creative, and more aggressive technical SMEs than the enemy possesses and also have access to better, more up-to-date knowledge than either the enemy or other competitors.

The U.S. military cannot assume it will always be superior to others in using technology—such arrogance could result in deleterious outcomes. Arrogance in technical analysis is extraordinarily dangerous, because when analysts become arrogant they tend to make false assumptions, their minds close to new ideas, and they engage in specious reasoning. Instead, people have to be honest and humble, recognizing that at times others will have advantages in either applied or new technologies. Enlightened advanced intelligence analysts must anticipate the future technological advantages an enemy might come to possess. These analysts will use a virtual community of SMEs and knowledge bases to figure out how to recognize ascendancy and superiority of a particular technical knowledge and how to negate or offset any advantages the technology might bring to our competitors.

As a final aspect of discussing technical analysis, we need to identify some of its difficulties and then discuss ways to overcome them. Technical challenges are not insurmountable. But, to work with them, analysts must know the challenges or problems, and they must have a strategy in mind for succeeding. As mentioned earlier, electrical and mechanical engineers, medical doctors, knowledge engineers, and data scientists will rarely be found in a tactical military headquarters. Yet, it is precisely these kinds of experts advanced analysts need for helping them perform the difficult cognitive and knowledge work of the modern analyst. So, what is an analyst to do?

As a first step, advanced analysts must know if they have the requisite knowledge or experience to perform the specific technical analysis required. This is an analytic challenge of the first order. It takes serious and honest introspection about their ability to think and know about the inner world of technology. To use technical analysis, advanced analysts will often need to use technical SMEs. Analysts can find military scientists in places like the National Ground Intelligence Center (NGIC). They can also seek such support in the interagency, the intelligence enterprise, and in a VKE. The analyst can also seek scientists and engineers from the host nation in which they are working. To increase the possibility of finding the right kind of technical support, analysts must know their problem set, ask the right question, and request the right technical expertise. A knowledge broker in a supporting VKE can help analysts decide upon the right question and the right level of expertise required for the problem at hand.

The analyst must be mentally organized. As such, they need to use a technical analysis thought template to help them think about this difficult subject in sufficient depth to leverage its amazing potential. To check their own thinking, they should engage in critical thinking with help from a VKE, red-teaming people, and intelligence wargaming specialists who can check the analysts' thinking and critically assess their hypotheses, hunches, expectations, and mysteries.

As a second problem, collection is very difficult against urban technical observables and signatures. This difficulty arises from developing the right technical observables, finding the collectors that meet the sometimes arduous standards of the tactical advanced analyst (timeliness, specificity, accuracy, relevance, and clarity), and finding and tasking the right mix of collectors to work against the invisible world of technology.

To improve analytic performance in the area of working with collection experts to collect information against technical targets, the analyst must use technical experts to decompose their information requirement into technical observables and crosswalk those observables with the others—cultural, functional, situational, and biometric. They will undoubtedly find analytic relationships among all five kinds of observables. The analyst and collection team will also need the support of technologists to match the technical observables with collection. Single collectors will not usually accomplish what is needed. Measurement and signatures intelligence (MASINT) will often be a key ingredient for technical analysis and collection requirements. Therefore, the analyst and collection team must work with technical people to use the right ground and air MASINT, in optimum mixes, at the right time and place to look for the right technical observables.

Technical collection will often require the combination of many collection capabilities. Even with optimum mixes, technical collection will often yield only "snippets" or wisps of data that will require fast fusing and expert interpretation. This machine and cognitive effort is called "recomposition" in advanced analysis parlance (recomposition will be discussed in depth in Chapter Seventeen). In this process and when turning resultant information into knowledge, technical experts will work with deployed analysts to make sense of data and eventually synthesize it into knowledge. As another way to help, advanced analysts will have to keep collection positions, people, and organizations informed of what they are looking for in a high degree of detail at the start of and during the actual collection effort.

They will also have to work with collection people to design data flows to meet standards of timeliness and specificity. In addition, all technical collection will need to communicate, tip, and cue with other types of collection. All collection will have to have a pathway for "coming to life," communicating among themselves in a tip and cue role, and sending data back to the DCGS or a cut-out server that is used for cleansing potentially dirty data.

As a third and final challenge, the advanced analyst must learn to think like the enemy. They will need to answer the following questions and understand the subsequent answers:

- *What is my perception of U.S. technical collection?* The enemy will assume American technology is very good. He will assume the American intelligence system will hear and see his activities unless he takes supreme acts of precaution. Thus, the U.S. analyst must anticipate the steps the enemy might take when thinking this way and when worrying about U.S. technical capabilities to find him as he performs his duties. But, he will also believe that the U.S. technical intelligence system will have blind spots, and he will take advantage of them, e.g., poor HUMINT to see very discreet occurrences of activities. In this respect, the enemy will assume U.S. technical collection cannot do things well in urban settings and that U.S. commanders rely too much on technical collection that is not always effective in urban settings.
- *How can I hide from his sensors?* He may conclude that he should not talk on the cell phone. He could choose to move only at night and then in the shadows if on foot or intermixed with other cars if driving an auto or taking mass transit. He will be careful about technical signatures, and he may use computers only from an Internet café, moving from machine to machine, and then only with semiotic codes and symbols on selected Web sites.
- *What will the Americans do technically that can cause my failure, and how might I surreptitiously counteract these efforts?* He will worry that the American intelligence system can pick up on subtle technical signatures and observables, watch specific houses or places for technical observables, and track cell phone transmissions. He will work hard to develop early warning and to design effective countermeasures.
- *Can the Americans' technology see me moving at night?* He will conclude—yes. Thus, he will stay in the shadows and mask his movements with other activities and disguise specific condition-setting activities.
- *Will I emit technical observables while the United States is looking for me?* He will conclude—yes. He will conclude the range of technical observables is vast—from cell phones, to television, to Internet traffic, to heat emissions, to thermal imaging, to use of technology from the infrastructure. This will make him wary and inclined to see and use low-tech solutions to communication and condition-setting challenges.

- *What is the best way to use technology to provide early warning of danger?* He will choose to use a mix of high- and low-technology and will rely heavily on HUMINT. But, that does not mean he will not use technology. Some of the technology he will use to provide security, intelligence collection, early warning, and countersurveillance includes cameras, IR alarms, texting, watchers with cell phones and magnification (day and night optics), and noise makers triggered to alert mechanisms.
- *How will I preclude the United States from finding the technical indications of my countersurveillance?* The smart insurgent will conclude that he must reduce his dependence on high technology and go to lower and older forms of technology. He will minimize use of technology and will use throw away phones. He will limit movement to important meetings or through the use of people to support his network. He will have supporters show up very early in the morning. The enemy will use low technology—semiotics, runners, and couriers—to overcome what he attributes to be U.S. technical collection capabilities.
- *Can the Americans use their technical sensors to detect the technical aspects of my resupply operations?* The answer will be yes. So, what will he do? He will limit movement of key vehicles unless embedded in normal traffic flows. He will limit communications. He will emplace supply vehicles in storage sheds.
- *How will I communicate so the U.S. intelligence people won't notice?* He will use semiotics, runners, couriers, carriers, and suppliers from the populace. He will think through the errors his supporters could make and set up alerts if they do make such technical mistakes. This enemy will also learn to set up deceptive technical aspects of supporting networks to confuse and slow U.S. intelligence and decision-making.

This chapter has introduced the notion of technical analysis. It is important to the advanced analyst for two reasons. *First,* the well-hidden insurgent must use some kind of technology, and its use cannot be totally obscured. *Second,* technology is important to the center of gravity in all insurgencies—the populace. How the populace thinks about technology and uses it is critically important not only for helping to locate the enemy but to assist in winning the hearts and minds of the population. The overall challenge of using technical analysis is, of course, finding the technical needle in a technical haystack of hundreds of needles. This is a difficult endeavor that is so complex it may escape the scrutiny of analysts and master analysts.

Interestingly, technical analysis is not new—signals intelligence (SIGINT), geospatial intelligence (GEOINT), technical intelligence (TECHINT), and MASINT specialists have been engaging in technical intelligence for years. What is new is the notion of purposefully -

developing technical observables to task a variety of collectors. What is new is the codified and disciplined use of technical analysis to decompose information requirements into the aforementioned observables, figure out what technical collectors or even HUMINT can best collect against the observables, and make sense of resultant data to turn into information and knowledge. What is new is the purposeful emphasis on technical intelligence to help make visible a sphere or world in a city that is largely invisible but immanently important in the chess game advanced analysts play with their highly skilled insurgent adversary. What is new is the notion that deployed analysts neither possess nor have at their disposal the wherewithal to find the right kind of expertise to help them use high-grade technical analysis to decompose requirements, to task collection and to engage in sense-making.

The insurgent will, of course, know U.S. intelligence services are looking for him all the time. He will also know that he must use technology, but the smart ones will be wary of its overuse. Thus, the wily insurgent will do several things to protect himself that the analyst using technical intelligence must know and understand:

> *First,* the insurgents will ambiguate their use of technology. As such, they will intermix their use of technology with the thousands of legitimate uses constantly occurring in a large urban setting.
>
> *Second,* they will use the dependence of the Americans on their technologies to be able to find patterns and to attack. T. E. Lawrence in *Seven Pillars of Wisdom* thought this to be so important in conducting insurgent operations that he made it one of the six principles for success.[3]
>
> *Third,* the insurgent will attempt to use a mixture of high- and low-tech approaches. For example, he might use cell phones, but he also might use a courier and a small, old-fashioned tape recorder for transmitting guidance to another cell.

The chapter made the important point about the necessary interaction between "what to think" about technology as well as "how to think" about technology and its influences. The how-to-think approach is particularly apropos to comprehending and visualizing in one's mind's eye the invisible world of technology and its manifestations. In this regard, the chapter advocates that analysts use a short model to help them with how to think about technology in a large urban setting. That is, to use the model of how people and organizations use technology to interact, act, transact, and behave. This aspect of technical analysis fits snugly with the need to use technical templates so as to facilitate anomaly analysis.

When faced with the double whammy of a need to possess scientific and engineering knowledge in order to use technical analysis and the need to use it against an adaptive, smart, and technologically savvy foe, the analyst has several techniques that the chapter discussed. The techniques can best be understood via rhetorical questions such as the following:

- What are the technological indicators of what we think the enemy is doing or planning to do?
- Is there a technical baseline available and is it up-to-date and accessible to me?
- Are there technical aspects and implications of situational, biometric, functional, and cultural observables?
- What are the technical aspects of cultural interaction, activities, transactions, and behaviors of people who live and work in the neighborhood in question?
- What are the technical aspects of the enemy's networks?
- What are the technical aspects of potential high-value targets (HVTs) and other surveillance targets, e.g., enemy condition-setting to attack a key element of the infrastructure supporting the city in question?

The chapter extolled the importance of the infrastructure. To know and understand the infrastructure, the intelligence analyst must understand the technical characteristics and integration of that infrastructure. In many ways, this supposition presents a vexing challenge to the analyst, as every infrastructure is different, which compounds the knowledge complexity requirements. The analyst must seek and find the support of SMEs—U.S. and indigenous engineers—to help with this kind of knowledge and understanding.

The enemy must use technology in his condition-setting before any kind of action he plans. Thus, technical analysis is closely entwined with anticipatory analysis, and both figure prominently in the continuous struggle for the initiative. This type of relationship is so important that the analyst must learn to meet the knowledge and thinking requirements in all mission rehearsal training at home station and at the combat training centers.

The analysts must realize their strengths and limitations when attempting to use technical analysis. The worst possible tack, however, is to avoid using technical analysis all together because the analyst might not have the requisite knowledge and experience to do so. Thus, they must be introspective and then knowledgeable of the intelligence enterprise and VKE to seek and find the right kind of experts to help in designing the use of technical analysis. The analyst will also be perplexed by the dizzying array of possible technical sensors that might be of use in collecting against technical targets. Once again, experts can help in this matter, and they can be found in the intelligence enterprise or at a stateside VKE. As another challenge, the analyst must realize that technical collection will never represent a total picture or the "truth" even when focused and empowered by the best possible technical observables. Instead, the outputs of such collection will be snippets and wisps that the analysts and their cognitive assistants must weave into a whole of meaning. Up-to-date technical baseline databases will assist in this function. Lastly, it is challenging to think like the enemy to the extent of how he intends to use technology and to mask its use. Thus, the analyst must seek the help of people very knowledgeable of both the enemy and of his use of technology as well as U.S. technical collection capabilities. Seeking and finding people to help in this matter is a significant requirement.

As a final note, technical analysis figures prominently in successful employment of tendency analysis. In fact, tendency analysis needs technical analysis to perform at its best. Thus, it is fitting that this chapter on technical analysis be followed by tendency analysis.

12

Tendency Analysis[1]

*Definition: Discerning meaning through thought and study of the general pro-
clivities of people, the behavioral and action inclinations of organizations,
mental snapshots of current environment or contextual situations, events,
activities, behaviors, the emanation dispersal of energy emissions, and what
the interaction and enmeshing of all could portend for the future.*

THE IMPORTANCE OF TENDENCY ANALYSIS

Tendency analysis involves inclinations of the subconscious and its workings. Imagine driving down a busy freeway when suddenly you know,
instinctively, that the person ahead of you is going to make a move. You do
not know for certain what move the person will make, but you are certain
it will be made all the same. How do you know that such a move or action
is coming? Or when encountering a detour while driving, why do we let our
subconscious lead us into an unknown area or street to get around whatever has been causing the detour, following "guidance" from something so
unscientific or, at the very least, so difficult to describe? Or what is it that
causes us to sense when someone is going to say something when there is
no indication they are going to do so. But we know all the same they will
be saying something, and we have a good idea of what it is they will say.
These are tendencies. Tendencies also involve the subatomic level of
physics. In this world of the minute, many things happen that suggest the
validity of including tendency analysis as a vital part of advanced analysis.
In this world, physicist Fritjof Capra tells us,

At the subatomic level, matter does not exist with certainty at definite places, but rather shows "tendencies to exist," and atomic events do not occur with certainty at definite times and in definite ways, but rather show "tendencies to occur . . . We can never predict an atomic event with certainty; we can say only how likely it is to happen . . . At the subatomic level, the solid material objects of classical physics dissolve into wavelike patterns of probabilities, and these patterns, ultimately, do not represent probabilities of things, but rather probabilities of interconnections.[2]

The human being (in our case the intelligence analyst) comes into play in this world. As such, Capra helps us once again to understand an abstract, complex subject by stating,

As we penetrate into matter, nature does not show us any isolated "basic building blocks," but rather appears as a complicated web of relations between the various parts of the whole. These relations always include the observer in an essential way. The human observer constitutes the final link in the chain of observational processes, and the properties of any atomic object can be understood only in terms of the object's interaction with the observer.[3]

These thoughts from Dr. Capra provide several corollary thoughts in our work with intelligence analysis. *First*, what the observer, whether a HUMINT agent or an analyst watching a flat-panel display, thinks about, watches for, and sees makes a great difference when looking for, noticing, and interpreting small, vague moves or activities. *Second*, there is a world of energy, relationships, and movement that is invisible. It is in this invisible world that tendencies occur. They manifest as slight changes tied to a moment in time and a particular place. *Third*, these relationships can be and will be perturbed. Nonetheless, the analyst and collector have to know what they are looking for to spot the microchanges.

As an illustration applicable to modern intelligence analysis, consider a HUMINT case officer in a Middle Eastern city who knows a particular street is "dirty" without any outward manifestations of illicit activity. When asked why or how he knows this, the officer answers that he really does not know—he just senses it. As a final illustration of tendency analysis, why is an Army noncommissioned officer (NCO) who has been leading patrols in Baghdad for nine months aware of danger when most of us see no such signs. When we ask him how he knows a street or neighborhood is dangerous or safe at any given time, he says "I don't know how, I just know." He cannot describe why, but knows there is danger all the same.

What do all of these scenarios have in common? *First*, tendencies occur and surface in the subconscious. They cause us to act certain ways. *Second*, people make decisions and act on what their subconscious is telling them.

Third, something is input into the subconscious that creates tendencies. In the examples above—in each scenario—the actors received inputs over time, and their personal subconscious discerned normal from abnormal, safety from danger, and truth from deceptive data, information, and eventually knowledge. *Fourth*, tendencies generally relate to experience. Over time we see things and process them in our subconscious; they form the basis for questions, musings, patterns, trends, and alarms. Within our subconscious we categorize and compare. If something is out of place or not "normal," our individual subconscious sends a message to our conscious mind, and we choose to respond or ignore. *Fifth*, tendencies relate strongly to both intuition and creativity. Thus, the intelligence analyst must not only have access to data as a stimulant for using tendency analysis, he or she must also use their own creative energies and

> bring into maximum contact the problem specification, the data, and one's own store of experience and expertise; allowing these to resonate together as intimately and as flexibly as possible, so that the full range of meaning and possibility of both current data and past experience are extracted. The good intuitive is the person who is ready, willing, and able to make a lot out of a little.[4]

How does this discussion relate to tendency analysis and fighting insurgents and terrorists? The answer is quite simple: Tendency analysis helps analysts know what to look for by way of subtle, nuanced indicators, signatures, and observables that lead to well-hidden and well-protected terrorists and their potential activities. Tendency analysis helps analysts anticipate an enemy's next moves and the activities and actions associated with such moves or activities. If analysts can determine tendencies beforehand, they will be equipped with the wherewithal to know and understand the most subtle and nuanced observables to watch for when looking for specific things at specific times and specific locations to form hypotheses, decompose those hypotheses, and develop functional and cultural observables to guide collection activities. In this regard, tendencies enable people to project where a car will be swerving, where the dirty streets are, and where danger could be lurking. It enables the human being to start to understand how, why, and where the enemy's networks will morph next and gives them the wherewithal to watch for signs confirming hypotheses involving the morphing.

THEORY BEHIND TENDENCY ANALYSIS

Actions, activities, and manifestations of energy emanating from people, machines, organizations, and networks generally begin in the subconscious. They appear in our conscious as thoughts, suggestions, implications, inference, and actions. Because tendency processes occur in the subconscious, their emergence only becomes known and clear to our conscious with extreme mental effort. But something is there. Something tells the beat cop that a robbery is going to occur without seeing anything truly specific. Something tells the HUMINT case officer that a street where a dead drop is going to occur is not safe when there is nothing specific to tell him so. Something tells the experienced squad leader leading a patrol against insurgents in a city that an attack is imminent when there is nothing specific to which he can connect his feeling of impending danger.

This "something," as discussed above, is what we are after with tendency analysis. This "something" involves energy, an anomaly, a movement, a slight change, an almost imperceptible activity, a cell phone call that is out of place, a sudden text message alert in a seemingly deserted alley, and, of course, the null—that is something expected or normal that does not appear or occur. This "something" is tendency analysis.

As a derivative thought, could it be that an upcoming event comes into being through even the minutest mental or physical activities of the participant? The central idea of tendency analysis comes forth in the following passage by some renowned physicists:

> May the universe in some strange sense be "brought into being" by the participation of those who participate? . . . The vital act is the act of participation. "Participator" is the incontrovertible new concept given by quantum mechanics.[5]

What this passage implies is the mere presence of perpetrators engaging in the mental act of planning and the physical acts of sustaining their network and setting conditions for attacks cause tendencies to occur.

Advanced analysts are interested in the indicants of future insurgent or even populace activities or actions or the presence of an enemy condition-setting operation that causes such a small ripple in a societal sea of movement that the activity means nothing to the uninformed or inexperienced person. The advanced analyst wants to tap into the slight and subtle changes and shifts in an OE that typically inputs into a human's subconscious and rarely makes its way into the conscious. The advanced analyst wants to tap into the world of quantum mechanics, for it is there that tendencies either exist or come to life. In this respect, author Gary Zukav provides us some insight into quantum mechanics by stating

> Quantum mechanics views subatomic particles as "tendencies to exist" or "tendencies to happen." How strong these tendencies are is expressed in terms of probabilities. A subatomic particle is a quantum, which means a quantity of something. What that something is, however, is a matter of speculation . . . the tendencies of subatomic phenomena . . . become manifest under certain conditions.[6]

But if an impending action becomes intuitively visible to people in whose neighborhoods the activity is occurring or soon to happen to the point of causing them to change their normal activities or to sense danger, it becomes a harbinger of action. This is a harbinger the advanced analyst wants to know about and follow, if nothing else, as an analytic mystery. Examples of such a harbinger could be a car parked with its wheels pointed in instead of out, a semiotic symbol that suddenly appears on a wall near an alley, or an absence of rugs being hung out to air at a usual time. Without knowing why, a mother might change the play patterns of her children because her subconscious is screaming that something is wrong and potentially dangerous.

The advanced analyst wants to know what these subtle and almost invisible observables mean. The analyst wants to anticipate action or behavior from the data being collected by collectors specifically watching for such specific observables. This is not some strange Freudian psychobabble. No, it is something that truly happens, and with thought, we can not only anticipate tendencies as they are about to happen and when happening, but our commanders can intercede to change or shape the outcome of the tendency's power. Author Malcolm Gladwell helps us think about this process with the following passage from the book *Blink*:

> [T]he adaptive unconscious, and the study of this kind of decision making is one of the most important new fields in psychology . . . The new notion of the adaptive unconscious is thought of . . . as a giant computer that quickly and quietly processes a lot of the data we need in order to keep functioning as human beings. When you walk out into the street and suddenly realize that a truck is bearing down on you, do you have time to think through all your options? Of course not.[7]

With such knowledge, the advanced analyst and his or her collection partner, working as a unified team, have something to focus on to disambiguate that portion of the neighborhood and to have their sensors and HUMINT source watch for the right activities at the right time. If advanced analysts can use tendency analysis correctly, they can produce knowledge that allows their commander to get ahead of the enemy's decision cycle and to preempt his condition-setting or attack execution before it can be brought to bear as a mature and dangerous action.

Thus, tendency analysis is very important to successful advanced analysis cognitive operations. Because of the complexity of the OE, the capability of the enemy to hide and blend, and the mental prowess of an enemy embedded in the culture, tendency analysis is important not only for direct action, but for focusing our analysis and collection to find suggestive and incriminating observables of enemy (or their network supporters') transactions, interactions, activities, and behaviors. With tendency analysis, we presage the enemy's actions by purposefully looking for and noticing small, imperceptible perturbations in a sea of normalcy, looking for and noticing the enemy's essential but subtle, well-hidden network activities and a neighborhood's or businesses' responses to those activities. When we use tendency analysis, we scour a neighborhood to compare what we see with three kinds of baselines—technical, functional, and cultural—and detect and identify even miniscule changes.

Tendencies appear as a situation unfolds, as people or organizations engage in interactions, activities, and transactions, and when they behave in a certain way. Tendencies often appear when condition-setting, direct actions, second- and third-order effects, friction (Clausewitzian), and accidents happen. Tendencies also come forth from the purposeful activities of U.S. intelligence people, machines, and organizations. That is, U.S. intelligence people and their partners (such as coalition or host nation governmental agencies) can either change the surroundings or perturb the enemy's network purposefully or accidentally to cause tendencies to surface. Tendencies can also occur as the result of both enemy and friendly condition-setting. Further, when tendencies do occur, their vibration or actual change can show in any of the three baselines upon which tendency analysis depends. In addition, tendencies are highly susceptible to perturbation caused by the conjoining of sensitive variables with always lurking windows of opportunity.

Tendency analysis is vital to winning the war of wits against a highly skilled and well-hidden enemy. Our goal is, of course, to outthink the enemy in and across every domain at all times. But, in a strange land, working against smart, well-hidden insurgents who are embedded in a population that often is opposed to U.S. troops and activities and who use a very capable network, this goal is difficult to achieve. Tendency analysis can help us achieve an intellectual advantage over any insurgent or irregular.

When we do not have the option to decline such mental engagement with a wily foe, how might we proceed? While not easy, tendency analysis can be a useful part of an advanced analyst's strategy and tool kit. For example, if we use tendency analysis to presage enemy activities and link both tangible and intangible direct action to preempt and usurp his intentions with our own, we can seize the initiative from him. As he attempts to adjust, he becomes more visible, enabling us to be continuously setting conditions to use tendencies to get ahead of his decision processes. As he becomes more visible through our efforts, we can anticipate his options and cover those most feasible with our ISR (including HUMINT) to confirm or deny our resultant analytic expectations. All along, we are setting conditions to keep the decision-making initiative by anticipating his next moves with the aggressive help of tendency analysis. Continuing along this line of thought, we can use tendency analysis to anticipate his trickery via deception. His attempts to deceive will be translucent as we use tendency analysis, and with it, spot the very subtle activities that will differentiate between truth and deceit. In addition, we can disturb his emotions and use such disturbance to decrease his belief in the viability of his own plans. We can slow his decision-making—enemy decision entropy is a positive aspect of tendency analysis for our decision makers. Finally, we can plant in the enemy leader's mind the notion that we are smarter, have better analysis and collection capabilities that will not let him hide or deceive us. We can lead him to believe that we have far better and faster decision-making capabilities than him, thereby enabling us to be ahead of his moves in every situation. Tendency analysis provides us the capabilities to dominate his thoughts because of their supposed impenetrability and inaccessibility to any people other than the most astute indigenous person.

People with direct experience in a neighborhood can often identify tendencies. They might not call the slight disturbances or perturbations tendencies, but they feel both consciously and subconsciously that something is wrong or out of place. Sometimes, however, very intuitive people with no experience in a particular place or doing a particular activity can also discern tendencies. Sometimes they recognize something is amiss, but their sensing becomes completely smothered by a tangle of space we call the subconscious.

Tendency analysis depends on the presence of three kinds of baselines as mentioned above—technical, cultural, and functional. But as part of our inquiry, we have to ask why baselines are so important to tendency analysis? The answer lies in comprehending what is normal so as to understand what is anomalous or abnormal. As a first step, let us review our working definitions of baselines and discuss how they influence tendency analysis. A *technical baseline* is a mental template with elements that serve as a normal technical standard with which to look for and find anomalies relating to technical processes, emanations, and emissions coming from a house, a portion of the infrastructure, activities, conveyances, a neighborhood, an aggregate of neighborhoods, and, in the macro, a city writ large. If tendencies are at work, slight fluctuations that are ever so brief or even periodic and lengthy will appear and disappear. A series of cell phone calls each occurring for 5 seconds when there usually are no cell phone calls serve as an example of a technical baseline deviation. A *functional baseline* is a mental template with elements that serve as a normal functional standard with which to look for and find differences relating to functions or the assigned actions, duties, and activities required or expected of a person or group processes. A person delivering something to a house when there are not usually deliveries serves to illustrate an example of a functional baseline deviation. A *cultural baseline* is a mental template that serves as a standard relating to the shared knowledge and values of an element of a society by which things in a particular neighborhood are measured or compared denoting or deriving from or distinctive of the ways of living of a distinctive group of people. Children not playing as they normally would is an example of a cultural baseline deviation. With this line of reasoning, it follows that there will be subtle differences arising in interactions, transactions, activities, and behaviors if tendencies are at work in a culturally endowed neighborhood. It is just as obvious that advanced analysts must use tendency analysis to drive the collection and to drive recomposition and synthesis to use tendencies to our advantage.

While tendency analysis looks for what is anomalous, it differs from another similar aspect of advanced analysis—*anomaly analysis*. Let us examine very briefly the differences between tendency and anomaly analysis to clarify our thinking. Tendency analysis is a snapshot in time. Anomaly analysis involves thinking about the past and about the future. As such, it is more inclusive than tendency analysis. Tendency analysis involves bringing into being what normally occurs only in a person's subconscious. Anomaly analysis is purposeful and deliberately conscious efforts to systematically differentiate normal from abnormal. Tendency analysis is generally extremely subtle and nuanced. Anomaly analysis may involve subtleties but also involves obvious differences between normal and abnormal. Tendency analysis most often involves a very specific location, such as a small portion of a neighborhood, while anomaly analysis can involve larger areas as well as entire neighborhoods or even a city.

Tendency analysis is closely related to *synthesis*. In fact, to perform tendency analysis, analysts must engage in synthesis at the front of the analytic process as well as its finality. It is through synthesis that tendencies first appear in the analyst's thought process. The analyst (often with the help of indigenous and functional SMEs) develops a mental snapshot of an alley, or a neighborhood, a residence, or a business, with respect to functions, technologies, culture, biometrics, and the context or situation. He or she pulls together these seemingly disparate elements and weaves them into a whole, which is the process of synthesis. The analyst decomposes the whole of tendency into observables, which go into the collection system. Once resultant data starts returning, the analyst first recomposes data to develop information and synthesizes information into actionable knowledge. More discussion about this important relationship will occur in Chapter 18, on synthesis.

Tendency analysis is also related to another element of advanced analysis—*trend analysis*—but the difference between the two lies in the mental and subconscious functions of the mind. Trends come forth from studying the past—activities, bombings, movements, etc.—to create a potential straight line into the future. Trend analysis uses an if-then logic: If *x* events in the past occurred, then *y* events in the future will occur. Tendency analysis, on the other hand, deals with the nature of what *might* happen, that is, to anticipate possibilities by understanding an affinity for something that is happening or not happening at a particular snapshot in time. Tendency analysis, therefore, does not generally involve that straight-line, linear thought of trend analysis and does not depend upon a detailed and richly recorded chronological past. It does do creative and exponential analysis to deduce what could be going to happen from a snapshot in time and ranging across a wider variety of creative possibilities. In addition, tendency analysis involves intuition, experience, and the culling of subtle snippets of data and abstruse changes in a particular location—the subtle cultural anomalies one ingests into the subconscious—to identify or recognize a future state of affairs or an event that may or may not appear on a straight line curve. An event prognosticated through tendency analysis can be anticipated through extrapolation or by making an off-the-wall creative mental leap.

But a problem remains: We cannot peer into another person's subconscious anymore than we can peer into our own. Unfortunately, this is where the bits and pieces and tangles of data and information lie, organized for recall only by a very unruly and disorganized subconscious. How can people start working with tendencies existing in their own subconscious minds as well as in others' minds? Several steps can help.

- Understand the phenomenon of tendency analysis and learn to use its powers.
- Put forth a significant effort to work with and talk to people who have experienced the challenge or problem under discussion. Spend time in debriefing, walking through simulated terrain in the areas being worked and "known to be dirty or dangerous," and coax out the bits and pieces of data and information contributing to the tendency in question.
- Study tendencies and experiment with their development, tasking into traditional and nontraditional sensor work and understanding forthcoming data as being related to and giving insights into tendency analysis.
- Use intelligence concept developers to ask people experienced in various aspects of counterinsurgency problem sets to visit their experiences and perceptions, via simulation and changing context, to notice what caused dissonance and subsequent decisions. Conduct structured interviews with these people, using well-thought-out questions, continually probing until identifying what caused the responder to conclude the street was dirty or dangerous. Ask participants to jot down anything that might have been out of place: actions a child took that aroused suspicion, a car's tires being turned out instead of in toward the curb, shades being pulled when normally open, women being covered when normally uncovered, absence of music and conversation when the norm is conversation and music, and so forth.
- Use models to help understand the influence of the phenomena of tendencies, which any force has to acknowledge, specifically on the enemy. Technologists can model some of the major functions and

activities terrorists and insurgents have to engage in to plan, gather supplies, collect HUMINT, rehearse, recruit, obtain materials, learn, communicate, hide, deceive, move, and so forth. They can feed into these models the specifics coming from debriefings and from working with very experienced people to unlock the practicality of tendency analysis. They can also work with people to gather the data they require for modeling, including analytic specialists, indigenous experts or ordinary people, interrogators, captured terrorists and insurgents, experienced case officers, anthropologists, indigenous police, multinational corporation people, patrol leaders, psychologists and psychiatrists with insurgency and terrorist experience, and counterterror analysts. Through these simulations they will be able to bring the context to the people whose subconscious we are trying to peer into and open the door into those subconscious so we can understand what is occurring and use such understanding to design cultural, situational, or functional observables and apply tendency analysis to recomposition and synthesis.

• Use data mining and knowledge discovery to identify patterns extant in the OE to design observables and to understand events. As people progress in their thinking, they bring forth patterns and trends that help in understanding the indications or observables leading to tendency analysis and thus to developing implications. From these implications analysts can probe into the consciousness of people to help them know why they knew something intuitively or subconsciously. Specifically, analysts can use organic or VKE data mining to reconstruct the data world, GIS three-dimensional (3D) simulation to reconstruct the visual world, and M&S to reconstruct the subconscious world, which together help the responder identify why he might have concluded a particular street was dangerous, why a person believed to be a perpetrator was hiding in a particular building, why a U.S. Army NCO knew an ambush was about to take place or that a mine was planted nearby, and so forth.

As the reader has undoubtedly surmised, tendency analysis is one of the most intellectually arduous aspects of advanced analysis. At best, it is abstract. At worst, it seems impenetrable owing to its clinging relationship to the subconscious and its manifestations as extremely subtle changes and perturbations in an existing snapshot in time that portend how the enemy may be acting or reacting. Thus, we need to delve into some of the major challenges in dealing with tendency analysis and some of the ways these challenges can be overcome. Some of the challenges when using tendency analysis include the following:

• Understand tendency analysis well enough to use it on a continuum when it is so abstract and complex.
• Finding and using constantly updating baselines.

- Discerning how to think about tendency analysis—front-end decomposition, back-end recomposition, and synthesis.
- Designing a strategy to "pull" the minute specifics of activities submerged in the subconscious of people that can be useful in designing tendency analysis observables.
- Bringing into comprehension the identification and then the understanding of tendencies seemingly invisible to Americans but not necessarily to people who have grown up in and lived in a particular neighborhood all their lives.
- Using tendency analysis to design the right observables to recognize the enemy's or the populace's subtle changes and perturbations owing to impending activity or action.
- Finding and using the optimum mix of sensors and HUMINT to watch for the right observables at the right time to notice the right activities that can lend understanding to abstruse happenings.
- Finding the current and specific knowledge to assist in the use of tendency analysis.

These challenges are very real. They often preclude people from venturing into this esoteric area of intelligence analysis. Regardless, we need to venture forth into this new area and continue to broaden our understanding so we can use tendency analysis to help us disambiguate, see what appears to be invisible, and portend an emerging future so our commanders can take preemptory actions. Keeping these challenges involved in the use of tendency analysis in mind, let us consider how one can meet and overcome the challenges.

- Mental organization—understand the basics of tendency analysis.
- Use a tendency analysis thought template.
- Seek help from experts. Analysts can find experts in the intelligence enterprise and overwatch system, in a VKE, through red-teaming, by engaging in wargaming, checking my thinking, murder-boarding hypotheses, hunches, expectations, and mysteries.
- Find or develop, but use baselines (cultural, technical, functional). Devise a strategy for keeping the baselines updated until no longer needed.
- Anticipate possible movements of the enemy—be aggressive, anticipate, work with collection people.
- Start early in the planning cycle to set up the right knowledge SMEs to help you develop the tendency analysis knowledge you need to recognize the subtle changes whose synthesis suggests the presence of a tendency.
- Pull in slivers of data and "knit" them into a tapestry of understanding. With this technique, the output is a tendency with enough definition to understand the potentialities of the future well enough to act and obtain an advantage over the enemy.

- Work as a team with collection people and technologists for latency standards and for meeting programming requirements.
- Know what you are after—right observables, right place, right time, and right activity.
- Avoid mirror imaging—recall what mirror imaging is. It is thinking about a problem and its outcomes from a western point of view and imposing your thoughts and values on an enemy who thinks, perceives, and has values quite different from an American.
- Develop sources and contacts that will serve as an indications and warning (I&W) net of sorts to tell you when cultural anomalies occur.
- Know and use the technical environment.
  - Understand the invisible world of technical emanations.
  - Seek the help of electrical engineers.
  - Design technical observables using technical analysis.
  - Work with technologists to design technical collection.
  - Work with technologists and SMEs to make sense out of data and to transform them into knowledge and understanding.
- Be creative—seek out low-tech and high-tech ways the enemy could use technology and be undetectable from his point of view.
- Understand how the enemy thinks.
  - Use indigenous people and SMEs to help you decompose requirements, particularly those dealing with culture, aggregation, anomaly, and semiotics.
  - Study trends and patterns but consider the enemy's creativity too.
  - Think seriously about how the enemy thinks about you.
  - Know the culture well enough to seek and find advantages.
  - Gain a working knowledge of the culture and recognize its uniqueness in the neighborhood you are working on.
- Think like the enemy and answer the following questions:
  - What is my perception of U.S. analytic capability to notice glacial change and to pick up upon and understand small, inevitable perturbations in baselines?
  - How can I hide from the Americans' sensors and HUMINT?
  - What will the Americans do that can cause my failure and how might I surreptitiously counteract?
  - Where and how will American HUMINT and technical collection be watching or looking for me?
  - Should I be using cell phones?
  - How will I know when the Americans are closing in?
  - When should I move?
  - How will I proceed with my countersurveillance and I&W ops while the United States is looking for me?
  - What is the best way to provide me with early warning of danger?

- How will I become resupplied with food and water without compromising my location and mission?
- How can I receive medical support without drawing attention?
- How will I hide my functional requirements—lights, food, water, electricity, refuse, water, and sewage?
- How will I recruit people to perform the many duties I need for sustaining my network and for performing tasks essential to my mission?
- How will I communicate so the U.S. intelligence people will not notice?

Some other techniques can assist the advanced analyst in using tendency analysis. Tendency analysis takes current, relevant knowledge. It takes an understanding by the analyst of change that is perpetual and sometimes latent. It takes people being patient and willing to watch for small changes or even perturbations that could be indicants of tendencies. To become proficient in tendency analysis, a U.S. advanced analyst must learn to use indigenous red team people who will help (1) understand the OE, (2) design cultural, situational, functional, biometric, and technical observables, (3) engage in act/react/counteract wargaming and be aware of one's own proclivities to mirror image when considering the enemy's thoughts, (4) search for, find, and use the three types of baselines discussed above—technical, cultural, and functional—that will help identify these small changes and intuit their meaning. In addition, the advanced analyst has to engage in rigorous critical thinking to understand tendency analysis. Further, to understand tendency analysis, the analyst has to understand the OE, its influences on friendly forces, the enemy, the host nation and its populace, and neutrals.

Finally, to use tendency analysis takes an aggressive, intellectually combative outlook of an analyst with an "*attitude.*" This attitude manifests as "I'm going to get ahead of my enemy through his own actions and conditions absolutely necessary for accomplishing his mission. The disturbances he creates in the normalcy of the culture, the technical domain of specific technical areas, and the necessary and adjunct functions that occur in the neighborhood and around my target or focal point of the enemy's activities are my allies and I can find them, use them to anticipate his activities, and preempt his decision/action/assessment cycle." Since tendencies and anomalies are so closely related, it makes sense to delve next into anomaly analysis, which happens to be the next chapter.

13

Anomaly Analysis

Definition: Discerning meaning in departures from the normal or common order, form, or rule; absence of that which is expected.

THEORY BEHIND ANOMALY ANALYSIS

The threats U.S. forces will face in large urban settings are embedded amongst the culture in which they conduct their activities. This is a theme that has surfaced again and again. Often, the insurgent will be from the culture or at least be able to blend with cultural people and activities. In addition, the city is always moving and changing. Thus, to seek and find insurgents in this sea of change involves an advanced level of thinking by even junior analysts to know what to look for, how to search for it, and when they have found what they are searching for. Unfortunately, the answers to our questions will never be totally obvious unless the insurgents are truly stupid. Thus, we will receive snippets of information and data that does not look like it makes sense, and we will feel cognitive dissonance in that we know things are occurring in the swirl of everyday life, but we cannot see what appears to be invisible. One of the best ways to think about this problem is using anomaly analysis. This chapter discusses anomaly analysis and explains its use, the power inherent to anomaly analysis, and what needs to occur to be able to use it.

Advanced analysts always have to consider the nature of what they are trying to find and understand. Since this discussion concentrates on COIN operations or actions against irregular units in large urban settings, our discussion has to involve people, their culture, their technology, and the functioning of their society. Fortunately, we have some good guides in counterinsurgency theory. One of the best is *Low-Intensity Operations* by Frank Kitson. In one telling passage, Kitson tells us

> It looked as if the company commander would have to start again and try and work out when next a sortie for food was likely to take place, and in fact he did start work along these lines. But there was one worth-while clue, which arose out of the ambush. Amongst several sacks of food taken from the bodies at the scene of the ambush was one, which contained some fruit, which was seldom grown in the area. The company commander and the inspector of the intelligence section discussed this and came to the conclusion that if a farm growing such fruit could be found near village D, there would be a chance of getting some useful information out of the owner.[1]

What the passage tells us is small abnormalities or differences can make a difference in our analytic work. But, sometimes thinking about and watching for the small differences is difficult owing to a lack of time, knowledge, and power to observe through the eyes and minds of people remote from the analyst. Therefore, to understand anomaly analysis, we have to decide upon the nature of what we seek and consider how we might approach it using anomaly analysis. Anomaly analysis works with cultural, technical, and functional observables that could involve the following:

- Cultural influences, aspects, manifestations, behavior
- Cultural influences on human characteristics or behavior
- Cultural influences on appearances—permanent or fleeting
- Cultural influences on degree of vagueness or ambiguity in speech and gestures
- Cultural influences on integrity, hyperbole, gestures, and speech
- Cultural influences on organizational and group dynamics
- Cultural response to outside stimuli
- Use of technology in the society by individuals and organizations
- Technical aspects of infrastructure support to the society
- Technical aspects of individual business and commerce
- Technical aspects of individual homes
- Technical aspects of infrastructure supporting home and business functions
- Day-to-day functions of the society (e.g., going to work) and specific neighborhoods (e.g., going to the market to purchase food and water)
- Day-to-day functions of homes, businesses, interactions, transactions, and activities

Understanding the nature of these elements of a culture, technology, and functions is not an easy endeavor, but it is essential in COIN and IW analytic work. Counterinsurgency theorist David Galula helps us reason along this line of thought with the following passage from *Counterinsurgency Warfare: Theory and Practice*:

> The aim of control is to cut off, or at least reduce significantly, the contacts between the population and the guerrillas. This is done by watching the population's activities; after a while, when the counterinsurgent personnel has become acquainted with the population and knows each inhabitant, unusual behavior can be spotted easily.[2]

Thus, advanced analysts have to use the powerful tool of anomaly analysis to help them first understand what normal is and then to search for and identify anomalies. Let us carry this thought a little further. Even the well-embedded threat cannot exist and perform missions without showing signs and making some kind of mistakes. But to notice the mistakes, the intelligence analyst must see the critical connections[3] in advance of their occurrence and know the essential elements of the problem. These essential elements and the aforementioned mistakes will most often be cultural (e.g., using an improper gesture or an out-of-place voice inflection), technical (e.g., making cell phone calls), and functional (e.g., performing reconnaissance). While not all deviations from the norm will indicate insurgent activities, the advanced analyst will have to identify legitimate from illegitimate activity. The analyst has to look for the signs that will become observables to find insurgents, understand their network, and "see" their activities and transactions. With anomaly analysis, we are looking for deviations from the norm that identify the presence and potential activities of a well-hidden enemy.

An anomaly is, as stated in the definition, a departure from the norm or common order, form, or rule; however, its importance lies in comparing normal with anomalous. Other fields of knowledge use anomaly analysis. In particular, medicine uses it to vigorously anticipate and attack health problems as they become differentiated from what is normal. This aggressive activity helps doctors head off fast-spreading problems before they become disastrous. An article in *Wired* helps us understand what the medical community is doing in this regard:

> What's normal matters because we're entering a new era of health care, one in which we look not for causes of illness but for risks. It's called predictive medicine, and its primary tool is the screening test. A good screening test should provide a range of results, distinguishing between a condition within normal parameters—which doesn't require intervention—and an anomaly, which demands it.[4]

This analogy works well to understand how U.S. military intelligence analysts can use anomalies to seek and attack the disease that is an insurgency, operating from a network early enough and with the right "medicine" to avoid harming the host while still being effective enough to drive out or kill the disease. Anomaly analysis helps find the proverbial "needles in a haystack" that are the mistakes and abnormal behavior and activity that will help advanced analysts form hypotheses and develop observables.

As discussed throughout this work, the local populace that provides support to insurgent or terrorist groups is relied on for basic security, sustenance, logistics, travel, intelligence collection, deception, operational security (OPSEC), and recruitment via transactions, activities, interactions, and behaviors. However, these network supporters will most likely not have perfect HUMINT tradecraft; therefore, sensor and HUMINT observation can notice them if the collectors "know" what to look for. This "what to look for" comes from in-depth knowledge of local communities, cultures, and customs to discern what is normal so as to look for and find what is abnormal. That which is abnormal could very well be the actions of people supporting an enemy network.

How can the advanced analyst use anomaly analysis? Anomaly analysis allows the analyst to search for nuanced, subtle, and ambiguous observables. Anomaly analysis also helps analysts understand and use change detection—changes in behavior, changes in the way people interact and transact, changes in ground temperature, and changes in activity patters. In fact, the causes for deviations of the enemy or his supporters come from elements of the population supporting the insurgent's network;—e.g., people of the neighborhood knowing a safe house is operating. These people will experience some degree of angst that will cause them to go about their daily lives differently than normal. These differences are anomalies. It also involves changes in the earth such as disturbances caused by digging or by something in the ground that is generating heat. Anomaly analysis also helps analysts understand why there has been change or perturbation in the three types of baselines—cultural, technical, and functional. In this regard, anomaly analysis assists the analyst to establish cause-and-effect relationships for changes and disturbances in normal activities and patterns. Finally, anomaly analysis, when working synergistically with synthesis and recomposition as well as semiotics, aggregation, and tendency analysis, greatly assists the advanced analyst in his or her effort to make sense out of collected data.

Anomaly analysis is closest to cultural and semiotics analysis in the system of thought presented here. *Cultural analysis* in advanced analysis is knowing a particular culture, its people, and their patterns of behavior deriving from traditional, culturally induced attitudes, behaviors, social norms, and conditions. *Semiotics analysis* is discerning meaning of cultural signs and symbols reflected in drawings, paintings, signs, symbols, photographs, syntax, words, sounds, body language, and graffiti. These two aspects of advanced analysis will be discussed in Chapters 14 and 15, respectively. Anomaly analysis on specific cultural neighborhoods and associated semiotics will be challenging to develop and collect against; however, its difficulty in no way diminishes its importance. Continuing with this line of thought, anomaly analysis relates to semiotics analysis through cultural analysis and the highlighting of what the semiotics mean and how they can manifest in a culture. The output can be anomalies. Thus, one of the most important implications we can deduce at this point in the chapter is that advanced analysts must keep their attention on local cultural intelligence and semiotics when using anomaly analysis to develop cultural and situational observables as well as functional observables. They must then make sense of incoming data, keeping in mind the importance of local culture and semiotics. They must use cultural and semiotics analysis to understand deviations in the baselines that we must understand and use in anomaly analysis.

Let us continue going into more depth and answer the following question: Why is semiotics analysis specifically important to anomaly analysis? Our answer is, in many urban COIN situations, that which is abnormal or anomalous will often appear and be noticeable in the realm of semiotics. Unfortunately, semiotics are not easy to understand. Thus, competent knowledge experts and, for certain local neighborhood, indigenous people need to identify and interpret semiotics continuously. Semiotics analysis is difficult and takes much knowledge of the culture to perform. Further, when anomaly analyses is working with semiotics, successful thinking will undoubtedly be supplemented by the knowledge and experience of indigenous people as well as VKE, SME, or even very experience FAOs.

When analysts use semiotics in relation to anomaly analysis, they must look for ambiguity, nuance, and subtlety in the populace's language, syntax, symbols, and signs. Anomaly analysis brings out some of these subtleties. Many aspects of human interaction, transactions, activities, and behaviors are subtle, nuanced, and ambiguous to the point of invisibility. But semiotics are not entirely invisible. Anomaly analysis helps us search for and find these seemingly invisible events or human activities or transactions. Anomaly analysis relates to semiotics analysis by pointing out the manifestation of semiotics—nonverbal behavior, symbols, syntax, language variation, and signs—we must search for and find as well as quickly exploit once discovered.

But before proceeding with our discussion of anomaly analysis, we have to discuss another influence on anomaly, cultural, and semiotics analysis—that is disambiguation. What does disambiguation mean? Disambiguation is "clarity that follows clearing up or removal of ambiguity."[5] Disambiguation is an important term in intelligence analysis that is focused against insurgents in an urban setting. In essence, with effective anomaly analysis, ambiguity disappears, enabling the analyst to know what he or she is looking for, seeing, or hearing when anomaly-induced data starts coming in. The object when thinking about and using disambiguation is to make what appears invisible, e.g., cultural, technical, or functional anomalies, visible and useable, thereby removing them from the list of enemy advantages. Can we come up with a more appropriate and understandable operational definition of disambiguation? Yes we can. Such a definition would be making visible what heretofore has been invisible. How does disambiguation relate to the invisibility of baselines and anomaly analysis? The answer is, we have to use advanced analysis—namely anomaly analysis—to develop the observables that will make visible that which appears invisible.

To effectively use anomaly analysis one has to consider several influences. For example, one has to know what is normal, but knowing what is normal is not an easy matter. Establishing "normal" takes the recording of and interpretation of interactions, transactions, activities, and behaviors people exhibit over time through developing an extensive baseline. Anomaly analysis will not work without three kinds of baselines—technical, cultural, and functional. So, let us spend some serious effort in understanding baselines and their relationship with anomaly analysis.

A *cultural baseline* is a mental template that serves as a standard relating to the shared knowledge and values of an element of a society by which things in a particular neighborhood are measured or compared denoting or deriving from or distinctive of the ways of living of a distinctive group of people. Anomalies with the cultural baseline will often appear as interactions, activities, transactions, and behaviors as well as semiotics (signs, symbols, nonverbal behavior, syntax, and intonations). The framework for a cultural baseline could include the following:

- Dress
- Nonverbal behavior
- Speech
- Walking, gait
- Displays of affection
- Treatment of women
- Home activities
- Religious observances
- Shopping patterns
- Recreation
- Marriage
- Death
- Birth
- Children's activities & treatment
- Home activities & functions
- Work activities & functions
- Semiotics
- Relationship with strangers

A *technical baseline* is a mental template with elements that serve as a normal technical standard with which to look for and find anomalies relating to technical processes, emanations, and emissions coming from a house, a portion of the infrastructure, activities, conveyances, neighborhood, aggregate of neighborhoods, and, from a macro perspective, from a city writ large. A framework for a technical baseline could include the following:

- Cell phone frequencies
- Heat expenditures of houses and businesses and cultural buildings
- Amperes being expended from buildings
- Water consumption
- Generator use
- Fuel sales
- Phone line usage
- TV/radio station broadcasts
- Light generation
- Electrons flowing over landlines
- Heat and cooling differentials, e.g., of a house with and without people
- Temperature of target
- Ground temperature
- Air temperature
- Refuse pile temperature
- RF energy from computers and even their clocks
- Fumes from latrines
- Fumes and smoke from refuse piles
- Smoke from cigarettes
- Sounds—metal, wood, carrying, lifting, digging, automobiles starting
- Animal excrement
- Human waste
- Music
- Cooking smells
- Energy from movement

A *functional baseline* is a mental template with elements that serve as a normal functional standard with which to look for and find anomalies relating to functions or the assigned actions, duties, and activities required or expected of a person or group processes. A framework for a functional baseline could include the following:

- Sustenance
- Water
- Security
- Deception and diversion
- Countersurveillance

- Communications
- Materiel
- Transportation
- Storage
- Intelligence collection
- Early warning/OPSEC
- Sleep and rest
- Medical care
- Training
- Physical exercise

Intelligence analysts have to either find the baselines discussed above or develop their own. Unfortunately, it takes time and extensive knowledge to develop any baseline. In addition, all baselines are local. To use existing baselines, analysts have to check veracity and how up to date the information in the baselines is. If no baselines exist, the analysts must develop their own. How will they do so? First, they have to decide why they are contemplating use of baselines. Then, they will search for existing baselines and check for relevance and usability. They will work with the intelligence enterprise and a VKE to fill out their baseline template to the extent possible within the constraints at hand such as a rigid time constraint. Finally, they will always seek to find a local person to help them either develop the baseline, check the developed baselines for accuracy, or to help develop a new baseline.

Baselines and anomaly analysis are important in any urban counterinsurgency (COIN) situation. Why is this so? Many of the changes we are searching for will be subtle, ambiguous, and fleeting. In some cases, only an indigenous person will be able to use existing baseline elements to spot and explain anomalies. In addition, some of the anomalies we seek could relate to something other than just enemy activity. For example, people seeking medical help per day and per week is an element in a local cultural baseline. If the numbers of people seeking medical help decreases from what is normal, it is an anomaly. But, the reason could be that a rumor is spreading about the doctor the people are seeking help from or a rumor could surface that women are being violated or molested by western doctors trying to provide medical support to various neighborhoods.

To use baselines and anomaly analysis, analysts first of all must know what they are looking for. They must also identify where they are looking and when they believe the anomalies will surface. They need to work with collection people to use many collectors to search for this most nuanced of observables. As a final suggestion, they must approach the use of anomaly analysis by thinking about the thread and the loom metaphor. That is, when multiple collectors look for observables that are anomalies, many sources of resultant data will come to the analyst for sense making. One source and one thread or "sliver" of data by itself will mean very little. But, many threads or "slivers" of data, from many different collectors, can be woven into an understandable tapestry of meaning.

Anomaly analysis is very intellectually arduous for several reasons:

- *First*, to engage in this intense activity, people have to know a lot. Searching for, updating, or developing new baselines takes cultural, technical, and functional knowledge to an extent far beyond the knowledge of most analysts. To use anomaly analysis to its full potential, analysts have to know a lot about the culture. Unfortunately, not many analysts will have the required knowledge and understanding to design the observables and to perform the resultant sense-making from incoming data. Cultural data will often be subtle, nuanced, vague, and fleeting. So, how does the analyst handle this dilemma? The analyst must have a way to work with indigenous SMEs from the neighborhood being worked on. In addition, the analyst must use U.S. cultural SMEs who speak the language and who have been recently on the ground in the vicinity of interest and under observation. The analyst involved can also work with a VKE and gain access to the far reaches of the Internet to answer specific questions and to help make sense of incoming data.
- *Second*, analysts who engage in anomaly analysis will need advanced analytic knowledge support. But, where will they get it? They will often seek and find such support from the intelligence enterprise or a VKE that is supporting them. Another way to seek and find such knowledge is among one's own staff, indigenous people supporting the staff who have proper security clearances, and coalition partners. As a continuing line of thought, analysts engaging in anomaly analysis can often seek help from multinational corporations (MNC), people working in the OE, and sometimes even nongovernment organizations (NGOs), which often have a bevy of highly educated knowledge specialists working as neutral supporters of humanitarian relief organizations.
- *Third*, analysts must know and use the technical environment. But, how many analysts have the requisite technical knowledge and understanding to work with anomaly analysis? The answer is very few. Why? Most of time what analysts will need will be an experienced electrical engineer, medical doctor, mechanical engineer, explosives expert, bridge expert, oil refinery expert, infrastructure expert, and so forth. Where do analysts find such expertise? They can look on the staff, but the likelihood of finding such expertise is not high. They can go to his supporting VKE, who can find the right kind of expert. Analysts can try and find indigenous technical SMEs but will often come up against security constraints. Analysts can also go to the coalition for help as well as to the intelligence enterprise.

In a general sense, when using anomaly analysis and baselines, the analyst must use a thought template, must seek the intellectual and knowledge assistance of experts, and must search for existing baselines and determine their worth. In addition, the analyst must engage in wargaming to help identify potential anomalies and required baselines. The analyst must also realize his or her knowledge shortfalls and seek the help of the organization's red team to critique his or her thinking and the outputs of that thinking. This work with the red team can be accomplished physically or virtually (with the VKE or an external red-teaming analytic service).

Our urban enemies will not be innate as we attempt to use anomaly analysis. We are in a duel against a wily and adaptive foe. The duel metaphor is apropos. Only this time, the duel is just as often mental as physical. As Clausewitz tells us,

> War, however, is not the action of a living force upon a lifeless mass (total nonresistance would be nor war at all) but always the collision of two living forces. The ultimate aim of waging war, as formulate here, must be taken as applying to both sides. Once again, there is interaction. So long as I have not overthrown my opponent I am bound to fear he may overthrow me. Thus I am not in control: he dictates to me as much as I dictate to him.[6]

Thus, we have to answer the question: How will the enemy *think we think* about anomalies? Given the proclivity of all humans to engage in mirror imaging, it is safe to posit that the enemy could very well believe U.S. intelligence analysts will not possess the depth of knowledge required to understand a society's cultural, functional, and technical anomalies. They will probably believe the U.S. intelligence analysts will see the more obvious anomalies, but miss the all-important subtle, nuanced, and fleeting observables prevalent in the interactions of any society, the observables that provide meaning to experienced, knowledgeable people who understand the OE and its cultural, technical, and functional interactions. This means the analyst has to think about how the enemy is thinking about *how his enemy (U.S. analyst) thinks about himself, the enemy, and the enemy's thinking.*

A good example of long-term observation involved with some cases of anomaly analysis (but useful more as a commercial indication and warning system) is the process by which credit card companies identify credit card theft. The software they use "knows" through learning what normal transactions are; when they determine an anomaly, they flag your card and a security person phones. In the same way, analysts must know the culture in detail or be capable of using reach back to find SMEs capable of providing such detailed knowledge.

Normalcy also depends on several other things. It depends on the weather and the time of the year. It depends on knowledge of existing businesses, infrastructures, and human interactions. It depends on the ebb and flow of traffic. It depends on a working knowledge of normal electrical and other infrastructure outages in various parts of cities and neighbor-hoods. It depends on knowing behaviors inherent to particular cultures and in particular the patterns and trends that should exist in given situations.

Often, analysts can search for some constants to help them think about anomalies. For example, when practicing Muslims pray five times a day, they face to the cardinal direction of Mecca. Prayer times exist and are announced—this is normal. If during prayer times a person or several people are not praying, an anomaly worthy of exploration has arisen. Or consider traffic and market patterns, which have cycles of normalcy. Activities at the market have normalcy patterns, such as time of day, bartering actions, use of carrying devices to transport purchases, the purc-hase of certain amounts of food to feed typical households—this is normalcy. People sleep on roofs during hot summer nights in the Persian Gulf region—this is normalcy. People meet in Internet cafes (particularly young people) to gossip, exchange information, and gain knowledge—this is normalcy. People wear particular clothing. So, when one (or many) of these signs is anomalous or out of the expected range of normalcy, it demands the attention of HUMINT collectors and technical sensors as well as the analysts, who take the incoming data and turn them into information and knowledge or form a hunch or mystery to solve or to find answers or solutions.

Thus the advanced analyst observes a curious duality that characterizes this aspect of advanced analysis: Normal and anomalous behaviors and transactions are always in play. Most interactions, transactions, activities, and behaviors will be normal. But buried in the sea of normalcy are the snippets of abnormality. A reasonable person can conclude very easily that the vastness of the sea of normalcy in an urban OE precludes one from searching for and finding the few instances of anomaly. And this would be a reasonable conclusion, except to the advanced analyst who purposefully sets out to look for anomalies using five kinds of observables developed through anomaly analysis.

How might the advanced analyst proceed to discern anomalous activities or behaviors? Several methods can help them work on this problem:

- Analysts can use geospatial information system (GIS) models to concen-trate on a particular area of study or geographic location. Cultural expertise, GIS foundation data, and layering can work together to help analysts understand normal and anomaly.
- Analysts must consider what mediums and domains to use for their quest into anomaly analysis. Examples include Internet and telephony in the information domain, transit (such as subways and buses in mass transit), electrical flows over the electricity grid, typical purchases at the market for individuals or families, methods of payment for goods and

services, transporting of purchases in the economic sphere, numbers and locations of police in the law enforcement sphere, refuse collection and meter reading in the government regulated sphere, mail delivery, taxi loitering, and distribution and delivery vehicles.

- Advanced analysts must decompose every aspect of religion peculiar to a particular neighborhood. Analysts need to understand how religion works in the culture in question, what the religious social order is, how homage is given to senior religious people, and how these people communicate. They must know when people attend the mosque, how long a service normally lasts, how attendees look when they enter, how they look when they leave, and the amount of social interaction taking place in and out of the mosque. Analysts also must know how people donate money, how the money is secured, where the money is safeguarded, and how it is dispersed and moved.
- Analysts must dissect aspects of the predominant culture, to know what elements of a culture are the most important and how these elements influence the way people interact, behave, engage in transactions, and conduct activities.
- Analysts have to assess how people in the culture in question relax and indulge in recreation. This involves understanding what people of a particular culture, tribe, or sect do to enjoy life and relax and how they typically engage in social and recreational activities.
- Analysts have to consider relationships between and among the sexes, between and among relatives, and between husbands and wives to identify anomalous behavior.
- Analysts must recognize the importance of semiotics and know the best they can how people and organizations use language (syntax, intonation, dialect, and gestures), signs, symbols, nonverbal behavior, and even graffiti.
- Analysts have to be familiar with people in general: how they think, perceive, exhibit emotion, and talk. For example, do they tell the truth, engage in hyperbole, or lie? What views do they hold of integrity and honesty? How do they view law enforcement and military security forces, how do they act in their presence, and how do they treat them?

These are just a few of the ways to think about anomalous activities, transactions, interactions, and behaviors, but it is only a start. To use anomaly analysis effectively, a question, while obscure, looms and eventually becomes clear: How will analysts ever develop the in-depth knowledge and understanding of the complex urban terrain, infrastructure, and culture in addition to the enemy, neutrals, and host nation government and services, sufficiently well to perform anomaly analysis? The answer is that not all analysts *will* ever advance sufficiently to perform anomaly analysis to a high degree of proficiency. Some individuals will not possess the breadth and depth of knowledge and experience necessary to perform anomaly analysis well. But under the auspices of advanced analysis, all advanced analysts will know something, and together they will have a cognitive framework to proceed in this complex mental landscape. In addition, analysts will know how to use a VKE of SMEs, COEs, and data scientists to help them with the more difficult parts of advanced analysis—in this case, anomaly analysis.

As an additional analytic consideration, advanced analysts can mimic what multinational corporations (MNCs) have been doing for years. That is, MNCs engage in forms of anomaly analysis, albeit probably under a different name. They consult with cultural SMEs and COEs to understand foreign cultures to market their products. In addition, these corporations have as corporate experts people knowledgeable in the social mores, predilections, culture, and biases of people around the world, all the way down to specific neighborhoods, or they find such experts and collaborate physically or virtually to discover or build the knowledge they need. The U.S. military and specifically advanced analysts need to engage in this same type of knowledge access and building work and find ways to gain insights into the specifics of foreign cultures specifically to help form the baseline of normalcy we have been discussing, and engage in anomaly analysis to begin to look for that which is abnormal. Analysts must intellectually couple with a wide variety of SMEs and COEs whose participation depends upon the questions being asked and the problem being worked. They must learn to work with people from all strata of the culture. Analysts pursuing the precepts of advanced analysis, in particular anomaly analysis, can also consult and work with data scientists and use their powerful machines and data to help meet this challenge. Analysts must also learn to work with indigenous people who can provide the extremely specific knowledge of neighborhoods, cultures, activities, transactions, interactions, and behaviors. If security concerns enter into whether or not analysts use indigenous people to help with anomaly analysis, analysts do not need to tell everything about the missions, but they can nevertheless still ask specific questions in search of in-depth answers that they can use to develop observables to drive collection.

Continuing with this discussion thread, U.S. intelligence analysts must engage in anomaly analysis to succeed in working against the terrorists and insurgents embedded in societies. These people do not want to be found. They blend with the society, and are masters in cover, concealment, security, and deception. U.S. intelligence analysts are interested in the populace not only for the "winning the hearts and minds" part of counterinsurgency work but also as an indirect approach to finding the enemy and his network. Often the populace supports insurgents' networks and sometimes makes mistakes or conducts unusual activities that will turn up as anomalies. Analysts will recognize these anomalies if they are looking for them with the right observable, the right sensors and HUMINT, at the right time, and at the right place. Advanced analysts and collection experts must look for the unusual or different or anomalous signs, behaviors, transactions, bodily functions, interactions, and activities to be successful. These signs and symbols will be present because all people interact, perform transactions, engage in activities, exhibit behaviors, and, most importantly, make mistakes. With the mistakes humans make, advanced analysts can begin to recognize nefarious enemy network activities even if fleeting and subtle. These mistakes, no matter how seemingly innocuous or unimportant, could carry the filaments, strains, or slight hints of what analysts and collection specialists must purposefully look for.

As a final aspect of our discussion on anomaly analysis, we need to discuss the challenges analysts will have when using anomaly analysis and ways to meet these challenges. First, let us discuss the challenges of anomaly analysis:

- Knowledge support is required.
- Analysts will require advanced analytic support.
- Knowledge support must come from indigenous SMEs, red teamers, VKE, knowledgeable analysts, and cultural, functional, and technical experts.
- Analysts must know and use the culture to achieve an advantage.
- Analysts must know and use the technical environment to achieve an advantage.
- Finding the right indigenous SMEs who know the particular neighborhood of interest is difficult but very important.

There are ways to overcome these challenges. Some of the best ways include the following:

- Mental organization—work with a thought template to facilitate conclusive and deep thinking.
- Seek support of and work with experts. Baseline development and the task of searching for anomalies takes cultural, technical, and functional (knowledge of threat and OE) knowledge to a very high degree.
- Search for existing baselines. Analysts can use existing baselines if they are available. Of course, odds are that even with existing baselines, analysts will have to modify them with updates and do some data manipulation to make them useful for the problems at hand. They will sometimes have to develop new baselines with which to use in anomaly analysis if they find none in existence. They must also pay extensive attention to cultural, technical, and functional baselines and engage in new, anticipatory baseline analysis work before they are needed.
- Find cultural SMEs. Analysts will want to seek and find some indigenous, some external, and some FAOs to help them consider the

challenges of anomaly analysis and to work with complex baselines. They will need to use indigenous SMEs to find the right neighborhood experts required to assist in the local nature of baselines and anomaly analysis.

- Engage in red-teaming, wargaming, and critical thinking. Analysts always need somebody to check their thinking for errors such as mirror imaging, over simplification, use of expert testimony, arrogance, and so forth.
- Use an anomaly analysis thought template.
- Get help from the intelligence enterprise and its overwatch capability, help from a VKE, and a thorough scrub by a red-teaming group or individuals.
- Engage in wargaming, constantly check thinking, and seek experts to murder board hypotheses, hunches, expectations, and mysteries. Analysts using anomaly analysis must always anticipate premature movement of the target and other sources of friction that can wreak havoc with the best thinking and planning.
- Think like the enemy and answer the following questions with the help of properly cleared indigenous people:
  - How can I make my necessary activities appear normal?
  - How can I thwart the U.S. intelligence system's attempts to disambiguate and find signs of my anomalies?
  - How can I make things in the neighborhood appear normal with no anomalies?
  - How can the Americans use anomaly analysis and cause my failure and how might I surreptitiously counteract?
  - Where and how will the Americans be watching or looking for me?
  - What part of the day should I move and perform my necessary functions so as to avoid anomalies?
  - How will I preclude the United States from finding indications of my countersurveillance through anomaly analysis?
  - Who can I use to perform early warning and countersurveillance duties around my safe house to avoid presenting anomalies?
  - How will I communicate so the U.S. intelligence people will not notice activities and anomalies?

In concluding, we must say that anomaly analysis is an interesting chapter. It is interesting because people have been trying to find anomalies for years, but they often come up short owing to challenges with their own thinking, finding the right kind of expertise and knowledge, using the right combinations of collection to find the anomalies, and coping with the vagaries of the OE. Regardless of difficulty and shortfalls that retard its success, if performed correctly, aggressively, and continuously, anomaly analysis makes superb contributions to advanced analysis and decision-making.

If intelligence analysts learn to perform anomaly analysis correctly, they commence the arduous process of disambiguation of the confusion, ambiguity, and chaos extant to an urban OE. They can turn what appears to be invisible into something visible and actionable. This disambiguation via anomaly analysis is an important aspect of support to commanders' decision-making activities.

Let's review some of the most important points in this chapter:

- When working with anomaly analysis, intelligence analysts must first know and understand what normal is for the neighborhood and activities they are thinking about and studying.
- To understand normalcy, intelligence analysts must use three types of baselines—technical, cultural, and functional. These baselines are local and must undergo constant updating. This is a difficult challenge for unit intelligence people hard pressed for time owing to the fluidity of the OE, the constant demands for high-grade, timely knowledge, and the heavy responsibility for finding an elusive, formidable, and well-hidden foe.
- Network supporters will not always be highly proficient in tradecraft. Thus, they will make mistakes. These mistakes will often be cultural in nature. Thus, to see, notice, and understand the mistakes (hence the observables associated with the mistakes), one has to know the culture in detail.
- Anomaly analysis is highly relational to cultural, semiotics, and tendency analysis.
- Disambiguation is turning what appears to be invisible into something that is visible. This mental function is essential in "seeing" difference, changes, and even the slightest perturbation-induced change. Arguably, this is a difficult process owing to the complexity of the OE, threat, network, populace, and other actors on the stage of an urban insurgency. To disambiguate, one has to know a lot about technology, functions, cultural activities, and interactions, transactions, and behaviors of specific areas. Without training, access to a VKE, and visualization machines, anomaly analysis is sometimes much more than a typical deployed staff can produce.
- To readily discern anomalies, one has to undergo several activities. Analysts can enhance their cognitive performance by using three-dimensional GIS modeling to help understand the OE, what normal looks like and in particular neighborhoods, alleys, and courtyards, and their variable activities and energy emissions.
- The intelligence analyst must look for anomalies across multiple domains—air, ground, information, and cyberspace. They must visualize in their minds what they seek. This is an anomaly related hypothesis or expectation. With this in mind, they engage in decomposition to

develop the observables with which to drive intelligence collection. Then, they must know and understand the culture, its technologies, and its functions to recompose resultant data into information and synthesize it into knowledge.

With anomalies, one looks for differences or subtle changes indicating an activity or action involving the threat. With anomaly analysis the advanced analyst is looking for a change-induced outcome or an action. When an insurgent is preparing for or actually executing an attack or a supporting action, there will be departures from the norm. These activities must occur or there would be not action. But U.S. intelligence sensors, HUMINT, and analysts may not see or notice these changes and subsequent activity deviation. What is the reason? The chapter on anomalies explains that U.S. intelligence people often do not know what to look for by way of change or anomaly, and if they look for some change in particular, they sometimes do not have the knowledge to understand what they are seeing let alone understand its relationships. Thus, knowledge and access to people who produce or add value to it becomes a preeminent activity for success in anomaly analysis.

Anomaly analysis is a cornerstone of advanced analysis. Any enemy activity will result in action. The action will cause perturbation in what heretofore has been normal. This perturbation will induce changes from participants in the endeavor, bystanders to said activity, infrastructure, business activities, child play, traffic patterns, the issuance of building permits, and so forth. Advanced analysis provides "a way" to notice change or movement through anomaly analysis. To use it wisely, however, the advanced analyst will always have to seek, update, and use cultural, technical, and functional baselines as a starting point of thought.

Since anomaly analysis is dependent upon cultural and semiotics analysis, it is logical that the next two chapters are cultural and semiotics analysis, respectively. Each element of advanced analysis will be explained and made practical for the reader.

14

Cultural Analysis[1]

Definition: Knowing a particular culture, its people, and their patterns of behavior deriving from traditional, culturally induced attitudes, behaviors, social norms, and conditions.

THEORY BEHIND CULTURAL INTELLIGENCE

Culture in anthropological terms means "the sum total of ways of living built up by a group of human beings and transmitted from one generation to another."[2] *Cultural intelligence analysis* (which is "cultural analysis" in this work) involves data, information, and knowledge of a particular people or grouping of people. Such insights are essential to advanced analysis; they are gained through observation, investigation, analysis, and understanding of integrated patterns of human behavior (thought, speech, artifacts, symbols, actions). These integrated patterns depend on the human capacity for learning and transmitting knowledge (beliefs, attitudes, behavior, social norms, and material traits) to members of an ethnic, religious, or social group and succeeding generations. Culture is the most important aspect of an insurgency bar none. As one author tells us, reinforcing this point, "Culture counts, and intelligence personnel need to understand the language, history, and culture of the area in which they must work."[3]

Cultural intelligence analysis involves the study, decomposition, knowledge, and understanding of a culture sufficiently enough to know how that culture works, how its elements function, how it influences thought, how its people live, think, perceive, and make decisions, and what values people, organizations, and leaders hold dear. Cultural intelligence analysis involves understanding how the culture influences the judicial, political, military, economic, security, diplomatic, and financial systems. Cultural intelligence is history; historical roots are always an important aspect of cultural analysis. It is vital to know it *to gain advantages*. Cultural intelligence has to cope with the phenomenon of globalization. Globalization presents opportunities for both sides in a conflict, which is well described by journalist author Thomas Friedman:

> what the flattening of the world means is that we are now connecting all the knowledge centers on the planet together into a single global network, which—if politics and terrorism do not get in the way—could usher in an amazing era of prosperity and innovation . . . My personal dread derived from the obvious fact that it's not only the software writers and computer geeks who get empowered to collaborate on work in a flat world. It's also al-Qaeda and other terrorist networks.[4]

Cultural intelligence analysis goes well beyond awareness. It is one thing to be aware of cultural idiosyncrasies. It is quite another to know how to design effects and execute coherent actions that take into account cultural perspectives and views. The U.S. military has acknowledged the importance of culture in any counterinsurgency operation (COIN) in its doctrine. In Army Field Manual 3–24 (U.S. Marine Corps 3–33.5), it acknowledges the importance of the culture and its relationship to intelligence in the following statement:

> Counterinsurgency (COIN) is an intelligence-endeavor. The function of intelligence in COIN is to facilitate understanding of the operational environment, with emphasis on the populace, host nation, and insurgents. Commanders require accurate intelligence about these three areas to best address the issues driving the insurgency. Both insurgents and counterinsurgents require an effective intelligence capability to be successful. Both attempt to create and maintain intelligence networks while trying to neutralize their opponent's intelligence capabilities.[5]

U.S. implementers of national power must possess a significant depth of understanding about the ways and means to influence how people, organizations, and leaders of a particular culture think, perceive, make decisions, act, assess actions, learn, and adjust. Because people are of primary importance in any insurgency, decision makers must take time to develop excruciatingly detailed plans for initiating successful, human-oriented effects and actions. Author David Galula, writing in *Counterinsurgency Warfare Theory and Practice*, helps us realize the importance of the populace and their culture by stating

If the insurgent manages to dissociate the population from the counterinsurgent, to control it physically, to get its active support, he will win the
war because, in the final analysis, the exercise of political power depends
on the tacit or explicit agreement of the population or, at worst, on its sub-
missiveness. Thus, the battle for the population is a major characteristic of
the revolutionary war.[6]

Of course, to win the population the intelligence analyst must understand
and use the culture in which the population lives and interacts with other
people and organizations. Continuing with this line of thought, General
David Petraeus wrote about the importance of understanding the culture in
Military Review in 2006, stating

cultural awareness is a force multiplier, reflects our recognition that
knowledge of the cultural "terrain" can be as important as, and sometimes
even more important than, knowledge of the geographic terrain. This
observation acknowledges that the people are, in many respects, the
decisive terrain, and that we must study that terrain in the same way that
we have always studied the geographic terrain. Working in another culture
is enormously difficult if one doesn't understand the ethnic groups, tribes,
religious elements, political parties, and other social groupings—and their
respective viewpoints; the relationships among the various groups;
governmental structures and processes; local and regional history; and, of
course, local and national leaders.[7]

Intelligence analysis, planning, collection, and condition-setting are critical
in the process of gaining knowledge and understanding about the OE, the
enemy, the population, and last, but certainly not least, the culture. Intelligence analysts must find or develop sufficient cultural knowledge and
background to be specific in planning intelligence operations and assessing
outcomes.

No matter how much schooling and no matter how many times people
visit a country, it is still difficult to think like the people of a particular
culture if one is not raised in that culture. Thus, as one consideration,
people engaging in advanced analysis and working with cultural intelligence need the wherewithal to seek, find, and successfully confer with
indigenous and U.S. cultural SMEs. When the cultural metrics that count
are atypical to one's own society, this interaction involves taking the right
steps to gain a sufficient breadth and depth of knowledge to design good
effects and actions and to know how to assess outcomes. Operations and
actions, even interpreting data that signify actions and outcomes, cannot be
adequately accomplished without help from trusted indigenous cultural
experts. Even when dealing with indigenous specialists, however, intelligence analysts must realize the limitations of knowledge any one person can

possess. Thus, the intelligence analyst, using the precepts of advanced analysis, must seek and use the help of a VKE knowledge broker to find and link analysts with a variety of trusted SMEs for helping with advanced analysis processes.

IMPORTANCE OF CULTURAL ANALYSIS

Along with what has already been discussed, cultural analysis is important for several reasons. It helps decision makers and their staffs understand the fundamentals of a culture, its institutions, its people, their perspectives, and their behaviors. Cultural analysis helps decision makers and their staffs anticipate the outcomes of actions and effects not only on an enemy but on the populace in which the interaction occurs. In addition, it provides people with the wherewithal to develop and use cultural observables. Cultural analysis develops cultural observables to guide very specific and detailed intelligence collection. It also helps advanced analysts make sense of incoming data and turn them into information and knowledge so the commander and other senior staff officers have the best possible opportunities for gaining situational understanding.

It is through cultural analysis that cultural observables come forth to guide all types of collection to collect on the right target at the right time and the right place with the right degree of specificity. As a quick review of an earlier part of our inquiry, *cultural observables* are observed or measured tangible or intangible properties deriving from the ways of living propagated by a particular ethnic group. Cultural observables are important to cultural analysis in that they provide indicants of activity or anomalies when searching for well-hidden and embedded enemies. It takes advanced analysis, with help from SMEs and indigenous people, to develop cultural observables in sufficient detail to be useful. Cultural observables are often subtle, nuanced, and fleeting; they are extremely difficult to plan for, execute against, and understand once collection-derived data is fused, integrated, and interpreted. The use of cultural observables quickly comes to the forefront of any cognitive efforts made by intelligence analysts participating in a counterinsurgency. As a final point, cultural observables help U.S. planners and decision makers understand the enemy, populace, and cultural setting in which the enemy interacts with the U.S. military, neutrals, multinational corporations, indigenous people, and elements of the culture.

In counterinsurgencies, decision makers always consider the effects of their decisions, actions, and outcomes on the populace. Such consideration involves designing cultural observables at the front of the analysis/collection process to drive collection and provide the data that cultural intelligence analysis helps to turn into information and usable knowledge. Of course, cultural intelligence analysis is the most important ingredient in interpreting outcomes of actions through the cultural "lens" of the people who will experience the direct results or side effects of the action in question.

Sometimes people support insurgents because their living conditions are so bad that they go with the side they believe will improve their lot. The long arm of day and night security continually looms over and influences the minds of these people. Security is perceptual—it depends upon thought and emotion—and it is physical. Thought and emotion, however, come from the culture and how it conditions people to think, perceive, feel, act, and behave.

As an example, how people cope with poor infrastructure support is a direct result of their longstanding expectations and is derived from a particular cultural perspective and the past. The analyst must engage in cultural analysis to understand what the populace believes their plight to be at the present and what they expect the future will be. Their expectations can come from information gleaned from the Internet, via telephones, and from television or other forms of information sharing or simply from what they have come to know through good or bad personal experience. Or, better yet, their expectations come from interviews, from HUMINT, and from the thoughts of indigenous and U.S. cultural SMEs. How a person interprets such data and information is, once again, dependent upon the way that person interprets all information. Again, perception is the result of a person's cultural lens. To understand perception, one has to figuratively get into the mind and culture of the person being studied. Regardless, expectations are important, and they derive from and depend upon cultural upbringing.

Interpretation, a close companion to expectation, is an important aspect of cultural intelligence analysis, but it is also complex and difficult to understand. This difficulty in understanding and using interpretation is precisely why, generally speaking, U.S. intelligence analysts cannot "go it alone." By way of reinforcement, consider how a city's infrastructure influences the perceptions and interpretative powers of the populace at a given location. Consider how actions by U.S. leaders and soldiers influence the people's perceptions and how they interpret the flow of incoming data. Consider the relationship between interpretation and perception. As an example, while September 11, 2001, was a traumatic event for all Americans, people from other countries interpreted it far differently. Some people in the Middle East, for example, believed the event came from a worldwide Zionist effort to drive Americans further away from Muslims. Terrorists viewed it as a God-ordained event. People in Europe sometimes held that the war-against-terror efforts after September 11 were an overreaction, particularly in light of the losses some of these people and their countries had experienced in their own counterterrorism efforts over the years. It follows that perspectives are an important aspect of cultural analysis. Author Michael Scheuer helps us understand this notion about perspectives:

we must accept that there are many Muslims in the world who believe that U.S. foreign policy is irretrievably biased in favor of Israel, trigger happy in attacking the poor and ill-defended Muslim countries . . . rapacious in controlling and consuming the Islamic world's energy resources; blasphemous in allowing Israel to occupy Jerusalem and U.S. troops to be based in Saudi Arabia; and hypocritical and cruel in its denial of Palestinian rights, use of economic sanctions against the Muslim people of Iraq, and support for the Muslim world's absolutist kings and dictators.[8]

At this point in this chapter on cultural analysis, we can draw three short conclusions. *First*, to succeed in using advanced analysis and its essential component—cultural analysis—an advanced analyst must be trained and educated and also have access to the right cultural SMEs to understand the subtleties, nuances, and ambiguities of cultural intelligence. In the absence of SMEs, analysts do the best that they can with the knowledge and experience at hand. *Second*, both perception and interpretation are important and highly relational, as one "feeds" upon the other. As such, analysts must perceive the world, the neighborhood, and the inputs coming from interactions, activities, transactions, goals, objectives, and ordinary and extraordinary happenings from the perception of the people in whose culture they find themselves. Interpretation is also culturally oriented. That is, it is important for advanced analysts to use cultural intelligence to understand how people interpret actions, communiqués, messages, and efforts to improve the lot of the populace. This is a cultural issue, and it is cultural intelligence and its direct lineage, cultural observables, that can help us understand how the people we are dealing with interpret what we are doing or have done. Advanced analysts use cultural analysis and seek assistance from indigenous and nonindigenous SMEs to gain requisite insights and understanding to use the culture for gaining advantages. *Third*, if advanced analysts do not design and use cultural observables with which to collect, they will miss out on a huge part of intelligence operations in urban settings.

Cultural analysis is closely related with other cognitive elements of advanced analysis. Some of the closest relationships include the relationship of cultural analysis with *anomaly, tendency, aggregation,* and *semiotics* analysis. Let us briefly discuss how cultural analysis relates to these other elements of advanced analysis.

- **Cultural analysis and anomaly analysis.** *Anomaly analysis* is discerning meaning in departures from the normal or common order, form, or rule; it is the absence of that which is expected. Anomaly analysis depends on cultural analysis and a cultural baseline to plan, look for, and understand what is collected and to make sense of it. By way of review, a *cultural baseline* is a mental template that serves as a standard relating to the shared knowledge and values of an element of a society by which things in a particular neighborhood are measured or compared denoting or deriving from or distinctive of the ways of living of a distinctive group of people. A cultural baseline is important because it establishes the cultural norm. With the cultural norm in mind, our analysts and collectors can then look for and understand the cultural aspects of anomalies. With anomalies, the analyst can rapidly explore cause/effect relationships. In addition, people supporting the enemy's network will make mistakes; these mistakes will come forth as cultural mistakes owing to nervousness, fear, increased adrenalin, increased sweating, agitated diction, poor manners, and hurrying when they usually saunter. Cultural analysis helps to develop cultural observables with which to look for anomalies. It provides the intellectual and knowledge wherewithal to develop and nurture the cultural baseline and to develop cultural observables.

- **Cultural analysis and tendency analysis.** *Tendency analysis* is discerning meaning through thought and study of the general proclivities of people, the behavioral and action inclinations of organizations, mental snapshots of current environment or contextual situations, events, activities, behaviors, the emanation dispersal of energy emissions, and what the interaction and enmeshing of all could portend for the future. Tendency analysis must work with a snapshot or a mental image of a current situation. Tendency analysis, therefore, depends on cultural analysis to understand what is normal and what is wrong with the conjured snapshot by way of perceived or real cultural anomalies. Tendency analysis portends the future, but for the most part, it needs to make such a projection in the context of the culture and subelements of the culture (such as semiotics) to be meaningful. Then, if portending the future, the advanced analyst using cultural analysis develops the observables that deal with the projected state of cultural being. Once observables are tasked to collection and collection starts producing output, it is often a combination of cultural, anomaly, and tendency analyses that helps the analyst to draw meaning from resultant data and to rapidly turn it into information and knowledge for commander's understanding and decision-making.
- **Cultural analysis and aggregation analysis.** *Aggregation analysis* is discerning meaning of several things numbering from a few to millions that are grouped, moving, working together, and considered as a whole. It is the culture that most often provides the "glue" that binds the parts and pieces of an aggregate and aggregates to other aggregates. Thus, it follows that advanced analysts have to know the culture, or find the people who do know, to understand it well enough to understand what "glues" together the essential elements of aggregates. This same understanding helps to understand, search for, and find the conditions conducive for aggregates to conjoin into larger aggregates. Some other

considerations of the relationship between aggregation and cultural analysis include that the enemy will use culture to mask his changes and morphing and that advanced analysts have to use indigenous SMEs to help anticipate where and how the culture will be changing and how the enemy could be using the change to mask his activity. Thus, advanced analysts will have to be cognitively agile to understand cultural adaptation and change so as to "see" and understand the cultural side of aggregation and where these aggregates will morph to in the future.

• **Cultural analysis and semiotics analysis.** Semiotics analysis is also closely related to cultural analysis. *Semiotics analysis* is discerning meaning of cultural signs and symbols reflected in drawings, paintings, signs, symbols, photographs, syntax, words, sounds, body language, and graffiti. As a close relative to cultural analysis, semiotics can suddenly appear and signal the formation of change or insights into the perceptions and interpretation of the populace. It is cultural analysis that provides meaning to semiotics. It also provides the knowledge and intellectual wherewithal to design cultural observables to watch for the appearance of, perturbation of existing, and interpretation of semiotics that come and go in any bustling and constantly changing city. Semiotics also help to provide hints of what comprises the cultural "glue" that binds aggregates. Why is semiotics analysis specifically important to cultural analysis? Our answer is, in many urban COIN situations, semiotics help the advanced analyst to identify something very culturally specific with which to search for, find, and interpret anomalies and tendencies. In fact, that which is abnormal or anomalous will often appear and be noticeable in the realm of semiotics, and it takes cultural analysis to interpret and apply semiotics. Many aspects of human interaction, transactions, activities, and behaviors are subtle, nuanced, and ambiguous to the point of invisibility to the western eye and mind. But semiotics are not entirely invisible. Cultural analysis helps us search for and find hard to notice, invisible events, human activities, or transactions. Cultural analysis relates to semiotics analysis by finding and identifying what semiotics mean—nonverbal behavior, symbols, syntax, language variation, and signs we must search for and find as well as quickly exploit once discovered.

As a next step along our path of understanding of cultural analysis, let us get into more specificity and consider some practical applications for how intelligence people and commanders can use cultural analysis. As an initial step, let us delve into some of the most important considerations for understanding the vagaries of cultural analysis. The following question can help guide us in this quest. What are some of the most important things to consider when thinking about the culture in relationship to urban intelligence operations?

- The neighborhood
- The actions that normally occur and what anomalies would look like
- The interaction of people—friends, men and women, couples, relatives, acquaintances, children, and adults
- How transactions occur
- How social, political, religious, and leisure activities of people occur
- How people behave
- Activities of people and organizations and cultural influences
- Cultural baseline of the neighborhood in question
- Influence of religion on activities, transactions, interactions, and behavior
- How people work with and defer to religious and cultural leaders
- Populace's views of the west, technology, and presence of foreign soldiers
- Populace's beliefs about security and hope for the future
- Populace's interpretation of U.S. military and western-provided data, information, and knowledge
- Populace's views on outsiders and trust among themselves
- Relationships—closest to most distant
- Leisure activities
- How people dress
- How people talk
- How people gesture

Advantages and disadvantages abound for all sides in an urban OE. In cultural analysis, it is important to understand these advantages and disadvantages for two reasons. *First*, what are disadvantages could easily be vulnerabilities. Vulnerabilities provide opportunity for the side that finds and employs the means to take advantage of the vulnerability. As friendly forces go through the process of cultural analysis to attempt to exploit a perceived vulnerability, they must watch for anticipation by the enemy commander of potential attacks against his vulnerability. In addition, friendly analysts must help their commander understand the cultural impacts of trying to take advantage of perceived vulnerabilities, particularly cultural vulnerabilities. *Second*, looking for enemy vulnerabilities should also cause friendly commanders to understand their own vulnerabilities and that the enemy and other competitors may try to exploit them.

Some of the enemy's cultural advantages could include the ease of blending with the culture and its many activities, interactions, transactions, and individual, group, and organizational behaviors. One of the most interesting aspects of the insurgent's networks involves the term "embeddedness." Terrorism expert Marc Sageman describes embeddedness as follows:

The term embeddedness refers to the rich nexus of social and economic linkages between members of an organization and its environment. Being embedded in society encourages trust in ongoing interactions. It makes people sensitive to local criticism. If grievances are aired, they are anchored in concerns that are close to home . . . The lack of such bonds frees people from these responsibilities and local concerns.[9]

This notion of embeddedness suggests how the insurgent or terrorist can exist within a community or neighborhood yet plan and execute the most horrific operations against the people who live there. It also implies that cultural alienation could be at play even when insurgents or irregulars are deeply embedded in a neighborhood and that there is potential to be able to search for and find them using cultural analysis to design observables and make sense from resultant collection data.

In many cases, the insurgent or irregular will look, talk, sound, behave, and act like ordinary people who are legitimate and integral parts of the culture in question. But he will be different in some subtle ways. In his book, *The Suicide of Reason*, author Lee Harris tells us

> Likewise, the virtues of the rational actor, such as the avoidance of violence, the willingness to compromise, tolerance of other tribes and their traditions, are looked upon as signs of cowardice, imbecility, or a traitorous lack of loyalty to one's tribe. Thus it is virtually impossible for those who follow the laws of the jungle to find a common ground with those whose highest ethical aim is to abolish these very laws and replace them with cultures of reason. What is day to one is night to the other; what is good to one is evil for the other. The fanaticism abhorred by the rational actor becomes the collective bond that keeps the tribal mind together.[10]

In addition the culture will provide people willing to support the enemy's network and hide the insurgents' activities. Further, discerning legitimate from illegitimate activities is very difficult for a western analyst. In addition, a city has masses of people who are involved in many activities every day. It is easy for an irregular warrior or insurgent to mask their activities by mingling with legitimate people doing legitimate things. Communication is also another advantage. The insurgent and irregular warrior can communicate through the use of high-tech cell phones and the Internet, or he can use the ageless technique of human couriers. The insurgent and irregular can also use semiotics to transmit culturally laden codes, symbols, and puzzles using myths, traditions, and icons only the people of a local culture would know. As a final point and thanks to enemy's and their supporters' capabilities to blend with the flow and use semiotics, discerning anomalies, tendencies, trends, aggregates, patterns, and links will be difficult even for the most proficient of advanced analysts.

When insurgent and irregular operatives operate in a large urban setting, they also have some disadvantages. For instance, they bring danger.

They upset the ordinary lives of the people in whose midst they reside. Thus people will act differently when insurgents are in their midst—observables will appear with such deviant behavior. For example, supporters of the network and ordinary people who are passive supporters of the insurgency will often feel the very real presence of danger, death, or prison. They could very well restrict the freedom of children to play in the streets, to move about, to be alone, and to walk to school. Women might not be able to dress freely at home and they might not be allowed to stay home alone when the husband is gone.

As another disadvantage, insurgents and irregular warriors must use the populace to perform many of the essential functions of their networks, such as providing food and water, medical care, transportation, and parts for bombs, and performing reconnaissance or intelligence collection. Some of these functions involve the all-important condition-setting the enemy must perform to accomplish his goals or missions successfully. With network support and condition-setting, people will make mistakes. With these mistakes properly guided U.S. collection will pick up the errors, and teams of advanced analysts and SMEs will take resultant data and quickly turn them into actionable knowledge for command decision-making. In addition, some of the people will be double agents. The potential for spies and double agents in and amongst network operations could cause increases in counterintelligence and countersurveillance, which have the cascading effect of inadvertently providing more observables for friendly forces to look for.

When any side has so many moving pieces that make up a network and its functioning, there is the very real possibility of discovery and neutralization for those trying to remain hidden and unnoticeable. The insurgent must be secretive to survive. When attempting to be secretive, the insurgent and his network become sensitive to natural or U.S.-induced sensitive variables. They cannot plan for all of these variables and when they may occur. If the U.S. advanced analysts and collection specialists have anticipated their ascendancy and power at the right time in the right window of opportunity, the insurgent is often exposed for study, for purposefully morphing, and/or for neutralization.

With the immensity of a large urban setting and the importance of the culture, is there any way that the advanced analyst can start narrowing his or her focus to search for, find, and make sense of data, information, and knowledge to provide situational awareness and understanding to the commander and the rest of the staff? Is there a way to organize his or her cognitive efforts so as to focus on culturally oriented and manageable specifics through the use of cultural analysis? The answer to both of these questions is yes. A usable thought template involves *interactions, activities, transactions,* and *behaviors.* But what do each of these mean and how do they relate to cultural analysis?

- **Interact.** To *interact* means to act together or towards others or with others.[11] People interact in social settings such as a city. They meet, greet, and exchange pleasantries or information. They share information. They conduct business, and they purchase the essentials of life. The way they normally interact is driven and influenced, indeed dictated, by the culture. When analysts know the culturally accepted and dedicated way of interacting, particularly between two men, between a man and a woman, between adults and children, between people purchasing and those selling, between acquaintances, and between relatives, they will find an enormously rich area for intelligence analysis, collection, and exploitation.
- **Act.** To *act* is to operate or function in a particular way; perform specific duties or functions.[12] The particularities or specifics, of course, come from the culture. How people normally act is dictated by the culture. Deviation from what are normal acts provides insight into change, into a disturbance in the individual or collective psyches of the people living and acting in the culture, or to a foreign element that could very well be a foreign and dangerous body in the collective organism that is the culture.
- **Transact.** To *transact* means to carry on or conduct (business, negotiations, activities, etc.) to a conclusion or settlement.[13] Transactions provide a focus for intelligence analysis and collection in a busy city life. People in the culture conduct transactions. People who support the insurgents' network conduct transactions too. Occasionally, they will make mistakes in these transactions and cause a ripple or perturbation in the cloth that is cultural normalcy. That is when U.S. analysts and collection specialists must be watching. Transactions are part of a cultural baseline. As such, the advanced analyst must understand how normal transactions occur across a swath of life in the city—religion, play, pleasure, marriage, death, birth, business, work, recreation, eating, exchanging information, and so forth. It is not enough to know and be able to recite these types of transactions. The advanced analyst must understand the cultural influences and historical applications of how people conduct transactions inherent to a particular culture and what differences would occur when people from a different culture try to conduct the same transaction. Analysts must delve into cultural detail to understand how the culture in question dictates the normal conduct of transactions so they can use machines and people to watch for abnormal or slightly deviant transactions, such as a person going to market slipping a packet of illicit cash to an insurgent's courier in a busy thoroughfare.
- **Behavior.** To *behave* means to act in a particular way; conduct or comport oneself or itself . . . to act or react under given circumstances.[14] Cultural habits and social mores drive behavior. Some societies have very strict codes of behavior, e.g., Saudi Arabia, while other countries

have less strict codes of behavior, e.g., United States. Cities, particularly in the Middle East, provide a fertile ground for both analysis and collection because of their rigid, culturally induced ways of behaving via a well-defined group of social mores (the accepted traditional customs and usages of a particular social group).[15] If the advanced analyst can use cultural analysis to design cultural observables dealing with culturally influenced behaviors under a wide range of conditions, behavior becomes a powerful analytic and collection tool for conducting COIN and IW in urban settings.

The reader will have concluded by now that cultural analysis is intellectually arduous and highly dependent upon knowledge of and relations in the culture in which U.S. soldiers are operating. Analysts must meet these challenges if they desire to use cultural analysis. Given the propensity of modern conflict to be in urban settings in cultures different from that of the United States, it follows that advanced analysts of the future will have no choice but to use cultural analysis to succeed. Thus, they will always need to be aware of difficulties and challenges and have well-planned strategies for their demise or mitigation. Let us take an excursion and discuss some of its challenges and then identify some ways to overcome them. First, let us identify some of the more difficult aspects of cultural analysis.

- **Cultural knowledge and understanding.** People have to know the culture or use people who do know it to use cultural analysis and cultural observables. This means advanced analysts have to know enough about the culture to discern how the enemy is using the culture to mask his movements, hide, and coordinate. In addition, advanced analysts must know much and understand the culture to anticipate, watch for, discern, and comprehend incoming data dealing with this subject.
- **Culturally induced perception and interpretation.** As mentioned previously, both perception and interpretation are critically important to commanders in the activities they plan, execute, and assess. But, intelligence analysts have to know a lot about the culture to provide the specifics in information and knowledge to help the commander make judgments.
- **Relationship with collection and finding the right collectors to pick up on cultural observables.** The observables discussed in this chapter are cultural observables. They are often nuanced, subtle, ambiguous, and fleeting. Mechanical sensors do not do well working against these types of observables. Unfortunately, HUMINT-produced collection often fails to see such observables unless the collector knows exactly what the analyst is looking for, including where, when, and operational context.
- **Designing and ensuring data flow architectures.** Source inputs will come from a wide variety of people, machines, and places. Some will be quite

ordinary, e.g., U2 coverage, but other sources will have to be commercial-off-the-shelf (COTS), and that will present immense challenges for moving data from this type of source to U.S. military processors such as the Army's DCGS-A.

- **Finding right indigenous SMEs who know particular neighborhoods.** All cultural intelligence is local. Along with knowing the culture writ large, the advanced analyst must be able to bore into specific neighborhoods, into specific sects, and into particular tribes to design, execute, and assess outcomes of analytic-driven intelligence operations. Two types of SMEs can help. One is an indigenous SME. This kind of SME has the local culture and background to help with cultural analysis. Unfortunately, this person is not always trustworthy. A second type is a U.S. cultural SME. Unfortunately, this person may not be a person from the culture we are discussing, and they will not have requisite knowledge and understanding of how the culture influences a specific neighborhood in question, but they can be of assistance in working with cultural intelligence.
- **Thinking.** Obviously, a wide chasm separates western thought processes and those of the people of a country in which the United States finds itself involved. It is imperative to understand how people from the country in question and the insurgents in their midst think. Finding ways to bridge this chasm is difficult at best and nearly impossible at worst. This difficulty does not obviate the problem.
- **Influence of media on populace's psyches.** All people have access to the news media. Unfortunately, how the data become information for consumption and interpretation by the masses is highly dependent upon cultural influences. U.S. commanders have to consider how to overcome this challenge and obstacle and convince the populace that they are telling the truth. The conveyance of such information and its medium has to be enshrouded by cultural influences or it will always fail.

Now, let us consider some of the ways advanced analysts can overcome the associated difficulties/challenges with cultural analysis.

- **Mental organization.** Work with a thought template. Quite frankly, there are too many considerations one has to make to think about cultural analysis from memory and experience. Thus, advanced analysts desiring to perform cultural analysis have to use a thought template of the major considerations. The thought template should not be a checklist with its associated restrictions on thinking. Checklists are fine for mechanical functions such as preflight inspections of an aircraft, but are not usable in working with the dictum "how to think" about complex problems. Instead, a thought template lists considerations that form a conceptual framework for the analyst to use, in this case, for cultural analysis.

- **Seek support of and work with experts.** Intelligence analysts attempting to use cultural analysis need to use SMEs. Some of these SMEs can be well-educated cultural anthropologists from the United States and coalition countries, given they speak the language, have spent years studying the culture in question, and have lots of time on the ground. Advanced analysts can also use the help of indigenous SMEs. They will be of two main types. *First*, the analyst can use properly cleared cultural specialists. *Second*, the analyst can seek the support of indigenous people from the neighborhood in question to help with the analytic work—decomposition, recomposition, synthesis, wargaming, and so forth. Advanced analysts can also seek the assistance of foreign area officers (FAOs) who have been schooled on the culture in question, speak the language, and have on-the-ground experience. Another source of expertise can be found in a supporting VKE. Here, the advanced analyst can find knowledge brokers, problem managers, SMEs, COEs, and scientists who can lend a hand in the cerebral chores of an advanced analyst. As a final point, the analyst can go to other sources such as interagency, nongovernment organizations (NGOs), and business organizations such as infrastructure repair, medical treatment, and security companies for assistance. Indigenous people can help the analyst think as the enemy or populace thinks, as can U.S. cultural specialists. In addition, FAOs can help in the work to understand how people think.
- **Use the culture for advantage.** The intelligence analyst must assist the commander by helping him understand cultural influences on perception and interpretation and how both concepts can help reduce his *cultural uncertainties* and manage *cultural risks*. In this sense, even the slightest cultural errors can cause enormous, almost irreparable, cultural *faux pas* and attendant damage.
- **Engage in red-teaming, wargaming, and critical thinking.** The military is slowly drifting toward embracing the need for red-teaming capabilities in each staff. Leavenworth-trained red-teaming people provide contrarian points of view, critique thinking and assumptions, and help people develop different ideas and approaches to problems. A large part of the Red Team University's curriculum involves anthropology and empathy for others' cultures. With such a capability, red-teaming people can help to murder board hypotheses and criticize thinking to help find cultural errors in logic and what to do about those errors. Using red teamers to help analysts think like the enemy and critique their thinking should be an early part of analytic condition-setting for successfully using cultural analysis. As a second step in analytic condition-setting for cultural analysis, the advanced analyst must be deeply involved in wargaming. This wargaming must be with and among four pairs—friendly, enemy, host nation, and neutrals. Each should be assigned goals, objectives, resources, tactics, techniques, and tools and should be represented by

red team people and people of appropriate ethnicity. Each aspect of this wargaming should discover effects, when control of the initiative moves from competing group to group. In our case, we are seeking help about how to use the culture for our advantage and how the enemy will be using it for his advantage. We also want to discern cultural reactions to our actions and effects. The advanced analyst will use resultant hypotheses (act, react, and counteract hypotheses) to help guide cultural analysis and collection. This type of wargaming will also help to guide the questioning of assumptions and their underpinning considerations, the potential for the ascendancy of second- and third-order effects, the opening and closing of windows of opportunity, and thought about the most important aspects of any conflict—initiative, freedom of maneuver, tempo, knowledge, momentum, position, and decision advantages.

- **Analysis and baselines.** Advanced analysts attempting to use cultural analysis must always use baselines of three types—*technical, cultural,* and *functional*. If these baselines do not exist, the advanced analyst must seek the help of people in the intelligence enterprise and a supporting VKE to help gather and organize data to form them. To do so, they must work with the other aspects of advanced analysis we have previously discussed—anomaly, tendency, aggregation, trend, link, and pattern analysis.

- **Collection.** The advanced analyst must work very closely with collection specialists to match observables with optimum mixes of collection. They must ensure that each collector knows analyst guidance, situational context, and sampling rates as well as the right time, right place, and right activity to look for the right observables and have the wherewithal to send pertinent data as directly as possible to the advanced analyst while meeting analytic-imposed standards—timeliness, specificity, accuracy, relevance, and clarity.

- **Think like the enemy and the populace that supports him.** To think like the enemy, the aspiring advanced analyst must answer the following questions (from the enemy's perspectives) with the help of properly cleared indigenous people and U.S. SMEs spread across a particular area of expertise:
  - How does culture affect my perception of U.S. analysis and collection?
  - How can I use the culture to hide from his sensors and HUMINT?
  - How can I use the culture to blend in and become "invisible"?
  - What will the Americans do with the culture that can cause my failure and how might I surreptitiously counteract?
  - How can I use cultural activity to move and deceive?
  - How can I plan and execute my condition-setting and operations by leveraging and taking advantage of the culture while the United States is looking for me?

- What are the best ways to use the culture to provide early warning of danger?
- How will I use the culture to preclude the United States from finding indications of my countersurveillance?
- How can I use the culture to enhance my bomb-making material resupply?
- How can I use the culture to recruit people to perform the many duties I need for sustaining my network and for performing tasks essential to my mission?
- How can I use the culture to communicate so the U.S. intelligence people will not notice—semiotics?
- As an additional step or way to help overcome the challenges involved in using cultural analysis, more techniques must be thought about and made available. In one way or another, all of the techniques listed below involve thinking. Thus, as a first step, analysts must think about their own thinking and understand that as a human beings they will make errors. Along this train of thought, analysts must be introspective about their knowledge of the culture and typical errors and mental traps they fall into. In an introspective way, they must answer the following question: What must I do to ensure I do not commit cultural thinking errors? Possible answers to this question include the following ideas:
  - Advanced analysts must be painfully aware of their biases, values, outlooks, open mindedness, and stereotyping and seek feedback from others to help identify their particular cognitive shortfalls, problems, and errors. As the reader can surmise, this is a most difficult task and one that is very easy to shunt off for a later time only to never address. The advanced analyst must know their proclivity to mirror image and recognize if others are falling into this trap. They must look for mirror imaging in wargaming and in others' thoughts and products.
  - Use U.S. and Iraqi SMEs to learn from and to check one's thinking. If these types of SMEs are unavailable, analysts can use a VKE. In addition, analysts can be creative and use people in non-intelligence roles and missions to help (e.g., maintenance people, LNOs, host nation military, and police).
  - What can analysts do to keep an open mind about cultural sensitivities, cultural influences on thinking and perceiving, and the importance of icons and religious holidays? Advanced analysts must use history when contemplating the influence of the culture. But, they also must attempt to identify and use new ways of thinking, perhaps even creative thinking, to come up with solutions in an environment that is built on cultural stasis in one respect and cultural dynamism in another respect. What commanders need are "new ideas . . . from the association of old elements in new combinations . . . [t]his ability to

bring previously unrelated information and ideas together in meaningful ways is what marks the open-minded, imaginative, creative analyst."[16] The advanced analyst can also use singular or combined approaches or techniques to keep the door of their mind open to new ideas or fresh approaches to old problems. Some of the more well-known techniques include:

- Role playing.
- Use of indigenous SMEs.
- Use of U.S. cultural anthropologists.
- Seeking and using a devil's advocate.
- Identifying possible cultural second- and third-order effects, with the purpose of mitigating adverse effects being the most important aspect of this technique.
- Addressing how the various players upon the stage of urban conflict perceive. Answer the question: How am I addressing how the competitor perceives his surroundings, his enemies, the host nation government, and the populace?
- Ask the right questions about cultural influences.

- Let us review some of the cognitive or logic errors in thinking an analyst can make when attempting to use cultural analysis and when engaging in the many considerations extant to effective intelligence analysis:
  - Mirror imaging
  - Inadequate or outdated knowledge
  - Biases and close mindedness
  - Poor use of and understanding of relationships
  - Non sequiturs
  - Incorrect cause/effect relationships when dissecting occurring or planning cultural second- and third-order effects
  - Cultural arrogance
  - Oversimplification of a society or culture

- Going another step along the pathway to understanding, the aspiring advanced analyst must answer the question: What are some of the personal errors analysts make as they try to use cultural analysis?
  - Did I consider my penchant to engage in mirror imaging?
  - Did I design cultural observables using cultural intelligence, anomaly analysis, aggregation analysis, and tendency analysis?
  - Did I seek and use the expertise of red teaming people?
  - Did I seek and use the expertise of indigenous SMEs?
  - Did I seek and use the expertise of the VKE's cultural SMEs and data scientists?
  - Did I use indigenous people to help me overcome my errors of thought about the culture?
  - Did I find the right SMEs who know the cultural peculiarities of the specific neighborhood in which I am interested?

- Did I use cultural SMEs familiar with the neighborhoods in question to work with me in wargaming, to identify points of friction, and pursue my expectations, mysteries, and hunches?

In concluding, this important discussion on cultural analysis will help the advanced analyst immensely. Many issues and complexities cloud the use of cultural analysis, and this chapter on cultural analysis seeks to help lift the veil of ignorance and corresponding lack of understanding. Two issues stand out in importance for the purposes of our inquiry. *First*, the U.S. military pushes "cultural awareness" when it should be pursuing "cultural competence" and knowledge. Arguably, not every intelligence analyst can be an expert in a given culture, but they can and should know enough to be more than "aware." *Second*, people rarely think about the U.S. military using culture knowledge *to gain advantages* and not merely to avoid offending the populace or to know how to communicate with people of the culture under discussion. To use the culture for advantage takes knowledge and a very different type of analysis—which is, of course, cultural analysis. Now, let us review some of the main points the chapter brings forth.

- It is difficult for Americans to think like the populace, the government, and the insurgents in a foreign culture. But, even with the difficulty, it must be done and accomplished with minimal bias, mirror imaging, and recognition of the ultimate subjectivity of everything people do. In addition, the analyst must realize that as they attempt to think like their adversary, they come to realize the insurgent has the same thinking biases and problems as us.
- Cultural intelligence is important because it helps us to know and understand the fundamentals of the culture in question and to use this knowledge to seek, find, and exploit advantages. Cultural intelligence helps the U.S. intelligence analyst anticipate outcomes of courses of action (COA), anticipate second- and third-order effects, develop and use cultural observables, and make sense of collection-derived data.
- Within the framework of advanced analysis, cultural intelligence relates most closely with anomaly, semiotics, tendency, and aggregation analysis.
- Working with the culture for advantage can often be successfully narrowed into interactions, activities, transactions, and behaving.

The chapter went through an elucidation drill dealing with challenges and meeting the challenges involved with cultural analysis. Some of the most important challenges included the following:

- Attaining cultural knowledge and understanding
- Understanding culturally induced perception and interpretation of influences and inputs into the indigenous population's minds and the government's collective brain

- Developing a close partnership with collection specialists and then having the wherewithal to collect against cultural observables
- Finding properly cleared and knowledgeable indigenous SME who know the particulars of specific neighborhoods is a significant challenge
- Finding an up-to-date cultural baseline

The chapter also offered some thoughts about ways to overcome challenges associated with cultural analysis. Some of the more important ways to overcome challenges include the following:

- Using a cultural analysis thought template
- Seeking and using support of cultural experts
- Learning to use the culture for U.S. advantages
- Engaging in cultural red-teaming, wargaming, and critical thinking
- Designing well-thought-out cultural observables and working with collection specialists to actually use optimum mixes of technical sensors and HUMINT to collect against those observables
- Using analytic baselines—cultural, technical, and functional—all of which relate to cultural analysis
- Learning to thinking like the enemy, the populace, and their political leaders and using these skills for creating and exploiting advantages

With completion of the chapter on cultural analysis, the reader is ready to proceed to the next chapter—semiotics analysis. Semiotics analysis is a close relative to cultural analysis but different and important enough to merit a separate discussion.

15

Semiotics Analysis[1]

Definition: Discerning meaning, knowledge, or understanding from cultural signs and symbols as reflected in drawings, paintings, photographs, syntax, words, sounds, and body language, plus the mediums upon which they ride and by which messages are delivered.

THEORY BEHIND SEMIOTICS ANALYSIS

The most direct application of semiotics analysis involves developing and understanding cultural specifics in urban settings. Semiotics have an important purpose in society—they help to identify and interpret the culture, and they serve to pass or transmit information via written, verbal, and visual communications. Semiotics represent the culture through its signs, symbols, history, myths, and the language they convey. So, how are semiotics and semiotics analysis relevant to advanced analysis? As we examine the culture in which our enemy resides, we must know the semiotics to know the culture. In addition, in our quest to know and understand COIN, our analysts have to understand, use semiotics and cultural analysis to design collection in urban settings, while working to discern the mood of the population, the outcomes of effects and actions the friendly commander has planned and executed, and understand how the insurgents and irregular warriors can use semiotics to pass information concerning alerts, codes, orders, descriptions, and courses of action.

U.S. advanced intelligence analysts must learn to use semiotics analysis to help think about, develop, and form conclusions, or at least tentative hypotheses awaiting confirmation or testing from cultural, semiotic-originated observables, and indicants of activities, transactions, interactions, and behavior. In an analytic context, semiotics analysis has a particular taxonomy involving but not limited to written words, spoken words and sentences, diction, intonation, inflection, semantics, emphasis, nonverbal behavior, nuance, subtleties in language and gestures, tone, graffiti, sounds, smells, group behavior, symbols, codes, and jokes to name but a few. Renowned Arab cultural specialist Bernard Lewis helps us understand how Islam influences semiotics with the following thoughts:

> Whatever the cause—political, social, economic—the form of expression to which most Muslims have hitherto had recourse to voice both their criticisms and their aspirations is Islamic. The slogans, the programs, and to a very large extent the leadership are Islamic.[2]

People must understand, not simply be aware, of the culture in which they work. Some aspects of the culture are in constant flux (the latest trend, the recent hot gossip), but others are semi-permanent or longstanding traditional aspects of culture. Semiotics involves cultural signs and symbols as well as body language, drawings, and even graffiti that are both short- and long-lived. The Arab's use of language is interesting and related to our work with semiotics analysis. When speaking, the Arab tends to exaggerate, and he

> has a predilection for repetition. If an Arab wishes to impress his interlocutor with having definitely made up his mind to embark on a certain course of action, he will state several times what he intends to do, using a series of repetitious asseverations, often with increasing emphasis, and always with slight stylistic variations.[3]

Just as important, all behavior is filtered through the prism of the observer's eyes and undergoes comprehension processes in that observer's mind. Those minds are heavily influenced by culture, surroundings, and context, and therefore could miss the meaning of semiotics and, in the case of the military, the ability to use semiotics analysis as a part of cultural observables and for recomposing data into information and knowledge.

The reason semiotics is an important aspect of advanced analysis is quite simple: counterinsurgency and counter-terror work must be centered on people, the specifics of their lives and activities, and the influences of the culture in which they live. However, even semiotics can be turned against the adversary if U.S. intelligence analysts know and understand the enemy. As I have previously written,

> It is particularly important to understand the information and knowledge inputs an opponent seeks, uses, and trusts. Why? If people understand

what information an opponent seeks, uses, and trusts, they can manipulate or create information inputs specifically designed to confuse, trick, or alter the opponent's perceptions.[4]

Semiotics helps provide some of the needed specificity to win in the war of wits the United States is currently engaged in with insurgents around the world. Intelligence analysts must be interested in the people whose homes and businesses constitute the insurgents' or terrorists' OE. Advanced analysts must be interested in people who can perform human sensor work as sources. This includes being interested in influencing people to avoid supporting the insurgents'/terrorists' networks. Thus, culture and its influence on what happens or doesn't happen are essential to all that occurs in an OE. This means that all activities, without question, stem from the culture enshrouding them. Signs and symbols are how people communicate within a culture. They are culturally peculiar. It follows that analysts working against an enemy who is embedded in a culture must know both semiotics and culture to be successful in analytic roles and missions.

Because the insurgent enemy is often embedded within a large population with identical or at least similar cultural orientations and characteristics, they are difficult to see, track, or trace. Because U.S. intelligence analysts don't come from the culture in question, they don't act, dress, think, or engage in pastimes like the local residents, nor do they think like the local populace unless they are prepared intellectually in training and education programs and have practical experience in the culture being discussed. Their perceptions of reality and the stimuli that influence their thoughts are dramatically different from those of local inhabitants. Moreover, without extensive training and education, U.S. intelligence analysts usually will not readily understand the signs, symbols, gestures, and other nonverbal behaviors that host nation citizens exhibit as part of their public routines and private lives. But these signs and symbols that indicate the presence of our enemies and that provide indications of population support are knowable and observable.

Arguably, at times analysts will not be able to use semiotics analysis against an embedded enemy per se. An insurgent may be so well hidden and paranoid that he will seldom venture forth into society for any kind of activity. But that same insurgent will still need support, regardless of his operational security. Wrapped in this support lies the indirect approach that has been surfaced and discussed previously. The movement and energy trails of people supporting the insurgents' networks will lead friendly hunters and gatherers to them like pheromones lead ants back to their anthill. Semiotics analysis helps in this hunt for hidden people in the vibrant foreign culture in motion that is a city.

As mentioned earlier, semiotics analysis relates to cultural analysis. Thus, we need to review the meaning of culture so we can better understand the meaning of semiotics and how the two relate. Culture is *the behaviors and beliefs characteristic of a particular social, ethnic, or age group; the sum total of ways of living built by a group of human beings and transmitted from one generation to another.*[5] How are humans involved with culture? Humans are the culture. They produce and develop culture. They change culture. People live within a culture and experience its changes. There are particular human manifestations of culture. One of them involves semiotics. What are some of the elements of any culture we need to consider for forming a framework with respect to semiotics? Some of the more important elements include:

- Religion
- Language
- Communication
- Education
- History
- Relationships
- Literature
- Television
- Marriage
- Internet
- Family life
- Myths
- Traditions
- Storytelling
- Symbols
- Dress
- Leisure activities
- Rest and relaxation
- Dining
- Technology
- Death
- Birth
- Tattooing
- Telephony
- Rituals

People relate to the culture with semiotics. As an example from American culture, street gangs use colors to denote turf or territory. People always communicate. Sometimes they use traditional means such as talking on the telephone or sending an e-mail message. But, people also communicate in a nontraditional way with what they wear or don't wear. For example, they wear traditional clothing if they are fundamentalists. They wear modern clothing if they are not strictly adhering to fundamentalist codes of apparel. They wear particular clothes in which to exercise. Women wear specific clothing to the market as well as to religious events. People wear specific clothing when they travel and relax or engage in leisure activities. They also wear clothing to commemorate death or birth celebrations. Clothing is an important aspect of culture and it can help transmit information via semiotics. The point is, even clothing is semiotics-laden and conveys messages if one knows what to look for and can analyze meaning from what they see.

People use semiotics to communicate. Some of the ways semiotics are transmitted include nonverbal behaviors such as gestures and grimaces. Other forms of nonverbal semiotics include lifting one's eye brows and making cognitive and emotional "gestures" with their eyes such as projecting incredulousness, fear, and signaling a more tenacious stance when presenting a point of view in an argument. In addition, people often use their hands and bodies to communicate emotions such as excitement or disagreement. They can also communicate their feelings in the way they stand and even the gait they choose as they walk or run.

People also exude semiotics as they communicate with their voices. They talk loudly or softly. They sing with great happiness or with sadness. They also whistle tunes of happiness or sadness. They raise inflection in their voices to convey meaning. They become silent when they are usually talkative—this also signals meaning. They become terse when they are usually verbose, which conveys either purposeful or inadvertent meaning. People exclaim with their voices and intonation, and they repeat words and ideas for emphasis. Some suicide bombers, for example, use chants and mantras in their preparation for death.

Semiotics also come forth through art. People paint or draw symbols or pictures to transmit their beliefs, feelings, or emotions at one end of a spectrum and to transmit purposeful and functional messages for the moment at its other end. The symbols people use in art are often difficult to understand by those not part of the culture. Even the colors people choose for their art can have cultural connotations that often prove difficult to spot, let alone to decipher. As an additional perspective of semiotic conveyance of meaning through art, drawings can convey symbolism, stories, codes, myths, histories, and encipherments. As another form of art that is chock full of semiotics, graffiti conveys meaning through cultural messages. What people draw or etch on walls, bridge underpasses, street signs, houses, and businesses by way of art, symbols, words, and even codes has meaning and is often symbolic of what is occurring in the minds of people living in a neighborhood of a particular culture. Written words also constitute art. What comes to us by way of written words when we consider semiotics? Some examples might be people's accomplishments, passing information, providing explanations, providing guidance, engaging in an angry diatribe, providing historical perspective, telling stories, and transmitting hidden messages.

Semiotics can also appear and be used for special meaning. Such culturally enshrouded meanings embedded in the semiotics are often unintelligible to people from the United States and other western cultures. What are some special-meaning semiotics that can be communicative in nature? In a general sense, they could be verbal, visual, audio, and nonverbal. They can include how people gesture, kiss when meeting, hold hands when talking, and even how they choose to shake hands. Even the presence of dead animals in cultures that typically don't dispose of dead animals can be used for semiotic communications. This way of conveying semiotic meaning could include position of the animal, pointing of limbs, arrangement of the head or even the torso, and the simplest meaning of all—dead animals can appear and disappear.

Semiotics analysis relates to some other elements of advanced analysis, with the most important being anomaly, aggregation, tendency, cultural analysis, and synthesis. Let us briefly discuss each of these highly relational elements of advanced analysis cognition.

- SEMIOTICS AND ANOMALY ANALYSIS. As a review, *anomaly analysis* is discerning meaning in departures from the normal or common order, form, or rule; absence of that which is expected. Semiotics analysis, often through the use of graffiti, helps identify anomalies. As such, it provides some of the basis for cultural and functional baseline work. Semiotics analysis also helps us think about what anomalies might look like and what we might see in a semiotic sense that could help us know change is occurring or about to occur. In addition, semiotics analysis also helps advanced analysts perform various types of change detection that are so important to searching for and discerning even the slightest changes. In fact, anomalies often appear as semiotics, and the advanced analyst must know how to use both semiotics and anomaly analysis as they work together and relate to other cognitive elements of advanced analysis.

- SEMIOTICS AND AGGREGATION ANALYSIS. *Aggregation analysis* involves groups, clusterings, and conglomerates numbering from a few to a million moving as one and exerting power with the strength of more than the power of single entities. Semiotics analysis helps us recognize the "glue" that holds aggregates together, and to comprehend the composition of the "glue" and how strong it is. Further, semiotics helps us to identify the "propellant" that projects aggregates and to know when it is more than simple energy or motion. Semiotics indicate the appearance of catalysts for propelling aggregates into higher levels and more advanced and powerful aggregates capable of inflicting harm and casualties on the U.S. or host nation populaces. In addition, semiotics helps us identify how sensitive aggregates are to perturbation and change. As a final comparison, semiotics analysis can alert us to the presence of nascent or even mature but latent aggregates and how they could combine to form larger, more powerful aggregates.

- SEMIOTICS ANALYSIS AND TENDENCY ANALYSIS. *Tendency analysis* is discerning meaning from the general proclivities of people, their activities, and their organizations, and snapshots in time to anticipate future states of things or activities. In our case, tendencies can yield insights into future attacks or activities and also indicate to commanders a strong case for selective and knowledge-driven intervention or preemption. Why? Semiotics analysis can indicate proclivities of people, their activities, and their organizations that tendencies rely upon. In addition, semiotics analyses are part of the mental snapshots so important to successful tendency analysis. The various kind of semiotics inherent to a cultural baseline can be observed for messages, symbols, and indications of change and movement owing to appearance or disappearance—this baseline work is critical to tendency analysis, and semiotics contribute significantly.

- SEMIOTICS AND CULTURAL ANALYSIS. *Cultural analysis* is knowing a particular culture, its people, and their patterns of behavior deriving from traditional, culturally induced attitudes, behaviors, social norms, and conditions. Semiotics and cultural analysis are inextricably entwined. Why is this relationship so strong? Semiotics are the language of the culture. Semiotics explain what people are doing, how they think, how they believe, and their state of tranquility or agitation all through communications inherent to the various types of semiotics. Semiotics present clues about the cultural influence on the psyche of people. In addition, to use semiotics takes watching, cataloging, combining, and using experts to help understand what they mean. One has to understand the culture or find people who do in sufficient levels of detail to understand how semiotics help explain the culture. Further, semiotics analysis adds more detail into cultural and anomaly analysis. It helps with recognizing and comprehending perturbation in the culture and can help in foreshadowing second- and third-order effects. As a final note of comparison, semiotics help identify the ascension of conditions in which sensitive cultural variables may come to life and influence the U.S. military and interagency operations.

- SEMIOTICS ANALYSIS AND SYNTHESIS. *Synthesis* is combining elements of substances to form a coherent whole. To be successful, any advanced analyst will have to engage in synthesis. The advanced analyst will have to combine several aspects of advanced analysis into a whole to understand the true meaning of the whole. Semiotics will often be what the analyst looks for and synthesize into a whole. Semiotics have linkages to the culture and to its people. Synthesis helps to identify relationships among people and their various means of communicating and transmitting stories, myths, and traditions thorough language, symbols, and cultural-specific codes. Semiotics help the analyst to comprehend the many types of communication that comprise the whole of the society and culture in question. The various types of semiotics will often appear unconnected in particular situations. However, through synthesis, semiotics will appear as a part of a much larger whole, thereby enabling meaning to come forth much more readily in the analyst's mind. When we combine the results of semiotics analysis with other aspects of advanced analysis and synthesize them into a whole for gaining insights and understanding, we start to gain higher levels of meaning than if we worked with each element individually.

Certain members of a populace will provide support to the enemy and their network. As they support, these people will exhibit signs in their talk, behavior, and action, which influence and identify pending and occurring enemy and network behaviors. Or, passive supporters will diverge from normal routines owing to the potential for trouble (thus provide watchers with other observables). In any type of counterinsurgency, it is vital to understand this active support and the passive acquiescence of people not actually supporting the network but not doing anything to counter it. The importance of this struggle for the hearts and minds of the population is brought to light in this statement by counterinsurgency theorist David Galula:

> The population, therefore, becomes the objective for the counterinsurgent as it was for his enemy. Its tacit support, its submission to law and order, its consensus—taken for granted in normal times—have been undermined by the insurgent's activity. And the truth is that the insurgent, with his organization at the grass roots, is tactically the strongest of opponents where it counts, at the population level.[6]

It is important for the counterinsurgent to understand both active and passive support and attempt to initiative activities and actions that help to separate the populace from the insurgent and his network. Famous military theorist T. E. Lawrence tells us of the importance of this struggle when he waged insurgent warfare against the Turkish army in World War I by stating

> It seemed to me proven that our rebellion had an unassailable base, guarded not only from attack, but from the fear of attack. It had a sophisticated alien enemy, disposed as an army of occupation in an area greater than could be dominated effectively from fortified posts. It had a friendly population, of which some two in the hundred were active, and the rest quietly sympathetic to the point of not betraying the movements of the minority. The active rebels had the virtues of secrecy and self-control, and the qualities of speed, endurance, and independence of arteries of supply.[7]

Semiotics can provide the communicative wherewithal to work on this aspect of the struggle between the United States and the insurgent for the hearts and minds of the populace. It is through semiotics analysis that intelligence analysts can track progress or setbacks through the communication and use of the semiotics of the populace. Thus, it follows that semiotics can also provide a form of communication for people to use with friendly forces without appearing to be in their support. The opposite also holds true. That is, elements of the populace could easily use semiotics to secretly communicate with the insurgents and among themselves. But this tack leaves them open to discovery and exploitation if advanced analysts use semiotics analysis constantly and effectively.

Often, semiotic observables will appear via cell phone activities (talking, pictures, chat, instant messaging, text messages), over the Internet, through newspapers, through jokes, dialects, and intonation, through argumentation and other forms of social intercourse, through graffiti, and even through word choice. The enemy will use cultural signs, symbols, tips, and cues to send messages over these and other mediums to warn, to direct, to disseminate, and to educate fellow insurgents and terrorists. This means, of course, friendly intelligence analysts have to understand signs and symbols in written, verbal, and nonverbal activities, or find the right combinations of expertise to help them interpret the recurring or recently occurring signs and symbols. If advanced analysts become good enough at semiotics, they can use those same signs for bait and switch, double agent, and ambush operations. But they will need to be on top of the cultural nuances and anomalous behaviors of very specific areas and tribal boundaries to use this aspect of a culture against the embedded enemy.

Advanced analysts use semiotics as a cognitive weapon in their search for a well-hidden and nuance-laden enemy. As such, advanced analysts work with data coming from observables they task to collection assets—these observables arrive in processing and C2 nodes as sensor and HUMINT data. Advanced analysts, with the help of VKE experts, use semiotics analysis to synthesize data into information and knowledge.

Two activities can help analysts learn and to use semiotics to search for and recognize the enemy as he hides or disguises himself among masses of people in large urban areas. First, intelligence analysts can use data that scientists and engineers provide when computers empower their efforts to conduct extremely fast searches for people, places, things, and activities in baselines, if they exist. It is though the cultural baseline that they can discern what the norm is, e.g., traffic flows, times of shopping, numbers of purchases, people in coffeehouses, children playing on the streets, typical dress for men and women, and other expected and "routine" signs. Second, data mining can lead to fast, interesting searches, accumulations of data, and relationships that intelligence analysts can use in their semiotics analysis work. Advanced analysts can also use knowledge discovery tools to assist in forming new cultural or social relationships and/or understanding existing relationships and associations. In addition, analysts must rely upon models to help them understand the characteristics of particular cultures and alternative ways to look for the enemy as he hides or moves surreptitiously. Patterns and trends will be laden with culturally induced semiotics. Thus, pattern and trend analysis help in this identification as analysts view the past, see trends and new patterns, and project where the semiotic trail will lead their thinking next. Also, social network analysis (SNA) helps analysts understand relationships, nth degree of separation, and what data scientists call "snowballing" (the identification of connections and relationships that ripple as more relationships branch from the initial query). Analysts will use subject matter experts, such as cultural anthropologists, indigenous functional experts, cultural and functional experts, and foreign area officer cultural experts to help them perform semiotics analysis to formulate observables during decomposition activities. These observables will be specifically designed to produce tasking to technical and HUMINT collection to look for cultural observables often showing as semiotics. They also can use such SMEs to learn what intelligence collection works the best against the derived observables in a variety of culturally peculiar situations. These SMEs can help analysts recompose and synthesize data into information and knowledge through the application of semiotics analysis. SMEs help analysts understand cultural norms and the activities innocent people would normally engage in, and what their behaviors, conversations, and nonverbal action should be, if normal. It is often through semiotics that signs of deviation from the norm come forth into our consciousness.

To delve into more specificity, consider if we were thinking about how suicide bombers might be planning to attack. If they are actually in the progress of attacking, how would we use semiotics? Five elements come to mind for using semiotics analysis in this situation:

- Some behaviors, physiological manifestations, language (written, verbal), and choices (message, picture, symbol color) could indicate a heightened state of aggression—something that a suicide bomber would have to possess or at a minimum find occurring within his or her physical body or occurring in his or her mind. These behaviors could very well become manifest as semiotic deviations that although subtle, could be excellent clues into future activities by particular people who exhibit the semiotic deviations.
- Some physiological characteristics and behaviors might be noticeable to highly trained subject matter experts but are ultimately difficult for unwitting, untrained, or culturally ignorant people to notice. For example, a suicide bomber may not blink, even in a culture in which people transmit emotion and other meanings through their eyes and

through blinking. Or the driver of a vehicle laden with improvised explosives device (VBIED) may avoid making any kind of gesture even when gestures dominate the nonverbal communication of a particular culture as its people drive automobiles. Or a suicide bomber may chant with only their lips moving, when ordinary people engaged in similar but legitimate activities would not.

- In addition, analysts could look for biometric observables influenced by semiotics dealing with stress, emotion, and physical characteristics such as profuse sweating, agitated hand gestures, abnormal gait, profuse body chemical emissions, and rapid eye movement.
- As another technique, analysts, in their direct analyst to collector communication, can ask linguists to listen for differences in voice—inflection, intonation, rapid or slow speech, the use of metaphors, a resignation in tone or an inordinately exuberant tone, or semantic changes that people familiar with the culture and language would be capable of hearing and highlighting as an important deviation from normal voice communications.
- Unusual discussions or manifestations of abnormal behavior could be linked to semiotics. For example, if a female happens to be sharing a room with two males and talking with them as equals, which is nearly unthinkable within some cultures (as was the case with the hotel bombing in Jordan), we should be suspicious.

Going even further into depth to help provide a practical explanation of semiotics analysis, let us postulate a scenario in which intelligence analysts are working against a terrorist network in Baghdad. The analytic mission is to find nodes and links of the enemy's network and decision-making apparatus, to learn from them and gain specific knowledge to enable intelligence analysts to discern the activities, transactions, behaviors, and interactions of the supporting network. Further, suppose that, owing to cultural analysis, the analysts have a hunch there is illicit activity in a particular house in a particular residential neighborhood. This neighborhood is his or her intellectual starting point or baseline. Then, suppose a bomb maker is embedded in the house, living and building bombs in a sympathizer's home, and it is this same house that an intelligence analyst has developed a hunch about—the house, its occupants, or its activities. As part of the setting, the sympathizer works outside of the dwelling, has a family and two children, and is a conservative Sunni Muslim. The wife is a traditional Muslim woman and the children are raised in accordance with strict Sunni Muslim tenets. The house and its occupants blend with the general populace and with the multitude of activities of the all-Sunni neighborhood.

The decision maker is constrained by the specter of second- and third-order effects and therefore cannot simply attack the house or search it just because an intelligence analyst has a hunch. He is faced with the dilemma of needing to aggressively search for and eliminate the enemy's network without alienating the civilian populace in the neighborhood. The U.S. decision maker is living with high risk and uncertainty, and the only way to reduce those risks lies in knowledge—good, high-grade, timely, and relevant knowledge that fits with the context of the OE. The decision maker has to work within the boundaries of this dilemma: it takes time to develop the knowledge he needs to reduce risk and uncertainty, but time is not on his side. One of the ways he can develop high-grade knowledge to help him make the best possible decisions while keeping both risk and uncertainty low is to use advanced analysis—specifically, semiotics analysis. He turns to his intelligence enterprise to work with advanced analysis to develop the high-grade semiotic-related knowledge he needs.

What options do intelligence analysts have in leading this operation? A first step is always to perform some difficult mental tasks, one of which is semiotics analysis. Through personal knowledge or with the help of SMEs, the analyst knows the culture and people in question. But she is not a native, and therefore does not know the intricate details of the society and culture well enough to identify specific cultural observables deriving from semiotics analysis to use for discerning the presence of an embedded enemy network. Thus, the analyst must seek help from the intelligence enterprise and the cultural and technical SMEs from a VKE, and also seek the help of a properly cleared Iraqi government official, a retired Iraqi police officer, a cultural anthropologist, and a retired HUMINT case officer once responsible for overseeing source networks in this particular neighborhood.

As another order of business, the advanced analyst must find an existing cultural baseline or build one to discern the cultural (semiotic) norm for the neighborhood and its individual homes and businesses. How do people talk, gesture, discuss, argue? How are signs and symbols displayed and do they change? What gestures are normal to people going about their business in their transactions, interactions, and behaviors? What is the normal state of graffiti in the neighborhood? How does the neighborhood sound by way of music and songs, loud conversations, and social intercourse during both day and by night? By nature, this must be a very detailed analysis. With the help of SMEs and through the use of 3D GIS products and data manipulation, the advanced analyst engages in high-level cognitive functions to discern graffiti, signs, symbols, sounds, manners, gestures, human intercourse noise levels, and discussion intonation of the neighborhood and its inhabitants to accurately judge if what she is observing is a normal situation, or contrarily, anomalous signs of enemy network activity. Each observable is associated with the transactions, activities, interactions, and behaviors occurring in a neighborhood and in particular associated with a particular household in a particular neighborhood. The analyst assesses the list thoroughly so she is fully equipped to confirm or deny the hypotheses that something untoward is occurring.

Next, the analyst works with the VKE of the enterprise's SMEs to identify the *functional observables* that must occur as *condition-setting* if in fact the house is dirty and/or if it is supporting some aspect of an IED network. The activities could include security, early warning, bringing food, providing transportation, providing parts for bombs, exchanging information, introductions, security screening, conducting reconnaissance and HUMINT operations, moving and storing completed bombs, and other logistics of making bombs—bringing the parts together for assembling, camouflaging, and hiding. In this respect, she decomposes each aspect of an insurgent's bomb-making requirements into functional observables, assesses them for semiotic potential, and keeps those observables "on ice." Of particular regard, the analyst thinks through the various steps in the insurgent's condition-setting activities and processes if a bomb factory is to succeed.

Next, the analyst and the VKE identify *cultural observables* (in this case, through semiotics and cultural analysis) of the people who live in, visit, and perform tasks in the neighborhood. Following the identification of cultural observables that are normal for the neighborhood, the analyst and the VKE decompose the activities of people who could be performing various functions, roles, and missions in support of the enemy's network to understand the semiotics involved with each of the five kinds of observables analysts use in advanced analysis. By using semiotics analysis to help develop the observables, U.S. analytic people and virtual SMEs are then able to "map" or task the observables into intelligence collectors, including observables deriving from extensive semiotics analysis, ensuring that all mission managers, sensor operators, and case officers know both the observables to look for (cultural, functional, situational, technical, biometric) and the rationale for this specific analytic focus (the why, when, and where to look). As another activity in semiotics analysis and observable use, the analyst would ask all collectors to report any unusual signs, symbols, verbal exchanges, or noticeable differences in people's gestures, intonation, syntax, and even the appearance or lack of graffiti. In this case the observables to look for are transitory and often appear and disappear rapidly—human beings hiding something may not provide indicators for a long or leisurely amount of time.

What we are discussing is using an indirect approach against the insurgents—that is, using the culture and semiotics of the people who must support the network for it to thrive, indeed survive. This approach, in which semiotics analysis provides assistance, dates to Sun Tzu. As a particular strength, the enemy makes his network shapeless and he hides it amongst the normal activities of a busy city. This approach is sound and makes it difficult for U.S. intelligence analysts and collectors to find the network. In a theoretical sense, the enemy is trying to follow an age-old dictum by remaining shapeless and thereby invisible. In this regard, the enemy is trying to do what Sun Tzu postulates:

> The ultimate in disposing one's troops is to be without ascertainable shape. Then the most penetrating spies cannot pry in, nor can the wise lay plans against you. It is according to the shapes that I lay the plans for victory, but the multitude does not comprehend this. Although everyone can see the outward aspects, none understands the way in which I have created victory.[8]

Nonetheless, any enemy taking this approach has an Achilles heel. That is, to survive, the insurgent has to have the passive and active support of the populace. It is through the populace that the indirect approach exists, ready for the advanced analyst to search for, find, exploit, or neutralize. To do so, that advanced analyst has to use both semiotics and cultural intelligence.

The semiotics approach presupposes the relevancy and connectivity of everything that happens among all aspects of life and commerce in a neighborhood and adjacent neighborhoods. As theorist M. Mitchell Waldrop tells us:

> In example after example the message was the same: everything is connected, and often with incredible sensitivity. Tiny perturbations won't always remain tiny. Under the right circumstances, the slightest uncertainty can grow until the system's future becomes utterly unpredictable.[9]

Semiotics often provide insights into how these relationships and connections are occurring and what they mean. This connectedness of all things that happen in a society and culture are critical to knowing how to develop observables with cultural analysis, in order to find relative semiotics and to understand what they mean and how their connections are relative to the whole that we strive to understand and find.

Analysts are looking for both normal and anomalous signs, symbols, and signals. It follows they must possess detailed and current cultural knowledge, access to the intimate experience that comes with living in a particular society, HUMINT to work subtle human interactions signified by facial expressions, jewelry, clothing, gestures, grimaces, and written words scrawled on a wall, as well as high-resolution sensors to provide overhead and ground imagery and night viewing of specific targets. The analyst also must have the capability to task and receive the outputs of SIGINT and be able to understand the outcomes of voices and discussions. The analyst synthesizes information from indigenous HUMINT watchers of specific sites, mobile watchers looking for physical, semiotic-oriented observables (such as differences in gestures), and strange, newly appearing cultural signs and symbols appearing in graffiti. The analyst/collection team needs an optimum of sensors, HUMINT sources, small, well-concealed ground cameras, MASINT devices, as well as data architectures that enable collectors to provide semiotic data to fusion centers for rapid development into information and knowledge.

Armed with this knowledge, the advanced analyst works with a VKE to develop appropriate observables. She also returns to the functions developed earlier that could be occurring if something nefarious was occurring at the home in question and sorts through them mentally using semiotics analysis. She applies cultural and semiotics analysis to develop the best combination of functional and cultural observables to have the best opportunity to locate what she is looking for. This analyst uses the resultant functional and cultural observables to look for the potential human semiotic error that HUMINT or electronic sensors could detect.

The analyst then begins to match the observables she has developed with advanced collection by working with collection specialists to devise a strategy for finding and using the best collection to task collection. The analyst and collection specialist task collection to collect against specific observables at precise times and locations. But this strategy and resultant action is different than most. This strategy is designed to look for cultural observables developed through semiotics analysis. This collection strategy, designed to collect on nuanced cultural observables and in particular, semiotics 1) uses a combination of sensors and HUMINT configured in an optimum mix; 2) employs persistent surveillance of a specific point, looking for specific observables with a sample rate sufficient to ensure occurrences do not go undetected; 3) uses a variety of HUMINT; and 4) uses a mixture of sensors and HUMINT, as well as nontraditional sources, such as indigenous police, looking for detailed observables at specific points where the analyst expects to see illicit activity.

Semiotics occupy a critical place in this effort. Looking for semiotic-laden cultural observables will usually have to fall to low-level HUMINT sources or informants who first see the neighborhood in sufficient depth and detail to notice fleeting appearances of nuanced observables and second to understand the culture and its specific activities well enough to recognize even the most subtle and fleeting cultural observables we are looking for. It is through semiotics analysis that even the most nuanced cultural subtleties can be found, leading to hidden nodes and links comprising the enemy's network.

Unfortunately, semiotics analysis is difficult to perform. It takes serious thought, relevant and up-to-date baselines, a creative approach to collection, and it takes seeking and using assistance from a variety of SMEs. To perform semiotics analysis, one has to know and understand the culture. It is a very subtle form of analysis. That is to say, semiotics analysis involves sometimes fleeting and culturally oriented observables and must employ a variety of collection capabilities to be most effective in using it. It will benefit our inquiry to now consider some of the more specific challenges and then discuss some of the ways advanced analysts can overcome them.

In a physical sense, people have to learn to guide sensors and HUMINT through the use of specially designed observables—designed to possess the specificity necessary to use semiotics analysis. People also have to learn to find the presence of semiotics and then to decipher what they mean. In this respect, advanced analysts must discern what particular or suspected codes, symbols, signs, intonations, inflections, etc., mean. Advanced analysts will have to seek semiotics help from cultural experts as well as from semiotics-related data and knowledge in relevant databases and baselines. Sometimes analysts seeking to use semiotics will seek assistance from people performing red-teaming duties to help watch for cognitive or knowledge error; however, not all red team people can provide this specific level of expertise. Collection will be particularly difficult with semiotics analysis even if analysts, with the help of SMEs, design the best possible indicators, observables, and signatures. To understand and exploit semiotics analysis, advanced analysts will have to prime experts to monitor cell phone calls and listen for signs of voice-related semiotics. Additionally, advanced analysts will have to engage in the difficult task of figuring out how to monitor Internet traffic to find symbols, codes, encipherments, and codes, and identify, flag, or tag those that could be relevant semiotics. This type of analysis and collection will transfer into the requirement to monitor Web sites constantly for culturally laden messages that could be codes, transfers of knowledge, orders, plans, codes, symbols, and encipherments. Further, to use semiotics analysis, the advanced analyst will have to know the culture sufficiently well to perform analysis and guide collection. Or, if they don't have the requisite knowledge and understanding of the culture in which they work, they must locate and employ U.S. or indigenous SMEs to help with 1) designing the front-end or in other words, developing observables; 2) interpreting data appearing from direct-feed data (e.g., UAV, FMV, EO) and back-end sense making (recomposition and synthesis). Finally, the advanced analyst using semiotics analysis will have to realize that most semiotics and the cultural intelligence they seek and use will be peculiar to the neighborhood they are working in. This will cause them to seek out a bevy of expert assistance to reach the necessary degree of knowledge and understanding to use semiotics analysis.

As the reader has undoubtedly surmised, using semiotics analysis is intellectually strenuous from two broad perspectives. Besides requiring specific knowledge of both culture and semiotics, semiotics analysis requires the capability to engage in higher-level thought. To use it to its fullest potential, semiotics analysis must conjoin with tendency, aggregation, anomaly, cultural analysis, and the most difficult of all—synthesis. Now, let us delve even further into some of the more toilsome challenges facing any advanced analyst aspiring to use semiotics analysis. These challenges can be decomposed into four parts.

ANALYSIS. The analyst must understand the culture and semiotics well enough to employ them in analysis and its close relative collection. The analyst is challenged to develop extremely specific cultural observables of sufficient clarity for tasking many different types of collectors to provide the "strands" or "threads" required to form meaning and relationships from semiotics. The analyst must know semiotics well enough to tell the collector exactly what, where, and when to look, along with the context, rationale, and finally the standards constraining or guiding the effort. The analyst must also find and use cultural baselines to use semiotics analysis. These baselines are rarely available because they are difficult to maintain and they are local. These two characteristics suggest the absolute requirement to either update existing cultural baselines or constantly develop new baselines. The analyst will most often have to find the right cultural expert to help him or her use semiotics for collection, sense-making, and turning data into information and knowledge.

COLLECTION. The advanced analyst and collection expert face trying tasks in devising collection strategies and then selecting tools to help find semiotics-driven observables. What do they need to optimize collection? They need sensors with high resolution. They need to find and task the right street-level HUMINT to provide the detailed specifics semiotics that analysis requires. They must collect with an optimum mix of sensors and HUMINT at the right time and place, as directed by the analyst in charge to find or notice the right semiotics. As a final challenge in collection, the analyst and collection specialist must learn how to task and request collection that produces a variety of semiotics data coming from cell phones, the Internet, chat rooms, and Web sites.

DATA FLOWS. The analyst and collection specialist must ensure that all collectors working on the semiotic problem flow data quickly and in a "straight pipe" configuration. The challenge is, of course, many of the sources reporting on semiotics will be low-level sources and informants who will not have properly cleared data transmission devices. The object is of course to move data into the DCGS or other data-processing device as quickly as humans and machines can do so to facilitate quick decision-making.

CULTURE. Along with all the other challenges we have discussed up to this point, other challenges still remain. As one, the analyst must understand the emotional, cognitive, and physical characteristics of the people who live in the culture as well as the insurgents who are embedded in it. As mentioned previously, the analyst has to have an up-to-date database and cultural baseline. Both will be laborious to find, ensure relevancy, and update. As another issue, it will be hard for any U.S. analyst to first notice semiotics and then to understand what they mean. In this respect, the analyst must know enough of the culture in question to discern normal from anomalous semiotics.

With these challenges in mind, how might the advanced analyst overcome them? As a first step, the analyst can work with improving their mental organization. As an example, advanced analysts should use a thought template to help guide their thinking about difficult subjects such as semiotics analysis. Seeking assistance from people who know the culture is another worthy approach to semiotics analysis. However, even the best cultural expert will be of little assistance without a good, up-to-date cultural baseline. If there is no baseline, the advanced analyst has to seek assistance in developing one from a VKE or the intelligence enterprise providing overwatch support to the analyst in question. As a final point in organization, the advanced analyst should work on figuring out in advance what particular or suspected codes, symbols, signs, intonation, inflections, and so forth would be normal and what he or she would or should see if anomalous semiotics suddenly appeared in the neighborhood in question.

Analysis is closely related to mental enhancement and organization. There are many ways or approaches analysts can employ to help with semiotics analysis. Analysts will seek help from the intelligence enterprise and from the overwatch support of a supporting VKE. The advanced analyst desiring to use semiotics analysis will want to use red team people to check his or her thinking, assumptions, and to check on the analytic proclivity to fall into the cognitive trap of mirror imaging. The analyst will always want other people such as peers or even people of senior rank to murder board (that is, to subject to organized scrutiny) his or her conclusions and methodology for pursuit of the requirement or analytic mystery. As with mental organization, in the realm of analysis, anybody wanting to use semiotics analysis will always have to use existing or develop new cultural baselines so as to determine normal semiotics from anomalous semiotics that could very well indicate something worth pursuit or an actual insurgent-induced semiotic anomaly. As another helpful approach, the advanced analyst will want to anticipate movement of the target, and with this change the analyst should be able to discern an associated flow of semiotics, which should be noticeable. Such anticipation will also suggest that the analyst should anticipate where the insurgents will morph and start the baseline work even in advance of the movement.

The advanced analyst will want to think like the enemy to understand how he might be thinking and attempting to remain nearly invisible to any and all efforts to find him as he operates in a particular culture. The analyst must think like the enemy as he considers his perceptions about U.S. analytic work and collection efforts. This insurgent will reason that he must never allow U.S. intelligence analysis and collection to pick up on his semiotics trail. The analyst who thinks like the enemy will certainly conclude that U.S. analysts and collectors will never know enough about the culture to be able to find and exploit semiotics. This enemy will probably not consider this indirect approach of finding those who support his network to get at the principal perpetrator, but he will be cautious and extremely wary of insider HUMINT or people having the potential to watch his moves. However, even this wary enemy will believe that visual, audio, and symbolic semiotics will allow him to move and communicate without much risk.

Continuing with this important line of thought, the enemy will be thinking about and wondering how he can hide from U.S. sensors and HUMINT. He will consider sowing real and dummy semiotics by a wide variety of media. He will use semiotics at will, however, if he discerns the United States does not have the capability to notice and report on semiotics. He will conclude that technical sensors will never have sufficient resolution and savvy operators to notice the semiotics he is using for his command and control, and for early warning or directions to elements of his operational network.

The smart insurgent will also be asking himself: What can the Americans do that can cause my failure, and how might I surreptitiously counteract such capabilities and efforts? He will reason that he is in trouble if the American analysts and their SMEs start looking for, finding, and understanding his semiotics codes, symbols, and warnings. He also reasons that he will be in trouble if the Americans start understanding the culture well enough to disambiguate what has heretofore seemed invisible to them, or begin finding people who have such knowledge to neutralize his use of the culture and semiotics. This smart insurgent will also be worried about early warning in his network. Providing good security and early warning is one of the most important functions of the insurgent network. Thus, he could very well reason that the Americans will not be knowledgeable of the culture to the extent necessary to see his semiotic signs of early warning (such as symbols), through his use of very repulsive dead animals for signs and symbols, and how he might communicate through routine semiotics such as rugs hanging out of windows and flags hanging from satellite antennas on the roof. This savvy insurgent will conclude that if he uses semiotics to communicate via cell phones and over the Internet, the odds are that no American will know enough about the culture to interpret what appears to be data of no real interest, but in fact is owing to the semiotics and how they transmit meaning.

As we approach the conclusion of this chapter, it seems useful to *think about how we should think* to use semiotics. Thinking about semiotics is trying. First of all, we must have some considerations about the task at hand—how we can use semiotics. We have to consider the culture. We have to consider semiotics and how they can be fleeting, subtle, or obvious. We have to consider how not only the perpetrator thinks and perceives, but also how the populace that supports his network thinks and perceives. Once we understand this, we can start anticipating their use of semiotics. We also have to consider how people in a particular culture communicate and how culture affects this communication. Our advanced analyst also has to consider what semiotics are normal and anomalous.

The advanced analyst has to consider his or her strengths and weaknesses when it comes to semiotics analysis and steps they can take to overcome their weaknesses. Our advanced analyst must consider whether his or her thinking is flawed when it comes specifically to semiotics analysis. They also have to consider how they might test their hypotheses, theories, and assumptions about the enemy's use of semiotics. The advanced analyst contemplating use of semiotics analysis must always have a coterie of people to turn to for critiquing his or her thinking—other analysts, SMEs from a VKE, red teamers, cleared indigenous people, and functions experts from the VKE immediately come to mind when pondering this question.

This marks the end of the chapter on semiotics. I hope this chapter has been as interesting to the reader as it has been for me to think about the subject and attempt to present its main ideas cogently. Semiotics analysis is yet another important aspect of advanced analysis. What sets semiotics analysis apart from many other aspects of advanced analysis is that semiotics analysis always involves subtleties and nuances. By way of explanation for why the book discusses cultural analysis and semiotics analysis in separate chapters, culture is much broader and easier to notice and look for than the often-overlooked semiotics. Semiotics are a subset of culture and are more toilsome to notice, understand, and exploit.

Why is semiotics analysis important? Quite simply, semiotics, along with cultural analysis, provide "a way" for the commander to take advantage of the culture and use it for advantage, such as taking control of the initiative by preempting an insurgent activity. Also, the intelligence analyst must know semiotics to truly know the culture. Semiotics analysis is an important part in decomposition and designing observables—particularly cultural observables. Semiotics analysis is also imperative for making sense of incoming collection data and turning it into information and actionable knowledge. However, the chapter admonished the reader to remember that some parts of semiotics are stable, and other parts are dynamic and constantly change. Regardless, cultural and semiotics analysis are as two conjoined rings—they never entirely separate, but one, as mentioned above, subsumes the other.

The chapter brought forth some interesting characteristics of semiotics analysis. As one, semiotics can be spoken, written, or nonverbal behavior, such as gestures, grimaces, and body stances. Semiotics can also be art, pictures, and even graffiti. Interestingly, even the clothes people wear communicate and thus are aspects of semiotics analysis. Along with being strongly related to cultural analysis, semiotics analysis is also highly relational to several other cognitive elements of advanced analysis. For example, semiotics analysis relates to anomaly, aggregation, tendency analysis, and synthesis. The chapter also brought forth the proposition that semiotics analysis must be a part of a cultural baseline.

As such, the semiotics baseline (as a subset of a cultural baseline) is critical to the advanced analysis because one of the most important aspects or characteristics of semiotics analysis is something called "glacial" change. That is, semiotics are constantly changing but westerners often do not recognize this, because the changes can be small. Semiotics are indicants of change, and change, of course, often indicates anomaly portending enemy action or attempts to gain influence. As another important proposition, the chapter brought forth the notion that if we believe everything is connected in some way, fashion, or form, it is through semiotics that we can start understanding these relationships and how they work.

Semiotics analysis is difficult to perform and has some challenging aspects. Some of the more important challenges include

- The number one challenge is to know enough about the culture to understand how semiotics work, communicate, influence, and can be used by the enemy as a semi-secure way of communicating.
- It is toilsome to find and employ collection specific enough to pick up on slowly or even quickly changing semiotics.
- To use semiotics analysis, the intelligence analyst must use SMEs. Sometimes the analyst will find it challenging to find the right SME and even to work with them to perform the knowledge work with which to work with semiotics analysis.
- Many technical challenges plague the analysts' use of semiotics analysis. As an example, to use semiotics analysis takes a holistic approach to the issue, including using what transpires on the Internet and Web sites.
- Compounding the challenges, semiotics are often peculiar to specific neighborhoods. This accentuates the requirement for indigenous SMEs, but increases the level of the challenge owing to the need to find SMEs with local experience.

With the challenges identified, what are some ways analysts can learn to overcome the influence of these challenges? Some of the more important ways include the following:

- The analyst must learn to use cultural SMEs. Often these SMEs will be in sanctuary. Learning to use SMEs to help with knowledge requirements for semiotics analysis needs to occur in all phases of an analysts' preparation for deployment.
- The intelligence analyst must learn to develop and use a constantly updating cultural baseline database, of which semiotics is a subset.
- The intelligence analyst must learn to anticipate enemy activities and their associated potential use of semiotics to hide their activities and attempts to communicate.

- The military needs to develop sensors and to train HUMINT people to collect on cultural observables developed through both cultural and semiotics analysis.
- Finally, the analyst can help himself or herself by learning to think like the enemy as he attempts to communicate, deceive, and provide command and control to his network.

With this chapter on semiotics analysis completed, the reader is ready to think about the next logical step in our intellectual journey. That is, the next chapter will discuss the extraordinarily interesting topic of aggregation analysis.

16

Aggregation Analysis

Definition: Discerning meaning, knowledge, or understanding of the energy and power of several things—numbering from a few to a million—that are grouped together, moving together, working together, and considered as a whole, although the parts may at times appear disassociated or disparate.

THEORY BEHIND AGGREGATION ANALYSIS

Aggregation analysis helps people understand how terrorists and insurgents function as a whole. In fact, aggregation analysis helps us to think about, search for, find, and influence wholes that constitute enemy networks, operations, and activities. It helps people understand the particulars of a shifting, morphing, constantly aggregating and disaggregating insurgent network. With mastery of aggregation analysis, analysts can anticipate the formation of aggregates and advise their commanders how to retard or contain their natural tendency toward growth.

With good thinking, advanced analysts can also cause the "glue" that holds the parts and pieces of aggregates together and that connects aggregates with other aggregates to decay more rapidly than the enemy would hope for. In addition, if advanced analysts find aggregations early enough, they can advise their commanders how to either neutralize or destroy the aggregate in question. Aggregation analysis also helps people identify possible second- and third-order effects, sensitive variables, and windows of opportunity or vulnerability. Aggregation analysis helps analysts discern possible outcomes with information operations (IO) aimed at the population, and how effects and actions might influence their moods, perspectives, and attitudes. Finally, if after suffering from the appearance and often paralyzing effects of large aggregates that appear as second- and third-order effects, aggregation analysis can help with the postmortem to find analytic error and failure in anticipating or in thinking about the arousal tendency of an embryonic aggregate, the appearance of and energy expended to combine into larger aggregates, the "glue" that binds aggregates, the fuel that "propels" aggregates, and decay of the aggregate that could have been induced by the advanced analyst if his or her thinking had been better.

An example will help explain aggregation analysis and its underpinning theory. If the U.S. military finds itself operating in a large urban setting against extremely aggressive insurgents and terrorists, aggregation analysis will be crucial to satisfactorily performing any analytic mission. To help explain aggregation analysis, consider the condition-setting either insurgents or terrorists must undergo before they can successfully accomplish their mission of say, establishing and operating a safehouse. To find, occupy, operate, and move from a safehouse, they have to perform several condition-setting activities. Various kinds of people perform such activities. For example, prior to occupying a safehouse, people who are intelligence collectors constantly gather and provide information to the insurgent leader to gain sufficient insights and knowledge for planning and execution of this mission. Insurgents operate from a functioning network and have people perform various missions. These missions can include conducting reconnaissance and intelligence collection; conducting security operations; supplying the safehouse with food and water; providing medical support; providing transportation; planning for and rehearsing escape; employing high- and low-tech communications; using well-concealed command and control; conducting countersurveillance operations; and conducting security operations.

At the smallest level of decomposition, we find individuals operating and doing things united by a mission, guidance, commonality of views, monetary reward, and purpose. These individuals aggregate into groups. The group in this case could be multiple people performing a countersurveillance or security mission 24/7. Groups aggregate into larger aggregations. In our case, the countersurveillance group would aggregate into the larger security aggregate. The security aggregate would aggregate into the network, the network into a larger aggregate that is a larger network. Of commonality, each aspect of the aggregate is bound by a "glue" and energized by a "propellant" that provides energy and motion. The importance of this description is severalfold. First, advanced analysts can disaggregate or decompose their requirements and what they seek to understand and make sense of into very small aggregates and the entities that comprise them, as well as combinations of aggregates. Second, advanced analysts can search for the "glue" that binds the elements comprising aggregates and that binds aggregates with other aggregates. Third, analysts can search for, find, and influence the "propellant" that provides energy and movement to the aggregate. Fourth, analysts can think about and understand the trends and patterns associated with past safehouses, and use their thoughts to identify associated aggregates that comprise what the safehouse does, how it sets up, and how it disbands. This is decomposition in advanced analysis. With decomposed observables coming from aggregation analysis, analysts and collectors start looking for traces or subtleties indicating the presence of small or large aggregates that indicate and in some cases define condition-setting for insurgent operations.

Unfortunately, aggregation analysis is one of the more trying aspects of advanced analysis for several reasons. It is abstract. Aggregation analysis is also conceptual and as a result often invisible to people unless the aggregation under study is induced to appear or if it exudes physical manifestations of its properties. Regardless of difficulty, aggregation is a critical aspect of understanding the enemy. Such understanding includes how the enemy might act (anticipation), how to watch for signs that the enemy is planning to act (condition-setting), why the enemy is preparing to act (intent and will), how the enemy views U.S. intelligence collection (countersurveillance), and how aggregates can influence somewhat obscure phenomena in the OE, such as comprehending how second- and third-order effects coming from the activities, action, and power of aggregates can influence friendly operations. But the relationships comprising aggregation are confoundingly challenging to anticipate and shape.

To use aggregation analysis, people have to comprehend wholes and aggregates. An *aggregate* is "a sum, mass, or assemblage of particulars; a total or gross amount."[1] An aggregation is, of course, a compilation of aggregates. Aggregates are bound by "glue." Aggregates move by a "propellant" of sorts that provides them velocity and gives them the capability to grow very quickly into something important. An aggregation "propellant" could be a cause, a belief, an emotion such as fear (e.g., panic in a movie theater when there is a fire or with the smell and appearance of smoke), hatred, revenge, or envy.

The "glue" that binds parts of the aggregate is important. It serves as the means for conjoining elements into the whole that is the aggregate. It identifies possible links with other aggregates. This "glue" decays with time and influences of the environment, thereby giving friendly leaders the opportunity to watch for and manipulate its decay rate. It identifies what is causing the aggregate to bond and thereby presents opportunities for friendly influences on the aggregate or even negation of the aggregate's power. So, determining the nature and characteristics of the "glue" bonding the aggregate together is important.

What is this "glue" that enables aggregates to develop, renew, and sometimes grow into exponential power and influence? Some aspects of this "glue" include the neighborhood, social groups, the society that provides common beliefs, common perceptions, common goals or activities, and common degrees of intensity about certain facts, myths, beliefs, or views. Other aspects of the "glue" that bond elements of the aggregate include similarities, dissimilarities, self-organization, needs to adapt, common interests, and religious motives. Some social aspects of the "glue" that bind aggregates include influences of the infrastructure, presence of money, availability of information and data, joblessness, and religion. The "glue" that binds the essential elements of aggregates can also be purpose, functional, rationale, law, intent, or mission orders, to name just a few.

Along with "glue" and "propellant," there is a third important consideration when thinking about aggregates and what they do. That is to say, there is an *"igniter."* An "igniter" is a catalyst that excites and explodes the propellant. The propellant, of course, moves the aggregate or causes it to grow in strength or impact. The notion of "igniter" is very abstract, some could say unfathomable. Regardless of abstraction, however, something causes the propellant to come alive and cause the aggregate or aggregates to move. The igniter could very well be variables that become extremely sensitive, often exploding into energy, e.g., something sets off a lynch mob, something causes hatred to boil over thereby bringing into life a riot of people, organizations, ideas—aggregates of CAS bonded or glued into wholes that connect and bond with larger wholes. The advanced analyst therefore has to understand the lingering presence of that which causes variables to arouse, to become sensitive, and to emit energy. Armed with such precognition, the advanced analyst is then prepared to collect against attendant observables to help people understand and see such conditions as they come into being so as to provide the commander with the wherewithal to preempt, mitigate, or to let the conglomerate of aggregates run its natural course.

Keeping these characteristics of aggregates in mind, let us digress for a moment and consider how advanced analysts can use aggregation analysis in their thinking. As a starting point for discussion, aggregation analysis is very much involved with envisioning, identifying, developing, and using relationships. Relationships cause things, events, activities, and behaviors to come together and combine into something often more capable or powerful than before the relationship developed. With aggregation analysis, advanced analysts seek to understand why certain environmental conditions are conducive to the development of aggregates. They also attempt to understand how things, events, emotions, technology, etc., come together in relationships to form aggregates and how these aggregates relate to other aggregates. When we search for and find the answer to the question of why relationships are relationships and why they stay together, even with man-made or environmentally induced perturbation, and why things become aggregates, we come to the essence of aggregation analysis. Thus, we have to answer the question—how do we find relationships?

Some relationships, of course, are obvious. The challenge of relationships and aggregation becomes more daunting with acknowledgement of the fact that some relationships appear unrelated but are actually related. Thus the inquisitive advanced analyst must search for seemingly disparate relationships to go along with more obvious relationships. When thinking about an existing aggregate or potential aggregate, the advanced analyst understands it is composed of *types of relationships*—people, organizations, functions, activities, roles, missions, technical, processes, and outcomes. Further, analysts must search for relationships and discern why they exist and what people can do to disaggregate and or disambiguate the more abstract connections, links, or, as we say in this work, "glue" that connects such relationships.

One of the more interesting explanatory aspects of aggregation analysis involves the potential for aggregates to become apparent in our consciousness through the presence or nascent manifestation of cascading or exponential outcomes. In military parlance, this phenomenon is a second- or third-order effect. In complexity theory, this phenomenon is often called the "butterfly theory," which is defined thus:

> Tiny differences in input could quickly become overwhelming differences in output—a phenomenon given the name "sensitive dependence on initial conditions." In weather . . . this translates into what is . . . known as the Butterfly Effect—the notion that a butterfly stirring the air today in Peking can transform storm systems next month in New York . . . In science as in life, it is well known that a chain of events can have a point of crisis that could magnify small changes.[2]

Translating the theory into something meaningful for aggregation analysis goes something like this. Military planners always should worry about the Clausewitzian friction we discussed previously, as well as unanticipated outcomes and unintended consequences. Over the past several years, these particular events have sometimes been labeled second- and third-order effects. However, military planners have rarely dealt with exponential or "butterfly" effects, and if they have, they have not conjoined these effects with anticipation wrought by the hard work of creative analysts who watch for the effects and collection experts who provide the means for such vigilance. To explain the butterfly effect and the phenomenon of uncontrollable second- and third-order effects, a passage in *For Whom the Bell Tolls* helps:

> He had the feeling of something that had started normally and had then brought great, outsized, giant repercussions. It was as though you had thrown a stone and the stone made a ripple and the ripple returned

roaring and toppling as a tidal wave . . . Or as though you struck one man
and he fell and as far as you could see other men rose up all armed and
armored.[3]

There is some justification for the reticence to delve deeply into
the world of which we speak. Complexity is difficult. Resources
(particularly time) are constrained, and the essence of aggregation theory
(relationships, "glue" that connects the elements of aggregates, and
aggregate "propellant"), as mentioned earlier, is intellectually arduous to
understand, let alone put into action. But in this day and age, people cannot afford to overlook or ignore this important force that is a significant
actor on any stage of strife. It is not "a tale told by an idiot."[4] With
aggregation analysis, we are working hard to peer behind the curtain to find
the inner workings of planned, rehearsed, and pointed actions to active
outcomes.

To help us understand aggregation analysis, we need to relate it to several other important elements of advanced analysis—*tendency, cultural,
anomaly analysis*, and *synthesis*. Let us spend some time to work on understanding these relationships.

- AGGREGATION ANALYSIS AND TENDENCY ANALYSIS. The definition of *tendency analysis*, for the purposes of this book is discerning meaning
  through thought and study of the general proclivities of people, the
  behavioral and action inclinations of organizations, mental snapshots of
  current environment or contextual situations, events, activities, behaviors, the emanation dispersal of energy emissions, and what the interaction and enmeshing of all could portend for the future. The analyst looks
  at wholes of a neighborhood or a business, or of a house, or of a planned
  action to sense and consider what is missing out of the whole. When
  people perform tendency analysis, they are looking for small variations
  in current pictures or mental snapshots to discern tendencies or movements. Sometimes, the aggregation of activities or events will be large,
  easy to see, and obvious. At other times and at the other end of the spectrum of size and importance, the tendencies will be so small as to deny
  recognition, let alone comprehension, or will cause confusion to those
  trying to use typical tendency analysis. Thus, the analyst must bring in
  aggregation analysis. Aggregates often appear as tendencies. Thus the
  appearance, movement, and influence of some aggregates will be obvious, although others will be more difficult to see, let along understand.
  Tendency analysis can help people discern the future from a "snapshot"
  of the present and understanding the slightest variations indicating what
  has changed or is changing in that mental picture.

  An advanced analyst who desires to use aggregation analysis with a supporting role by tendency analysis must start by decomposing requirements,

which manifest as PIR, IR, hypotheses, expectations, hunches, and mysteries. This analyst takes the result of the decomposition and identifies four things pertinent to aggregation analysis and indirectly relating to tendency analysis: 1) the parts and pieces comprising the aggregates; 2) the "glue" that binds both parts and larger wholes; 3) the catalyst or "propellant" for smaller wholes to combine to become larger wholes or aggregates, and for aggregates to grow and increase in speed or die; and 4) the tendency that portends a future state of being or the goal of the aggregate. It also suggests the need for mental exploration of complex adaptive systems (CAS), sensitive variables, windows of opportunity, and the ascendancy and influence of second- and third-order effects whose potential power can have an enormous influences on U.S. combat commanders.

- AGGREGATION ANALYSIS AND CULTURAL ANALYSIS. As a reminder from an earlier discussion, *cultural analysis* is knowing a particular culture, its people, and their patterns of behavior deriving from traditional, culturally induced attitudes, behaviors, social norms, and conditions. The "glue" that binds the parts and pieces of aggregates to one another and aggregates to other aggregates is often cultural. Thus, it follows that advanced analysts have to know the culture or find the people who do know in order to understand it well enough to comprehend what "glues" the essential elements of aggregates together. This same understanding helps to search for and find the conditions conducive for aggregates to conjoin into larger aggregates. The advanced analyst therefore provides the commander with recommendations, ideas about risk mitigation, and opportunities to reduce uncertainty. This occurs through well-conceived preemption by using soft and hard actions, activities, and effects to thwart the development of aggregates in their formative stages when they are easier to manipulate, change, destroy, or hasten their decay and eventual death.

  - As a close relative to cultural analysis and highly influential with aggregation analysis, semiotics can suddenly appear and signal the formation of new aggregates. They can also signal the presence of conditions enabling dormant aggregates to come to life, and provide hints of what comprises the cultural "glue" that binds aggregates.

  - Some other considerations of the relationship between aggregation and cultural analysis include the following tendencies: the enemy will use culture to mask his changes and morphing; advanced analysts have to use indigenous SMEs to help anticipate where and how the culture will be changing and how the enemy could be using the change to mask his activity. Thus, advanced analysts will have to be cognitively agile to understand cultural adaptation and change so as to "see" and understand the cultural side of aggregation.

- AGGREGATION ANALYSIS AND ANOMALY ANALYSIS. As a review, the definition for *anomaly analysis* in this book is discerning meaning in departures from the normal or common order, form, or rule; absence of that which is expected. The outputs from anomaly analysis can identify when aggregates are moving and changing (either growing into larger aggregates or becoming increasingly diminutive and inconsequential). Anomaly analysis involves baselines of three types—cultural, technical, and functional. Anomaly analysis depends on baselines to identify what is "normal." Often the formation, growth, influence, and eventually demise of aggregates is what causes perturbation in baselines. Aggregates involve the formation, growth, connectedness with other aggregates, movement, and influence—each of these steps involves change in the baselines. These changes are sometimes easily noticeable, but at other times they are imperceptible to human consciousness. This is where anomaly analysis and its dependence on baselines intersects with aggregation analysis.

- AGGREGATION ANALYSIS AND SYNTHESIS. *Synthesis* is the human cognitive activity that combines elements of substances, events, activities, or energy to form a coherent whole. A dictionary definition of synthesis is "the combining of the constituent elements of separate material or abstract entities into a single or unified entity."[5] The *Department of Defense Dictionary of Military and Associated Terms* defines synthesis as "In intelligence usage, the examining and combining of processed information with other information and intelligence for final interpretation."

  - Synthesis is the mental construct for conceptualizing aggregates. Synthesis helps the analyst understand what comprises aggregates, comprehend how aggregates relate and connect to other aggregates, obtain insights into the composition of the "glue" that holds aggregates together, and identify and understand the "propellant" that projects aggregates in terms of speed, velocity, and tangible and intangible mass.

  - Synthesis also helps the analyst understand how an already forming aggregate or aggregation might be *preempted* to keep aggregation and its inherent power from coming into being. Embedded in this thought about synthesis, one can find the concept of *holism*—the theory that "the parts of any whole cannot exist and cannot be understood except in their relation to the whole; holism holds that the whole is greater than the sum of its parts."[6] Synthesis and its close "relative" holism help the analyst understand how the enemy can attempt to bring together parts and pieces to create aggregates. Comprehending synthesis and holism helps the analyst understand how the enemy could hope to keep these aggregates together. The relationship between aggregation and synthesis helps the analyst understand how the "glue" that bonds the wholes of the aggregate or aggregation in question can hold together even seemingly disparate parts and pieces of aggregates. Synthesis also helps the analyst understand aggregation sufficiently well to anticipate events and to reverse engineer outcomes into causal relationships. Synthesis provides the intellectual wherewithal to design mitigating effects and actions to thwart the commingling of activities and interactions that can lead to the output of power in aggregates. Further, synthesis helps the analyst understand evolving or future relationships that could become aggregates and some techniques for shaping or "strangling" the aggregate coming into being by taking away one, some, or all of the aggregating parts that must work, move, and act together for an aggregate to fulfill its potential.

Now that we have thought about the relationships between aggregation and other elements of advanced analysis, the next step in the effort in understanding aggregation analysis is to go into more depth and to discern more relationships. As an example, aggregation analysis and complex adaptive systems (CAS) are closely related. To start this line of thought, we need to review what a CAS is. It is

a dynamic network of many agents (which may represent cells, species, individuals, firms, nations) acting in parallel, constantly acting and reacting to what the other agents are doing. The control of a CAS tends to be highly dispersed and decentralized. If there is to be any coherent behavior in the system, it has to arise from competition and cooperation among the agents themselves. The overall behavior of the system is the result of a huge number of decisions made every moment by many individual agents.[7]

Then, we have to answer the question of why are CAS and their interactions important for aggregation analysis? A CAS in our counterinsurgency discussion is a person, a group of people, a network, or an organization—friendly, enemy, neutral, and host nation. CAS perform activities, interactions, and transactions. When CAS of any kind meet and intermingle, there are a variety of possible outcomes. None of the outcomes are entirely predictable. For example, when a person goes to a food market, the interaction with the owner or sales clerk will generally be peaceful. The identity of the person seeking to purchase something or if that same person will purchase what we have predicted is another question because of the unpredictability of CAS and the play of chance in all CAS transactions. Therefore, the transaction becomes susceptible to the imposition of variables—price fluctuations, amount of money the person has, stockage of food, hunger—some ordinary, and some sensitive. Other types of CAS interaction are hostile and dangerous. Some of these interactions could be an assassin gunning down a politician (e.g., Ms. Bhutto in Pakistan), a suicide bomber detonating his bomb in a large public setting (e.g., suicide bomber in a hotel in Amman Jordan), or, on a more delayed but nonetheless dangerous note, an individual supporting a network by conducting condition-setting operations.

In busy settings, such as a large city, CAS constantly move and interact. When they interact, they have four outcomes the advanced analyst is interested in. They *collide*. They *intersect*. They *careen* off of each other. They *conjoin* and form an aggregate. For the purposes of this discussion, we are most interested in when CAS conjoin and form an aggregate. This is one of the most important aspects of aggregation analysis.

When CAS interact, they often have an additive effect. A person is recruited to a network. An insurgent case officer adds a source to his list of sources. A team joins the insurgent movement. A tribe joins the insurgent movement. A sect joins a tribe. A group or business joins an insurgent network. This is conjoining and is why CAS relate to aggregates. It is an aggregate that occurs when CAS conjoin and connect with other CAS (aggregates). Their importance, strength, lifespan, and extent of influence depends on the strength of the "glue" holding the aggregates together, the renewal and adaptation of the CAS, its anticipation and resultant change, and the "flammability" of the aggregates' "propellant." Yes, insurgents' cells, links, and networks are examples of the aggregates/CAS our troops face in urban settings today and will face in the future. This notion of the enemy network as CAS and aggregates will be a topic of further discussion in a few paragraphs.

Let's explore some other interrelationships of CAS pertinent to our inquiry and discussion. CAS involves aggregation as a way of simplifying complex systems. To exemplify what CAS do, it concerns the emergence of complex, large-scale behaviors from the aggregate interactions of less complex agents.[8] They also self-organize. When a single CAS combines with another CAS or a group of CAS, it becomes an aggregate or aggregation. This aggregation also adapts, and because of adaptation, self-organizes, with no real direction from a higher authority. Self-organization is when CAS evolve, adapt, and choose a different or new organization for the purpose of gaining advantage or even survival. In the modern world, very diverse companies often merge for purposes of profitability, greater financial power, or for the purpose of beating a mutual competitor. M. Mitchell Waldrop discusses this phenomenon of self-organization as

> people trying to satisfy their material needs unconsciously organize themselves into an economy through myriad individual acts of buying and selling; it happens without anyone being in charge or consciously planning it. . . . Flying birds adapt to the actions of their neighbors, unconsciously organizing themselves into a flock. Organisms constantly adapt to each other through evolution, thereby organizing themselves into an exquisitely tuned ecosystem. Atoms search for a minimum energy state by forming chemical bonds with each other, thereby organizing themselves into structures known as molecules. In every case, groups of agents seeking mutual accommodation and self-consistency somehow manage to transcend

themselves, acquiring collective properties such as life, thought, and purpose that they might never have possessed individually.[9]

CAS are adaptable. They intermingle and adapt to the environment and to other CAS. In this regard, any insurgent's network is, at its basic essence, a CAS. This CAS will survive or die/extinguish by its ability to anticipate change, danger, and opportunities for self-aggrandizement, but they also must adapt to circumstances, adversaries, functions, and activities in a constantly fluctuating environment. When CAS evolve over long periods of time, they become very capable of not only acting, but of constantly anticipating and adapting to changing circumstances. CAS can also be diverse. This means the parts and pieces of aggregates that we might think of as too diverse for partnerships, combining, or joining can happen.[10] John Holland again helps us understand this complex phenomenon by writing

> This diversity is neither accidental nor random. The persistence of any individual agent, whether organism, neuron, or firm, depends on the context provided by other agents. . . . If we remove one kind of agent from the system, creating a "hole," the system typically responds with a cascade of adaptations resulting in a new agent that "fills the hole." The new agent typically occupies the same niche as the deleted agent and provides most of the missing interactions.[11]

Diversity of CAS is important for this discussion because the way aggregates form is not just with similar people, organizations, functions, roles, and missions. They also combine and form relationships with dissimilar CAS. As such, they combine because of a unifying purpose or "glue," such as a coincidental goal, a common purpose, self-interest such as a criminal element joining with an insurgent group, which joins with a terrorist group for a short period of time to accomplish a singular mission. This phenomenon could also be called self-organization.

Often, aggregation does not occur easily. Sometimes aggregation remains in the formative stage until the appearance and influence of sensitive variables. Examples of this could be youngsters in a Madrassa whose social group is on the brink of joining with an insurgent group but is still hesitating at the precipice of choice. Suddenly, a sensitive variable appears and exerts tremendous influence. In this case, the sensitive variable could be the sudden death of a well-respected Mullah by an errant friendly precision guided missile. Although the act causes a short-term bonding of people in a small riot in protesting the accidental death of the Mullah, the long-term effect is for the aggregate to jell and bond. The "glue" holding it together is the highly emotional backlash and release of the inner hatred, energy, and the long-term xenophobia of the youngsters in the Madrassa.

Let us explore this phenomenon more to understand its relationship with aggregation analysis. Aggregation theory lies at the heart of what we are speaking; therefore, we must understand this theory in another measure of depth. That is, when most actions occur, effects and outcomes are contained by a lack of will, insufficient motive, shortages in resources, laws, environmental conditions, and potential outcomes. However, interestingly, when other actions occur at the right time and place and when under the influence of sensitive variables within limited "windows of opportunity," outcomes occur that are far more powerful than people ever imagine, let alone anticipate. Thus the impact of aggregates and aggregation will sometimes produce a tsunami-type effect where relatively small inputs create large outputs.

Let us take our thoughts to the subject of sensitive variables and how they relate to aggregation analysis. What are sensitive variables? How do we know if conditions are ripe for them to come into being? Why can they influence the appearance and power of an aggregate and enhance and expand the "glue" that holds the elements comprising an aggregate as a whole?

Let us answer and shed some light on these questions. A variable is something prone to change or fluctuation. A sensitive variable is something prone to change or fluctuation, but is easily perturbed, excited, or excessively affected by stimuli. Although difficult to notice the ascendency of a sensitive variable and discern its potential influence, we can more easily watch for and understand the *appearance of the conditions conducive for the surfacing and influence of sensitive variables.* These conditions can be emotional (fear of foreigners, hatred between sects, desire for revenge if numerous people have died as a result of errant precision guided munitions), physical (lack of water and sewage, intermittent electricity), weather (heat, humidity, wind, dust), or personal (appearance of a charismatic demagogue). Once a sensitive variable appears or a normal variable becomes sensitive, they can cause the fast conjoining of aggregates, hence the unforeseen appearance of second- and third-order effects. The appearance of sensitive variables can enable aggregates to grow faster, become more powerful, and through growth and power gather many seemingly disparate aggregates into the field of what is being aggregated.

As a closely related thought, we also need to discuss a sensitive variable *window of opportunity.* What is such a window of opportunity? It is a time in which variables can become or have become sensitive. It is during this time that either the enemy, friendly, neutrals, or host nation are most vulnerable to being exploited by the appearance of sensitive variables. Thus, friendly forces have to know themselves and their enemies as well as the neutrals and host nation in an OE. Even though he was writing military theory thousands of years ago, the words of the military philosopher Sun Tzu still are crystal clear and help us understand this thought:

> And therefore I say: Know the enemy, know yourself; your victory will
> never be endangered. Know the ground, know the weather; your victory
> will then be total.[12]

However, to know the enemy, we also have to know the populace, the
neutrals, the host nation government, and the infrastructure. Our analysts
have to purposefully think about and watch for these conditions, and
inform the decision maker of the imminent appearance of sensitive
variables and how they could influence the development and influence of
aggregates.

Watching for and striking or influencing the opponent, neutrals, or host
nation government, police, or populace during the windows of opportunity
in which sensitive variables have the greatest potential of creating intended
effects is using what Sun Tzu calls *ordinary* and *extraordinary forces*. In
modern parlance, this is using an indirect approach to take advantage of a
weakness or an opening the enemy, neutrals, or the host nation present. In
this regard, Sun Tzu says,

> In battle there are only the normal and extraordinary forces, but their com-
> binations are limitless; none can comprehend them all. For these two
> forces are mutually reproductive; their interaction as endless as that of
> interlocked rings. Who can determine where one ends and the other
> begins?[13]

Using an indirect approach is how friendly forces can use their own version of aggregation to strike or influence the weakness presented by the sensitive variables and windows of opportunity. However, at the same time,
friendly decision makers have to anticipate similar efforts by the enemy
against their weaknesses, as the enemy, neutral, or host nation leader perceives. Although complicated, this mental work is vital for anticipating and
using the power of aggregates to set conditions, create effects, and to
accomplish goals while ensuring friendly forces do not fall victim to the
same strategy. If our commanders fail to understand and use this phenomena—that is, the relationship between sensitive variables, windows of
opportunity, and aggregation—they will never seize, let alone hold the initiative, and they will always be victims to the enormous and sometimes out
of control effects of aggregation.

Continuing with this line of thought and taking another mental step
along the path toward understanding aggregation analysis, we find ourselves needing to ponder and answer yet another pressing question. Given
that I want to use and protect myself from the influences of aggregation and
sensitive variables, how do I know and understand what makes variables
sensitive? The answer lies in understanding three influential aspects of life—
the culture, the OE, and the weather. How people are educated, how they

comprehend and believe in religion, and discerning what in a particular culture is sensitive and therefore likely to cause second- and third-order effects
if appearing could help to anticipate what makes variables sensitive. The
answer also lies in understanding what makes people emotional or irrational. The answer lies in working with past situations to find if sensitive
variables were the catalysts of unanticipated outcomes or consequences and
watching for similar conditions and appearances in the current situation. In
addition, we have to know the weather and OE well enough to understand
how they commingle with and influence the culture and its inhabitants.
When all three (culture, weather, OE) combine at the right time, with the
right conditions, and with the right variables, aggregates could suddenly
appear and cause mission failure, surprise, or both.

The ascension of second- and third-order effects comes from the complex behavior and interactions of aggregates in urban environments.
Second- and third-order effects sometimes come from the imposition of sensitive variables at just the right time to create exponential effects. Thus, a
very pressing and practical use of aggregation analysis lies in anticipating
the kinds of activities that could form their own energies, seek alliances,
anticipate the adversary's counter, and adapt to the environment and the
enemy. Aggregation analysis also enables commanders and staffs to understand the appearance of conditions extant in the OE that foment the development of aggregates, and to watch for the appearance of small and
seemingly insignificant inputs that could have a direct, causal relationship
with huge outcomes out of proportion to the inputs.

By now the case has been made and the reader will surely agree with
the proposition that aggregation analysis is mentally taxing to understand,
to put into concrete terms, and to apply. However, who can deny the influence and importance of aggregation analysis? This isn't the forum for delving into reasons aggregation analysis is neither a common phrase nor why
there is such a dearth of knowledge about this aspect of analytic cognition.
As such, aggregation analysis hasn't been and isn't used extensively, but we
can conclude that its difficulty is undoubtedly a contributing factor. Practically speaking though, we must work on how to use aggregation analysis to
help us work in urban settings against the many adversaries, competitors,
people, and organizations we need to influence, complete with, or neutralize.

As another step along our journey to understand aggregation analysis,
we must first inquire—can early recognition and intervention or manipulation of aggregates help control their ultimate shape, power, and decay? The
answer is yes, but recognition and determining the degree of maturation of
the aggregate(s) in question is difficult. One has to anticipate the appearance of the aggregate, determine whether or not the aggregation has the
potential to grow and how fast, and dissect and understand the "glue" that
binds the aggregate's essential elements. In addition, the analyst has to

determine the potential outcomes of second- and third-order effects and design observables and collection to watch for and report on their appearance and potential influences. Further, the analyst must watch for the appearance of aggregates or the sudden inexplicable power and influence of events, activities, or groups of people that can only come from the subtle and often invisible appearance and influence of aggregates. However, even if advanced analysts miss anticipating the appearance and influence of nascent aggregates, they can still take action to cause their early decay, to neutralize their effects, and to negate their influence, if they first use aggregation analysis to understand the aggregate and also use a wide variety of experts to design strategies for causing the offending aggregate's demise or the early neutralization of its influence.

To recapitulate in simple terms, the advanced analyst using aggregation analysis has to decide exactly how he or she can use aggregation analysis against the enemy or other competitors in an urban OE. As such, the analyst in question has to both anticipate the surfacing of aggregates that can influence either friendly or enemy via immediate or delayed effects and determine if sensitive variables are influencing the aggregates. If they deem the presence of conditions and sensitive variables conducive to the ascendency of aggregates, they have to estimate potential outcomes on the commanders' mission and activities. They also have to determine how the ascendency of sensitive variables that give rise to aggregates could influence the friendly commander's actions. These same advanced analysts have to search for, find, and take advantage of windows of opportunity in which the enemy is vulnerable to manipulation or to preemption. To accomplish all of these mental and physical activities takes an ISR system attuned to sensitive fluctuations and changes, and a decision cycle that is agile and capable of acting very quickly once sensitive variables and the forming and clotting of aggregates starts.

Some examples help illustrate aggregation theory and its second- and third-order effects. Consider, for example, the images of dead soldiers being dragged through the streets of Mogadishu, Somalia in 1993. CNN piped the image to a U.S. distribution center in New York or Atlanta. If the image had been redirected to only one, ten, or twenty homes, it would have had no effect on national policy. But the image went to millions of homes. Because of this aggregation and the immense power in the form of the public outcry it unleashed, a single tactical event caused national policy to change. Or consider the images of the maltreatment of prisoners at Abu Ghraib prison. If the story had reached just a few people there would have been little hue and cry. But the story spread rapidly around the world via the Internet and caused an immense political storm.

As another example of aggregation, psychological operations (PSYOPS) affect the intellects and psyches of many people just enough to cause perturbations in morale, which has a first-order effect on the fighting quality of the opponent. The second-order effect is to cause cognitive dissonance in the minds of commanders whose command and control systems friendly forces seek to affect. The struggle in these competitive endeavors lies in the invisible realm of manipulating collective (that is, aggregate) intellects. The third-order effect is to use attacks and influences on the aggregate psyches of enemy soldiers to indirectly create cognitive dissonance in the psyche of the commander and affect his decision-making cycle and capability. Influencing the intellects of one or a few enemy soldiers or commanders has little influence on the whole, but if friendly forces are able to influence many hundreds of psyches, intellects, or a majority of the enemy commanders, *will* becomes susceptible to friendly effects and actions.

Further, consider how advertising works. If an advertisement affects just a few people it is meaningless. But if an advertisement affects a million people it becomes significant by the exponential power ingrained in the spread of ideas among many people. Encouraged by repetition of ideas and reinforcement by famous people, an idea spreads among individuals, groups, collections, and communities—that is, it aggregates.

Or consider the strength and functioning of an enemy network. Networks come together and disband; at times they appear as nodes and links and at other times there is nothing signifying their existence. Yet people physically and emotionally support perpetrators in a network. Thus, they come and go, and they provide food, shelter, logistics, transportation, security, communications, intelligence, security, and countless other necessities. When looking at just one of the support functions these people perform, they are almost invisible and generally the support is meaningless. Yet when looking at the situation using aggregation analysis, one begins to notice multiple support transactions, activities, interactions, and a collective psychic affliction (the semiotics and physiological manifestations of people when they know they are doing something untoward or they have an innate fear of being captured and sent to prison).

Indeed, second- and third-order effects become more important with aggregation. For example, if a killer application (app)[14] (e.g., a new, powerful computer application) takes hold, it must not influence just one or a few people. For the innovation to be a true killer app it must affect millions of people and collectively change the way those millions do their business. The second- and third-order effects coming from the impact and implications of killer apps often are unintended. Such was the invention of the simple stirrup for the horse, which led to reconnaissance, cavalry, maneuver, and so forth. No doubt the person who invented this killer app would have been surprised at all of the second- and third-order effects coming from it.[15] The same notion holds true for other killer apps: television, telephone, wireless communications, airplanes, and computers.

Another example would be the phenomenon of driving 70 mph along a busy highway and suddenly coming to a stop. The reason for the stop can help describe aggregation theory. Suppose the driver of the lead vehicle in a busy six-lane highway with over 5,000 vehicles going the same direction sees an animal get hit by another car. The lead car then slows down by a few seconds per mile. By itself this slowdown is meaningless. But magnifying the effect by 5,000 means the last car in the line will grind to a halt. The driver of the lead car has no idea of the second-order effect created on the person driving the last vehicle in the line. The last driver stopping knows nothing about the cause of the stoppage but knows whatever happened has caused an enormous outcome in the rear.

Will terrorists in the twenty-first century seize upon aggregation theory to manipulate the public psyche of our country or our friends to further their goals? This notion of many orchestrated, violent activities occurring at many places in the country, particularly with near simultaneous occurrences, could create effects of massive and sustained hysteria. If one terrorist activity similar to the 2002 suburban Virginia, Maryland, and Washington DC sniper incident occurred, it would elicit a small, localized response. In the case of the sniper, the response was localized but the economic impact on the area was great, as people stayed in their homes and didn't shop, and many did not go to work. If the activities stretched across several cities and caused thousands of casualties, the effect would grow exponentially and would soon affect public opinion, which in turn would affect public policy. The implications for this particular aspect of the phenomena of aggregation include the fear that a single terrorist using biological weapons can create in the collective psyche of numerous people: those directly affected by the biological agent, those whose close relatives or friends could be affected, as well as those potentially influenced by the spread of disease and ensuing panic.

Aggregation analysis will undoubtedly never be a favorite element of advanced analysts. Some will say it is too abstract and too intellectually strenuous. However, we must become good at it because it is though aggregation that the enemy can surge enough power to conduct attacks. It is though aggregation that a host nation populace supports the insurgent. It is though aggregates that second- and third-order effects arise to create huge problems and often mission failure for our commanders. So, let us identify a few of the more significant difficulties or challenges with advanced analysis and then identify how the advanced analyst can overcome these difficulties. Some of the more difficult aspects of aggregation analysis include:

- The urban OE is complex.
- The subject is abstract.
- The decision to search for, find, and do something with a newly formed aggregate is trying to think about, let alone to act upon.
- Aggregation analysis takes high-grade, current, and sometimes abstruse knowledge for success.

- We have to think like the people who are either part of an aggregate or who are using the aggregate, if we want to affect it.
- The act of thinking about and watching for signs of the birth of an aggregate or the decay of the glue that binds its parts into a whole, and the propellant that projects the aggregate is difficult—subtleties, ambiguities, and nuances abound and affect thinking.

So, let us explore ever so briefly what analysts can do to help themselves set their personal conditions for success with aggregation analysis. Several things come to mind.

- THE MIND. Intellectually, the advanced analyst can use an aggregation analysis thought template that helps him or her think and ensure they aren't forgetting some important aspect of thinking about aggregation analysis. Their minds cannot be uncomfortable with invisible abstractions involving aggregation analysis, such as the "glue" that binds aggregates into wholes and the "propellant" that causes aggregates to move, grow, and influence. In particular, the advanced analyst using aggregation analysis has to understand, seek, and use relationships, as aggregates come together and disband through relationships. Sometimes these relationships are obvious, but with adaptive CAS as parts of aggregates, many times advanced analysis will have to search for, find, and understand the most obscure and evolving relationships imaginable.
- KNOWLEDGE. Advanced analysts can seek assistance from the SME and COE, and scientists of a VKE to help provide the knowledge they need for engaging in aggregation analysis. These people have the cognitive "horsepower," knowledge, and practical experience to help the deployed or preparing to deploy analyst think. They can help the advanced analyst gain the knowledge he or she needs to engage in the vagaries and often arcane art and science of aggregation analysis.
- THINKING PROCESSES. There has to be good and effective deep thinking early in any effort to use aggregation analysis to its fullest capability. Analysts using aggregation analysis have to not only use a thought template but baselines of three types—technical, cultural, and functional. They also have to recall the strong relationships among aggregation, anomaly, tendency, cultural analysis, and synthesis (including holism). The analyst has to be curious about aggregation analysis and actively seek to use its intellectual processes. We need to use a good red team to check our thinking as we consider aggregates and attempt to use aggregation analysis.
- COMPLEXITY THEORY. The advanced analyst must have a modicum of knowledge about complexity theory to understand and use aggregation analysis. In particular, the advanced analyst must understand nonlinearity; small inputs cause large outputs; the presence and influence of

sensitive variables and windows of opportunity; the notion of complex adaptive systems (CAS); understanding that CAS anticipate, adapt, evolve, and mutate; understanding that during mutation, the CAS often conjoin with dissimilar CAS; CAS engage in self-organization; and of course the relationships between CAS and aggregation. Of equal importance, the advanced analyst must have the wherewithal to take his or her modicum of knowledge about complexity in urban OE and seek help from the scientists of the VKE for performing many of the functions involved with aggregation analysis and advanced analysis writ large.

AGGREGATION IMPLICATIONS

Aggregation analysis gives us several implications to consider and ponder. Some of the more important implications include

- Consider the implications of multiple low-level insurgent-induced events in a city such as Baghdad. Some are small and seem like pinpricks; they seem disjointed, and—in the doctrinal parlance—at the low-end of tactics (and not very hurtful at that). But other considerations must occur in the thinker's mind. These "pinpricks" in an aggregated sense can have immense influence on the political spectrum. They contribute to perception and thoughts that lead people to conclude, in an aggregated sense, that chaos reigns. When looked at in isolation, the deaths, carnage, and damage to property in urban military operations appear appalling but tolerable. But viewing a situation through the lens of aggregation analysis, when the numbers of killed and wounded civilians and the property destroyed or damaged add up to serious numbers, the physical damage to people's homes and property on its own becomes an overwhelming issue. The carnage becomes a true issue because of widespread fear and distrust of the government's ability to maintain order and the supporting country's disgust with the lost time, money, and lives.
- What often appears disjointed in complex urban operations is in reality a unified, related whole, with order buried within the apparent chaos. Author M. Mitchell Waldrop helps us understand this phenomenon, called the edge of chaos:

> all these complex systems have somehow acquired the ability to bring order and chaos into a special kind of balance. This balance point—often called the edge of chaos—is where the components of a system never quite lock into place, and yet never quite dissolve into turbulence, either. The edge of chaos is where life has enough stability to sustain itself and enough creativity to deserve the name of life. The edge of chaos is where new ideas and innovative genotypes are forever nibbling away at the edges of the status quo, and where even

the most entrenched old guard will eventually be overthrown. . . . The edge of chaos is the constantly shifting battle zone between stagnation and anarchy, the one place where a complex system can be spontaneous, adaptive, and alive.[16]

- Unfortunately, the order and stability we seek is often alien to our rationale; stability is camouflaged by chaos, so we see only the collisions, intersections, careening, conjoining, and random emanations of energy, whose resultant pieces and characteristics can seem quite the opposite of order—that is, this mix seems like, smells like, and looks like chaos. However, the threads of stability are masked by the culture in which they embed (which we may not understand), and the specific, local activities and actions that when taken in isolation appear insignificant. But through aggregation analysis, the power of actions in an aggregated whole help the analyst to find order in chaos, and to understand the appearance of and the stage of maturity and possible influence of sensitive variables.

- When looking at an enemy network, several constants come into play. For one, the network will change and morph. The links between and among nodes will appear and disappear, sometimes quickly. People are the network, and they have needs. They must eat, sleep, relieve themselves, and move from point A to point B. The populace performs functions to support the network—security, transportation, logistics, intelligence collection, food, shelter, communications, storage, and so forth. People using autos, motorcycles, scooters, and walking move around and provide such support often under the guise of normal activities. As such they are like ants, which leave invisible chemical trails entomologists call pheromones. Analysts can have trouble noticing or visualizing human support network "pheromones" because people tend to look at things in isolation, or if they don't recognize or understand what they see, to pass it by and ignore it. To see the human network support "pheromones," analysts must understand the culture in which the enemy is operating, but they also have to view human support network activities not as isolated actions but as many continuous efforts flowing into one single or multiple aggregates relating visibly and invisibly among other aspects of other networks.

- As a final implication, advanced analysts must be able to disaggregate challenges into essential elements and understand parts and how each part relates to an aggregate so he or she can disambiguate and disaggregate for the purpose of negation or manipulation. As such, an enemy's network must be disaggregated into its nodes, links, functions, characteristics, means of connectedness, and purposes, and the analyst must understand each element individually and how each element relates to the entire aggregate. The analyst must gain an understanding of how one network unfolds into a more elaborate network and enfolds smaller and more insignificant networks. When one piece of a network linked in this way begins to move, other pieces move or morph too. Unfortunately, it is difficult to reach this level and sophistication of thinking without deeply delving into and understanding aggregation analysis.

This chapter presents an abstract but important subject in the totality of advanced analysis. Regardless of its high degree of abstraction, which sometimes blocks understanding, it is through various forms of aggregation that wholes such as attack, defend, occupy, operate a safehouse, set off an IED, and so forth come into being from a mere glimmer in the imagination of an insurgent. Aggregation analysis also works against more subtle indicants of preparation for action, such as condition-setting. In such a sequence of activities or events, aggregated wholes come together, exude energy toward a goal, emanate emissions, and eventually disaggregate or die. The chapter also emphasizes the importance of aggressively thinking about how aggregates unfold into other, larger aggregates and enfold smaller aggregates, and then hold or bond what we can call sub-aggregates into a whole.

In this chapter, the author takes a measure of liberty and asks for the indulgence of the reader to allow some thoughts to come forth involving some new but meaningful approaches to thinking about aggregates and aggregation. As one idea, the chapter introduces the notion of "glue" that binds aggregates into a whole. This glue can be an idea, a mission, hatred, or intent. It can also be a neighborhood's subcultural perspectives, social groups, common beliefs, common perceptions, common goals, and common degrees of intensity about myths, facts, beliefs, or views. As an interesting aside, the glue of aggregation always decays, but its decay rate varies. It follows that the advanced analyst must not only understand the aggregate in general and its essential parts, but how it congeals and disaggregates, and of course the nature of the "invisible glue" that bonds aggregates.

As another idea, the chapter brings forth the notion of an aggregation "propellant" that hurls aggregates in varying degrees of speed, velocity, influence, and intensity toward their destiny of impact, influence, or death. Along this train of thought, the chapter emphasizes the importance of discerning, understanding, influencing, or simply monitoring the volatility and overall condition of the propellant that fuels aggregates over time, particularly when considered in relation to the ebb and flow of sensitive variables and windows of opportunity, which provide the conditions for an aggregate's influence and degree of intensity and influence. This type of thinking provides the analysts' mind's eye with an incredible insight into the birth, influence, and death of second- and third-order effects that have caused and continue to cause commanders so much trouble in urban irregular warfare. Clearly, intelligence analysts must purposefully expend cognitive energy in thinking about and understanding the "glue" and the "propellant" of aggregation theory.

Aggregation theory is also important in thinking about and turning into operational reality the largely intangible realm of information operations. It is in this realm that the struggle for hearts and minds of the center of gravity (the populace) in any urban conflict is won or lost. It is here, through aggregates comprising the totality of moods, thoughts, and perceptions that shape the numerous interactions, transactions, activities, and behaviors occurring in an urban setting that effective IO planners and advanced analysts can defuse the potential for an exponential leap into strategic influence by a seemingly innocuous event. It is in the mind's eye of the effective advanced analyst in which an apparition can appear as an aggregate, not as a separate event. Advanced analysis and its high-powered cognitive activities must play a major role in IO; therefore, intelligence analysts must understand how it should relate with the function of IO and more specifically, how the notions of "glue," "glue decay," "propellant," and "propellant flammability" all conjoin into a very powerful and critical force for the friendly commander.

With the passage of this chapter, the reader is now ready for studying the next element of advanced analysis, which is recomposition. Recomposition, of course, is an essential step in producing outcomes or products of advanced analysis. Recomposition connects with synthesis, which is the essential cognitive aspect of producing actionable decision-grade knowledge and understanding.

17

Recomposition

Definition: Human- and machine-driven recompilation of collected data to gain information, knowledge, and understanding.

THEORY BEHIND RECOMPOSITION

Recomposition is a cognition- and machine-driven compilation and recompilation of parts, components, basic elements, and data to gain insight, information, knowledge, and understanding of the whole. Recomposition is a direct descendant from decomposition, which we discussed earlier in this book. Once analysts successfully engage in decomposition and develop five kinds of observables, they articulate the detailed observables (times, locations, and suspected activities) to collection experts and machines. With the commencement of collection activities, data returns to be processed, correlated, and distributed. It is upon the receipt of collected data that intelligence analysts and their machines begin to recompose. This is a "must do" step to develop knowledge, which comes with the human cognitive function called synthesis. Interestingly, the best analysts have an end state in mind as they decompose requirements. That is, they have a vision, a hypothesis, an expectation, hunch, or mystery in mind they are working with as they start the decomposition process. As such, they have specific outcomes in mind that they constantly strive for during recomposition. Nonetheless, they will not let their vision of the end state corrupt facts and inferences. They will keep their analytic effort unassailable by the waves of human cognitive error and bias even when they have an idea in mind as they start the process of decomposition that will eventually lead to recomposition. The analysts will use other people and organizations to critique their work so as to avoid falling into logic traps and errors in thinking.

Though it sounds simple, recomposition is complex and presents challenges to advanced analysts for several reasons. First, analysts have to know a lot about what they are looking for to start the process of turning data into information and eventually knowledge. Unfortunately, as mentioned earlier, analysts on deployed staffs sometimes lack sufficient expertise in all 14 areas of advanced analysis, the threat, and the OE to drive the development of observables, let alone recompose seemingly innocuous and disparate threads of data into usable information and knowledge. In this way of thinking, the analyst is attempting to run several strands through the entire web of human activity[1] in an urban OE and combine the strands to make sense of combinations and relationships of strands through recomposition and eventually synthesis. The wise advanced analyst knows his or her own cognitive limitations and seeks help in areas in which they lack proficiency. Second, the analyst uses advanced machine work to help knit seemingly disparate threads, or metaphorically speaking, gossamers, into a unified whole or "tapestry" to create information that foreshadows the framework of nascent, usable knowledge. Third, advanced analysts must engage knowledgeable, experienced SMEs, along with military analysts performing an analytic overwatch role, to provide the knowledge, experience, and cognition necessary for successfully engaging in recomposition. In this regard, they need the cognitive capabilities necessary for understanding not only military aspects of situations but also diplomatic, informational, and economic actions and effects aimed at the enemy's political, military, economic, social, and informational infrastructure (PMESII).

Interestingly, if this process is performed correctly, collection outputs coming to an analyst will usually be cultural, functional, situational, technical, or biometric—after all, they come from these same types of observables. The outputs will match or challenge what analysts expect, test their hypotheses, call their assumptions into question, or solve an ongoing analytic mystery. Recomposition becomes easier if the person doing the recomposing also performs the decomposition at the front end of the analytic/collection process. Because data coming from collectors requires making sense of it, the analyst that decomposed requirements at the front end of the process will undoubtedly aggregate and manipulate pertinent data in more depth and faster than a person unfamiliar with the work that went into the decomposition process.

To recompose effectively, an analyst must know and understand the highly interactive strengths, weaknesses, and characteristics of both sides in a competition. The analyst will have to know the culture, infrastructure, nature, and thinking proclivities of the populace, and of course the enemy, to engage successfully in recomposition. The analyst must also understand

and search for a capability to see what is invisible. Decision theorist Gary Klein provides the following thoughts that help us understand what the analyst must do during recomposition and specifically when searching for what appears to be invisible:

> Experts see the world differently. They see things the rest of us cannot. Often experts do not realize that the rest of us are unable to detect what seems obvious to them . . . There are many things experts can see that are invisible to everyone else: patterns that novices do not notice; anomalies— events that did not happen and other violations of expectancies; the big picture (situation awareness); the way things work; opportunities and improvisation; events that either already happened (the past) or are going to happen (the future); differences that are too small for novices to detect; their own limitations.[2]

This knowledge of the enemy and what is invisible will help the advanced analyst recognize activities or non-activities coming forth for what they are. This knowledge will also help the analyst relate these activities, because during collection much data will seem disparate and unrelated but in reality they are highly relational. When using advanced analysis though, an analyst can combine these seemingly disparate data fragments into increasingly meaningful aggregates that over time become usable information. Eventually, with perseverance and after taking the results of recomposition and using the advanced analysis element called synthesis, an analyst derives knowledge, which the commander requires to lower uncertainty and help manage risk.

Some associated definitions will help the reader more fully comprehend the notion of recomposition. *Recomposition*, as we recall, is human- and machine-driven recompilation of collected data to gain information, knowledge, and understanding. There is a difference between recomposition and fusion. *Fusion* in the context of this work is machine work that brings together data and turns it into what is intelligible to the human being. In this respect, fusion is the merging of different elements into a union.[3] Recomposition takes results from fusing data and turns it into information. Recomposition uses machine work to support the human intellect. In *Stray Voltage: War in the Information Age*, I provide additional insights into this notion; it is the principal reason that recomposition differs from synthesis:

> They must learn to search for and find both obvious and disparate relationships. Intelligent agents and fast processors can help in such endeavors. . . . a man-machine symbiosis will have to occur with the two operating as one, each capturing the strengths and minimizing the weaknesses of the other. Such symbiosis can occur through the growing competence of intelligent agents and other learning software.[4]

Synthesis is the human cognitive activity that combines elements of substances, events, activities, or energy to form a coherent whole.[5] It is, as mentioned earlier, a distinctively human function. It is essential to advanced analysis, as it is what occurs in the human mind alone that turns information into knowledge that commanders require for their decision-making. It is synthesis that produces actionable intelligence. Sense-making is a final related element of recomposition that requires some explanation in our quest to understand recomposition. *Sense-making* is for the most part a cognitive activity involving understanding the current situation, discerning how it will evolve, and the threats, constraints, opportunities or limitations, and potential actions that could be taken in response or in anticipation, along with the projected outcomes and the assumptions and values driving COA. Analysts and supporting machines make sense of data. Analysts think about the data and try to make sense of it from their minds' perspectives and experiences, and most important, from the reason they are engaging in analysis in the first place—to support the commander's planning and decision processes. When possible, they enjoin the knowledge and experience of others to help make sense of often vague and culturally or technically ambiguous data that has been either gathered by machines or collected by sensors and HUMINT. To help them, they use one, two, combinations of, or all 14 elements of advanced analysis to recompose data into information on the journey toward developing actionable knowledge.

There are some trials and tribulations the advanced analyst must endure and overcome in sense-making. They must be on the lookout for these potential problems and take immediate corrective action if they discover their appearance and feel their influences. As one example, sometimes an analyst uses the wrong data, thereby causing the wrong sense-making. Sometimes data appears impenetrable; therefore analysts give up and discard the data. Sometimes analysts cannot handle all the data available, thereby leaving valuable data on the "cutting room floor," to borrow a metaphor from the filmmaker's repertoire of activities. Sometimes the analyst has to comply with ill-founded priorities to narrow the hunt for relevant data. Sometimes being afflicted with the wrong data can even contribute to the wrong decision. Even when the data is good and not contaminated, the analyst must still think correctly. However, the busy, tired, stressed analyst can make faulty assumptions about data, interpret it incorrectly, and even evaluate it incorrectly.

As the intelligence analyst recomposes data into information, they will find themselves making some important considerations. First, they will revisit their comprehension of the difference between information and knowledge. They will recall that information applies to facts told, read, or communicated that may be unorganized and even unrelated. Knowledge is an organized body of information, or the comprehension and understanding consequent on having acquired and organized a body of facts. Wisdom is a knowledge of people, life, and conduct, with the facts so thoroughly assimilated as to have produced sagacity, judgment, and insight.[6] The analyst will also recall that there are three kinds of knowledge—existing, existing but with value-added comments and applications, and new knowledge. Often, the analyst will try to find existing knowledge all the while knowing that he or she and other SMEs will have to massage the knowledge and add value to it to make it useful to the task at hand. The analyst will also have to consider the commander's mission, guidance, intent, and PIR/IR. As such, they will use their commander's guidance to answer these questions—What am I looking for? Why am I looking? Am I thinking about and looking for the right answers? Is what I'm looking for relevant to the commander's planning and decision cycle? Along with the commander's information requirements, the analyst will also keep in mind his or her analytic requirements. These requirements come forth as hypotheses, expectations, hunches, and mysteries. When recomposing, the analyst also must keep in mind the constraints and standards, which enshroud and influence the effort to recompose and to produce a product. They will also have to consider standards for the information they are recomposing. As a reminder, throughout this work we have used the standards of timeliness, accuracy, specificity, relevance, and clarity. The metrics applied to these standards will, of course, change upon movement through the levels of command. As the analyst becomes more and more involved with recomposition, he or she will think about some other aspects of the OE. Some of these considerations include

- ENEMY SITUATION: The enemy is always moving and operating. He uses a network that is very difficult to see or notice. He is embedded in the society. Thus, the analyst has to comprehend how the enemy's fluidity affects his and friendly operations. The analyst has to know and understand how the enemy perceives and thinks, as well as the enemy's tactics, techniques, and his network operations so as to pull the right data from the masses of data available and to work with machines to turn it into information. The enemy will complicate the intelligence analyst's life, as he will view his struggle with us as Sun Tzu articulates:

  Therefore, against those skilled in attack, an enemy does not know where to defend; against the experts in defense, the enemy does not know where to attack. Subtle and insubstantial, the expert leaves no trace; divinely mysterious, he is inaudible. Thus he is master of his enemy's fate.[7]

- CHANGES IN THE OE: Analysts have to realize the fluid nature of the OE. Fluidity has a significant impact on the staff responsible for planning, conducting, and assessing outcomes of stability operations. A constantly changing OE means changing missions. With changing missions come decision variations. With fluctuation in decisions, commanders will demand more high-quality knowledge owing to the requirement to lower uncertainty and risk. With the demand for high-quality information and knowledge, the ISR system becomes stressed to meet the standards. The analyst and the collection will be the most stressed. Thus, they need to make their considerations early and seize the intellectual initiative instead of waiting until the time arrives for the information and knowledge to come forth. This requirement ties back into analytic condition-setting we discussed earlier in this work.

As the analyst becomes involved with recomposition, there are some techniques that will assist. As one, the analyst should always answer the question— what does this data mean? Answering this question causes their minds to work to apply meaning to the data and to appreciate the elements and magnitude of the challenges they face when dealing with masses of data. Additionally, they should answer the question—what could this mean? Answering this question causes their minds to explore possibilities and options from their view as well as that of the adversary, the neutral, and friendly indigenous SMEs as well as American SMEs. Continuing with this train of thought, they must answer the question, what are the implications? Engaging in implication analysis is an excellent way to engender higher-level thinking, which will make their transition into the realm of synthesis much easier. Thinking about implications "switches" on the portion of the analyst's brain involving relationships and creative thinking. Implications help with "what ifs" and actions the commander or his staff should take to preempt the adversary, protect themselves, or think about solutions to long-range problems and challenges. They must also understand the culture and its people, including the infrastructure, the role and influence of religion, power structures, commerce, views and use of technology, and views of foreigners. Most importantly, the analyst must discern how the indigenous populace perceives, thinks, feels, communicates, and how they express themselves. This work with the people and their culture, however, should be worked through the thought processes of the people and the culture. Most often, the analyst will need the assistance of indigenous SMEs to help him or her perform these considerations.

To the inquisitive analyst, there are some ways to evaluate the quality of data, information, and knowledge. As one way, they must always evaluate this type of information in relation to their commander's mission and his or her intent. Further, they are obliged to evaluate the information in relation to the five types of standards—timeliness, specificity, accuracy, relevance, and clarity. Then, they must evaluate the information in terms of usability—that is, can the information contribute to the immediate or near-term future of the problem at hand? The analyst can also review and judge the credibility of the source of the information and in the process attempt to judge its veracity or truthfulness. To help in their quest to judge the worth of the data coming to them, they can find experts to work with to check on the validity of the data and for its possible problems so as to judge the risk of it being corrupted or deceptive information.

The output of recomposition is important. It connects to and drives the quality of information and knowledge so important to decision-making and in anticipating enemy activities and actions. However, even with its importance and the supreme effort analysts and collection specialists and their SMEs put forth, recomposition will almost always be fragmentary. This state of affairs is particularly apropos in urban conflict, owing to the fluidity of the OE, the nature and capabilities of well-hidden insurgents, and the motion and activities of people who live in the contested city. So, what does fragmentary mean in this context? Quite simply, fragmentary data and information mean that there will never be a complete "whole," for which the analyst searches. Although somewhat abstract, the term "whole" is apropos to what we are after with recomposition. This idea is explained more in the following passage:

> What are wholes? Wholes are constructs—mental and physical. Wholes represent things (physical) and ideas (mental). Wholes compose smaller wholes and comprise larger wholes. Wholes nest within each other and unfold, much the way paper dolls do, each separate yet connected, when we cut them out of a newspaper for our children. Wholes aren't simple, discrete entities; they always either relate to or connect with other entities. Sometimes these connections or relationships are hard to find, but they exist.[8]

Clausewitz also helps us understand the term "wholes" from yet another perspective. In this regard Clausewitz tells us:

> Combat is not a contest between individuals. It is a whole made up of many parts, and in that whole two elements may be distinguished, one determined by the subject, the other by the objective. . . . The whole of military activity must therefore relate directly or indirectly to the engagement. The end for which a soldier is recruited, clothed, armed, and trained, the whole object of his sleeping, eating, drinking, and marching is simply that he should fight at the right place and the right time.[9]

In addition, the analyst can rest assured that in this environment working against an insurgent or irregular threat, truth will be difficult to come by and when found "truth will change." Thus, both analyst and commander must deal with partial wholes. That is, there will be enough information and knowledge that the bold commander can make a decision and act. However, with this situation, the commander will know that his risk and uncertainty are entwined and high. The other choice is to wait until high-grade knowledge is available, when wholes are developed, and when risk and uncertainty are low. Unfortunately, this is a recipe for disaster in urban COIN and IW operations. It is the decision maker's dilemma. This dilemma goes as follows. The commander will have in his mind a *sweet spot of decision-making* in which he is comfortable with the recomposition effort and its outputs, in which his tolerance for risk and uncertainty are as low as he requires, and he approaches the problem with the sure knowledge that if he doesn't act quickly, the enemy network will morph, and when the commander does strike, it will be at nothing. If the tactical and operational commanders wait upon recomposition and its relative, synthesis, to provide high-grade knowledge sufficient to push risk and uncertainty to a very low point on a sliding scale of acceptability, the enemy could also act first and thereby seize the initiative. The commander and his analysts must have a relationship in which the analysts know their commander's tolerance for risk and uncertainty, and act accordingly during the recomposition process. Together, they will find the sweet spot of decision-making in which the commander is comfortable with the partial wholes of risk and uncertainty, and acts rather than waiting and waiting for the last piece to the knowledge puzzle.

Next, let us delve into some of the challenges of recomposition and how the analyst can overcome them. The challenges come first followed by a short discussion of ways to overcome them.

- KNOWLEDGE. As mentioned earlier, the analyst engaging in recomposition will need to possess a vast range of knowledge to be effective. This is particularly true for analysts at the tactical level who often won't have the luxury of seeking and finding a "great mind" knowledge expert of the type required. Analysts will need to know a lot to recompose data into information and set conditions for the building of knowledge through synthesis. In addition, in many cases, the analyst will lack the knowledge required to use appropriate tools of advanced analysis. As yet another challenge, the analysts will not have the experience, cultural knowledge, technical knowledge, or even the functional knowledge with which to perform recomposition.
- TECHNICAL ENVIRONMENT. For the most part, the technical environment is invisible but critically important. Most analysts won't have sufficient technical knowledge to use and exploit it against the enemy and to work with the populace. Thus, the analysts must learn how the enemy uses it, how the populace uses and thinks about it, how enemy and populace think we think about our use of technology, as well as how we think about the enemy's and populace's use of technology.
- BASELINES. In many cases, the analyst will find that nobody has developed the baselines he or she needs to serve as a model of normalcy for efforts to recompose data into information. As we discussed previously,

baselines are local. They must be developed or updated constantly to be of use in establishing normalcy with which to employ anomaly, aggregation, tendency, cultural, and semiotics analysis. These developmental and maintenance functions of baseline databases must be updated constantly as a purposeful function clearly driven by advanced analysis and in particular by the cognitive element of recomposition.

- ANALYTIC SUPPORT. A significant analytic challenge with recomposition involves time. Unfortunately, analysts at the tactical level will often be too stressed and busy with multi-tasking to take the time to perform the deep thinking recomposition requires. The time constraint for thinking also applies to the use of tools. That is, the analyst will face severe challenges to find time to perform the functions of the various kinds of tools that can make their work with recomposition easier. In addition, skills with tools quickly atrophy. Thus, although the analyst might have learned how to use the tool at some point in their learning history, they could very easily have lost their proficiency with the tool.
- KNOWING THE CULTURE. This is a significant challenge. Succinctly put, the analyst must know the culture and understand how it works and influences people to use it in advanced analysis, but in particular when engaging in recomposition. There is a difference among knowing, understanding, and simply being aware. As such, the challenge is that the analyst must know the culture well enough to use it for seeking, gaining, and finding advantages. In this case, the advantages being sought lie in knowledge, thinking, and decision advantages—all coming into being if the analyst knows and understands enough to use the culture as described. It takes even more knowledge to understand how the culture influences relationships that can range from personal, to business, to religious, to familial. Developing such knowledge and understanding sufficiently well to apply it in recomposition is a prodigious challenge. Why is this the case? Quite simply, the culture in which U.S. advanced analysts will find themselves will be influenced by the science of complexity, and in many cases will be culturally alien to the analysts' ways of perceiving, thinking, making decisions, and acting. The analysts must learn how the enemy thinks, operates, assesses outcomes, and adjusts. Such knowledge is often culturally oriented and beyond the cognitive reach of the advanced analyst.
- RELATIONSHIP WITH COLLECTION. A relationship with collection is an indirect challenge when considering recomposition. It ties to an earlier admonition for engaging in decomposition—that is the analysts performing decomposition should be the same analysts that are performing recomposition. As such, the analyst must view the process as an assembly line, but with the analyst performing the duties and functions of the decomposition to work with collectors to the actual recomposition and eventually the synthesis of information into

knowledge. Why is this cognitive process such a challenge? The challenges are many and varied. For example, people often are not organized for this type of continuity. The analyst who engages in decomposition might not work with collection specialists or might move on to something else before recomposition occurs. In addition, collection and analysis currently exist in their own stovepiped worlds and do not mix with one another to the extent needed. Further, when analysts and collection specialists are busy, they most often default to what they have always done and what they know—stovepipes and functional knowledge. Organizationally, the cooperation of analysts and collection people is inhibited by structures such as MTOE, physical space, separate training, rewards, and feedback on how well they are doing (as individuals and not as teams).

Arguably, the challenges listed above can tax even the most effective analyst, but ways to meet these challenges head on and to learn to ameliorate their impact on analytic operations certainly exist. This next section covers how the analyst can consider meeting and overcoming the challenges.

- KNOWLEDGE. For starters, the analyst needs to keep the requirement for knowledge firmly in their mind. With understanding of knowledge challenges, the analyst will understand the three types of knowledge and how to work with each. Analysts will have to find help to assist in recomposing data into information and synthesizing information into knowledge. The first place to go for help is on their staff. However, it will be extremely difficult to find the right kind of knowledge SMEs in the organic headquarters. Therefore, the advanced analyst will seek help from other places, including the intelligence enterprise, the interagency and nongovernment organizations supporting the operation, trusted indigenous SMEs, and an external VKE. Of particular importance, the analyst will need to find and use reliable, skilled indigenous SMEs to help them gain required knowledge and understanding sufficient to engage in recomposition. Regardless of cultural and language differences, the U.S. analyst must put forth a purposeful effort to know the culture well enough to seek and find numerous advantages—they can often do this through working with an indigenous source who has the right trust and clearances with which to help. Analytic overwatch can also help the deployed analyst with specific tasks dealing with the three types of knowledge listed and discussed earlier. As part of a disciplined and trained overwatch, clear roles, missions, and supervision need to drive the work of a distributed analytic overwatch system specifically designed to work knowledge requirements for the deployed analysts. Even the overwatch analysts, however, will often not have the right experience, education, or maturity to provide the detailed and local knowledge that deployed analysts require. Thus, they will need access to the country's great scientific, technical, and cultural minds to help work with and provide the knowledge and its applications that deployed analysts need for working effectively in a large urban setting. With any external support, the effort must be characterized by discipline, correct articulation of requirements, critiquing forthcoming knowledge products, reliance, and bona fide authorities in their fields of knowledge. A system has to be set in place to supervise this type of requirement, as the deployed analyst will not have the time.

- KNOWING THE TECHNICAL ENVIRONMENT. The technical environment is extremely important to advanced analysis. As a first step in meeting the challenges associated with technology, the analyst must understand and work with the existence of two worlds, in the context of this discussion. One world is what the analyst can see and touch—it is the physical world. The other world is the invisible world in which millions of activities and interactions are occurring (e.g., electrons flowing, heat emanating, smells occurring), all of which the analyst cannot see, sense, or touch. However, just because something is invisible and can neither be seen nor touched does not diminish its importance. These two worlds represent the technical environment, and the advanced analyst must learn to work with each. Therefore, recognition of the challenge of knowing the technical environment is the first and most important step in meeting this challenge. Second, because the advanced analyst will not usually be an engineer, he or she must seek assistance from engineers who are on the staff, in the intelligence enterprise, among interagency organizations, at work in the civilian populace of the country and city in question, or in a supporting VKE. As such, the analyst must learn to seek help and to use scientists and engineers to help them not only design technical observables, but also to help design the right collection, and ultimately to engage in recomposition. The third way the analyst can meet the technical challenge is to view it as a continuum of decom-position, technical observables, collection, recomposition, and synthesis. Recognition of and work with this continuum suggests the advanced analyst must seek help early and keep the same people working through-out the cycle of analysis, collection, and recomposition/synthesis.
- BASELINES. We have discussed baselines a lot in this work. Baselines are important for effective recomposition. The analyst has to find what baselines exist to support his or her analytic work very early in the planning cycle. Often, they will find that baselines don't exist, and if in existence, they will most often be outdated. In addition, many times baseline databases will not have the right fields, as there is no accepted, doctrinal field organization in the three types of baselines—technical, cultural, and functional. Thus, the challenges in using up-to-date

baselines are immense. What is an analyst to do to meet and overcome these challenges? As one approach, the analyst can identify the need for three types of baselines during his or her analytic condition-setting. During condition-setting, the analyst needs to think through what is required for updating or establishing new baseline databases and make the requirement known through both command and intelligence channels. As another related approach, the analyst can work within the intelligence enterprise and make requests for baseline production to support his or her requirements. Also, the analyst can request direct support from the supporting VKE for dedicated work to either maintain baseline databases in the unlikely case of finding them current, or adjusting existing baselines, or, in a worst-case scenario, building new baseline databases.

- KNOWING THE CULTURE. The analyst must know the culture to engage in effective recomposition. Software will not help him or her know the culture—it is the human being that will know culture and understand its relationships with how people and organizations perceive, think, make decisions, act, assess outcomes, and engage in interactions, activities, transactions, and behavior. Advanced analysts are intellectually introspective; therefore, they will know if they have depth of knowledge of the culture sufficient to recompose data into information. If they do not possess sufficient knowledge of the culture to perform rapid and meaningful recomposition, they have some options to follow for finding assistance. First, they can sometimes find cultural experts in their organization. Such expertise can come from other analysts, civil affairs, engineers, and combat arms specialists who have been on the street. They can also come from human terrain teams and from assigned FAOs. Second, they can seek the help of indigenous people who have proper security clearances. These people might work in the headquarters. Or, the analyst can attempt to use indigenous people who, as members of the society in question, perform their daily work as professional people such as doctors, engineers, and accountants. Because much of the work the analyst does is local, it is best that indigenous support be local too. Third, the intelligence analyst can consult with the intelligence enterprise and in particular analytic overwatch people who often have access to outside cultural experts. Fourth, the intelligence analyst can seek assistance from a VKE with its bevy of SMEs and SME contacts throughout the United States and the world in general. The important aspect of knowing and understanding the culture is that the analyst in question knows he must use the culture to perform his or her analytic work—in particular, to perform recomposition and its close relative, synthesis.
- COLLECTION AND ANALYSIS. Analysts and collection specialists must work as a team. Although it is not the purpose of this work to identify how to

overcome the organizational frameworks that cause a schism in two natural functions, suffice it to say that our military units need to bring analysts and collectors together on a continuum, and not just for brief moments in time. Analysts who decompose and then recompose need the same person or people to be a part of the problem team from the beginning to the end of the operation, and if possible, for subsequent intelligence operations. Additionally, analysts and collection people should train as a team before deploying and should work with the distributed collection and analytic systems before, during, and after deployment. To help in such a teaming endeavor, the intelligence analyst must learn the rudimentary aspects of collection and vice versa. As such, the analyst must ensure that each collector knows analyst guidance, rationale, and sampling rates to collect at the right time, right place, look for the right activity, and search diligently for the right observable.

- ANALYSIS. To help with advanced analysis sufficient to perform recomposition, analysts must enter into decomposition with recomposition in mind, but in particular, with the well-defined standards of specificity, timeliness, accuracy, relevance, and clarity. Such a synergistic effort will drive the early requirements to design data flow architectures coming from tasked collectors. In addition, the busy deployed analyst will need organized and disciplined support that he or she can count on. This support is necessary in several respects:
  - First, the analyst will need detailed, relevant knowledge support.
  - Second, the deployed analyst *will lack sufficient time* to perform many analytic functions.
  - Third, more specifically, the analyst will need *specialized analytic support*. This support can come from a VKE that will either have the requisite analytic talent on hand or will have the contacts in a community of interest that they will bring to bear on working the analyst's requirements and problems.

Analytic support efforts, for reasons discussed throughout this work, will be among analysts, collection specialists, technologists, and SMEs from an intelligence enterprise, indigenous SMEs, interagency and NGO SMEs, and a distributed VKE. Analysts can also help themselves by engaging in red-teaming, wargaming, and critical thinking. This critical thinking effort will come from red team experts with the staff or in a higher headquarters, or SMEs external to the deployed analyst's organization. During this process, trained experts will challenge the deployed analyst's assumptions and aggressively seek to discover errors in logic (e.g., mirror imaging, expert opinion, over-simplification, circular reasoning, etc.). To help with recomposition, analysts must set out to test, confirm, or deny hypotheses and confirm or deny their expectations and hunches, and resolve to solve their analytic mysteries from the start of an operation. In addition, they must look for creative and innovative solutions and insights, often with help from the external intelligence enterprise and a distributed VKE. Other approaches that analysts can take to help with recomposition include identifying or noticing signs of emerging sensitive variables and their related windows of opportunity. The analyst must consider and watch for the emergence of second- and third-order effects that should have been identified as possible in the commander's course of action feasibility wargaming.

- THINK LIKE THE ENEMY. During recomposition, the analyst, with help from indigenous and external SMEs, works diligently to think like the enemy, develop, and answer the following questions from enemy leaders' perspectives:
  - Will American analysts be capable of recomposing obscure activities into meaning in time to cause me harm?
  - How will I know they are looking for me and how they are looking?
  - When should I move to avoid their recomposition activities?
  - How will I proceed with my condition-setting to avoid the American's ability to recompose data into information?
  - What kind of deception will most likely confuse the American analysts' recomposition efforts?
  - Will my necessary countersurveillance operations inadvertently help the American analyst involved in recomposition?
  - How will I recruit people to perform the many duties I need for sustaining my network and for performing tasks essential to my mission without showing up in the American analyst's recomposition activities?

In closing this chapter, the discussion of recomposition explains why it is the first point of output for advanced analysis that ties directly with decision-making. It is where collected and gathered data flow to fusion centers and are worked with first by machines and then by the analyst's intellect and focused machine effort. Recomposition is the continuation of an intellectual maturation process of sense-making that started with many unknowns, uncertainties, and risks as commander's intent and PIR, or as analysts pursued their hunches and mysteries. Fittingly, only synthesis follows the recomposition chapter of the substantive cognitive elements of advanced analysis. The discussion of synthesis will pull the essential element of advanced analysis into a whole of meaning, output of knowledge, contribution of knowledge to understanding and decisions, and culminate in knowledge-driven action.

The discussion in this chapter brought forth an important distinction in meaning between recomposition and synthesis. Recomposition involves the human mind but depends on and cannot do without machines. It is with recomposition that the important bridge between seemingly meaningless technical data (zeros and ones) becomes meaningful. Synthesis is a uniquely human cognitive function that can occur with or without machine support. But with synthesis, the output is knowledge, which in military parlance is actionable intelligence. Recomposition is also tightly related with sense-making. Sense-making involves machines and people working as a "team" to start turning data into information. It takes a "knowledge team" to perform sense-making, owing to the heavy cognitive and knowledge requirements to know and then to start understanding the strands of relationships leading to the synthesis of information into knowledge and understanding. Recomposition is often challenging in the subject areas of knowledge, knowing the technical environment, finding and using base-lines, and knowing the culture, collection, and analysis. Fortunately, there are ways the analyst can meet and overcome these challenges; this chapter identified some of those ways.

The next chapter continues from the discussion of recomposition. It discusses synthesis and the transformation of information into knowledge and understanding. The chapter on synthesis is the culminating point of the book and will help the reader pull together the parts and pieces of the 14 chapters, which discussed the cognitive elements of advanced analysis, into a meaningful whole.

18

Synthesis

Definitions: The human cognitive activity that combines elements of sub-
stances, events, activities, or energy to form a coherent whole.[1]
    The DOD Dictionary of Military and Associated Terms says synthesis is
"In intelligence usage, the examining and combining of processed informa-
tion with other information and intelligence for final interpretation."

When people synthesize, they combine seemingly disparate and obviously
related things into a whole whose characteristics are greater than the sum
of the individual parts. Traditional analysis involves breaking or dividing
something into its constituent parts to know functions and characteristics.
Over time, analysts have proven to be quite adept at pure analysis. But
shortfalls in thinking start surfacing when analysts are content with the
results derived through pure analysis; when analysts don't search for relationships, meaning, trends, implications, and higher-level thinking; and
when they don't synthesize what they learned from analysis into a new state
or condition of meaning. We need synthesis, not just analysis, to reach a
higher level of thinking than our adversaries and therefore to achieve and
sustain intellectual advantage over the adversary.

    Let's discuss a few specific reasons why synthesis is crucial to effective
advanced analysis. Without synthesis, analysts will, from habit and ease,
often tilt or default to analysis, which is breaking something into its constituent parts. This means people performing analysis sometimes stop at
decomposing a requirement or a hypothesis into its parts to achieve

understanding but will not engage in the more difficult cognitive act that is synthesis. If this is the case, they will miss the opportunity to understand an entirely different perspective, indeed, a new world, and to create new ideas and combinations of activities, organizations, people, and continuing upward spirals of thought. In addition, synthesis helps the advanced analyst search for and find relationships and combinations needed to develop broader and more vivid perspectives. Along with being good at the point of impact or the point of contact, or the here and now, we need to have broad horizons and peer behind the curtain that veils the future. We need to understand the many complex relationships that comprise our particular situation and this larger vista we are discussing in the abstract. Additionally, synthesis helps us gain knowledge and understanding about the enemy and other competitors, and helps us discern their intent in relationships and combinations, how they think and perceive, and how they make decisions. Synthesis helps the analyst understand opportunities for friendly deception activities as well as opportunities for such activities from both enemies and competitors. We need synthesis to pull together seemingly disparate relationships and use them for gaining an advantage. Often, relationships will not be readily apparent. Synthesis helps us first of all to be aware of relationships, second to look for them, third to understand their additive power when combined, and fourth to use them to create new approaches or new wholes (aggregates). As a final aspect of the importance of synthesis, it is a key element of creativity. In the difficult and complex world humans face every day, we need a constant influx of new, creative ideas because what we did well in the past will not always work well in the future. Synthesis provides such creativity.

An effective advanced analyst possesses the desire to perform synthesis well. If people aren't good with synthesis, they need to find people on their staffs or in a virtual knowledge environment who are talented synthesizers to help. When decomposing requirements, hypotheses, expectations, hunches, and mysteries, analysts need to keep in mind the whole they have theorized to be truth. They seek data and information to come to them to confirm or deny or at least add clarity to their analytic postulations. It is within this returning data they will search for and find relationships and combinations, and synthesize them into something more effective than what they started with.

When engaging in synthesis, people often start out being intellectually uncomfortable. In their minds, they intuitively know there must be more than the results of analysis. They intuitively understand that a better answer exists, a broader perspective is possible, a more creative solution looms, and a different approach could be just a thought away. As a catalyst for thought, they self-impose a strain on their minds to answer—so what, what is the relevance, what are the implications, and force themselves to answer the question, are there better ways or thoughts that could be coming forth if we think differently? This uncomfortable feeling results in varying degrees of confusion and cognitive dissonance.

As they enter the next step in sophistication and difficulty of thought, analysts enter into the cognitive world of synthesis. To do so, analysts must first consider and understand the abstraction of wholes and connections. One expert, Fritjof Capra, helps us understand this notion of wholeness and connectedness by stating

> The most characteristic of the Eastern world view—one could almost say the essence of it—is the awareness of the unity and mutual interrelation of all things and events, the experience of all phenomena in the world as manifestations of a basic oneness.[2]

As human minds strive to put bits and pieces of information into wholes or combine wholes with other wholes to discover increasingly higher levels of meaning, the cacophony in their mind starts becoming more melodic and the dissonance and confusion inherent to the more limited cognitive process of analysis dissipates. To enter this world of thought, advanced analysts have to search for and find connections that currently link the parts of wholes or aggregates and then link them with other larger or smaller wholes or aggregates. A useful thought to help us understand how the advanced analyst thinks about the theory of wholes postulates what people engaging in synthesis can achieve in a cognitive sense:

> he looks at the world, completely coherent, without a loophole, clear as crystal . . . the unity of the world, the coherence of all events, the embracing of the big and the small from the same stream, from the same law of cause, of becoming and dying.[3]

Effective advanced analysts strive to bring together fragmented, seemingly incoherent, unrelated pieces of behaviors, functions, transactions, or interactions into new, coherent wholes in a never-ending cycle. Their minds attempt to make sense out of chaos inherent to military operations by searching for order. Order is present in even the most chaotic situation, as attested to by both Sun Tzu and Clausewitz. Sun Tzu, for example, tells the advanced analyst that order lies in chaos even when appearing to be in a state of chaos.[4] Clausewitz believes it is in the mind of the discerning commander where one can find order in the chaos of the battle space.[5] The object for the intelligence analyst using synthesis is, of course, to form understandable or at least recognizable combinations of relationships, leading to increasingly higher levels of meaning and creativity so as to provide his or her commander with consistently high-grade, actionable knowledge.

This ideal thought process, however, often fails. Instead of using synthesis, analysts inadvertently slip into reductionist thinking without taking the more difficult path that leads toward a higher level of meaning in what is being analyzed. Reductionism is the practice of simplifying a complex idea, issue, condition, or the like, especially to the point of minimizing, obscuring, or distorting it.[6] This type of thought occurs frequently as it typically is a much easier and more immediately gratifying mental skill than synthesis. When analysts engage in traditional analysis and work in isolation, they stop searching for relationships and higher-level meaning. Synthesis, on the other hand, involves a process of combining parts that have been broken into constituent elements during analysis into a whole whose capabilities or powers are more than simply adding one piece with another. Synthesis takes data and combines it into a whole that has meaning—this is information—then combines information with other information—this is knowledge. Synthesis bonds its pieces through the process of connectedness. Connectedness is what keeps wholes together and is one of the elements of the "glue" that binds pieces, functions, activities, or substances into aggregates and then into even larger and more diverse aggregates. Being cognizant of connectedness allows analysts the capability to work on understanding wholes and aggregates, and to view them as the foci of intelligence collection and analysis. In this regard, synthesis combines existing knowledge, current contextual data, and information with postulated future states and dimensions to form a whole greater than the simple addition of its elements.

Synthesis occurs when human beings ponder meaning of complex data and seek understanding. It is the blending of data, information, and knowledge, and from that mental process, forming conclusions. There are three complementary mental functions essential to synthesis. As one, synthesis involves thinking about *relationships*. Synthesis asks us to search for and combine things already related in some way. Sometimes events, people, or incoming data don't appear to relate, but synthesis requires us to attempt to pull together both related and seemingly unrelated things and activities into a higher level of meaning. Another necessary mental function for synthesis to work properly is the requirement for our minds to work with *combinations*. That is, we must purposefully look for, find, discover, or develop combinations of like and unlike things, e.g., sensors, people, organizations, books, ideas, and combine them with other sensors, people, organizations, books, and ideas, into a larger whole. A final mental function essential to synthesis involves *synergy*. Synergy is the *interaction of two or more agents or forces so that their combined effect is greater than the sum of their individual effects*.[7] With intelligence, it is the wise analyst who seeks mental and physical instances of synergy, as the outcomes they can achieve are often astounding. Synergy occurs with machines such as sensors; it occurs with thought, as with many people thinking as a team on a difficult problem; it occurs with the synchronization of actions that cause effects. It generally does not happen of its own accord. Synergy, however, is very powerful and apropos to modern and future intelligence analysis and collection. It follows that effective advanced analysts must purposefully seek synergy in synthesizing parts, the activities of people, capabilities of organizations, the functions of software, the activities sensors, combinatorial thinking, expanded knowledge, and highly attenuated and sensitive cognitive skills.

It doesn't take a stretch of the imagination to postulate synthesis to be the essential element of intelligence; it causes the analyst to think and combine events, activities, and interactions into a meaningful whole with direct linkage to commanders' C^2. It enables analysts to relate decision-making to will, coherency, and human factors and is the essential element in forming a vision or envisioning an outcome. It is also an important mental skill in creative thinking. Synthesis creatively combines, restructures, and depicts what is going through a person's mind or occurring in a physical or emotional setting to find a different, more useful, more powerful whole, or an entirely new way of performing a task. In addition, synthesis is either recognizing or developing new combinations from those in existence to form a new whole or a new organization, way of doing business, or process.

Synthesis relates to some other cognitive elements of advanced analysis, including anticipation, tendency analysis, cultural analysis, anomaly analysis, aggregation analysis, and semiotics analysis. Let us take some time to discuss these relationships further.

- SYNTHESIS AND ANTICIPATORY ANALYSIS. Let us recall the definition of anticipatory analysis. It is *intuition, foreknowledge, or prescience*. It is *understanding and realization of an activity or action in advance*. If we look at entire events (e.g., an IED explosion) and decompose them and consider what must happen before such events can occur, we can easily break each event into pieces and study them. Once we have sufficient knowledge and understanding, we knit them into a whole that is greater than the sum of its parts. That is, along with breaking apart the IED attack with its many intertwining parts, activities, and interactions, with synthesis, we can develop when and where the attack might be, where the necessary condition-setting aspects of the attack might be and occur, and the implications of the attack from the enemy's perspective. Such thought can give us insights into how we can make the attack more costly, how we can thwart the enemy's attack through anticipation and denial, or even making his life difficult with a simple counter-synchronization operation.
- SYNTHESIS AND TENDENCY ANALYSIS. Let us review tendency analysis before venturing into its relationship with synthesis. It is *discerning meaning through thought and study of the general proclivities of people, the behavioral and action inclinations of organizations, mental snapshots of current environment or context situations, events, activities,*

behaviors, the emanation dispersal of energy emissions, and what the interaction and enmeshing of all could portend for the future. Tendencies are usually not noticeable as singular events or activities. Thus, it is through mental activities, conscious and unconscious, that the mind knits activities, interactions, transactions, or behaviors into a whole that, with inducement by an analyst engaging in synthesis, can bring the light of reason and meaning. When we take a mental snapshot or uncontrollably engage in a double take when presented with a situation appearing perfectly normal but still causing us dissonance signifying that something is deviant from normalcy, it is the starting point of a journey that involves the transformation of something seemingly innocuous to a unified whole of meaning. In this situation, the mind is ravaged by strange feelings and sensings springing forth from its primordial intuitive base. What the mind yearns for is a whole of vivid reality to come rushing into its consciousness to provide meaning. Unfortunately, in most situations, acquiring such insight will never be that forthright or simple. Thus, these sensings will most often result in neither vividness nor understanding and will subsequently fade into oblivion. However, with the bright shining light of synthesis, the meaning of the ongoing, imperceptible activities, regardless of subtlety, can come into and through our subconsciousness into our conscious mind with meaning coming from flashes of insight or epiphany. It follows that one must synthesize to recognize and learn how to cope with and exploit tendencies. With the tendency of choice in mind thanks to the art of synthesis, the analyst can start decomposing it into its parts, many which are one or more of the five kinds of observables discussed earlier. Once they have the observables in hand, analysts task them to collection, and start receiving the resultant data. Then, the analyst starts recomposing the data into information and synthesizing the information into knowledge. With knowledge, the analyst can anticipate and set conditions for gaining situational understanding.

- SYNTHESIS AND CULTURAL ANALYSIS. What is cultural analysis? It is *knowing a particular culture and people, as well as their patterns of behavior deriving from traditional, culturally induced attitudes, behaviors, social norms, and conditions.* Most of the interactions, activities, behaviors, and transactions occurring in a culture relate to other things, interactions, or people in the culture in question. Although important in and among themselves, the money people exchange, the gossip they share, their movement to the mosque, their leisure activities, all relate to each other and other things, events, and people. It is through synthesis that we can start combining parts and pieces of a culture into wholes of sufficient size and understanding to gain insight and knowledge and use the its advantage through decomposition (analysis), collection, recomposition, and eventually synthesis.

- SYNTHESIS AND ANOMALY ANALYSIS. What is anomaly analysis? It is *discerning meaning in departures from the normal or common order, form, or rule, and it is the absence of that which is expected.* Anomaly analysis works with baselines (technical, cultural, and functional) to find what is normal and then to watch with observables and collection for what is anomalous. The baselines can be viewed narrowly in isolation or as parts that when combined and synthesized result in setting the conditions that allow an analyst to start seeing the normal whole that is the neighborhood and a house in the anomalous whole that is a house in which the anomalies stand forth in their difference from the baseline. Analysts must also learn to look for the antithesis of a suspected activity, which is no activity or no whole. As an example, consider a suspected bomb factory in a large urban setting. If after decomposing the requirement that drove us to seek the bomb factory, we find that nothing has occurred in the past or the present that would lead us to conclude the presence of a bomb factory, this could be the antithesis of our original thesis. But if we decide to set different conditions for the perturbation we tried originally and once again consider the contradictions inherent to our belief that the house is "dirty," and if we perturb the network surrounding the house at a different time and in a different manner than what we did with our original situation and now begin to recognize the change caused by the perturbation, we then have a new situation—a synthesis that stands until it too is overtaken by contradictions and a new thesis. The interaction of the thesis, antithesis, and synthesis is a useful construct with which to think about synthesis.
- SYNTHESIS AND AGGREGATION ANALYSIS. What is aggregation analysis? It is *discerning meaning of several things, numbering from a few to millions that are grouped, moving, working together, and considered as a whole.* We must synthesize to understand aggregates, as aggregates are wholes. We must understand what comprises the glue that binds things, events, activities, people, and organizations into aggregates. We must understand what propels or urges the aggregate to form and gather speed or to die. Synthesizing how more and more aggregates could join and when this conjoining could occur can in turn lead to anticipation of the forming aggregate. We must also understand the appearance and power of sensitive variables and how and when they may appear and affect aggregates. When conditions are right, sensitive variables often cause aggregates to career out of control or assume huge effects when compared to small inputs. As complexity theory driven effects, sensitive variables cause aggregates to disintegrate into apparent nothingness, and to reform into new aggregates. Synthesis is important in anticipating all of these aggregation-related functions and then understanding what they are and what they mean when they appear.

- SEMIOTICS ANALYSIS. What is semiotics analysis? It is *discerning meaning of cultural signs and symbols reflected in drawings, paintings, photographs, syntax, words, sounds, body language, and graffiti. Semiotics is the language of the culture.* As such, semiotics relate to synthesis. Semiotics are part of the whole of a culture. Sometimes, to find meaning in semiotics, we have to combine language, written syntax, graffiti, tone, and inflection of voice, symbols, and nonverbal behavior. Taken one at a time or in isolation, each of these aspects of semiotics might mean nothing. However, when we synthesize them, they might add up to a whole greater than the pure sum of the parts. Therefore, when synthesizing, semiotics have to be examined and combined with other aspects of semiotics.

SYNTHESIS AND CONDITION-SETTING

In a more concrete and practical sense, synthesis is critical to setting conditions for analytic success. Why is this so? Some reasons exist that are worthy of discussion. Advanced analysts must consider condition-setting from two respects. First, the advanced analyst must consider the enemy's *condition-setting.* When they or their network supporters perform particular aspects of necessary condition-setting to accomplish a mission or task, the isolated act of one aspect of condition-setting, say, surveiling a potential IED site, is probably not noticed and if noticed probably discounted. This seemingly insignificant act probably disappears in the noise of a busy urban environment. However, if the analyst synthesizes the act of surveillance with the sound of digging, and spurious but brief stray electrons that identify a suddenly emanating electronic signature, the appearance and disappearance of vehicles in a neighborhood in vicinity of the site, and the report of IEDs being moved into the neighborhood in question, then an analyst using synthesis can produce an additive conclusion that can often be acted upon by way of direct action or at least closer monitoring.

Second, the act of condition-setting involves thinking about, planning for, and putting into action data, sensor, and knowledge architectures. This type of condition-setting must occur for the analyst to be successful. However, they work best if the analyst synthesizes the capabilities and potential outputs of all three for a *combined condition-setting schema* rather than setting up one or even two. This higher capability or power that comes into being when the elements combine creates a new capability whose potential can only appear in the mind of an analyst who has the original vision and who is intellectually capable of realizing what that vision has yielded.

For sake of clarification, let us consider an example. In ISR work, analysts can set conditions for using sensors as a shaping mechanism. If their decision maker's intent is to use intelligence (namely ISR) to shape a distant adversary's perceptions or to gain valuable data and information about a locale that is far from the United States, intelligence analysts must work with collection people to set analytic conditions and inputs. What are some of the essential conditions that have to be set to succeed in this type of analytic condition-setting endeavor? The answers to this question might be 1) identifying data processing requirements to prepare data so analysts can turn it into information and knowledge; 2) identifying the commander's information and knowledge requirements in advance from the study of potential courses of action and attendant decision criteria, e.g., constraints such as timeliness; 3)identifying and hiring appropriate people to perform analysis and to operate machines (some physically present, others in sanctuary); 4) identifying architecture requirements and coordination to support the venture (data, sensor, and knowledge); 5) identifying the right language mix, subject matter expertise, and analytic skills to task the machines and make sense out of collected data; and 6) knowing the culture, thought processes of leaders, and technology of the country or area in question. When the analyst combines these six seemingly disparate shaping activities or functions, he or she has a new tapestry of intelligence analysis capability brought about through the higher-level cognitive skill that is synthesis—the synthesis of organizations and functions with intent.

Synthesis closely relates to another aspect of advanced analysis: *recomposition*. But the two functions are different. Recomposition involves a partnership between machine work and human cognition that combines data coming from HUMINT, technical sensors, open sources, and nontraditional sources and aggregates, and interprets the data to discern information. Recomposition is a precursor to the human cognition function of synthesis. In recomposition, however, the data being turned into information and knowledge comes from intelligence collection and open-source data mining that has originated from a very purposeful decomposition of PIR, IR, hypotheses from wargaming, expectations, hunches, and mysteries. The resultant observables are pushed into intelligence and open-source collection systems and the data coming back, therefore, has a lineage reaching back to the original requirement. Recomposition is a combined machine and human cognition function.

Synthesis, on the other hand, is not so narrowly constrained. Synthesis takes the results of recomposition, and through human cognition, turns it into knowledge and understanding. Synthesis can come from a multitude of sources and does not necessarily relate to the stream of requirements and data outputs just mentioned. Synthesis pulls together data, information, and existing knowledge to form new information and new knowledge. Synthesis applies meaning to whatever is gained through recomposition, but the aperture of perspective and sources are much wider and deeper than recomposition alone can give. Although recomposition is a combination of human cognition and machines, synthesis and its end-state—knowledge— is a uniquely human mental function.

Synthesis can use the mechanics of another element of advanced analysis—*aggregation*—to combine related and unrelated thoughts into a larger and more significant meaning. Synthesizing means pulling data, information, and knowledge into ever-larger pictures or new looks at a situation, striving to be creative by adding multiple aspects, parts, pieces, and views together into a broader whole. This type of purposeful mental work often is done by a person who is adept at synthesizing and who works with a small group of people and adds or combines the views of various members into a different or similar, but larger, perspective view of a situation.

Synthesis to an intelligence analyst means the analyst is always working with aggregations, patterns, trends, significant activities, will, intent, outlooks, perspectives, and decision-making, and combining them to find a conclusion or to tell a decision maker the meaning of data. Because determining truth is extremely problematic, the analyst is wise to take the newly established conclusion and again subject it to decomposition and collection to confirm or deny the validity of synthesis if time permits.

Consider the 1983 television mini-series *The Winds of War*, which included a situation that the hero of the story relates. In the early portion of the show, Commander Pug Henry, the naval attaché in pre-World War II Berlin, visits a German submarine installation. The German Navy shows Commander Henry a submarine in immaculate condition. What Commander Henry concludes, though, is that the German Navy was not in a high state of readiness. How did he arrive at the conclusion when it was antithetical to the facts as presented by the Germans? In its most simple state, he understood the submarine as one of many data points, noting, for example, that the shipyard workers all went home at 5:00 p.m., with no one working overtime. He noted a lack of sense of urgency among the tour guides, briefers, and naval officers he met. He also noted some problems with maintenance of the submarine he visited and other ships in the yard. He noted a general state of disrepair in a country whose fastidiousness typically bordered on psychosis. He assessed the numbers of ships being built (as stated in German economic publications) and the number of tanks being built (from classified intelligence reports) and compared those numbers with steel production and deliveries. He also talked to many people about the German Navy and its capabilities. Commander Henry pulled together many sources of data and information and through synthesis formed a conclusion that the German Navy did not have one hundred submarines as they claimed; instead he projected the number of submarines as less than fifty and concluded that the German Navy was not in a high state of readiness. He further concluded that the German Navy would have difficulty waging a long war.

Implications are important because when one develops them from an event or activity and attempts to ponder a larger meaning, they are synthesizing. When people ponder questions or problems, and answers and solutions to those problems, they need to recognize the significant possibility that they could be missing the meaning of those questions and solutions, not only for the task or problem at hand but for other tasks, other domains, and other problem areas. Thus, an analyst engaged in synthesis should wonder about the rhetorical questions that follow: Could it be that what they have concluded presumes an impact or influence on another function or activity? Could this be the wrong presumption or implication? What other data or information could help ensure that a conclusion or implication is correct or incorrect?

Machines can help in synthesis by fusing data and providing the platform on which the capability to visualize data can rest, enabling the human being to start the difficult mental process involved. Machines help to integrate disparate data and information into a whole so humans can apply meaning. Machines help discern hidden relationships so humans can engage in synthesis. Hidden relationships are an interesting adjunct to the use of synthesis. Hidden relationships are activities and transactions that occur almost invisibly to the human eye.[8] Hidden relationships often appear only to the practiced eye of an expert or a person with lots of experience in the matter under consideration. However, if they use synthesis, advanced analysts can identify not only the hidden relationship, but they can also understand how it relates to other relationships and how these relationships combine into practical uses. Machines can help identify hidden relationships. As an example, data mining and knowledge discovery software search for, find, extract, organize, and identify relationships that the human mind can neither find nor interpret. Thus, machines help the advanced analyst search for and identify the hidden relationships we are speaking of. But only the human mind is capable of taking what machines create and applying value, meaning, nuance, and subtleties.

Modeling helps people perform synthesis, particularly models used in act–react–counteract wargaming, course of action analysis, and attempts to portend and understand the appearance and influence of second- and third-order effects. Modeling helps people discern effect decay, where actions and effects start to lose power and influence. Modeling then helps people decide on optimum combinations of actions and effects that could result in the outcome (whole) they seek. Modeling helps discern how an enemy leader synthesizes data into information and then into knowledge so intelligence analysts can help commanders engage in sophisticated deception.

Synthesis is an essential part of designing and describing: 1) vision, 2) intent, 3) concepts of operations, and 4) end states or desired states of continuity. These four mental functions occur in the minds of decision makers and their staff officers. Envisioning the interplay of engagements, battles, and campaigns is one way to describe the relationship between synthesis and vision.[9] Analysts have to think like the enemy and design a vision, a concept of operation, an end state within the mind, a thought process, emotions, and even an idea of the subconscious of the opposition or enemy. Analysts also need to know how to use synthesis and vision to understand a commander's view of the battlespace and how that commander intends to impose his will on an opponent. Analysts must use synthesis to anticipate enemy activities, interactions, behaviors, and transactions. They have to be able to think like the enemy thinks and envision the end state of what he is trying to accomplish, whether at the tactical level or at the grand strategic level, and then decompose his vision into actionable items. Analysts must use risk analysis and coordination to pull all the actions into a whole that the enemy's vision or course of action represents, and then decompose the hypothesized actions, interactions, activities, and behaviors into observables. Analysts must inject these observables into the collection system and, when resultant data starts appearing, recompose the data into an understandable whole. Synthesis follows this recomposition once the analyst is able to expand outside the original thrust to include other areas of interest, events occurring in other domains, past histories, and a broad array of open source data and information.

Analysts will not find synthesis easy to perform. Thus, it is helpful to engage in a personal question and answer session to trigger synthesis sessions. Let us take some time and think through some of these questions and answers.

- WHAT IS THE WHOLE I'M THINKING ABOUT? When we start with the whole, we can break it apart into finite pieces and turn those pieces into signatures and observables. However, we must keep in mind the whole from whence the parts, pieces, and observables came. When we task for intelligence collection support, we must think about the whole we have conjectured or hypothesized in our minds. When data starts to arrive ostensibly coming from tasking of decomposed wholes, the resultant data starts filling out the whole(s) in our minds. We can do this mechanically with a pie chart, but most of the time we form the whole in our minds. When we get enough of a picture of the whole, we can start making decisions or at least keeping our commander and ourselves informed and knowledgeable of how the situation is evolving.
- WHAT ARE RELATIONSHIPS IN THE WHOLE? To relate means to establish an association or connection. Unfortunately and particularly in a large urban setting, associations or connections can seem unassociated or even disparate. However, with the right conditions in the OE, sometimes even the strangest attractors can form obvious relationships and eventually a whole. Often like-things, people, or organizations form relationships for self-interest or to facilitate the interests of a perceived or real whole. Thus, when synthesizing, we must think about, search for, and identify relationships. If important for the whole or aggregate, we have to develop signatures and observables, and watch for the appearance of relationships (even those that appear improbable) and with their appearance in our minds, the ascendance of wholes.

- **WHAT BINDS PIECES OF A WHOLE (AGGREGATE) TOGETHER?** A type of "glue" holds the pieces of wholes (aggregates) together. The substance of the glue can be purpose, functionality, self-interest, xenophobia, religion, organizational ethos, nationalism, fear, strength through unity, etc.
- **HOW DOES SYNTHESIS AND FRONT-END (DECOMPOSITION) RELATE TO BACK-END (RECOMPOSITION) WORK?** We decompose our wholes, which come from requirements, hypotheses, expectations, hunches, and mysteries. To work with something both understandable and manageable, we have to disaggregate, disintegrate, or disambiguate. We start this process by engaging in deep thought about the requirement(s) and then engaging in the mental act of decomposition. We perform decomposition with the whole or end state in mind. When resultant collection data comes to us, we have to use our minds to turn relationships, combinations, and synthesis data into information and knowledge in relation to the mental whole we started our decomposition efforts with.

Another interesting aspect of synthesis involves its relationship with wargaming. Wargaming, according to the 2007 version of the DOD Dictionary of Military and Associated Terms is: "A simulation, by whatever means, of a military operation involving two or more opposing forces using rules, data, and procedures designed to depict an actual or assumed real-life situation." A wargame allows the analysts to find ways to seek, find, and sustain the initiative. Wargaming provides the means to identify possible second- and third-order effects from friendly actions. Wargaming helps identify sensitive variables and windows of opportunity. It also helps identify commander's future missions and knowledge requirements. All of these aspects of conflict involve synthesizing.

In a more abstract sense, wargaming is important for synthesis in understanding how aggregates or wholes might come together and form larger, stronger, and more influential aggregates. This is a particularly important thought in looking at the potential power of second- and third-order effects, and even when attempting to anticipate and prepare for Clausewitzian friction. In addition, wargaming and synthesis work well together in that wargaming helps people synthesize by understanding potential outcomes of small inputs that could cause large outputs owing to aggregation. Wargaming allows analysts to understand how to look for and find seemingly disparate pieces that might remain disparate except for wargaming and its act-react-counteract modeling that produces the need to carefully study emerging relationships, combinations, "glue" that holds aggregates and wholes together, the impact of "fuel" to propel the aggregate or whole, and the sensitive variables and windows of opportunity that could turn a seemingly insignificant, isolated outcome into a second- or third-order threat of immense significance. Finally, wargaming stimulates synthesis in the analyst's mind, which helps him or her to understand how the enemy might try to attack and influence friendly nodes and links, possible formation of combinations of power, relationships among echelons and organic units, and how they might try to take advantage of the appearance of sensitive variables and windows of opportunity to strike at any perceived moments of friendly vulnerability.

Two of the most important aspects of any modern conflict involve the notions of knowledge and situational understanding. Both depend upon synthesis to come into being and to prove useful. How is this so? The answer lies in comprehending that knowledge and situational understanding can only come forth with synthesis. Knowledge is built through using the relationships of concepts and ideas to build new knowledge, through the use of thought aggregates whose powers come to life through synthesis, and through links with other knowledge. Situational understanding comes forth like a beacon in a fog-enshrouded sea with a wise and experienced commander's synthesis of the situation, the OE, knowledge, intuition, experience, and sense or touch of the battle space. To use situational understanding takes people who can synthesize pieces of various wholes (such as Clausewitz's defense and offense continuum, and Clausewitz's engagement, battle, and campaign schema), rapidly changing knowledge, and a fluctuating OE, and who can combine and transform all of this potpourri into sensible decisions, effects, actions, and assessments of outcomes. The philosopher Nietzsche helps us understand the importance of wholes and relationships with the following thought:

> We have no right to isolated acts of any kind: we may not make isolated errors or hit upon isolated truths. Rather, do our ideas, our values, our yeas and nays, our ifs and buts, grow out of us with the necessity with which a tree bears fruit—related and each with an affinity to each, and evidence of one will, one health, one sail, one sun.[10]

As a final topic of discussion for synthesis, we have to examine challenges inherent to synthesis and then discuss ways to overcome the challenges. Some of the more important challenges facing analysts attempting to use synthesis include the following:

- Finding the right knowledge support.
- Understanding relationships and combinations.
- Driving collection to find the parts and pieces of wholes with which to combine and synthesize.
- Thinking about second- and third-order effects.
- Thinking about sensitive variables, possible windows of opportunity, and their relationships with outcomes for friendly, enemy, and host nation government and its populace.
- Considering assumptions.

- Considering connections and their relationship with synthesis.
- Avoiding the trap of reductionism.

The challenges inherent to synthesis, although difficult, are not insurmountable. Let us proceed to briefly identify ways to overcome the challenges.

- Analysts must be organized for mental combat to use synthesis to think. This thought means analysts must either have a thought template firmly etched in their thought processes or use a physical thought template to help them consider the many complexities of synthesis.
- Analysts must possess the desire to perform synthesis and set about to do so. If analysts aren't particularly good with synthesis, they need to find people on their staffs possessing this mental skill.
- When decomposing requirements, hypotheses, expectations, hunches, and mysteries, the analyst needs to keep in mind what we want the whole to be. The pieces of this whole will come back to us as data in which we search for and find relationships and combinations.
- The analyst must look for combinations with which to synthesize in several ways.
  - *First*, the analyst thinks about combinations that comprise the whole(s) or aggregate(s) he or she is looking for.
  - *Second*, the analyst thinks about the wholes comprising the enemy's actions and how he seeks synergy among the related parts of the whole to gain power and energy sufficient to accomplish his mission.
  - *Third*, the analyst thinks about combinations with his collection specialist partner to find the right combinations of collection, to create maximum sampling rates, to optimize the sensors, and to create a collection synergy in which sensors and human collectors work in a coherent way to offset their weaknesses and capitalize on their combined strengths.
- The analyst identifies, studies, and works with linkages between and among parts (aggregates) of the larger whole as an aid in synthesizing.
  - The analyst looks for links connecting parts of wholes, wholes with other wholes, and even larger wholes.
  - The analyst looks for linkages connecting friendly wholes and aggregates, and advises how the enemy might attempt to fracture the links to attack the whole.
  - Analysts use synthesis to help identify second- and third-order effects.
  - Analysts recognize that friendly and enemy effects and actions will have consequences appearing as wholes and aggregates.
  - Analysts work designed effects and related actions through a wargaming sequence with different people possessing the initiative.
  - Analysts compare wargaming hypotheses with outcomes they envision.

- Analysts work their hypotheses through a red team and through indigenous people to ensure they are not mirror-imaging.
- The analyst must think like the enemy and answer the following questions about ways to disrupt or denigrate U.S. intelligence analysts' capabilities to synthesize. Some questions and answers designed to stimulate thought follow.
  - How can I negate the U.S. capability to use patterns and synthesize?
    - Don't show patterns.
    - Obscure relationships. Hide or obscure personal, organizational, and familial relationships.
    - Don't let any part of my condition-setting know about other parts of my condition-setting, all of which are parts of a whole.
  - How can I thwart the U.S. intelligence system's attempts to disambiguate and therefore find the disparate signs of my presence or activities and synthesize them into a whole that is my network or condition-setting?
    - Keep my activities subtle and obscure.
    - Use semiotics for signs, symbols, warnings, and other forms of communications.
    - Anticipate what the United States could be seeing via baselines and obscure the view with false perturbation and the creation of anomalies away from where I am actually operating.
  - How can I attempt to anticipate how the United States will think about my combinations and attempt to disaggregate all that I'm attempting to aggregate so as to facilitate synthesis?
    - Recognize in advance that U.S. people will be seeking to learn how I combine and relate things as part of how I think.
    - Think about how U.S. analysts think about how I synthesize.
    - Show mistakes as part of deception.
    - Assume the Americans do not have good HUMINT, and therefore will have a difficult time seeing things that I'm doing that are fleeting, nuanced, ambiguous, and vague at best.
    - Break connections between and among relationships comprising combinations. As an example, shut down a safehouse. Don't use electronics as part of countersurveillance providing indications and warning (I&W) to a bomb factory.
  - What is my perception of U.S. analysis and its capability to engage in synthesis?
    - U.S. intelligence analysts do not perform synthesis well.
    - They do not search for and find my patterns, relationships, and combinations.
    - They do not understand the culture and therefore will never understand how I use the culture to obscure my wholes, my intent, and my condition-setting.

- They will keep trying to use technical sensors to see what is invisible to technical sensors.
- They will not be sophisticated enough to see how I'm using synthesis in my deception, planning, and execution.

In closing this chapter, the discussion about synthesis is critically important to the total notion of advanced analysis. Why is this the case? Synthesis is more than analysis—it is taking the results of analysis and developing a new whole or different insight, or an alternative approach. Without synthesis, analysts can fall prey to the "intellectual predators" of reductionism and increment incomprehension. Richards Heuer tells us more about this danger:

> The receipt of information in small increments over time also facilitates assimilation of this information into the analyst's existing views. No one item of information may be sufficient to prompt the analyst to change a previous view. The cumulative message inherent in many pieces of information may be significant but is attenuated when this information is not examined as a whole.[11]

Analysts must be cognizant of this danger and purposefully work their minds to synthesize information continuously.

Synthesis is the human unique mental activity that brings forth knowledge, which is of course the precursor to situational understanding. In addition, synthesis is the output of dialectic thinking we discussed in the chapter on critical thinking. In this context, not even synthesis is viewed in isolation. It is part of a larger whole that is the dialectic. The dialectic, as a whole, is the constant movement, change, interaction, and creation involved with the interlocking notions of thesis, antithesis, and synthesis, fueled by the all-important contradiction.

The chapter also discussed the relationship between synthesis and recomposition. Although similar in some respects, synthesis is more than recomposition in that it produces knowledge, and recomposition only produces information. Recomposition also involves the combined efforts of the human intellect and machines. Synthesis takes us into the world of connections and holism in which all things, people, and activities are in some fashion connected, and when the parts congeal, the whole is truly greater than the sum of the individual parts. Synthesis is the "stuff" of dreams—synthesis is how we develop visions. It is the mechanism for those who aspire to prescience. It is also the way people make sense of confusing situations and how they eventually engage in creative thinking. In fact, creative thinking is impossible without synthesis of some degree of sophistication. As a final note, synthesis is critically important in winning the all-important fight for the initiative. To engage in this constant struggle, the analyst has to first of all know what initiative is. The analyst also has to understand what advantages accrue to people or organizations that hold the initiative. As such, it provides what Mao Tse-tung called all-important and gives an antagonist "liberty of action."[12] However, in studying Mao's thoughts as a supreme theoretician of guerrilla warfare, the analyst must also understand that Mao's concept of the initiative dealt with a synthesis of tactical, operational, and strategic initiative. While early in China's war with the invader Japan in WWII, Japan had the operational and strategic initiative; however, Mao and his guerrillas held the tactical initiative. Eventually, he gained the operational initiative and eventually the strategic initiative. We cannot understand the impact of what Mao meant and did with respect to the initiative without being able to synthesize the three types and how they related, indeed interacted. Other theorists were obviously good synthesizers. As an example, Sun Tzu talked about ordinary and extraordinary forces interlocked in a series of connected rings,[13] which is a fine example of synthesis.

It is through synthesis that the cognitive elements of advanced analysis come to life; therefore, it is fitting that the topic of synthesis is the last of 14 cognitive elements to be discussed in this book. Each of the elements of advanced analysis are powerful in their own right, but when synthesized into a whole of use in developing vision, pulling bits and pieces of data and information into a unified whole, or engaging in anticipating the enemy's thoughts, decisions, and actions and thwarting him at every move, synthesis is much more powerful than working the singular strands of advanced analysis.

It is through synthesizing that people provide creative solutions to problems. With synthesis, people can envision and describe alternatives and fresh approaches to difficult problems. In an operational sense, it is through synthesis that analysts can go after the enemy's networks. As such, when synthesizing, the analyst can combine seemingly disparate data and information into patterns and trends. With synthesis, the analyst can start to understand the types of network links and how they decay and morph.

The next chapter presents Dr. Gary Citrenbaum's work on discussing the technology to support advanced analysis. It comes at this point in the book owing to the need to present all 14 cognitive elements of advanced analysis before connecting specific aspects of technology to each.

19

Technology for Advanced Analysis

> Because of limits in human mental capacity . . . the mind cannot cope directly
> with the complexity of the world. Rather, we construct a simplified mental
> model of reality and then work with this model.[1]

Although advanced analysis is for the most part a cognitive process, it
stands to benefit significantly from technological enablers. These enablers
can serve not only to reduce analysts' workloads, but perhaps more
significantly, they can improve the quality of analysts' products.

   This section identifies the key advanced analysis enablers and examines
them from three perspectives: 1) why they are needed and what they offer,
2) how they might work, now and in the future, and 3) the challenges, if
any, that will have to be faced in developing and deploying them. To
facilitate discussion, we divide the space of enablers into 14 areas: 1) simple query and search, e.g., Googling from free text and tables, including
meta-data search, etc., 2) concept based search, 3) multi-lingual search, 4)
linkage analysis, 5) social network analysis (SNA), 6) attribute monitoring,
7) pattern detection, including cluster analysis and collaborative filtering
techniques, 8) timeline/chronology analysis, 9) event and change detection:
e.g., from video, 10) taxonomy creation, 11) modeling, 12) fusion, model-
based in particular, 13) argumentation support, and 14) optimization.
In addition, we identify "enablers of enablers"—those lower-level capabilities needed to realize the enablers upon which advanced analysis relies.

To the extent possible the discussions attempt to indicate how the various areas draw upon, and sometimes depend upon each other. Unfortunately, as will become apparent, the cross-dependencies are such that this ordering is not as clean as one might like, and all that can be reasonably done is to identify this situation where appropriate and hope it does not detract significantly from interpretability.

Before delving into specifics, several caveats are appropriate. First, it's important to observe that although the discussions below allude to technology, they do not venture into the underpinning technical theory. The focus is on requirements and usage—specifically those associated with advanced analysis. There are, in fact, an abundance of texts dealing with the theory underpinning the technologies identified here, and we reference these when appropriate. Second, the treatment of each topic reflects its relative importance to advanced analysis and the needs of analysts potentially interested in exploiting particular technologies.

SIMPLE SEARCH AND MONITORING

Analysis often entails locating particular tidbits of data from within relatively large corpula. In some cases, the data is formatted, tabulated, or semantically marked-up, but in others it is freeform. Furthermore, the data may take a variety of forms—written text, audio, pictures, or even video. Regardless of the form, the underlying search challenge is similar—to find data with high probability of relevance to a problem in the most expeditious manner, while minimizing the return irrelevant data.

This section deals with what is generally considered to be the simplest case of search—database reference in which the database or corpus has been physically and logically prepared to support classes of queries known in advance to be of interest. This constraint permits the application of a variety of techniques that greatly accelerate (often by many orders of magnitude) the speed with which a search can be performed. When this constraint applies—as it often does for advanced analysis—vast amounts of data can be rapidly culled to small product sets highly tailored to the specific needs and interests of the analyst.

The classic example of such a search engine is Google, which essentially "inverts" the entire Internet, allows indexed searches by key words, and returns ranked "hits"—seemingly in a matter of a few milliseconds. The reason Google is able to perform the search so rapidly is that the indices in various Web pages have been prepared and sorted in advance of any particular query. This permits logarithmic search times instead of linear search times; and, when large datasets are involved, the difference in run time can be several orders of magnitude.

This basic approach can be extended to datasets that are not primarily text. For instance, for many years, relational databases have allowed users to specify "key" fields, which can be "inverted" to speed search and augmentation operations. This approach also extends to other data types, e.g., geographic, video, audio, and a variety of intelligence disciplines (what we refer to here as "INTs"). The idea, again, is to preprocess the data in appropriate ways and to prepare a corresponding metadata entry that records key information for each data element. The metadata entries, or records, can then be searched just as a relational database is searched. When the information about the underlying data set has been extracted and placed into the metadata record in an efficiently searchable form, extremely high rates of retrieval are possible.

Another approach for speeding database searches is through specially constructed data types that reflect the underlying mathematical structure of the data. A good example of this is geospatial information systems (GIS) in which data is often stored hierarchically, closely mimicking increasing levels of geographic accuracy and precision. At the top of the tree, small, easily searched fields permit users to cover large areas. By selecting sub-regions within a large area, however, users can quickly designate smaller, more focused areas of interest. Sitting behind this sophisticated user interface, the actual physical data architecture mimics this hierarchical logical arrangement in such a way that the "next" level of interest has almost always been cached into fast local memory, ready for instantaneous retrieval and review. Imagery archives can benefit from this technique, as can historical archives using "slow" retrieval devices (e.g., tape).

The common feature that all these approaches share lies in the search criteria (queries). The needed query is known in advance, thus speeding the process. This will usually be the case in advanced analysis, but not always. Significantly, it is sometimes possible for the search engine to learn the interests of the user on its own by observing user searches over a period of time. Amazon performs this capability today. There is no reason such computer work cannot be done for individual analysts with peculiar problem sets or in analytic condition-setting such as establishing knowledge architectures (discussed earlier in this book). In such cases, the engine can, without explicit prompting from the user, invert and cache the data of interest before the user actually requests it. When well implemented and tuned, such an approach can lead to enormous run time efficiencies and greatly benefit analysts or a VKE when working against stringent timelines.

A capability closely related to simple search is *monitoring* and *alerting*. The case here involves systems in which new data is continually being input from a known set of sources. The data entering the system may include societal or military events taking place in an area of interest. In such cases, the analyst can design and emplace a so-called "standing query" to be applied to all new incoming data. Whenever data matching the search criteria enters the system, the analyst will be automatically notified—and the system will, in effect, have served as his or her personal "surveiller" or filter. This ongoing query capability happens completely in the background without the need for further effort by the analyst except when a reorientation is required. Moreover, because the query capability has been placed in the data ingest flow, it happens rapidly and with high confidence. And again, because the system has been told in advance the type of data of interest, it can rapidly and effectively perform the search on an ongoing basis without further analyst intervention.

It is possible to take this capability forward yet another step. Consider, for example, a data source comprising news feeds from newspapers, television, and reporting services. Some systems permit an analyst to request daily customized products consisting only of items of specific interest. This can include place names, persons, and types of event (terrorist activity, economic activity, political activity, etc.). The tool monitors all the input data streams, extracting those news items that match the specified criteria, and then prepares for analyst review of a set of customized products—in effect, an analyst's personalized *New York Times*. Sophisticated investors have been using such a capability for many years now. Their topics of interest concern events and transactions in the worlds of finance, manufacturing, shipping, and investment. Surprisingly, insofar as we can tell, such a capability is not yet available to most intelligence analysts.

Needs and Desires

Practitioners of advanced analysis must rapidly search large data sources specifically structured to support rapid retrieval and comprehensive display. As a minimum, the search capability should efficiently handle queries dealing with any of the following:

- Records dealing with any date within a specified range, regardless of the internal form of date specification;
- Records dealing with a specific geographical region, e.g., a radius of x hundred feet around a specified latitude/longitude, regardless of the internal form of the locations (i.e., address, latitude/longitude, UTM, map directions, etc.);
- Records based on complex Boolean relationships; records that employ different wordings or synonyms for a similar attribute; people by name, regardless of spelling or translation idiosyncrasies; organization by name, regardless of spelling idiosyncrasies; and
- Records based on the automated query of an nth degree of separation algorithm.

The capability should permit analysts to specify their own product ranking and sorting criteria (e.g., by date, by location, or by quantity of times referenced by others); the criteria should automatically index all of an analyst's work (in the manner of the new desktop search engines), and should, to the degree practical, be jargon and even language independent.

Analysts will benefit from the fact that their detailed analyses often focus on a single area at a time. Tools exploit this analytic characteristic by adding a set of implicit specifications to an explicit search request based on current interests. When this is automatically performed in the background, analysts are able to expose any hidden filters in case they should suddenly change their interest.

Approach

Near-Term. Ideally, a single engine will provide all the capabilities listed above. The capability might, for instance, take the form of a sequence of filters (e.g., one for dates, one for geographic region, etc.), with the data being successively pared down at each step. Another useful approach is to integrate the search of multiple data sources via logical augmentation operations that make transparent the underlying heterogeneous nature of data sources from the analyst. To the analyst, the data sources will appear as a single, unified relation data source against which standard search techniques and filters can be applied. Using current technologies for unified ontologies and schema (e.g., XML and its derivatives, OWL, Tim Berners-Lee's semantic web), such a capability is within the approaching state of the art. Discussions with several search engine vendors suggest that the technology defined here could be provided at small cost; a few million dollars for upgrades to their technology and perhaps $10,000 per workstation. Thus, the challenge in simple search does not lie in the realm of search technology per se.

Far-Term. Due to the massively parallel nature of the techniques used in data search and retrieval, the performance and capabilities of any system can be expected to grow at an extremely fast rate. This will allow for much larger data sets, higher fidelity filters, more background automation (indexing/translation/clustering) and increased search and retrieval speeds. Looking into the future, data search and retrieval capabilities will improve along the same performance curve as the underlying support hardware (e.g., a doubling of capability every 18 months or so). This improvement, in turn, means both the size of the data sets and speed for search, display, and analysis will accelerate.

As suggested above, one important direction for such capabilities is the use of artificial intelligence (AI) or machine learning (ML) techniques to observe analyst search patterns and interests, and to anticipate data sources and relations likely to be of interest. Even when the AI tools are wrong, little will lost by the suggestion of an irrelevant data source when more powerful computers are available; the computational cycles will, in effect, be available "for free." And importantly, when a "hit" occurs, the reduced latency of the complex search that results will more than pay for the cost of the unused cycles. Much will be gained. As the AI/ML tools get better, one can expect a corresponding increase in the accuracy of these pre-fetch suggestions. The future of this capability is very bright.

Another interesting variant of search is the automatic "dialog" in which the search engine verbally prompts the analyst in the manner of a question-and-answer exchange, similar to the AI Expert System approach. When the search engine "gets an idea" about something useful, it suggests the approach and provides a pre-fetched sample of data that might be of interest. Instead of having to do all the creative work alone, the analyst can make use of the AI capabilities inherent in the search software to search for new ideas or unusual connections or correlations. People are even now beginning to employ such approaches in brainstorming activities.

Clearly, in a perfect world, all of these tools would be integrated into a single user interface with standard accesses across many different data types and data sources, and would employ a wide variety of search techniques. The analyst's job, then, would entail mastering a single "standard search" tool set. Differences in the underlying data sources would be masked: location, physical and logical data architecture, access pathway particularities, etc. In effect, the entire world of accessible data would be available "on demand" via a rapid, standardized, fully capable collection of search and analysis tools. Technical capability limitations do not currently allow this capability, but the data search world is definitely moving in this direction.

Challenges

A significant challenge not addressed above is data security, including access authorization and labeling. A "system high" solution requires that all analysts be cleared to the highest level of the data even though the particular data of interest to any particular analyst may require little or no special protection. Multi-level security appears to be the technology always "just around the corner," but these systems require significant resources to tag and classify data, quite contrary to the free-text/unformatted approach this system describes. At this point, it would be unwise to put forward a system architecture for which true multi-level security is a critical requirement.

Another security concern revolves around the "fact of" of a particular organization's interest in a topic. With Internet providers now selling the search profiles of their users to any interested buyer, it has become possible for malevolent parties to assess and continuously monitor various organizations' interest in them. This can be inconvenient to say the least, and could prove a very significant hindrance should adversaries begin "gaming" our analysis approach. Accordingly, it will often be desirable for research organizations to hide their interest by whatever means is appropriate—e.g., the anonymizers readily available for business and private use.

Another challenge concerns the economics of access to privately maintained data sources. In prototype demonstrations of the military utility of advanced analysis, there were a number of data sources that would have been useful, but required substantial access fees. The owners of these data sets spend considerable time, money, and effort gathering the data and developing the specialized tools needed to access it efficiently, and were understandably unwilling to just give away the "fruits of their labor." System architectures for advanced analysis, particularly in the early stages, will have to take these costs into consideration when deciding which data sources are likely to be of most value to the envisioned operational support.

Process and technique present a challenge all their own. Referring to the current state of the art, a unified, standardized user interface that successfully hides much of the data's internal characteristics is not yet generally available. Accordingly, in the near term, advanced analysis practitioners must be "power users" of a variety a search capabilities—a demand that will severely limit the utility of search.

CONCEPT-BASED SEARCH

Sometimes analysts will not be sufficiently knowledgeable of their topic to initiate effective search processes. They may, for instance, be new to a subject area and not well versed in the jargon, terminology, or acronyms, or they may simply not have sufficient technical, cultural, or theoretical background to do the search justice. In such cases, concept-based search and extraction is appropriate. By working at a level of abstraction well above that of simple keywords or phrase matching, this approach frees analysts from the need to think in terms of domain specific keywords.

The rationale behind concept-based search and extraction lies in the recognition that distinct concepts tend to manifest as distinct sets of word-level components. A concept associated with a nation's ability to wage war, for instance, would tend to include a significant subset of the following synonym sets:{war, battle, conflict}, {victory, win, defeat}, {soldier, marine, airman, sailor}. Although the job of identifying these sets generally requires relatively sophisticated linear algebra techniques, the techniques can now be abstracted to the degree they can be applied blindly by non-mathematically inclined analysts.

This form of concept–based search extraction can be employed in several ways. Given a set of articles designated as being of interest, the approach can automatically define the underlying concepts, and in turn the search criteria. And, if an analyst wishes to designate seemingly relevant articles as not being of interest, the approach can employ this information as well to further customize searches. This approach can be thought of as a technological extension of the process known as "search by example."

A special case of concept-based extraction of interest involves finding sets of words satisfying well-defined relationships; e.g., abc murdered xyz. In this case, the product of the search is a simple table specifying all identified instances of some subject "abc" murdering a victim "xyz." Well implemented, the search is tolerant of specific wording; for instance, it will correctly identify actions referred to as "killed, assassinated, whacked, put down," and so forth. Moreover, it is not overly sensitive to precise phrase structuring, and will even locate wordings such as "xyz was murdered; abc is the key suspect." Tools providing such extraction are now appearing on the market and assuming valuable roles in daily analysis. Most significant for our purposes here, it allows analysts to investigate problems in unfamiliar domains.

Needs and Desires

What advanced analysis requires is a capability to conduct effective search (high probability of detection, low probability of incorrect hit) without specifying specific keywords. To the extent feasible, the search should be tolerant of writing style and grammatical irregularities. The search may involve types of actions or logical, physical entities. By allowing the analyst to search and retrieve data coming from general concepts, and not simply domain-specific keywords, the analyst can gather information faster and more efficiently while learning topic vocabulary.

Approach

Near-Term. In the near-term, concept-based search will likely be based upon indication by analysts of documents of interest or not of interest to them, and natural language processing/sentence parsing to identify relationships such as subject-action-object groupings, or thesauruses/synonym dictionaries.

Far-Term. The far-term for concept-based extraction resembles, at least in certain ways, that of simple search. In particular, analysts can look forward to search tools that analyze past searches to identify patterns of likely interest to the current tasks, and employ these patterns to either extend or delimit current searches. The tools will make analysts aware of these assistance efforts, so they can turn off this "feature" when it proves undesirable. Ultimately, search will likely take the form of a continuous dialog: "Was this extension useful, yes or no? Is the current ranking useful? Yes or no? If not, please rank a few articles as you would like to see them displayed," and so forth.

Concept-based search will also enable a new category of tools capable of supporting ad hoc brainstorming. Such tools will analyze the concepts employed in a search to identify ideas and concepts potentially related to—but not identical to—those of current interest, and will bring these to the attention of analysts to stimulate their thinking. This approach, currently in its infancy, has been shown to be instrumental in avoiding analysts' version of writer's block.

Challenges

In view of its greater degree of abstraction vis-à-vis simple search, it should come as no surprise that concept-based search presents additional challenges. Chief among these is the need to keep it "tuned" to a specific analyst's needs. Unless an analyst is willing to expend effort to maintain his toolset, it will ultimately become dated and will provide less and less pertinent results. Ultimately, some form of machine learning will mitigate this problem, but in the near-term it will detract from the technique's usefulness in the eyes of many potential users.

MULTILINGUAL SEARCH

Multilingual search refers to a capability for analysts to locate potentially pertinent documents in languages others than those they speak. It also involves using the retrieved documents for preliminary analysis.

Needs and Desires

Advanced analysis requires a capability for analysts to employ reference material in any language. The material of interest will include newspapers, reports, and even informal discussion groups and blogs. The needs and requirements of a multilingual search system are similar to those of the concept-based search. In fact, from a high level, concept-based search can be viewed as a subset of multilingual search. At a minimum, the capability should identify articles of potential interest and provide sufficient gisting that analysts use to confirm or deny its selections and determine whether or not rigorous translation is warranted. Better yet, it should provide adequate translation for automated attribute monitoring and automated chronology creation (described later).

Approach

Near-Term. In the near-term, analysts can employ rudimentary capabilities that involve translating keywords into the target language, and translating the products of the search back to the analyst's language. A variety of engines are available for such an approach, and the process serves a useful role. However, it suffers in several areas. Translation of queries is often insufficient for accurate search. A recent query aimed at locating news articles relating to the 2005 North Korean nuclear "test," for instance, resulted in a set of articles focused on the training of nuclear engineers in North Korea. The problem, as it turned out, was that the word test was translated as "examination." A more appropriate term (as we determined through experimentation) was "demonstration." Many of the multilingual search problems can be remedied to a degree by some manner of "supervision," e.g., analyst specific dictionaries of words and phrases, and by customized, topic domain-specific dictionaries (e.g., military, medical, or engineering)

The current state-of-the-art in automated translation technologies is statistical machine translation (SMT). The concepts behind SMT originated back in the late 1940s and early 1950s, but it's only recently that computing power has reached the point where the approach is feasible. SMT relies on a "Rosetta Stone" type approach, where the system is trained on pairs of documents containing the same content, but in different languages. Given a large corpus, the system learns to associate words and phrases in one language with that in the other. A primary benefit of the SMT approach is that it doesn't require any "understanding" of the structure of the languages, and simply throwing more documents and processing power into the system increases its accuracy and robustness. Defense Advanced Research Projects Agency's (DARPA's) Global Autonomous Language Exploitation (GALE), and Google's translation engine employ this methodology.

Far-Term. In the far-term one can expect automated, statistical-based, machine-learning techniques to improve to the point their usage become transparent. End users might not ever need to know the language in which the document was originally written.

Challenges

Machine translation is an incredibly difficult problem. Philosophically, some argue it's not actually possible, but, ignoring this esoteric technicality, we are fast approaching the development of tools and techniques that are "good enough." The challenge now lies in integrating these tools and techniques seamlessly into search systems. Until comprehensive cross-language, topic-specific dictionaries become available, idioms will continue to be problematic.

LINK ANALYSIS

As the preceding sections indicate, retrieving data based on an explicit filter is a relatively straightforward process. Anyone on the Internet does it all the time using some manner of search engine. However, advanced analysts will often deal with a more sophisticated retrieval process—one in which the analyst is looking for patterns vis-à-vis specific words, or even cases in which an analyst has no clear idea of the patterns of interest ahead of time. This endeavor requires a different class of algorithm that is technically challenging. Despite the challenges, tools are continually appearing on the market that presume to handle at least portions of this problem. Research is ongoing in industry and academia, and great strides are being made. One field of particular interest is network theory.

Generally speaking, network theory is about *connecting the dots to discover and analyze hidden relationships among people, objects, data, and activities.* Just as the meaning of words is dependant on the meaning of other words, and differs in the context of other words, actions and associations differ in the context of other entities and actions. Although the technology is still somewhat immature, it finds extensive use in a wide range of pertinent fields; e.g., intelligence, law enforcement, homeland security, the social sciences, public health, epidemiology, politics, insurance, banking and finance, information technology, and security. Advanced analysts tend to be interested in these fields and more. Our current thoughts regarding link analysis follow.

Needs and Desires

Some of the link analysis capabilities needed for advanced analysis are unique, or at least esoteric. Consider, for instance, the job of anticipating an improvised explosive device (IED) strike. The problem here is that many, perhaps most, of a bomb maker's condition-setting activities take forms that are in themselves benign. For example, there are all kinds of good reasons for good citizens—"average Joes"—to purchase cell phones, fertilizer, household chemicals, nails, or even blasting caps, especially if one is a farmer or a construction worker. However, when members of a potential terrorist organization purchase all, or at least most of these items, an analyst would clearly like to know it. But this is generally very difficult because one must not only determine specific items of potential interest were purchased, but that people that have both a strong tie and a malevolent intent were the purchasers. This implies analysts must somehow link ad hoc combinations of people, organizations, behaviors, activities, events, and locations to determine if, in the aggregate, the connections represent some criminal or terrorist activity. This kind of link analysis is one of the cognitive elements of advanced analysis and relates to aggregation, tendency, trend, pattern, and anomaly analysis. The capability to determine such linkage—as well as many similar linkages—is a key requirement of link analysis. The advanced analyst's other link analysis needs are similar to those of existing link analysis practitioners: e.g., determining the path of tainted money, identifying patient one zero in a pandemic, locating the source of a new virus technology, and so on. All in all, the need is hugely diverse, vitally important, and incredibly challenging.

Approach

Near-term. Link analysis is an important contributor to many analytical domains and even a cursory survey of its potential applications would require far more space than is available here. More important, the existing work does not provide the answers advanced analysts require. Accordingly, we highlight below a few cases in which link analysis might prove helpful to advanced analysts and indicate briefly where this technical field is heading and how the technology might improve in the future.

- TRAFFIC ANALYSIS. Traffic analysis is concerned with deducing information such as the frequency of contacts and the importance of particular nodes from patterns of communications connectivity. Traffic analysis can be applied to any means of communication and is particularly important because it does not require the decryption of content. Traffic analysis is particularly useful for developing patterns that provide evidence of activities of likely interest, hence its direct influence on pattern analysis in advanced analysis. Frequent communications, for example, can indicate planning, and rapid and short communications can indicate negotiations or coordination. Furthermore, the directivity of calls or messages can reflect an organizational hierarchy or a network, and a sudden break in a communications pattern may indicate plans have been scrapped or reached a final stage. As with several of the topics dealt with here, experts have written many books on this topic and elements of the intelligence community are dedicated to its practice. The important point is simply to ensure advanced analysts know what traffic analysis is, what it offers, how to request it, and how to employ it effectively. This is a need that can and must be met.
- INFLUENCE NETWORKS. Influence networks and social influence network theory applies formal mathematical methods to understanding the interpersonal influence occurring in groups, as they strive to reach a consensus. Influence networks help analysts identify real power brokers within an organization so the analysts and their commanders can plan appropriate strategies for interdiction. This type of analysis can be very important, for instance, when one wishes to know whether "removing" the leader of a terrorist cell is likely to result in the disintegration of the cell or in the fragmentation of the cell into two equally powerful cells. Such analysis is an active field of endeavor in academia and the business and marketing industry, as well as the intelligence community.
- INFRASTRUCTURE NETWORKS. Analysts must be equipped to support planners in answering questions regarding infrastructure vulnerabilities or, conversely, the impact of reconstruction. This requires they understand the network nature of all elements of a societal infrastructure—power, fuel, communications, transportation, medical, sanitation, food, water, and so forth. Moreover, given the typical interconnectedness of these networks, they must understand each network not only in isolation but also as a network within networks. The development and population of such a "model" is no small task and requires all manners of link analysis. This analysis and modeling is the focus of a large

number of research efforts within the Department of Defense (DoD)—notably DARPA's conflict modeling and outcome experimentation (COMPOEX) activity.

- FINANCIAL NETWORKS. Network analysis is applied to financial networks to discover mechanisms for getting funds to terrorist cells and determining roles played by the different nodes of a link analysis. In particular, network analysis can reveal how insurgents or terrorists launder financial assets, who or what charitable organizations and businesses may be involved, and associated timelines to "cleanse" money and turn it around for use in insurgency or terrorist operations and associated security and functional interactions. Law enforcement people use network analyses of financial networks in particular in organized crime investigations and counter-narcotics activities. As links between crime and terrorism grow, the use of financial analysis will likely continue to grow as well.

The Challenges

Surprisingly, algorithms per se do not appear to be the current bottleneck with link analysis. Some link analysis practitioners argue that technologists can do virtually all one could theoretically expect to do with the current data. However, these practitioners also argue that future work will yield only marginal returns. Why is this? The key challenge in link analysis lies in data acquisition. Large networks are very complex; therefore, it is rarely possible to obtain needed characterization data. Infrastructure data, for instance, is often divided among various geopolitical entities, from national government to its smallest town and village governments, and although some data sources are available to analysts, many are not. This requires analysts to fill the gaps using models or assumptions, and this leads, in turn, to a second challenge—that of understanding the sensitivity of conclusions to model uncertainties. This is where careful modeling and statistical analyses come in play. These capabilities are discussed later in this chapter.

SOCIAL NETWORK ANALYSIS (SNA)

Social Network Analysis (SNA) is an important subset of link/network analysis. Due to the limited focus of SNA, as opposed to generic network analysis, special tools and techniques can be brought to bear. An example of this is the work being done by several organizations in designing metrics that are associated with organization vulnerability. These metrics permit modeling of an organization's evolution as it is influenced from the outside, and support the creation of interdiction plans. Researchers are also developing tools to support data needs of these algorithms. These include tools for characterizing organizations based on communications intercepts and traffic analysis. For example, with even simple traffic monitoring, an analyst could determine if the organization is hierarchical or cell-based, deep or shallow.

Not surprisingly perhaps, the principles of network connectedness extend beyond people. A recent study, in fact, found that two unrelated Web pages were separated, on average, by only 19 Internet links. Also not surprisingly, social networks are capable of providing valuable insights to intelligence and law enforcement analysts. One example that has gained notoriety is the work of Valdis Krebs, who produced a social network of the September 11 hijackers. Krebs began his search with two of the hijackers, Khalid al-Midhar and Nawaf Alhazmi, and, using accounts in the open source media and public records—including, in particular, addresses, telephone numbers, and frequent-flier numbers—found that all of the 19 hijackers were closely connected to each other. Moreover, he found that a disproportionate number of links converged on Mohamed Atta, which suggested Atta was the group's leader. Although this discovery process was finding the linkages after the fact and attempting to connect known entities, this doesn't discount the use of these techniques to discover unknown networks.

Able Danger—a once-classified Special Operations Command (SOCOM) program, provides a second example of SNA. In 2000, a full year before 9/11, this program purportedly characterized Mohamed Atta as a likely terrorist strike leader and identified at least three of the nineteen 9/11 perpetrators. Able Danger's purpose was limited to developing an Information Operations (IO) campaign against al Qaeda and transnational terrorism. Thus, the discovery of this information was not shared with the counterterrorism community. Still, the work serves to show that, under at least some circumstances, link analysis can provide potentially useful information. How useful is a key issue here: obviously the information was not so compelling as to provoke an interdiction operation.

Needs and Desires

As a minimum, advanced analysis requires a process that automatically identifies and characterizes an organization based on all available data. The characterization should include generic roles, high-level modus operandi, chain of command, relative importance of specific positions, and the like. The data exploitable should include communications intelligence, proximity, and any other form of intelligence available for a specific case. Ultimately, advanced analysts should be able to employ SNA to characterize organizations sufficiently that analysts can identify structural strengths and weaknesses, and develop appropriate interdiction approaches. These approaches should be designed not only to maximize immediate mission success objectives but also to ensure they don't make things worse in the long-term; e.g., by fractionating a group into two equally capable groups.

Approach

Near-Term. In the near-term, analysts will continue to employ communications and observable interaction patterns in order to characterize potential organizations in terms of SNA metrics such as betweenness, closeness, and structural cohesion (to name a few). The primary focus of the analysis will be on identifying relationships indicative of person-to-person cooperation in support of nefarious activities of interest. When organizations are positively identified, the focus will be on assessing their importance and on gauging the value of appropriate interdiction approaches.

Far-Term. In the far-term, one can anticipate the use of modeling and structured hypothesis testing, ultimately employing optimization technology, to support the determination and analysis of organization structures and operations methods. This approach will apply whatever constraints might apply in a specific case—physical, social, economic, and so forth—to make informed, educated guesses as to what an organization is all about, given available data.

Challenges

The key challenge to SNA will generally revolve around the availability of data. Although the data of interest will generally exist in someone's database, privacy and security considerations will often render it unavailable for routine use by analysts. There is, unfortunately, no simple solution to this problem; thus, effective SNA may be limited to certain categories of problems.

ATTRIBUTE MONITORING

Advanced analysis often involves monitoring some attribute for the purpose of identifying and characterizing changes and trends. For a typical analysis there may be dozens or even hundreds of data items that need to be monitored to ensure analysis currency and accuracy. In some cases, monitoring of an attribute is straightforward because the state of the attribute can be readily derived from the raw data. For example, the condition of worldwide financial markets can be understood at a glance by looking at various indices (e.g., attributes such as the Dow Jones Industrial Average, Nikkei 225 Index). Comparing the indexes with those of the prior day, yearly average, or some similar metric could, of course, accomplish further analysis; however, the index itself is self-describing. Much economics data are of a similar ilk; it is usually published regularly in an easily accessible form.

Qualitative attributes (e.g., populace attitudes and sentiments) are more difficult to assess. Tabulation of qualitative, intangible data in a useful and consistent form is not likely to exist; consequently, tracking in this case becomes a matter of interpretation and establishment of "goodness"— something computers are not particularly good at. Fortunately, technology is improving in this regard. A new class of monitoring technique is appearing, which seems to be capable of doing a respectable job of monitoring intangible attributes. This technique is based on the content analysis of media. Content analysis technology can deal with any attribute that an analyst can describe by rules or patterns. Current tools are capable of monitoring attributes as diverse as world and regional reactions to government policies, nuclear tensions, and economic conditions. Consequently, there is every reason to believe this capability will prove useful for advanced analysis.

Needs and Desires

Analysts must be able to monitor any attribute they are able to quantitatively or qualitatively define. In the case of quantitative monitoring, they must be able to assess instantaneous values (e.g., absolute statuses such as value of a currency or fraction of the population unemployed) or rates of change (e.g., population growth rate). Also, in the case of qualitative attributes (e.g., the degree of positive or negative sentiment associated with a particular idea) they must be able to monitor, as a minimum, relative values and trends.

Approach

Near-Term. Although trend characterization will likely always require some manual intervention, much of the analysis can be automated. The key algorithms employed today employ an assessment based on a subject matter expert's choice of status-defining words. In essence, the process entails four steps in which an expert 1) identifies the words he or she would expect to be used in describing a specific attribute, 2) defines or weights the words, positive or negative, to indicate whether the words represent a positive or negative status relative to a specified baseline, 3) employs content analysis and entity extraction to locate articles of interest and status-defining words of interest, and 4) applies some manner of weighted sum to the status words to develop an attribute status for the article. The approach is simplistic at best, but, if well tuned, it produces reasonable and useful results. Unfortunately, the process is not always cost effective and viable—not only does it require true subject expertise but it is time-consuming. Some researchers are employing more sophisticated approaches using sentence parsing and natural language understanding approaches.

Far-Term. Over time, it is reasonable to assume that libraries of attribute monitors will be created for many, perhaps most of the situations of interest. Customization for a particular analysis will entail supplying specifics such as the precise time frame of interest and the geographic region of interest. Furthermore, the more sophisticated approaches may be expected to mature and become routinely available. These will enhance attribute model development in the same way that content-based analysis enhanced simple search.

Challenges

A key challenge in attribute monitoring—at least with the near-term approaches—will be in handling noun-phrases that change the meaning of attribute defining words. For instance, the words "depression" and "recession" within an article on a region's economy will generally be interpreted as negative; however, paired with a qualifier such as "little chance of" or "fear of . . . have passed," the meaning can be exactly the opposite. A review of a movie could state "everyone thought I would hate this movie, that it was horrible, but they were wrong." This would appear to be a negative review, but in fact it is positive. Interestingly, it is very difficult to accurately identify all instances of such attribute morphing; thus, current attribute monitoring approaches attempt to de-weight the importance of such cases by taking averages over many articles. One would hope that ultimately more powerful algorithms and language parsing techniques would dispense with this need.

PATTERN DETECTION

Working with patterns is important in advanced analysis. In fact, please recall in an earlier discussion that pattern analysis is one of the 14 cognitive elements of advanced analysis. Retrieving databases on an explicit filter is conceptually a straightforward process, i.e., compare data elements against the filter criteria and return matching elements. However, analysts must often work at a higher level than simple data retrieval. For instance, they may find themselves looking not for simple word patterns, but for patterns of actions that an entity takes, e.g., enemy condition-setting patterns for attacking an important bridge. In some cases, these patterns may be predefined, in others they may not be. In still other cases, analysts may not be certain whether or not a pattern even exists, or if it does, what its form and predictive accuracy will be. In these cases, the construction of indexes for rapid retrieval is not possible because the desired query cannot be known in advance. The extraction of such patterns and their use in data retrieval and analysis requires a significantly different class of algorithm and a physical data architecture that permits very high rates of input and output (I/O).

Despite the challenge, commercial tools continue to appear that address specific portions of the broad problem and an active research program is ongoing in government, industry, and the U.S. Academy of Sciences to improve this important function. Again, the relevance in this work ties to advanced analysis, as pattern analysis is an essential aspect of conducting advanced analysis in the urban OE.

Needs and Desires

Advanced analysis requires analysts to identify trends or patterns and to employ these for forecasting or inductive reasoning. Here are a few examples:

- *Example 1.* A new type of IED appears in a specific neighborhood of Baghdad. The advanced analyst examines recent historical records to determine statistically significant precursor events that, in retrospect, could be predictors or used to help identify and/or locate the responsible organization.
  - *Approach.* Here, a stable background condition must be established against which potential indicators stand out as "signals." Some signals can be hypothesized, but a complete search of all possible indicators, singly and in combination, has better potential for finding actionable information within the large, noisy urban background.
- *Example 2.* A high-ranking officer in a local insurgency group has been captured and his aliases over the past five years are now known. The advanced analyst analyzes a variety of data sources (financial, medical, market/economic, law enforcement, travel) to determine whether significant patterns of behavior can be identified and to correlate these, if possible, with known insurgency attacks.
  - *Approach.* The very general nature of the assignment means that a variety of possible patterns, not known in advance, might potentially be of interest. These correlations might span geographic, organizational, financial, and political boundaries. In the absence of any other search goals, an open-ended examination of statistical anomalies (when compared to say, to a nominal background) offers the best hope of progress.

As can be seen from these examples, the domain of possible trends or patterns is large. But it is manageable. For the situations of interest, it generally includes space (the location of events of interest), time (the times of events of interest), modus operandi (linked sequences of events culminating in an attack), actors (and all of their identifying information and personal history), equipment (type, purchase information, maintenance, etc.), materials (type, movement, storage, preparation, etc.), proxy's (related persons or groups, witting or unwitting), and combinations of the above.

As the first and simple case, advanced analysis must handle specified patterns—e.g., find cases in which events employing similar modus operandi took place within a given distance. As the more general and difficult case, advanced analysis searches for persistent relationships between or among event elements across a specified set of events. The unspecified case is more challenging but also more valuable, as relationships of value are sometimes totally unexpected. Ideally, the capability will accommodate any available data. As a minimum, this must include unstructured as well as structured text and associated metadata. Depending on the problem at hand, it may also be useful to accept imagery, video, or audio inputs with the associated capability to do voice-to-text and recognition including language translation.

Given the variety of possible uses, the accommodation need not involve a single tool or a totally automated process. More likely, it will entail bringing to bear a suite of tools that, individually or collectively, can be rapidly composed to enable the type of pattern detection required for the case at hand. This suite would include, as a minimum, tools for 1) extracting individual elements/signatures; 2) characterizing potential patterns in a form that facilitates comparison/clustering; 3) restructuring the physical data architecture to support very high data input/output bandwidth; and 4) performing comparison, assessment, and clustering. The front-end to this process typically includes data extraction, reformatting, and a physical/logical data architecture to support the back end process—i.e., the very same high-performance demands that pattern recognition engines require.

Approach

Near-Term. Pattern detection presents two key issues. The first concerns construction of the training data to develop the pattern detection algorithm. The second concerns the application of this algorithm to search potentially large and heterogeneous data sets. Regarding the first issue, if training data is available, then the construct of patterns is difficult but does not require large storage or computational resources. The reason is that pattern recognizers can be trained on selected subsets of the available training data; there is no need to train on all the data. In a typical case, a small carefully chosen subset of the data is used for training purposes and the resulting search pattern is then validated against all or some of the remaining data. The technical challenge, then, is not computational complexity but the goodness of the pattern matches that come forth. By goodness, we mean the ability to accurately discriminate between valid matches (true positives) and invalid matches (true negatives). In each case, errors (false positives or false negatives) add overhead to the system, which in the some cases can actually render the approach nonviable in a practical sense. Very large amounts of time and effort can go into the construction of these pattern-matching algorithms, and only sometimes does the effort result in a satisfactory product. The difficulty often lies in the fact that, for reasons of computational efficiency (e.g., compression) or algorithmic requirements, significant heuristic content can be lost, which results in reduced signal-to-noise and increased error rates.

A wide variety of pattern-matching approaches are available, including neural nets, rule induction, support vector machines, singular value decomposition, probabilistic singular value decomposition, and optimized subspace projection techniques. Each or any of these may be appropriate depending on the particular characteristics of the problem at hand, and all have been successfully employed in various applications. There is, however, no "one size fits all," because success often depends on data peculiarities that vary greatly among data sources.

An important sub-case must also be identified—that in which training data is not available, and in which the algorithm must both identify important clusters in the data and construct efficient filters or patterns that can identify data elements that belong to the cluster. Two types of algorithms are commonly used when this more challenging type of problem is encountered: clustering and statistical analysis. Clustering projects data onto a suitably chosen subspace so the data, when projected, naturally decomposes into distinct groupings. When this happens, there is often a heuristic reason why, and a SME can examine the data and quickly determine the underlying causality. The next step, assuming this step has been successful, is to use this grouping to construct training data and train a good pattern-matching engine. A similar approach also applies when statistics help identify significant subgroups. Here, the goal is to find groupings within the data that exhibit strong non-random correlations (positive or negative). Again, the heuristic significance of such an occurring phenomenon is often clear to a SME.

An important operational constraint that attaches to this type of "bootstrapping" is the need for a SME to examine the groupings or clusterings the algorithm produces. In some cases, the algorithm will find clustering criteria that are simply not useful, or that in hindsight are obvious. In other cases, the algorithm may have found statistical groupings to be artifacts of the training set that has been used, and disappear when a larger set of data is employed. Ideally, however, the groupings found by the algorithm (when and if they appear) will point to an underlying heuristic causality that is significant and usable for analysis purposes. Often, only a SME will be sufficiently qualified to decide inapplicability to a specific case.

The second issue involves the application of a useful complex pattern to a large data set or group of data sets. The problem is no longer to construct the pattern, as it was above, but to apply the pattern to the data. The difficulty that arises here is that the type of indexing that makes structured data searches so rapid cannot ordinarily be done in this case. The reason for this limitation is that the pattern is complex and may only have been constructed recently (say, as part of the problem-solution process itself) so that the construction of a corresponding index simply could not have been done in advance. Another problem is that in many cases the search to be performed spans a number of heterogeneous data sources that were constructed and maintained independently of each other. A simple connecting operation across such databases is logically possible but computationally infeasible, because key fields may employ different naming conventions or units, and the physical order in which the key fields are stored in the two machines may be incompatible.

In such cases, a significant initial step is usually performed in which the data from the sources is physically copied into a central location where the pattern search will be performed. During this copying process, a number of significant data preparation activities take place. Incompatible data storage conventions are mapped onto the single convention that will be used by the central location. Unwanted data fields are discarded and data compression schemes can be undone or applied as appropriate. The physical architecture of the data at the central location is constructed to facilitate the very high input/output bandwidths needed once the pattern-matching algorithm has been initiated. Missing or conflicting data is manipulated so the algorithm will receive a single, clean stream on which to operate. The point is that without such data preparation steps, the complex pattern matching software will run too slowly to be of much practical use, and speed in counterinsurgency operations is important. Once a clean, unified data set has been prepared centrally, the complex search pattern (and important variants of it) can be applied to the data, and the analysis can be accomplished.

Far-Term. In the future, many of the difficulties described above will to some extent be addressed. What cannot be addressed, of course, is the nature of the underlying data sources themselves. If there are no inherently important patterns in the data, then no algorithm is going to find what is not present ("you can't put in what the gods left out"). Some improvement in clustering or training algorithms may take place, but a great deal of research effort has already been spent in this area and the returns are diminishing. It is unlikely that training or clustering algorithms will experience a major breakthrough. What can be done, however, is to greatly improve the preprocessing step that permits application of complex patterns and queries to heterogeneous data sets. All of the processes involved in this pre-processing operation—data cleaning, standardizing units and naming conventions, compression, missing or conflicting data, etc.—can be significantly improved, both in terms of speed and quality of product. Ideally, it should be possible to make the end-to-end process entirely seamless through the use of rich annotations (e.g., extensible mark-up language or XML). The XML version can then be mapped onto computationally efficient physical architectures tuned to accelerate the search process; once the search is complete, the data can simply evaporate. Such a "blue sky" picture is not yet a reality, but is on the way.

Challenges

Before pattern matching can become a routine element of advanced analysis, three key challenges will have to be overcome: 1) acceptable error rates must be achieved; 2) the required search engines will have to be made available; and 3) effective concept of operations (CONOPS) have to be developed. These topics are worthy of entire books in themselves, so we will limit ourselves here to an observation that the need for effective pattern detection is important enough to anticipate work in these areas will progress at the same feverish pace as now, and that both our near and far term expectations will be achieved.

EVENT DETECTION AND TIMELINE/CHRONOLOGY ANALYSIS

Timelines are a convenient mechanism—often the preferred mechanism for visualizing the evolution of situations and for identifying and analyzing cause and effect relationships. Unfortunately, timeline generation has until now been a predominantly manual process. The reason for this is threefold: First, there is the problem of locating the time specification in free text. In many news articles the byline works fine. However, often the date of interest is embedded in the article. Also, this specification can take a wide range of forms—e.g., today, yesterday, tomorrow, 9/11, 9/11/01, 11 September 2001, etc. Second, there is the problem of identifying cause and effect relationships. Third is the problem of characterizing events accurately in terms of the subject, action, and object.

Emerging technologies are poised to tackle each of these three problems. Pattern recognition-based entity extraction, for instance, can recognize a huge variety of date/time formats, numeric as well as textual; relationship-based entity extraction engines can identify many subject-verb-object constructs, even when they span sentences; and a relatively new technology known as topic detection and tracking (TDT) can now accurately identify and characterize many event types of interest. There is still a long way to go before a totally automated event characterization capability is available, but as long as one is willing to iterate on and refine a computer's initial cut, a useful semi-automated capability is possible. The product of TDT often takes the form of a timeline, such as is employed by news media, i.e., a sequence of actions taken by various actors in response to each other.

TDT can be employed in a variety of ways. For historical analysis, it can be employed to compare past situations in order to determine why and how things evolved differently in different cases. This information can be employed to determine general tendencies or, when sufficient information is available, to "profile" key actors. For current analysis, it can assist analysts in tracking events as they occur, determining possible cause and effect relationships, and in developing an understanding of what's going on "behind the green door," so to speak. These types of information will support a host of advanced analysis elements, including, among others, tendency analysis, anomaly analysis, and anticipatory analysis.

Needs and Desires

Advanced analysis requires a capability to create high-level timelines automatically. As a minimum these would take the form of annotated stock market timelines; i.e., prices versus time, with generally pertinent articles that may or may not explain the cause of the prices. Eventually, a more robust capability would be advantageous—one in which cause and effect as well as subject-verb-object are clearly indicated. The desired product would take the form of the timelines or chronologies published in news magazines.

Approach

Near-Term. The near-term approach is to identify the time of actions described in articles and produce a chronologically ordered list of articles regarding those actions. This will assist analysts in identifying topics of interest and will stimulate valuable analysis, but it will do little to support the in-depth analysis needed in advanced analysis.

Far-Term. Ultimately, what's needed is a powerful TDT capability—one that infers, automatically and on the fly, cause and effect between events of interest. Specifically, the capability would ingest a comprehensive corpus relating to a topic, and subject to analyst specification and direction, produce a timeline and supporting data indicating how a situation evolved.

Challenges

Event identification is not easy. The problem lies in the tendency for the news media, or any analyst/reporter, to continually revisit a topic of interest well after a significant event has occurred. This results in many articles relating to a single event—appearing from days to weeks after the original event occurred—and a blurring of distinction between that original event and subsequent events. This blurring makes it difficult to identify events based on simple criteria, for instance a large spike in the quantity of articles relating to a topic, and forces an event detector algorithm to delve deeply in the text of pertinent articles to identify distinct new events. TDT attempts this deep understanding, but the process still requires careful topic-specific "calibration" on the part of analysts.

EVENT AND CHANGE DETECTION FROM PHOTOS AND VIDEO

In addition to events involving large organizations and large groups of people, advanced analysts must deal with low-level events. These can include anything from seemingly chance encounters of individuals to perpetrators emplacing IEDs. Although trained observers easily accomplish the detection of such events, accomplishing it automatically, rapidly, and effectively enough to handle large quantities of streaming data is currently beyond the state of the art. There is no algorithm for reliably detecting the wide range of actions of potential interest.

Needs and Desires

What advanced analysis could use is an effective capability to monitor photos or video in order to detect actions of interest or to identify specific people, activities, or objects.

Approach

Near-Term. Currently the event and change detection is predominantly manual. Tools permit analysts to scan streaming input rapidly, process it to accentuate features of potential interest, and slow-down, single-step forward, or stop the data stream to permit precise mensuration. However, little if any automation is employed for analysis per se. Accordingly, the process works to a degree, but it is time consuming and tedious, and in many cases impractical.

Far-Term. In the far-term a modicum of automated event detection should occur. Existing programs, DARPA video and image retrieval and analysis tool (VIRAT) for instance, are focusing on this capability, and expectations are high. However, whether event and change detection will become routine components of an advanced analyst's tool box in the next decade is unknown.

Challenges

Given a shortage of the experts needed to vet a machine's identification, the challenge will be in maximizing the probability of detection for a specified probability of false alarm. Unless the false alarm rate can be made small enough to improve overall performance, the process will not achieve wide operational acceptance.

TAXONOMY CREATION

Taxonomies are useful tools for many analysis needs. Just as a hierarchically structured inventory list can help buyers identify all the types of products available from a supplier, a good taxonomy can help analysts identify information of potential interest for a specific analysis. However, taxonomy generation is no simple matter. It is a laborious, time-consuming endeavor requiring SME expertise and skills in taxonomy creation per se. But this situation is changing. Semi-automated taxonomy generators are appearing that create an excellent first draft of a taxonomy with remarkably little effort. Employing these generators entails providing a corpus certain to include the taxonomy elements of interest, and a filter specifying the taxonomy scope. The algorithms then provide a draft of the taxonomy and a set of business rules to allow users to refine the draft. The approach is expected to improve as it proliferates, and one can anticipate robust capabilities within a few years.

Needs and Desires

What's needed for advanced analysis is a capability that permits analysts to rapidly determine all information of potential interest to a topic.

Approach

Near-Term. Currently, customized rule sets and clustering algorithms can automatically create taxonomies. In essence, the process involves providing the algorithms with a corpus certain to contain all the taxonomy elements of potential interest and employing a clustering algorithm to identify the categories of information present and some measure of the various categories' closeness to each other.

Far-Term. In the far-term, analysts can anticipate algorithms that learn from past analyses. These algorithms will assist the basic taxonomy algorithms in determining the range of an analyst's interest, as well as perhaps geographical or cultural boundaries.

Challenges

Any approach will reflect, to a large degree, the scope of the analyst's knowledge. In the near-term case, this will be reflected in the corpus initially provided, and in the long-term case, in the analyst's case history. Consequently, there is always the possibility that a taxonomy will be incomplete, breadth-wise as well as depth-wise. There is no simple answer to this dilemma—an analyst doesn't know what he or she doesn't know—thus, the trick in taxonomy creation will be in inviting analysts with related, but not identical interest to vet the inputs to the creation process.

Modeling

Modeling is one of those terms that means very different things to different people—everything from a small scale mockup of a system, to a representation of a process, to a software package projecting a situation forward in time to permit analysts' examination of a range of possible futures. Also, although these appear very different on the surface, they in fact have much in common—namely, all capture the essence of a complex system and, as intelligence analysts will be quick to point out, all can be deployed to facilitate analysis.

Generally, advanced analysts will deal with two categories of models: dynamic and static. Dynamic models support advanced analysts in projecting the current state into the future, in gaining insight into the underlying causal mechanisms of events that have occurred, and in identifying and analyzing second- and third-order consequences of proposed actions even when these consequences are nonintuitive (e.g., a subtle, emergent behavior) or operating on different time scales than the actions themselves. Static models, on the other hand, enable them to understand relationships and causal connections that often go unexposed. This, in turn, will enable them to create robust theories of conflict, identify organizations and individuals of potential interest, and examine the likely consequences of influencing an organization in a specific manner.

This section elaborates on these possibilities and describes some of the important ways in which modeling can support the various elements of the advanced analysis process. It will then propose both near- and far-term approaches to meeting these needs and identify and discuss some of the important challenges facing modelers and model users.

Needs and Desires

In surveying the 14 components constituting the advanced analysis ensemble of capabilities, it is evident that almost all elements can benefit from the application of selected modeling techniques. Here are some examples:

- DECOMPOSITION can be significantly enhanced via process modeling. Models will help the advanced analyst decompose intelligence requirements into the five types of observables we have discussed throughout the book. Supported by visualization/manipulation tools such as USJF-COM's Real Time Business Rules Engine (BRE) G2 modeling tool, process modeling could assist analysts in identifying gaps in their understanding of an adversary process. By hypothesizing that the adversary is attempting to accomplish Task X, the model can suggest possible sequences of actions needed to achieve the goal. Associated with these actions are observables, which can then be collected against and resultant data examined to become information or knowledge sufficient to confirm or deny the hypothesis. The model is critical in identifying both intermediate task sequences and associated observables. It can also provide a mathematic basis for specifying such ISR-related issues as frequency of revisit (sampling rate), necessary resolution, and achieved level of confidence.

- CRITICAL THINKING. Models can help the advanced analyst think like the enemy. They can also help the analyst engage in four-pair wargaming (as explained earlier) with the help of SMEs and indigenous experts to rid the tendency to engage in mirror imaging. Models can help with analysts' preparation for deployment by presenting a synthetic environment complete with infrastructure, data environment, and cause/effect relationships with planned U.S. tangible and intangible activities and effects. Three-dimensional/GIS models can help the advanced analyst consider the enemy's countersurveillance operations and to determine line of sight and field of view from the enemy's humans and sensors, accordingly identifying dead space that could become the field of play for U.S. HUMINT and technical collection operations. Models can help too with use of automated thought templates by analysts considering the use of the elements of advanced analysis. Models will help the commander to monitor conditions for his pre-defined statuses of both risk and uncertainty. One of the capabilities of modeling that will come into being in the near future is cognitive amplification. Such models will help analysts know when they are making errors in logic and unexpected consequences of thought, and a range of alternatives the analyst could choose from.
- CHANGE/TREND/TENDENCY ASSESSMENT. Analysis in support of operations performance assessment is currently limited. Models can support the design as well as the assessment. In support of the design, they can help identify effective methods of effectiveness indices (MoEIs). This can be particularly valuable when the model indicates sensitivities well before the key state changes of interest are readily apparent. In support of the assessment, they provide a baseline (the evolution of the plan) from which to gauge progress. In this respect, models can help to identify and monitor link, pattern, trend, and knowledge decay, and provide a range of options a commander can consider to intercede in the decay process and possible outcomes. Models will provide an alarm for the possible ascendancy of sensitive variables and provide a range of possible impacts on the commander's decisions.
- LINK ANALYSIS. Static models show *interconnections,* human connectedness, and influence linkages between and among people, organizations, functions, activities, and transactions between significant individual-to-individual, individual-to-organizations, and among the organizations to which they belong. The models can help analysts understand and employ each of the six types of links discussed in chapter seven. These models, in turn, enable analysts to understand the current state as well as to assess how the social network might respond to new stimuli and appear in the future.
- PATTERN ANALYSIS. The use of automatic computational tools to identify patterns and apply them to new data often requires a formal mathematical model of the process that is a derivative of advanced analysis.

Models can also help the advanced analyst understand the six kinds of patterns identified in the book and possible outcomes when attempting to influence their appearance, operation, decay, and demise.

- ANTICIPATORY ANALYSIS. Models can help in anticipating enemy activities. Most importantly, models can help describe necessary enemy condition-setting, and the range of preemptive options and their possible outcomes to stop, shape, or desynchronize the necessary enemy condition-setting. Models can help the analyst understand the range of possibilities owing to the play of sensitive variables, the conditions for their arousal, the windows of opportunity for their influence (friendly and enemy), and second- and third-order effects when the commander chooses to use preemptive strategies.

- TECHNICAL ANALYSIS. Formal models in this arena are widely available off-the-shelf. Models will, however, contribute to understanding of the invisible domain of large urban OEs. Models help people understand electrical emanations, flow of data, plumes, fumes, smells, incandescent heat, the movement of electrons, radio frequency (RF) energy, energy emissions from nuclear material, and invisible bodily emanations coming from human beings.

- ANOMALY ANALYSIS. By formulating and validating a solid model of the current steady-state background environment (also known as a baseline), modeling can enable a rapid and high-confidence detection of significant departures from the norm and help analysts understand likely causes. Baselines in this book are three kinds—technical, cultural, and functional. Models can help with finding the right baselines, providing assessments of their state of usability (e.g., how up-to-date they are), and identify ways to ensure they are current.

- CULTURAL INTELLIGENCE ANALYSIS. Recent advances in the social sciences have generated a variety of models that can be "fit" to match and mimic the peculiarities and particularities of any given operational domain. Models need to help advanced analysts anticipate the thoughts, perceptions, behaviors, goals, motives, intent, and corollary activities of people from a cultural perspective. Models of cultural activities overlaid on actual OEs will greatly assist advanced analysts. Models can help analysts understand the "what if" and "if then" ruminations of people who think differently from them. Models can help advanced analysts understand the enemy's perspectives of sensitive variables and windows of opportunity for exploitation and denial. Unfortunately, technology is not advanced enough to perform as discussed here. Nonetheless, these articulated hopes must become requirements for the technology and scientific communities to unleash the full cerebral power of people practicing advanced analysis.

- SEMIOTICS ANALYSIS. Models of cross-cultural similarities in iconography, for example, can provide structure, correlation, and completeness metrics for understanding the significance of semiotic signals in a complex economically and politically diverse urban environment.

- AGGREGATION ANALYSIS. A variety of modeling techniques are available that assemble simple components into complex global structures. These structures exhibit unexpected significant emergent behaviors or disassemble behavior, expectations, or activities into essential elements, confirm or deny causality, and ultimately link causes to effects or outcomes. Modeling can help analysts identify the "glue" and "propellant" as discussed earlier, the influence of sensitive variables and windows of opportunity, and even possibilities for command-induced preemptive moves to shape the aggregate as it comes into being.

- RECOMPOSITION. In a manner similar to decomposition, a model can be used to reassemble the constituents of a process or an argument into abstract conceptual wholes, with internal structure and causal interconnections that can be synthesized until they are well understood. Models can take incoming data, fuse it with other data, and provide visualization of the results. Models help the analyst provide sufficient meaning to turn data into information and to set conditions for synthesis to turn information into knowledge. Models can help people understand the partial and eventually the entire whole of the focus of reassembling data via the analytic/collection synergy that advanced analysis postulates as the principal connecting glue and impetus for successful intelligence operations against insurgents in an urban OE.

- SYNTHESIS. Formal modeling supports synthesis by structuring the analyst's conceptual view of the problem at hand, threading relationships into a whole, filling in missing portions of problems, bringing possible combinations into consciousness, permitting analytic *Fingerspitzengefuhl* (an intellectual and intuitive sensing of a whole or totality), and providing formal mathematical means to validate proposed hypotheses. This process of synthesizing information into knowledge can be enhanced by three-dimensional/GIS visualization models should the analyst desire to proceed along this pathway.

The use of models is not solely confined to the 14 elements of advanced analysis. It permeates well into the operational processes being supported—e.g., decision-making, surveillance, situation shaping, analytic condition-setting, and crisis mitigation. Although the potential contribution of models is large, so are the challenges. If one delves a bit deeper than we have above, they quickly realize that advanced analysis poses requirements for just about every type of modeling technology available. Below, we elaborate on what can be done in this area.

Needed modeling technologies are available, many within analyst-friendly commercial-off-the-shelf (COTS) packages; the advanced analysis software suite should in fact incorporate most of these. In particular, the suite should include capabilities for system dynamics—agent based, discrete event, Bayesian net, Markov modeling—and should be capable of bringing all of the models to bear on all political, military, economic, social information, and infrastructure (PMESII) elements, individually as well as in the aggregate. Here are our thoughts regarding the near- and far-term.

Approach

Near-Term. In the near-term, model quality will be limited. In this role, the use of models will be restricted to analyses to identify and characterize, but not necessarily quantify, likely situations of interest. All of the needs identified in the needs and desires paragraph—i.e., all elements of advanced analysis—will be addressed, but limits of capabilities and even potential exist.

An example of the use of modeling and its inherent limitations is the employment of advanced analysis in support of operations planning. The challenge is this. For any action planners consider, it is imperative they identify and understand all-important consequences, undesirable as well as desirable. But this mental process is often difficult—the PMESII elements of an environment are often tightly connected, and nonlinear effects often result in all manner of nonintuitive, difficult-to-anticipate impacts. Models, on the other hand, are to a large extent immune to the limits of intuition. If a model is reasonably well constructed—in particular, if it contains the proper connections, even if not the correct connection magnitude—it will often exhibit the correct types of consequences, though the details can be blurred and of the ilk of fuzzy logic. However, the mere existence of these consequences should be sufficient to trigger an analyst's, and in turn, a planner's thinking—serving, in effect, as a significant, potentially important supplement to the planner's intuition. This has in fact been the preferred method of model usage in recent model research activities, such as recent collaborative modeling/operations efforts between USJFCOM and DARPA.

Here, in brief, are some of the many ways in which advanced analysis-based modeling might support operations planning and execution:

- THEORIES OF CONFLICT. This form of modeling, which is currently seeing considerable interest in the interagency community, focuses on the key actors in a conflict (or crisis)—in particular, their goals, strengths, intent, will, and modus operandi. However, in contrast to conventional modeling, it also takes into consideration the actors' passions, values, decision-making processes, dependencies, and influences, thus providing a much more comprehensive understanding of pertinent interactions than was previously possible. In cases where the theory of conflict is not clear, candidate models can be used within a maximum likelihood process to determine which best fits the observational data and the most likely representative of the real world.

- EMERGING SITUATIONS. Modeling can determine how an emerging situation is likely to unfold. Such modeling, based in large measure on an accepted theory of conflict, could indicate possible paths a crisis might take, and support analysts and decision makers in assessing the merits/demerits of friendly force intervention.
- VALIDITY OF ASSUMPTIONS AND VETTING. Models, supported by Bayesian or maximum likelihood techniques, can support analysts in determining how well various assumptions fit the OE, current situation, and facts bearing on the challenges and problems at hand.
- COURSE OF ACTION DEVELOPMENT AND ASSESSMENT. Models can support analysts and planners in identifying potentially beneficial actions and effects, as well as determining impacts of these actions and effects, undesirable as well as desirable.
- SENSITIVITY ANALYSIS. As discussed throughout this work, in an urban OE, sensitive variables will suddenly rise to create outcomes far more influential than ever anticipated. These variables can affect all competitors in an urban OE—neither force nor operation is immune. Sensitive variables often appear out of nowhere to influence all activities and operations for all competitors. They can lead to large, disproportionate outcomes and emergent behaviors. Future models, effectively focused, can help analysts and planners identify vulnerabilities for defense and plan attacks and manipulations of sensitive variables within the decision and action realms of all competitors.
- ADVERSARY INITIATIVE CONSIDERATION. This model-based activity could attempt to view the situation from the adversary's perspective and analyze his likely initiatives as well as his response to our initiatives. It could then help identify the various ways in which an adversary's plans might unfold, and in turn, support analysts in the creation of intelligence needs, surveillance plans, contingency plans, etc.
- EFFECT DECAY ANALYSIS. This analysis could model both friendly and adversary plans in a PMESII-wide context and could determine how long various effects are likely to endure. Such analysis could be critical in determining maintenance needs, vis-à-vis initial state attainment requirements.
- 4-PAIR WARGAMING—i.e., conducting 4- (even n) sided wargaming, that is, wargaming in which all key players (adversaries, friendlies, neutrals, host nation, and so forth) are represented and often possess the initiative. This gaming, heavily supported by models, permits analysts to study and anticipate not only friendly initiatives but also to anticipate and analyze adversary, host nation, and neutral party initiatives and resultant effects and actions.

The bottom line regarding modeling is this: As with advanced analysis per se, the potential use of advanced analysis–based modeling within operation planning and execution is potentially huge. Despite limitations due to quality, the potential role of models is quite significant. Thus, modeling should certainly be a key element of an advanced analyst's toolbox, even in the near term. So how about the far term?

Far-Term. In the far-term, modeling fidelity will likely improve, and perhaps more interesting, models that learn could come into play. Standardization of data capture will make it possible to rapidly and conveniently draw on historical experiences, to correlate these experiences with current events, and to use this data to calibrate models (via post-diction) in support of projection. Currently, finding related events from the past requires search, but by standardizing the end-to-end modeling process, it will become possible to discover relevant past events automatically. For example, the machine might suggest: "In a similar process in the past, this step was accomplished in such-and-such a way, increasing greatly the likelihood of the following scenario. . . ." As time goes on, the potential benefits from this self-learning process will grow.

Another far-term benefit will come from improvements in immersive visualization and virtual reality—literally putting the analyst "into" the context proposed by the model. Such capabilities are already appearing on the scene. One package, for example, draws an analyst's attention to regions in a complex data space of greatest potential interest and then assists the analyst in drilling down to discover unexpected causal or structural connections. Advanced analysis could employ such a capability and its successors very productively.

Yet another far-term improvement is the ability to replay dynamic models many times with a variety of probabilistically determined intermediate branching points. The idea is to fully explore the complex underlying probability space using Monte Carlo techniques. With ongoing improvements in hardware and software, such a capability (now available only at great expense on supercomputers) will become a routine feature of many dynamic event-driven models and simulations.

Challenges

Modeling is subject to the garbage-in-garbage-out (GIGO) principle—that is, the goodness of results achieved will strongly reflect both the validity of the abstract model and the accuracy of parameter values it has been given. Thus, it is important to create models with specific objectives in mind and to continuously monitor and assess them to determine how good they actually are at supporting that objective.

A second challenge in modeling is that of avoiding mirror imaging. Our modelers, similar to most of us, tend to bastardize the principle of "rationale actor." Their tendency is to assume, often incorrectly, that not only will subjects act similarly to us in response to an attack on their value set, but also their value sets per se are in fact similar to ours (mirror-imaging). This, as we are finding out the hard way, is not always the case. In all too many instances we do not understand our adversaries' values and goals (e.g., suicide bombers and sincere religious fundamentalists) and, by blindly assuming they are similar to our own, we draw conclusions and make decisions that have proven tragic. What's required is recognition that cultural modeling—e.g., avatar "tuning" in our dynamic and static models—must be done by cultural experts, preferably indigenous people. This sounds easy, but it engenders two problems: deploying the needed experts, and interestingly, ensuring that our analysts recognize situations in which the experts are needed. Often, their mindset regarding values, goals, and likely reactions is so strong that they don't even recognize that some of these might vary dramatically from one culture to the next. Consequently, they go it alone without even recognizing a missed opportunity for support. Clearly, the problem of mirror imaging must be given serious attention.

Yet a third challenge is actually creating the model. Models can take many forms, with different pros and cons, and selection almost always entails a compromise. In addition to the factors discussed above, other issues include data requirements vis-à-vis availability, user interface needs vis-à-vis user types, timeliness, and analyst familiarity with the associated analytic tools. Books can be written on this topic (we are in fact doing one ourselves) but the bottom line is this: anything can be modeled, but unless the characteristic of the model is well understood, the model will not necessarily be useful.

Independent of the model per se is the problem of populating and maintaining the model. There are a number of elements to this challenge: data availability, data uncertainty, data veracity, ISR characteristics, missing or inconsistent data, and specification of desired levels of confidence. For example, data may be available, but collection is difficult, costly, or time-consuming. Thus, compromises must be made. When certainty or uncertainty is not easily gauged, it may be possible to minimize the reliance on certainty by using models with known acceptable error bounds. The point is that the selection, instantiation, maintenance, and use of the model each come with their own set of constraints that must be considered when putting together a feasible and effective modeling strategy.

FUSION

Fusion is the process of bringing together tidbits of data to vet individual tidbits or to discern information not available from individual tidbits. The data corpus to be fused may comprise several forms of data: data of a similar nature, but collected at different times or places, data of different types, or data of the same or different types collected by different platforms or sensors.

Moreover, the data collection mechanism can vary. Data may have been deliberately collected for purposes of fusion, portions may have been collected based on tip-off, or collection of portions may have been serendipitous.

Regardless of the type of data and the collection means, the challenge is to exploit the data to its fullest potential. This generally requires something more than the raw data. As a minimum, it requires a mental model or a hypothesis to be confirmed or denied. In the case of a hypothesis, an analyst will attempt to identify clear discriminators between the hypotheses and will inject data into the various hypotheses until a clear decision is possible—i.e. a contradiction occurs with all but one hypothesis. In the case of a mental model the process is similar in principle, but less formal.

Advanced analysis employs this approach, but favors a third one when it is available—i.e., formal modeling, static, or when appropriate, dynamic. The advantages of such an approach, at least when it is effectively employed, are three-fold: rigor, traceability, and adaptability. However, as is indicated below, effective implementation and employment does not come for free.

Needs and Desires

What advanced analysis needs is an efficient and effective fusion process that 1) takes into appropriate consideration all the information available, 2) does not overburden operators with required interactions (in particular, actions that might be performed automatically), 3) provides an assessment of its performance on a specific problem, and 4) permits analysts to trace all results and override those they disagree with. Unfortunately, this is a classic example of a problem that appears easy to perform but proves incredibly difficult to solve.

Approach

Near-Term. In the near-term, advanced analysis will rely primarily on manual (highly interactive) fusion based on static models. These models will constitute, in essence, mappings between the activities to be observed and the signatures to be collected, and will support both information collection in support of fusion and fusion per se. Creation of these models will entail a process such as the following:

- For each key adversary activity (something the adversary absolutely has to do) and each general location and time, a tabulation of the different approaches that the adversary might take for the activity; i.e., the different "who, what, where, and when."
- For each alternative approach, a tabulation of the actions required.
- For each action, a characterization with respect to observables (action elements) and signatures (what the sensor would actually collect).

- For each signature, a specification of the sensors that could possibly collect it at the location of interest (taking into account field of view (FOV), line of sight (LOS), link budget, dwell, spatial resolution, and environmental noise). This would be derived automatically, employing the Blue ISR database and the National Signatures Program (NSP) signatures database.
- For each signature, 1) the probability that the signature would actually be emitted (actually, the probability that the action which would cause it will be executed), 2) the duration of the signature, 3) the probability that the signature, if emitted, would be collected by a particular sensor or platform in a nominal (but specified) interval, and 4) the probability that the signature would be emitted as a result of benign actions at a specific location type and time.

Collection planning. In support of a particular fusion case, the model created in this manner will be employed to identify the signatures to focus on, individually and in combination. These will be those that exhibited that highest (joint) probability of being detected and of being discriminated (from benign activities) at the particular location and time of interest.

The later point is a particularly important one. Analysts must never lose sight of the fact that signatures of interest, even seemingly damning ones, will rarely be unique to a single activity. Consider, for instance, several key constituents of homemade explosives—urea nitrate and nitric acid. Although it would be nice to conclude that the presence of their signatures was concrete evidence of an IED manufacturing activity, such a conclusion would be naive. A meaningful analysis would take into consideration the locale in which the signatures were collected. If it happened to have been a residential neighborhood, there is a excellent chance that something interesting has been discovered; however, if it is an industrial area, then little, if anything, can be concluded. The same sorts of arguments apply for signatures associated with equipment employed for nefarious activities, cultural signatures, functional signatures, and so forth.

Accordingly, the probability of discrimination must be estimated in planning collection and in conducting fusion. This will be done in either of two ways: via model-based estimation based on the best understanding of the collection environment and via real-time collection and comparison of specific signatures from the remaining background. In the former case, analysts will employ the best available information to characterize the locale of current interest in terms of its occupants and their activities, and will employ models such as the one above to determine the types and quantities of benign signatures that should be anticipated. In the latter case, analysts will attempt to qualify the background on the fly, as analysis progresses. This will involve analyzing the potentially nefarious signatures in terms of quantities, locations, and times of collection, and determining whether this characterization is consistent with the type of nefarious activities of interest or of benign activities that might be expected.

Once the collection needs and ancillary characterizations are defined, advanced analysts, in conjunction with intelligence collection managers, will employ this information to determine an effective multi-INT/fusion-based collection plan. Their planning approach will take into account cross-signature coordination needs, link budgets, and discrimination probabilities. The approach will be an extension of the current approach and would be joint and interagency as well as multi-INT, and multi-collection domain (i.e., space, air, ground, . . .). It would probably resemble the DARPA accelerated insertion of materials (AIM)/morphing aircraft structure (MAS) algorithm.

Fusion will involve the same sort of model as was employed for collection planning, but in an inverted fashion. In other words, the process would start with the signatures that were collected and identify from these the actions that likely produced them. The process would work something like this:

- The collection plan created above would be executed, signatures would be collected, and grouped according to location type/time.
- For each collection location type/time set, the appropriate portion of the functional model would be employed to determine the signatures, individual and combo, that would be expected from each action/observable.
- Some manner of matching scheme (there are many possibilities, including various types of Bayesian nets) would be employed to identify pairings/matches between signature sets from the model and the collected sets. Importantly, the matching scheme would take into proper consideration probabilities of detection and of discrimination.

The result would be a suggestion as to which specific nefarious activities were detected, and importantly, a statistics-based estimate of the confidence associated with the suggestion. Initially, this approach will be person-in-the-loop intensive. The tools would provide guidance to analysts, but analysts would be heavily involved every step of the way. Ultimately, however, the process would be automated.

Far-Term. In the far-term approach, analysts can expect a degree of automation at each step of the fusion process; collection plan development, fusion per se, and interestingly, even model development. Of course, analysts will still be required at every step, but their role will be that of developing the overall processes, tuning the processes, vetting results, and identifying, or at least vetting, needs for process and model updating, and working with recomposition and synthesis.

Challenges

Fusion, as described here, does not come easily. As is evidenced by current fusion activities, the development of the tools is expensive and time consuming, and the process of gaining acceptance is very difficult, for social and political as well as technical reasons. Moreover, except in the case of occasional but notable instances, the value added of technology-based fusion engines vis-à-vis tool-barren analysis has not been well demonstrated. This is not really surprising. Except within computer-based simulations—which are not always as pristine as one would like—it is very difficult to rigorously demonstrate the value-added of high-performance fusion. Consequently, as with many technologies, acceptance will likely not occur in one fell swoop, but gradually, as bits and pieces of the underpinning technologies find their way into accepted systems and processes.

ARGUMENTATION SUPPORT

A key feature of advanced analysis is the ability to rapidly form hypotheses relating to events or circumstances that cannot be directly observed, and then to marshal evidence to support or reject such hypotheses. In this way, a deeper understanding of the OE is obtained than is possible when observations remain "at the surface." Typically, posing a hypothesis requires the invocation of a model of some sort—either a mental model in the mind of the analyst based on training or experience, or a formal mathematical model in which the relationships between entities are explicit. Such a model enables surface observables to be linked to other entities of interest not directly observable so analysts can draw inferences (subject to the constraints of the model) about what is "really" going on. In the sciences, this process is routine and goes by the name of "experiment design." The experiment is constructed so that observed data is linked, via the model or hypothesis, to conjectured entities whose existence or properties cannot themselves be directly observed. Ideally, the observations then confirm or deny the validity of the hypothesis so that new "knowledge" is generated.

Argumentation support in advanced analysis applies this same technique, in a formal and repeatable way, to the analysis of intelligence data. Models are invoked, hypotheses concerning underlying causal connections are put forward, and the data is then collected and examined to determine the extent to which these hypotheses can be confirmed or denied. In an urban OE, the scope of available evidence is potentially quite large and the kinds of causal connections that may be of interest span the entire diplomatic, information, military, and economic (DIME)/PMESII spectrum. Further, these causal connections may, at times, require specialized knowledge or training not ordinarily within the experience of any given analyst or even among people of various headquarters. Further, the timeframe for such analysis can be quite short compared to the more leisurely pace of investigation in an academic laboratory. Finally, the fact that the adversary is intelligent and adaptive adds additional complexity and uncertainty. The following discussion identifies and discusses the need for this capability, identifies near- and far-term solution strategies, and discusses significant remaining challenges.

Needs and Desires

Advanced analysis' need for argumentation falls into six areas: taxonomy/ontology, argumentation templates, hypothesis creation, structured argumentation, interface to ISR, and validation metrics. Here, in brief, is what each of these entails:

> TAXONOMY/ONTOLOGY. The need here is for a standardized way in which to formalize or specify a pattern or type of argument. This is a meta-structure that sits above or behind a given argument and explains how its constituent parts (that is, the factual statements and their logical connections) go together to produce a convincing conclusion. The ability to formalize such a structure serves two important functions. First, it enables analysts to communicate in an unambiguous way about how their proposed argument will be assembled and how the evidence used will be marshaled to defend the conclusion. Second, it enables the automation of some of this work because the formal structure of the argument can be captured and analyzed in data structures.
>
> ARGUMENTATION TEMPLATES. Although the space of successful argumentation is large, the structure of most successful arguments falls within a fairly limited range. What varies from argument to argument is not its logical form but rather the specifics of the data produced in support of one or another constituent proposition. We might, therefore, imagine a system in which the major types of argumentation have been identified and assembled into a template library. This library would begin with a good set of well-known and understood examples but might then grow over time as new successful strategies were developed, identified, and stored for future reference. A priori, there is no reason why the process of argument template creation, identification, storage, and retrieval could not be partially or even fully automated.
>
> HYPOTHESIS CREATION. A hypothesis can be considered to be the intersection of two independent processes: (1) a model (either a mental model or a formal model), and (2) data to populate portions of the model in such a way that remaining values of model entities can be logically or mathematically inferred. The difficulty of hypothesis creation comes from both these contributors. However, the analyst may not have a model on hand that can help explain the observations. In that case, hypothesis creation must focus on generating such a model—a process that can be time-consuming and uncertain. In addition, the data to populate the model may not be readily available, for a number of

reasons: sensor limitations, sensor availability, denial and deception actions by the adversary, and so forth. It does not help to have a hypothesis if the data needed to confirm or deny it cannot be obtained in a timely manner and with the required confidence. Further, it is often the case that multiple hypotheses may account for the observations. Some sense of the breadth of coverage of the hypotheses under consideration is required and support is needed to help eliminate blinkered vision (that is, the consideration of only one or a few options based on the limited experience or bias of the analyst).

STRUCTURED ARGUMENTATION. Given a hypothesis, structured argumentation is the process of experimental confirmation or denial. The hypothesis identifies the model to be used and the data to be collected to populate the model so reliable inferences can be drawn. Structured argumentation then carries out this process on the particular problem at hand. Data sources are accessed, sensors are tasked, the resulting data (with its uncertainties and conflicts) is inserted into the logical framework, and degrees of confidence are computed and assessed. In some cases, for example, a probing action may be appropriate—that is, an action may be taken to stimulate adversarial response, which is then observed and used as evidence within the argumentation framework. Structured argumentation is also explicitly aware of the difference between statistical correlation on the one hand and causal connection on the other. The congruity of two events may point to a third, hidden event to which both are related rather than to a causal connection between the events themselves.

INTERFACE TO ISR. There is an ongoing need for a capability to task ISR collection capabilities in support of structured argumentation. The structure of the argument can be used to specify a variety of collection parameters: sampling intervals, precision, fusion techniques, cross-cueing, etc. Ideally, the hypothesis to be tested can be specified in enough detail that these tasking parameters can be automatically extracted and passed to the appropriate collectors. Further supporting such a vision is the ability to rapidly search existing archives. When the necessary data already exists, it can be found and used without the need to task scarce ISR resources.

METRICS FOR ASSESSMENT OF CONFIDENCE. Finally, a commander who will make a decision must understand with a level of confidence that he has made the correct decision. Sources of error or uncertainty must be explicitly identified, and their contribution to the overall assessment must be clearly and intuitively visible. A structured argumentation process can provide a firm theoretical and mathematical grounding for such estimates, and can help structure the collection process in such a way as to ensure that confidence thresholds have been met.

Approach

Near-Term. DARPA and its sister research and development (R&D) organizations have been actively pursuing a number of technologies addressing one or more of the requirement areas for structured argumentation. One that is particularly relevant is the GENOA[2] program, initiated in DARPA and now being pursued elsewhere. Supporting technology includes the use of intelligent agents, cognitive machine intelligence, associative memory, neural networks, pattern matching, Bayesian inference networks, and biologically inspired algorithms.

A key goal of GENOA is to assist analysts in accessing and searching very large, unstructured, and heterogeneous data sources. Evidence extraction and link discovery (EELD) has provided technologies and tools for automated discovery, extraction and linking of sparse evidence contained in large amounts of classified and unclassified data sources. These detection capabilities can extract relevant data and relationships about people, organizations, and activities from message traffic and open source data. By understanding or inferring how the analyst intends to use the information, the intelligent search engine can offload much of the routine work of query formulation and display of returned results. Ideally, it can even preemptively search and cache, so required data is pre-loaded, locally cached, and made rapidly available for analysis, thereby greatly reducing search latency. Early versions of a formalized structured argumentation approach have been successfully used to achieve this kind of capability. The argument pattern employed by the analyst, expressed as a template, permits inference of the type and characteristics of data needed to complete the argument (that is, to confirm or disconfirm the active hypothesis). In this connection, EELD has developed two promising techniques—learning patterns of activity and initiating the collection and characterization of documents for technology evaluations.

GENOA also addresses the issue of breadth and variety of hypothesis generation through a structured collaboration process involving human participants. Experts from a variety of fields are brought together within this virtual environment, and software monitors the interactions among the participants and suggests potential areas of weakness or omission in hypothesis "coverage" of the problem space. The latest generation of taxonomy/ontology languages has provided the technical framework within which a formal standard for specifying argumentation and hypothesis can emerge. In particular, this framework provides a robust infrastructure in which argumentation templates expressed as formal data structures can be stored, searched, merged, and populated. Early experience in GENOA is promising and provides a firm basis for a significant subset of the argumentation strategies needed by analysts—however, industry-accepted standards in this area do not yet exist.

Intelligent search- and pattern-matching algorithms now routinely incorporate mathematical and statistical techniques for dealing with the error, noise, uncertainty, and conflicting or missing data associated with argumentation. Bayesian analysis, using a Bayes net model, for example, allows uncertainty estimates for hidden variables to be inferred from downstream probabilistic observables. When such modeling is used, the commander can be provided with error bars indicating the level of confidence associated with recommendations and supporting evidence. Fuzzy logic, neural nets, and support vector machines are potentially applicable as well, but these approaches require extensive validated training data to calibrate their customized internal discrimination engines. The impact of false positives when such approaches are employed can be substantial in a stressful crisis environment.

Far-Term. A large number of active R&D projects have the potential to revolutionize this area. One of the most promising of these involves bringing to bear a genetic algorithm (GA) to perform a structured search through "hypothesis space." A hypothesis is the linking of model to data in such a way that observations have the potential, via an argumentation template, to confirm or disconfirm the hypothesized causal connection. The search process performed by the GA considers a very large number of models that, singly or in combination, might be used to explain some phenomena of interest or hidden variable. When the algorithm considers a proposed linkage and supporting argument, it evaluates the "ability to validate/likelihood of being able to validate" using models for ISR collection and historical database search results. Hypotheses with high likelihood of 1) explaining the data, and 2) being validated by an optimized collection strategy "survival" in the Darwinian contest are pursued (via collection and analysis) until they either produce a viable explanation or are discarded for one reason or another.

All of the essential pieces for such a "blue sky" vision have already been proved in laboratory R&D settings. The preferred approach, in the current state of research, involves intelligent agent "wizards." The analyst would interact with the wizard posing the top-level problem and tasking it to set about making progress as best he can. The wizard then autonomously begins the process of formulating hypotheses, selecting the most promising, formulating confirm/disconfirm argumentation strategies, assembling data both from databases and ISR capabilities, and determining which of the hypotheses appears to best "answer the question" posed by the analyst. During the course of this process, the wizard may return to the analyst to report intermediate results and/or ask for additional guidance (e.g., to resolve competing priorities). An analyst might have several such wizards active at once, and the analyst's job description becomes a kind of orchestra leader overseeing and performing ongoing quality control on the suite of active search agents.

Challenges

What are the potential "gotchas" that might slow progress in this area? Three difficulties cloud the future of the types of modeling discussed above:

dependence on other technologies, user acceptance, and validation. Here are our thoughts regarding these:

- DEPENDENCE ON OTHER TECHNOLOGIES. The near- and far-term technologies discussed above assume the existence of a variety of supporting technologies to furnish key components or functionality. These include continuing cost/performance hardware advances in computation, networking, and storage; multi-language capabilities to enable effective searches of unstructured data from many different sources; search capabilities (as described elsewhere); computer security, labeling, and assurance; continuing advances in ISR collection/exploitation capabilities, including accuracy, coverage, and timeliness; validated DIME/PMESII models, including models for economic, social, cultural, infrastructure, and political entities; seamless access to heterogeneous databases, including unstructured, GIS, and content-based retrieval of ISR archives; and visualization to permit rapid user assimilation of large amounts of related information from many data sources, including displaying levels of uncertainty.

- USER ACCEPTANCE. The technical approach (near- and far-term) described above will require dramatic changes to the current way of doing business, and may meet with a variety of kinds of resistance from the user community. As one example, analysts may not be used to thinking about their own reasoning processes in a structured way, and using a standardized taxonomy/ontology to capture the resulting logical structure. Initially it will appear to be an obstacle; it is only when such patterns have been identified, stored, and retrieved for appropriate use that their value will become apparent.

- VALIDATION AND UTILITY. The final challenge to be discussed here concerns how to validate the utility of the proposed technology. By definition, the types of events and entities that are of concern are uncertain, and often not directly observable. How, then, can the utility of these methods be formally demonstrated? Artificial test cases, where "ground truth" is known, have an artificial, cookbook quality that may be a far cry from the complexity of real-world operations. Further, even in the best of systems there will remain a degree of uncertainty. Indeed, one of the advantages of this approach is to bring uncertainty into the open for explicit consideration by the commander in the decision-making process. But what level of uncertainty is acceptable? When does increased certainty about uncertainty stop paying dividends, and start feeling more like an anchor than a balloon? These questions are difficult to answer in advance and in the abstract. It seems clear that as of the current state-of-the-art, there are still substantial effectiveness and efficiency gains to be had. At what point will the cost/benefit margin slope change? Again, that question can only be answered with actual experience under stressful operational conditions.

OPTIMIZATION

Aside from those technologies we now take for granted (word processing, spreadsheets, and so forth) one of the most important for advanced analysis is cavalierly referred to as optimization. This often unappreciated technology lies at the core of just about every process identified previously in this chapter—from content-based search (in which it can help with "tuning"), to rule development for automated categorization (for which it can develop the best rules subject to user criteria), to collection facilitation (for which it can develop plans that provide the best "bang per buck," in terms of collection versus resource)—and has a potential role in every element of advanced analysis. Also, interestingly, it is only within the last two decades that this enabler has matured to the point where it can support advanced analysis.

The challenge with optimization has always been two-fold: problem size and problem structure. The size problem revolves around the quantity of variables and constraints imposed by real-world problems. In the case of advanced analysis this requirement ranges from hundreds of variables (e.g., for simple plan sequencing) to many millions (e.g., for collection planning involving many platforms, sensors, and targets). Unfortunately, prior to the advent of modern algorithms and proliferation of high-power workstations, problems were limited, for the most part to between dozens and hundreds of variables; thus, there was a significant gap between capabilities and desires.

The situation with problem form was equally daunting. In the past, the only sizable problems that could be tackled were those that either conformed to certain convenient structures or those important enough from an application perspective to garner that attention of expert algorithm developers. In the latter case informal contests often evolved in which teams competed to develop the best algorithm in terms of answer quality versus run time, and application users wound up the big winners. Thanks to the advent and continuing refinement of what are termed evolutionary algorithms (because they tend to mimic Darwinian natural selection), things have changed. A competent operations researcher can now tackle real-world problems of previously intractable size confident in the knowledge that some manner of algorithm will be able to supply a useful—albeit not necessarily optimal—result.

What does this mean insofar as advanced analysis is concerned? Several important things come to mind. First, advanced analysts should be continually on the lookout for opportunities for optimization—cases in which optimization can improve their analysis. Also, given the wide range of possibilities, this will require training and familiarization. Specifically, advanced analysts must be made aware of what optimization can do in particular cases, how to specify their needs, and where to go to get these needs met. Second, advanced analysts should be made aware of the limits of optimization, and how this may negatively impact their analysis. These limits include (1) bounds on the quantity and quality of data collectable in support of a specific problem, and (2) run times needed to develop certain results. Aggressiveness on the part of analysts is generally good, but unwarranted optimism is not.

As anyone who keeps current with popular science knows, many astounding projections are being made regarding where optimization is headed. Between molecular computing, quantum computing, and new massively parallel computing architectures, it's just possible that some of these projections will eventually be realized. But in the meantime, advanced analysts should count on the capability of optimization growing just a bit faster than Moore's law—the algorithms and architectures will be advanced, as well as the basic chip capabilities. Thus, more and larger problems will become tractable.

ENABLERS OF ENABLERS

In addition to the technical enablers described above, there is also a category of lower-level enablers we have dubbed, for lack of a better name, "enablers of enablers." Although these are of less interest to analysts than the primary enablers, this section would be incomplete without at least introducing them.

COMPUTING INFRASTRUCTURE. The key enabler of enablers is the computing infrastructure. Analysts engaged in advanced analysis activities are faced daily with the challenges of rapidly producing accurate products useful to field commanders. They must have the tools and the infrastructure to streamline the process of marshalling evidence, aggregating data from disparate sources, and evaluating information that is in a constant state of flux. Moreover, the software and interface services provided by the computing infrastructure of the future must provide seamless collaboration—analyst to analyst, analysts to SME, and analysts to planner/decision maker—and must facilitate analyst activities in an ever more complex and time-urgent environment.

ANALYTIC INFRASTRUCTURE. The analytical infrastructure must provide instant access to applications, services, and data. The access to these facilities must be seamless and transparent—seamless, so the analyst will be able to call any application, service, or access any data with a single login; transparent so that data format and application compatibility issues are managed by the computer without human intervention. The analyst must be capable of combining data of different types, such as images, text, video, signals internal and external, and geospatial and temporal information to accomplish synthesis or conversely decompose an event into different data types for analysis (e.g., extract a sound track for processing) without needing to search for applications or services to perform the task.

DATA MARKUP SCHEMATA. At present it is a major task to prepare data for ingestion into many applications. XML is one approach to identifying structures within documents. XML is a meta-language because it does not specify either the tags or the semantics, leaving both to the user to define. There are thousands of application languages that have been developed through developer-added semantic constraints. Among the more popular are Really Simple Syndication (RSS) used to feed information such as news items over the Web, MathML used to describe mathematical notation and capture its structure and content, scalable vector graphics (SVG) for describing 2-dimensional static and animated graphics, and TalkML, a language for call center, mobile phone, and similar voice browsers. The XML family is indeed a major step forward in solving the data ingest problem; however, developing appropriate XML languages, tagging documents, and data files is a time-intensive process. There needs to be a service that enables nonprogrammers to construct and use XML languages.

HUMAN INTERFACE. Another area where improvement is needed is interface development. Current applications require a substantial amount of keyboard data entry and command selection from menus and palettes. The infrastructure of the future needs to be accessible through interfaces that recognize gestures, track eye movements, lip read, and understand speech. These components exist today. In fact, speech interfaces are common and embodied in many commercial applications, but major applications deploying an integrated interface have yet to be developed. For example, eye tracking using both reflectance methods and electro-oculography (EOG) have been demonstrated for virtual reality, video game, and applications for the physically disabled. Interfaces for the most part are still wedded to the keyboard and mouse. The integration of acoustic signal processing with visual information (lip-reading) for speech recognition is the subject of considerable research in academia and at companies like Intel and Microsoft. The advent of the Apple iPhone demonstrates some of the potential for gesture interfaces that enable seamless interaction with multiple applications.

Current client-server and Web-based infrastructures are unable to meet analyst needs for seamless and transparent access to applications and data. Distributed computing resolves some issues but current instantiations such as virtual private network (VPN) access to storage or application service providers are not dynamic and do not facilitate the scalable virtual organizations. What is needed is a high-performance "grid" computing environment that can provide secure and flexible resource sharing among dynamic, multi-institutional virtual organizations and that enables people and machines to work cooperatively and smarter. Resource sharing means that one user has direct access to computing facilities at another installation, not simply access to data. A virtual organization could be assembled anywhere and through sharing rules be provided immediately with all the tools and access to data needed to accomplish analysis. The concept of resource sharing is what separates grid computing from other forms of distributed computing. Working cooperatively is about an extension to grid computing called the semantic grid.

Cluster-Based Computing

In the future semantic grid computing environment, an analyst will not need to search for resources. All resources would be described; new ones would be automatically discoverable, and users would be connected with a minimum of negotiation and effort. Workflows to support the analytical processes, particularly for large virtual organizations, would be generated from process descriptions. The network would be self-healing; in the event of equipment or communications failures, the virtual organization would be maintained with minimal disruption. The grid environment would find people in transit and manage communities of interest in accordance with extant security regulations and procedures. The semantic grid takes care of mapping between concepts in different domains and facilitates queries across domains. The end result is that information is presented to users in the correct format with the correct visualization at the correct time.

Are these enabler of enabler technologies available to support our vision? Not quite, but things are moving ahead quickly. For instance, Web services have been providing loosely coupled software components with significant potential for enhancing the grid environment. The Open Grid Services Architecture has advanced the concept of using Web services within a grid computing environment and is responsible for specifying conventions and specifications. A variety of frameworks, e.g., Internet Reasoning Service, have been designed to enable applications to semantically describe and execute Web services. Such frameworks provide the development tools to devise analyst-friendly services, with the eventual goal being for analysts to describe a service needed in purely domain terms and to have a constructor service build and deploy the component. Other analysts would learn of the new service through the discovery service.

Software agent technology is being used by the military to enhance M&S. Considerable research is being undertaken to use software agents in the modeling of information operations and behavioral phenomena associated with military activities. A software agent is an autonomous or semi-autonomous goal-oriented software program, usually small, that performs specified tasks and provides its results to a user. For example, a search agent may periodically query some sources that its owner wants to monitor and provide reports of its findings in a format its owner desires. Such an agent simplifies the work of an analyst to periodically monitor a large number of sources for information on a specified topic. Embedded with appropriate artificial intelligence, agents can be a very powerful way to assist the analytical process, enabling the analyst to work through issues requiring cognitive skills.

The genome analysis research environment (GNARE) system at Argonne National Laboratories is a distributed network operating over the TeraGrid and Open Science Grid, which supports service-oriented science. GNARE periodically searches through worldwide DNA and protein databases to identify new or updated genomes. Upon finding data of interest it processes the data through several tools, and reports results to the scientific community. A semantic grid for intelligence analysis would similarly be proactive. It would continuously search data from conventional sources and assign sensors for data of interest to the active virtual organizations. Software agents designed to monitor snippets of data could autonomously join virtual communities and present what they have found to cue other agents to begin tasks such as recomposition or decomposition to reduce the analyst's workload and enable them to focus on problems requiring their cognitive skills.

WRAP-UP

As previous sections have emphasized, advanced analysis is sorely needed if we are to make headway against emerging, and even current threats. However, as has been shown here, advanced analysis does not come for free. It requires a range of critical enablers, and some of these are not yet ready for real-world use. The enabler discussions above are not, of course, comprehensive insofar as these requirements are concerned. As was pointed out at the onset, they are intended to provide a flavor of what is needed by focusing on key requirements. Reading between the lines, one can quickly identify a host of additional requirements, implicit and derived, that must be analyzed before beginning any manner of advanced analysis architecture definition.

In closing, an admonition is appropriate. Like computers themselves, computing infrastructure technology, and in turn computer-based enabler technologies, are driving forward at a rapid pace, and the enabler situation can be expected to change radically in the next few years. At some point, however, advanced analysts and the intelligence community must make a decision as to the way to go, and must "go for it." The indispensable variables at that point will be adaptability and extensibility. Whichever approach is taken, the structure must be ready and capable of accepting new technologies and paradigms as they become available. To do otherwise could seriously diminish the future advanced analysis enterprise.

This marks the end of the explanation of the cognitive elements of advanced analysis. As the reader can surmise, advanced analysis has a broad approach as well as one that is deep in thought and in using technology to help people think. With this background in mind, the next chapter presents a system of thought. This system is the culmination of all that the book has discussed, as well as providing a philosophy of advanced analysis, a synthesis of ideas, and implications that include doctrine, organizations, training and education, materiel, leadership, and people.

Part III

System of Thought

20

On a System of Thought

We are now ready to synthesize the thoughts into a whole, provide a philosophy of advanced analysis, as well as provide readers with some implications. The first part of this final chapter deals with the philosophy of advanced analysis. Then the chapter provides a synthesis of the big ideas in the book before drawing the reader's attention and deep thinking into some of the important implications.

While you have been musing through these many pages, in reality you have been slowly introduced to a new system of thought for dealing with a particular challenging and perplexing problem. That is, providing the thinking capable of competing with and winning a war of wits against insurgents using irregular warfare in complex terrain including, of course, the most difficult OE of all—the urban setting. Renowned thinker David Bohm helps us think about a system of thought and its constant change and motion:

> Similarly, thought is a system. . .A system is constantly engaged in a process of development, change, evolution, and structure changes, and so forth, although there are certain features of the system which become relatively fixed. . .We have some structure in thought as well—some relatively fixed features.[1]

Dr. Bohm believed that the system of thought influencing the world was incoherent because people choose to think and live in fragmented ways. What Bohm argues is for people to realize the natural, holistic, and connectedness of all nature and that all humans should view and live in the world in a similar fashion. Author Michael Talbot provides some more interpretation of David Bohm's thinking with the following passage:

> Indeed, Bohm believes that our almost universal tendency to fragment the world and ignore the dynamic interconnectedness of all things is responsible for many of our problems, not only in science but in our lives and our society as well.[2]

But suffice it to say, Dr. Bohm's point that is most relevant to this book about the incoherence of thought and his proposed new system of thought recognizes the impending nature of the system even as it is coming into being. In this way, we are laying the seeds for change even as we are bringing forth a new system of thought. In addition, *Intelligence Analysis: How to Think in Complex Environments* strives for coherence, not on a grand, global scale espoused by Dr. Bohm, but in a much narrower field of knowledge—intelligence analysis.

While some parts of this chapter are not new, the notion of pulling the pieces of intelligence analysis into a new system of thought is different. In addition, providing a philosophy of advanced analysis is a new step to help intelligence people and commanders move with assurance and confidence into a dangerous, nebulous, and rapidly changing future.

PHILOSOPHY OF ADVANCED ANALYSIS

So why must we have a philosophy of advanced analysis? The answer is straightforward. Anything of value must have at its core a philosophy. Advanced analysis possesses such a philosophy; it influences all of characteristics and cognitive activities. A philosophy of analysis is the bedrock upon which the system of thought is erected; it is a powerful beacon of light in a stormy sea to help analysts in their darkest and most trying moments, as it is something they can turn to for advice, nurturing, and reemphasis of what is important. The philosophy of advanced analysis gives meaning to the strong currents of energy coursing through the "veins" of analytic thought. Through advanced analysis the twin engines of knowledge advantage—*imagination* and *innovation*—grow in strength and perspective, if people recognize their importance and nurture their ability to come forth and influence thought.

Advanced analysis has a positive purpose. That is, advanced analysis provides commanders and their subordinates with knowledge sufficient to think, plan, decide, and act faster than their opponent, regardless of the difficulty of the OE and capabilities of the foe. Similarly, intelligence collection must also have a specific purpose or purposes, in the case of IW or COIN operations in a large urban setting. Advanced analysis provides collection with the positive energy of purpose and a pointed, specific driving force, and it makes sense out of what collection produces, thereby sustaining the positive energy connections with which it started. As such, advanced analysis provides meaning to the outputs of analytically driven intelligence collection. It is for knowledge that advanced analysis exists—knowledge for gaining understanding, making decisions, anticipating the enemy's actions, and wresting the initiative from him.

Mercifully, this discussion of philosophy will be short. Arguably, a philosophy of advanced analysis could be an entire book in its own right. For the purposes of this book, however, the philosophy of advanced analysis is but one of the essential elements of a system of thought. But, as a disclaimer, this philosophy is limited in scope. That is, the philosophy underpinning advanced analysis orients on the tactical and operational levels of war and intelligence analysis to support decision makers who are either planning, preparing, or actually fighting against insurgents and irregulars in large urban settings. It is beyond the scope of this work to present a philosophy of strategic intelligence, regardless of how much it is needed.

For the purpose of our inquiry, philosophy is "a set of ideas or beliefs relating to a particular field or activity."[3] We want to think critically about urban COIN and IW and espouse an influencing philosophy that affects all intellectual activity coming forth from the cognitive efforts of intelligence analysts. In this light, advanced analysis is a *basic branch of knowledge* that does have a philosophical foundation with which to think about and use such knowledge. The philosophy of advanced analysis has several parts; each will receive some discussion. These parts are *propositions*, *elements*, *principles*, and *axioms*.

Some philosophical propositions underpin advanced analysis. Please recall that a proposition is the act of offering or suggesting something to be considered, accepted, adopted, or done.[4] Thus, these propositions, while important for the philosophy of advanced analysis, are thereby important for the optimum functioning of advanced analysis. The important propositions underpinning advanced analysis include the following:

- Intelligence analysis always supports leaders' decision-making as its top priority.
- The indirect approach operates against the enemy's network and its supporters.
- Specific knowledge and thinking are required to win in conflicts with irregular warriors, insurgents, and terrorists.
- Analysts know the culture or find and employ people who do to gain advantages.
- One, all, or a mixture of five kinds of observables must always drive collection.
- The struggle for initiative is the preeminent battle in an urban COIN or IW operation.

- A war of wits is difficult and is related to friendly, enemy, and host nation "will."
- Advanced analysis creates advantages for commanders—*initiative, decision, knowledge, position, freedom of maneuver* (in all domains including information), *technology, tempo,* and *momentum.*
- Advanced analysts must think like the enemy to win the war of wits.
- Aggressive thinking is a necessity for winning a war of wits.
- Truth changes, particularly in an urban OE.
- Analysts must tell collection people the specifics on which they want concentration.
- Relationships are important and must be pursued and understood.
- The OE is visible and invisible.
- Analysts must always respect the enemy—he is smart, adaptive, and flexible.
- Synthesis brings a degree of closure to the actions of advanced analysis.
- Uncertainty cannot be eradicated, but it can be lowered.
- Risk is a constant owing to unpredictability, volatile variables, and the sheer energy and change of an urban OE. Uncertainty is also a constant owing to a rapidly changing, complex environment. Knowledge assuages the negative impacts of both.

Any philosophy has *elements,* and the philosophy of advanced analysis is no different. Elements are the parts comprising a whole that is the philosophy of advanced analysis.

- *People* are the most important parts of this philosophy. This is particularly true in both counterinsurgencies and operations against irregular forces. Of course, the populace and their political leaders are preeminent in such struggle, as they are the prizes, so to speak, over which the struggle occurs. Intelligence analysts always keep their minds focused on people—themselves, enemy, populace, host nation government, interagency, and neutrals.
- *Organizations* are another element of philosophy. The organizations in which analysts operate are chock full of a wide variety of cultures that influence how people think and work. The enemy has organizations too, but they are most often networks. Thus the shape, form, functions, and processes of organizations are important to each advanced analyst. In addition, analysts work in an organization and depend on other organizations to help their analytic efforts. In this regard, analysts have a personal philosophy of aggressive thought, collaboration, and sharing within their organization and presuppose, indeed depend upon, other organizations possessing a similar philosophy.
- Advanced analysis has *14 elements;* their definitions appeared earlier in the book and do not need to be repeated. On a philosophical note, the

elements of advanced analysis are not sacrosanct. They merely provide a starting point for discussion and improvements. The philosophy of advanced analysis will always allow additions or deletions to these fourteen elements. The philosophy calls for a constantly improving concept of advanced analysis and encourages all analysts to seek its improvement. These cognitive elements work best in combinations, as rarely will a single element work most effectively by itself. The complexity and knowledge involved when using these elements requires a variety of SMEs and machines to assist advanced analysts.

- *Wargaming* is an important philosophical element of advanced analysis. In a philosophical sense, when one wargames, it is with an understanding that the United States is in an interactive struggle and that no outcomes of collisions or intersections with the enemy can be predicted with accuracy. Engaging in wargaming means the analysts' or the organizations' philosophy recognizes that U.S. forces will not always have the initiative, the enemy will do unexpected things, the enemy can and will surprise us, and he cannot and will not be boxed into a stereotype of constant inferiority to U.S. military forces. Wargaming also demonstrates the belief in and importance of friction (unexpected chance events). Wargaming helps the analyst understand the possibilities of second- and third-order effects, the influence of sensitive variables, and possible windows of opportunity in which the variables might influence opposing sides of a conflict and helps them anticipate the enemy's moves and countermoves and the ascendancy of "butterfly" effects. Wargaming is a vital aspect of seeking and fighting for the initiative, and its use posits the importance of surprise, chance, enemy options, and the ominous presence of friction.
- Advanced analysis and commanders depend on *knowledge*. That said, the philosophy of advanced analysis recognizes the difference between and among data, information, and knowledge. Because of the importance of knowledge, the philosophy of advanced analysis recognizes its preeminent position in the hierarchy of needs that enable advanced analysis to be successful. This means analysts must think about their access to, gathering, and use of data and information. It means analysts must set conditions for developing knowledge in fluid, future situations. The philosophy also puts forth the proposition that data transform into information through human cognition and machine work, and information transforms into knowledge through the unique human cognitive function of synthesis.
- As another element of the philosophy of advanced analysis, *technical tools* contribute to the analytic mission. Thus, advanced analysts must be proficient in and use technical tools. When they do not have either the time or expertise, they must look to external knowledge environment SMEs to assist in efforts that require sophisticated tools,

scientific expertise, and more time than they possess. Technical tools will always change with advances in technology; therefore, analysts must stay abreast of technological change and view finding and learning to use new tools as a constant renewal effort.

- *Analytic condition-setting* is, as discussed earlier, vital to successful analytic mission accomplishment. In this regard, analysts have a philosophy for how to think about a constantly changing OE, changing roles and missions, changing command decision-making, and changing knowledge requirements. Thus, analysts always look ahead and set conditions for success. While the analyst is not directly responsible for any of the three kinds of analytic condition-setting, they must aggressively engage in setting conditions upon which their success depends—developing data architectures, sensor architectures, and knowledge architectures. Much of this work occurs in the military decision-making process and becomes part of future plans and operations.

- Providing *specific guidance to collection people,* enterprise analysts, and VKE SMEs is an essential element in the philosophy of advanced analysis. People work better when they know and understand what the analyst needs and where and on what he or she wants their attention focused. Personal involvement and direction by analysts to people they cannot physically see is acceptable and fits with individual and organizational elements of the philosophy of advanced analysis. The philosophy calls for assisting those in need in collaborating and sharing ideas, engaging in red-teaming, conducting organized debates, and performing serious wargaming to mitigate errors in critical thinking.

Every philosophy has an *organized set of interrelated ideas or principles.* Advanced analysis is no exception. Its principles are

- Influence the enemy's thoughts, planning, and decisions.
- Influence the populace so they do not support the enemy.
- Disambiguate the environment to make its activities visible.
- Aggressively seek engagement with the enemy's source of power—his network.
- Seize and sustain the initiative through anticipatory analysis and pre-emptive action.
- Seek analytic and collection synergy.
- Use an indirect approach—affect the enemy's network supporters.
- Recognize inherent complexity in urban OE and use it for creating advantages and mitigating both risk and uncertainty.
- Know and understand the enemy, the culture, and the infrastructure.
- Use combinations of five kinds of observables.

- Seek and work with up-to-date baselines of three types—technical, cultural, and functional.
- Develop a close partnership with collection specialists.
- Use an organized and disciplined VKE, when necessary.
- Call upon red-teaming for help with critical thinking.
- Use cultural and technical indigenous SMEs when possible.

As the last aspect of the philosophy of advanced analysis, axioms are important. In this effort, an *axiom* is "a self-evident and necessary truth, or a proposition whose truth is so evident at first sight that no reasoning or demonstration can make it plainer."[5] The axioms of the philosophy of advanced analysis are

- To win, discern how the enemy thinks about how U.S. analysts and commanders think about him.
- To find the enemy, confirm where he is and entrap him.
- To understand the enemy, verify he is performing anticipated activities.
- To understand the enemy's background, discern from whence he came, when he came, and why he came.
- To understand with whom the enemy is close, identify his family, acquaintances, and friends.
- To understand how the adversary functions now or in the past, find his business ties.
- To understand the enemy's personal beliefs and motives, discern his religious activities and political inclinations.
- To anticipate the enemy's activities and determine his strengths and weaknesses and how he thinks about them.
- To understand the enemy's strengths and weaknesses, learn from the enemy himself and the people who know him.
- To take advantage of the milieu where both friendly and enemy operate, understand the culture.
- To win the struggle for the initiative, discern what it means to the enemy.
- To beat the enemy by denying him the initiative, anticipate what he is likely to do next and in so doing, attack his intent.
- To defeat the enemy's goals, know his criteria for success.
- To desynchronize the enemy's plans, understand what conditions he must set and disrupt or desynchronize this process.
- To win the information war, aggressively attack the enemy's use of that domain.
- To gain a decision advantage, learn how the enemy thinks, perceives, and makes decisions and then attack or manipulate these capabilities.
- To defeat the enemy's thinking, decisions, and plans, outwit and deceive him.

- To defeat the enemy, use an indirect approach—find, track, and attack or manipulate his network support and condition-setting.
- To impose the friendly will upon the enemy, understand what it means from the enemy's perspective, discern elements of his will, and then design culturally, technically, and situationally feasible ways to attack, or manipulate those elements.

SYNTHESIS OF IDEAS

The absolute need to improve thinking is not an isolated problem at the low tactical levels of command. What this book asks the reader to consider involves the thinking of intelligence analysts at all levels of thought, operation, and command. Additionally, the book suggests the absolute need for commanders to learn the thinking of advanced analysis as well as they learn other combat and noncombat functions. This is a leader's C^2 challenge. Thought is surely a form of engaging in and winning conflict and competition of all kinds. But, analysts should not and cannot be left on their own to think about the challenges that confront them.

So, as a first and foremost conclusion, advanced analysis is a leadership challenge. How well analysts think and contribute to the conflict and in particular the commander's decision-making depends upon the guidance, mentoring, and support of intellectually strong leaders. Leaders of all walks of life need schooling and mentoring to at least understand the precepts of advanced analysis and to know the capabilities of their advanced analysts to perform advanced analysis. In addition, we face an intelligence system challenge in that all analysts, regardless of location or analytic function, need to learn to perform advanced analysis, as it is the strongest and most essential beam in the house that is the totality of ISR. All levels, people, and organizations of the U.S. military intelligence analysis functional area and field of knowledge need improved thinking processes; advanced analysis provides the conceptual wherewithal to do so.

Intelligence Analysis: How to Think in Complex Environments advocates the pressing requirement to train and educate the analytic force, their supervisors, and to a sufficient extent, combat commanders, and operations officers for understanding advanced analysis and its underpinnings. What will the benefits be with such an improvement in thinking? Four benefits come to mind.

- Improved thinking will help analysts and commanders *anticipate the enemy's intent* and the actions (condition-setting) he must take to implement his intent. This improvement will lead to seeking, finding, and sustaining the initiative, which, according to many great theorists (Mao, Galula, Trinquier, Kitson) is essential to winning any insurgency. With the initiative, the commander has options, such as preempting, using more ISR to test a hunch or hypothesis, or presenting confusing activities to alter the state of thinking in the enemy commander's mind. In this regard, improved thinking of the kind this book advocates will help commanders and staffs design activities to influence an adversary's actions, manipulate or influence his thoughts and decisions, and be a step ahead of him, thereby commandeering and sustaining the initiative across a wide variety of domain activities and actions.

- Improved thinking will help U.S. commanders and staffs *understand the culture* they are working in and learn to use its strangeness and subtleties to create advantages. In this respect, using the culture for advantages is an active, positive, and thus preferred force, while only understanding enough of the culture to avoid offending people is essentially a neutral force. Continuing, advanced analysis will bring increased understanding about a host populace that shelters an insurgent's motives. It will help analysts and commanders understand possible outcomes of activities to thwart insurgent and terrorist attacks and how to assess those outcomes.
- In addition, improved thinking will help analysts understand the *decay of actions and effects* and help them create altered or new effects to supplant those that are either dead or decaying. It will also help them understand how links, patterns, trends, and knowledge decay and how such decay affects each and every type of each action.
- Improved thinking will help U.S. intelligence analysts understand and *sense how the enemy will adjust and morph* and cause entropy within the enemy's decision-making activities. It is a slowdown and confusion in the enemy's mind and decision processes that the friendly analyst and commander strive to create.

Improving thinking through advanced analysis should be one of the most serious friendly short- and long-term training and education goals. Such thinking cannot be relegated to happenstance. Instead, all cognitive elements in analytic thinking need to improve via well-resourced and dedicated learning to develop advanced analysis as a skill, a philosophy, and, even more importantly, a method to determine "how to think" about an extraordinarily challenging problem. Specifically, advanced analysis training must improve our analysts' cognition of the relational aspects of everything they do, touch, or think about. All of us know relationships exist and are powerful, yet we cannot see or touch them. Frequently, analysts will engage the enemy and the civilian populace in a struggle involving invisible relationships. To help them understand this abstraction, consider nature. Nature consists of webs of relationships. Linkages connect the webs and show up in our world as patterns, networks, and connections. Similarly, to understand the enemy's networks better than we do today, the thought processes of U.S. intelligence analysts should mimic nature and emulate its natural coherencies, relationships, and strengths in manifestations of the network and its activities in the human mind. The ordinary cobweb serves as a useful example of unity and relationship in nature.

Consider that a cobweb's constituent parts are cells; cells connect and relate to each other physically and abstractly—physically by way of connections (webs and gossamers) and abstractly by way of relationship and purpose. Each cell contributes to the purpose of the whole web. But a cell's strength lies in its interconnectedness with other cells as part of the whole. If a cell breaks or weakens, the cobweb loses either proportionate or disproportionate strength. If cells remain linked, the cobweb has strength— stronger together as a whole than as a single cell or the simple sum of cells.

Along this line of thought, analysts must know how the enemy's networks operate, hide, exist, and morph in the cultures in which they find sanctuary and in the relationships (e.g., link to cell) the networks depend upon. For insurgents to survive and flourish, the populace must either actively or passively aid or abet them. It follows that to use the culture to gain such advantages, intelligence analysts must know the culture in which they function in sufficient depth to understand nuances and subtleties of the actions, transactions, interactions, and behaviors of the portion of the population supporting the enemy network (either directly or indirectly). It is not sufficient for analysts to know the culture well enough to cope; analysts must know the culture well enough to use its cultural vagaries to develop advantages. In the abstraction of duality, *the local population's support, while an enemy strength, can also be a vulnerability and constitute the enemy's Achilles heel of their networks, decisive points, and key nodes and cells.*

Thinking also has to go into the abstract world of information and thought to be of use in COIN operations in large urban settings. In this respect, advanced analysts learn to understand the power of information— it is the means to power. It is through information that hearts and minds are won or lost. It is through information that commanders can lose a fight even after winning a tactical but physical battle. It is through information that commanders manage risk and reduce uncertainty sufficient to make decisions and execute. Information fuels thought, and thought fuels information in never-ending, spinning, entwining circles of interaction, whose resultant energy, velocity, and power increase with access to and the skillful use of information.

One of the most important implications from this book is that intelligence analysts must assess outcomes of information activities quickly after inception and execution. Unfortunately, assessment of outcomes of activities and effects in the information domain is difficult to perform. Thus, to work with the information domain, thinking has to consider tangible and intangible actions and effects and measure outcomes to adjust activities and alter decisions. Without such intellectual rigor, commanders and government leaders will never know if their intended audience or target perceives policies, media broadcasts, and explanations for activities correctly and whether these activities actually make a difference.

As a recurring theme in *Intelligence Analysis: How to Think in Complex Environments*, analysts learn to *think like the enemy through their own intellects and those of cultural role players,* not only at low level of command and operations, but also at higher levels. Thinking like the enemy is particularly important in planning, wargaming, execution, assessments, and adjustment. Owing to its difficulty and the human propensity to fall into logic traps, the advanced analyst learns to habitually *employ red team people, indigenous SMEs, and the SMEs of a VKE* to help with the act of thinking to ensure that it is as objective as possible in a subjective world. In *Intelligence Analysis: How to Think in Complex Environments*, we find this skill to be vital and part of all planning, execution, and assessment operations. Thinking like the enemy must be more than just saying that it was "done in our heads." To think like the enemy, intelligence analysts vigorously and purposefully avoid mirror imaging and oversimplifying complex situations. They purposefully set out to improve their thinking and to attack their own intellectual weaknesses—in this respect they defeat their own thoughts and planning, which is similar to Klein's pre-mortem notion.[6] To assist in this difficult effort, advanced analysts use indigenous people to think, decide, and act like the enemy and to be brutally candid in wargaming. In addition, the analyst realistically identifies the enemy's goals, objectives, strategies, resources, constraints, strengths, vulnerabilities, will, intent, and views and how he thinks. Even the most cellular, distributed enemy will depend upon and engage in a similar thought process when attempting to perform meaningful operations to support his goals. Additionally, even the most flattened, networked enemy will engage in condition-setting to plan and execute his daily activities and operations as well as to prepare for and execute his attacks and other operations. These thoughts provide the means to power over the enemy not directly, but through a gaping opening in their "back door."

By now, the reader should have concluded that while vitally important and powerful in itself, advanced analysis takes a team effort to be at maximum proficiency. Individuals can use advanced analysis whether they are isolated or if a support team is available. Advanced analysis provides powerful cognitive skills to think through problems and to develop and execute plans and actions. By itself, in isolation, advanced analysis is far better than traditional ways of thinking. But, to maximize its potential, advanced analysis depends upon collaboration and working with knowledge experts and SMEs.

Advanced intelligence analysis is abstract and creative on one hand but grounded in the physics, people, and relationships of specific places and neighborhoods on the other. Contradictions between theory and on-the-ground reality exist; advanced analysts work diligently to satisfy or overcome contradictions. Out of this challenging machine and mental work a new synthesis arises that is a combination of theory and reality. It helps people to understand accurately the shifting sands that are the culture, neighborhood, enemy, variables, and operating environment. This means U.S. forces fight the enemy's network with good minds, a network philosophy of moving quickly after being focused by fast decisions, all the while employing a variety of lethal and nonlethal tools to adversely affect the enemy while ensuring minimal damage to the populace and their belongings.

The demand for high-quality knowledge and its corollary provision of the means to power through understanding of the OE and its essential elements to lower uncertainty and mitigate risk signals a need for a significant change in how the U.S. military and the intelligence community (IC) provide information support to tactical and operational-level units. Traditionally left to fend for themselves, tactical and lower level operational units sometimes have trouble sorting out the complexities of the OE during actual time on the ground and when passing knowledge along during unit transitions. In the past, commanders and their organizations made do in their planning and decision-making cycles with few real experts, except in certain fortunate circumstances where resident experts were available to provide specific required knowledge. Most of the time, however, lower level units have been on their own when it came to accessing great minds and knowledge experts. This situation shows signs of changing and must expand rapidly to be of assistance to the forward-deployed analyst.

The knowledge and experience residing in the minds of deployed personnel may restrict any given commander's knowledge base and can be understandably narrow. No one could possibly have the kind of expertise needed in every given decision-making situation given the fluidity of modern urban OEs, the potential for unintended consequences, the complexity in full motion, and a world of constantly changing situational variables. Arguably, the quality of knowledge in a deployed headquarters improves with time as people learn more about their OE; unfortunately, this unspoken, embedded knowledge often departs with people as units rotate in and out of an OE.

Nonetheless, after all the excuses such as "Tactical units have never had the wherewithal to connect with world-class minds to work on their knowledge challenges," a stark fact remains. The lack of access to cultural, technical, infrastructure, collection, and counterinsurgency expertise is debilitating to decision processes and situational understanding. A corollary lack of suitable mentoring accentuates this shortfall as new units and personnel rotate in and out of contested areas. Unfortunately, the National Training Center (NTC), 29 Palms, and the Joint Readiness Training Center (JRTC) provide only limited intelligence analysis mission rehearsal for intelligence analysts preparing to deploy to combat situations in urban settings. Thus, analysts remain firmly wedded and dependent to on-the-job training, discovery learning through trial and error, and pick-up strategies once they arrive in country. This preparedness methodology must change by adding extensive, realistic mission rehearsal training to learn and employ advanced analysis.

In most OEs—which are unforgiving of inexperience and knowledge shortfalls for any number of reasons—mission transition is dangerous in a variety of functional areas but in none more so than intelligence analysis. Part of this danger can be mitigated with preparatory training at home station or at mission rehearsal locations such as 29 Palms and the NTC. But mission rehearsal for intelligence analysts and collection specialists remains curiously and sadly inadequate. Let us examine what this conclusion means.

As one deficiency, intelligence analysts and collection experts do not have an adequate data environment that replicates realities they will face on the ground in the objective area to prepare them for the existing OE. In addition, they are not armed with the fundamentals of advanced analysis and its precepts. They do not work against adequate replications of enemy networks enmeshed in an urban OE to the extent required for "hitting the ground running." There is no M&S that allows individual analysts and collection people to learn new skills like analytic condition-setting, searching for sensitive variables and windows of opportunity, wargaming for the initiative, or seeking and finding the enemy condition-setting activities. As an obvious conclusion, deploying intelligence people (in particular analysts and collection specialists) need home station and CTC mission rehearsal training that includes the use of advanced analysis to perform urban ISR roles and missions.

Furthermore, national intelligence systems do not provide specific enough data, information, or knowledge to help on-the-ground tactical commanders make fast, effective decisions (with a prominent exception in signals intelligence and geospatial intelligence). Over time, the reason for this inability of national intelligence to support commanders on the ground has been attributed to the inability of the system to meet the exacting standards for knowledge commanders on the ground impose. This problem has been partially mitigated by emplacing forward deployed teams from various intelligence agencies. This has been a very positive step in the right direction. But distance, organizational location and unfamiliarity with a culture should not preclude "droves" of smart analysts from providing "direct" or "general" support to both advanced analysts and commanders forward deployed in objective areas. These direct support analysts could perform many analytic jobs that forward-deployed analysts need but do not have time for. Examples of such work include (1) starting baselines or keeping baselines current, (2) performing other database chores, (3) setting conditions for future operations, (4) exploring analytic mysteries, (5) anticipating knowledge, sensor, and data requirements, (6) searching for and preparing knowledge for ingestion by commanders and analysts, (7) detailed wargaming, and (8) red-teaming. Commanders need decision support to manage risk and to reduce uncertainty that only focused, current, and actionable knowledge can bring, but they must have such knowledge quickly and it must be accurate, timely, specific, easy to understand (clarity), and relevant to the particular situation.

Commanders also need help in sorting data; in performing data analysis, statistical analysis, and visualization; in determining the truthfulness of data; and in data mining for trends, patterns, and other relationships. Commanders need people who can engage in the more difficult elements of advanced intelligence analysis (i.e., semiotic, anomaly, tendency, cultural, and aggregation analysis) that typical staffs are not trained to produce. Commanders need help from world-class minds in anticipating an enemy's moves and discovering his efforts to deceive friendly forces. Commanders need assistance in designing creative ways to use commercial, off-the-shelf sensors against a nearly invisible enemy enmeshed in a culture. They need intelligence support that is sufficiently agile to refocus their efforts to other functional elements of a shifting environment in the blink of an eye. Finally, commanders need access to a continually changing breadth and depth of expertise owing to the constantly changing OE, changing missions, and corresponding changing knowledge requirements for decision-making, and they need to interact with such expertise quickly and directly.

Analysts who work against insurgents and irregulars in urban OEs are aggressive and activist by nature. They constantly engage in a chess game of wits with insurgents and the populace that supports them. Intelligence analysts in their new roles and missions take the mental fight to the enemy and other competitors. As such, they become an action and operational arm of a weapon system that is ISR. The aggressive, activist, advanced analyst in this schema pointedly takes on and purposefully competes with the enemy as he thinks, plans, decides, acts, and seeks feedback. The analyst who leads this war of wits is first and foremost a thinker, a person who knows how to find or develop knowledge and who uses M&S and synthetic gaming environments to discern possible enemy COA. Activist intelligence analysts often lead operations as they study and anticipate enemy activities, guide collection to confirm or deny their hypotheses/hunches, and work with machines and a VKE to confirm or deny their hypotheses. They work hard to anticipate the enemy's thoughts and actions and deny or manipulate those thoughts and perceptions to seek entropy (a slowing of the enemy's decision processes as the friendly decision cycle gains in speed).

Advanced analysts have a deep understanding of their knowledge and cognitive shortfalls. They understand the impracticality, indeed the impossibility, of attempting to know every pertinent aspect of operating in a volatile, fluid urban OE. They realize they cannot fully understand and use all 14 elements of advanced analysis to a perfect state of proficiency. Thus, to find knowledge, obtain advice, and provide expertise not resident in forward-deployed unit staffs, they seek help from analytic overwatch, analytic self-organization swarming, and through the good offices of a VKE and its knowledge brokers.

Modern advanced analysts understand traditional, nontraditional, technical, and low-technology analytic methods and techniques for assisting the analytic process. Not all solutions or aids for thinking are "high tech." Some involve age-old reasoning, such as the dialectic and critical thinking skills that great thinkers and theorists have been espousing and using for centuries. Regardless, the advanced intelligence analyst understands the goal—that is, the rapid transformation of data into information and information into actionable knowledge for command decision-making—and doing it faster than the enemy and other competitors. The goal seeks to attain and sustain a knowledge advantage. In essence, developing and providing high-value knowledge to a skilled leader will enable him or her to seek, find, and sustain not only a knowledge advantage but also an initiative advantage, which forces the competitor to recognize his disadvantages and to morph as the analyst desires.

IMPLICATIONS

Implications have to be a part of any synthesis. They form the bridge between the preceding thoughts in *Intelligence Analysis: How to Think in Complex Environments* and recommendations explained in the closing thoughts. At this stage in our intellectual journey, a few implications emerge as most important, warranting the reader's attention and consideration. These implications are as follows.

Doctrine

Doctrine must include, elucidate, and expand upon the themes and thoughts of advanced analysis. Doctrine must provide the detailed concepts and underpinnings for a common way of thinking about and executing intelligence operations. It is through doctrine that force developers and trainers will have the wherewithal and understanding to design organizations, training, and materiel to bring advanced analysis into being. Advanced analysis doctrine needs to permeate across all combat functions and seep vertically and deeply into even the lowest tactical levels of command and war. Doctrine (the broad capstone doctrine as well as specific functional doctrine) must adopt and explain specific aspects of advanced analysis:

1. It must include and explain the philosophy of advanced analysis.
2. It must provide for the presence and activities of very aggressive intelligence analysts.
3. Doctrine must recognize intelligence operations as a war-fighting function, as ISR is a weapons system.

4. Doctrine must explain the 14 elements of advanced analysis and how one uses them to help think, plan, decide, act, assess, and modify. These elements are: *decomposition, critical thinking, link, pattern, trend, anticipatory, technical, anomaly, tendency, cultural, semiotics, aggregation analysis, recomposition,* and *synthesis.*

5. Doctrine must recognize the importance of wargaming for the initiative among many "players" on a field of strife in a busy urban setting. This is multipair wargaming.

6. Doctrine must recognize the importance of the initiative particularly in IW and COIN operational situations in urban OE and how its possession leads to advantages for exploitation such as decision, position, freedom of movement or maneuver, knowledge, decision, tempo, momentum, and use of technology.

7. Doctrine must ingrain and instantiate five kinds of observables—technical, cultural, functional, situational, and biometric—for use in complex OE.

8. Doctrine must acknowledge and explain the presence of complexity theory in its lexicon and thoughts. In particular, doctrine must explain the presence and influence of sensitive variables and windows of opportunity; the butterfly effect of inputs and outputs; how order can be found and used even in the most chaotic situations; how very little can be predicted; the importance of CAS as they intersect, collide, and careen; the importance of relationships and connectedness in all things; and how things nest, enfold, and unfold.

9. Recognition of the absolute requirement for using red-teaming to challenge assumptions, advocate creative thought, search for and find errors in both logic and thought, and assist with wargaming must be a part of advanced analysis doctrine.

10. Intelligence analysis doctrine must advocate the use of a VKE and its scientists, cultural specialists (including indigenous), and other experts to provide the expertise commanders need for effective decision-making.

11. Doctrine needs to address the absolute requirement for the development and use of three types of baseline databases—*cultural, technical,* and *functional*—and identify requirements and responsibilities for keeping these essential databases up to date.

12. Doctrine needs to explain the three types of analytic condition-setting that advanced analysis postulates as essential to analytic success—*data, sensor,* and *knowledge architectures.*

13. Doctrine needs to introduce and explain the indirect approach to thinking about and operating against insurgents' networks. That is, the indirect approach to these difficult to find networks lies in the people and functions that support the nodes/cells and links of the network.

Organization

Advanced analysis implies the need for three major changes in organization:

1. Develop an organized and disciplined *virtual knowledge environment (VKE)*. This organization and its emphasis on producing knowledge products to help deployed analysts and commanders is an absolute must. While expensive to set up and operate, all future OEs will be so complicated that access to knowledge experts must be present all the time to supplement what analysts think, know, and do and in some cases even pick up the tasks that deployed analysts do not have time to perform. However, with this need stated, a VKE must be organized, disciplined, and trained. It must be responsible; for example, when it supports a unit in action, it has to stay with that unit regardless of competing priorities. In addition, any VKE must have all administrative details worked and transparent to the requesting unit, e.g., clearances, contracting, and access to and use of proprietary, SME, and COE databases. Further, commanders will want to know the bona fides of SMEs and the veracity (truthfulness) of data, information, and knowledge. Internally, any VKE supporting a deployed force will have to understand the fundamentals of advanced analysis, the basics of collection, how to engage in wargaming, how to work in a virtual, collaborative environment, and basics of military planning, decision-making, and execution. Knowledge brokers can help with such understanding, particularly with academics and corporate people who probably will not understand the military. Finally, the VKE will need both forward-deployed and virtual knowledge brokers to help identify requirements and ensure the requestor's knowledge requirements are met to include analyst imposed standards (specificity, timeliness, accuracy, relevance, and clarity).

2. Organize as an *intelligence enterprise* that goes from the lowest tactical level in which intelligence people operate (an intelligence support team or IST at the Army's company level) to the national level. This means in an organizational sense, people at the strategic level could very easily provide analytic support to a sergeant at the company IST who is involved in combat. Key among these types of organizational activities include alignment with similar functions, e.g., advanced analysts and collectors working as a team with direct action people, self-similarity or fractal commonalities among all levels, analytic overwatch (as well as collection overwatch), self-organization (meaning that analysts rush to deployed analysts in need without any direction), and help analysts perform functions they do not have time or knowledge to do.

3. Analysts and collection specialists form permanent organizational *analytic/collection teams* and work in the same or virtual workspaces. Their functions are well documented and understood in doctrine, concepts of operation, and standing operating procedures (SOPs). This relationship is natural and needed. As such, both advanced analysts and

advanced collectors must form habitual teaming relationships to have the capabilities to think about, decompose, develop observables, map observables into collection, recompose data into information, and turn information into knowledge. Analysts and collection specialists should know much about each other's thinking, knowledge, and functions. Advanced analysts must learn to design very specific observables and work with collection people to work against the observables. Advanced analysts must work with collection specialists and technologists as a team to design the right data, sensor, and knowledge architectures to ensure success in the urban OE. Analysts and collection people must function in a team during both analytic and collection wargaming that seeks to find ways to achieve the initiative and to anticipate enemy actions, reactions, and counteractions.

Training and Education

Intelligence Analysis: How to Think in Complex Environments implies a distinct need to train and educate analysts to perform advanced analysis in small group settings led by mentors. Such training and education must have a low student-to-mentor ratio, hands-on, performance-oriented training, M&S, cognitive amplification software, role-playing, and practical exercises. Realizing that advanced analysis takes a great deal of cerebral effort and several years in which to develop proficiency, decision makers must invest in analysts' long-term intellectual development to provide them the capability to engage in the high-level cognition discussed throughout this book. In addition, a coherent investment strategy needs to be in place, complete with goals and action plans, to implement changes in training and education sufficient to bring advanced analysis into being. Individual analysts will not have the capability to perform all of advanced analysis' 14 cognitive functions. Even the best analysts will be good at a few cognitive functions and will have but a working knowledge of the others. Analysts will therefore need to learn to seek the help of others who are skilled in the areas of cognition they are not skilled in to assist in using the totality of advanced analysis.

Materiel

Machines can help people think when using advanced analysis. But in many situations analysts will not possess the data manipulation skills required and will thus require the aid of skilled, experienced data scientists in data work-ups and condition-setting, e.g., data mining, knowledge discovery, veracity, statistical analysis, three-dimensional GIS renditions, and modeling. Advanced analysts will be busy, tired, stressed, and sometimes even fearful (particularly at the company IST and battalion levels) as they attempt to use the higher-order thinking skills that advanced analysis demands. Thus, technology can be of great assistance to the thinking required for excelling in the complex OE against the skilled insurgent and irregular warrior in future conflict. Some of the more meaningful materiel aids in winning the war of wits include the following.

Synthetic Environments

To operate and succeed in urban settings, intelligence analysts need a synthetic environment and numerous models to help them engage in mission rehearsal, understand what an asymmetric, adaptive threat may do or be doing, and engage in intelligence "rock drills" before an event occurs. Using the right models will go far in helping analysts understand how the enemy thinks and perceives and what his important relationships, links, and connections might be. Models will help advanced analysts anticipate second- and third-order effects, sensitive variables, and windows of opportunity that the variables expose for all sides to attempt to exploit in a conflict or even in competition. Models will help intelligence analysts think through the act-react-counteract cycles of enemy, friendly, and neutral operations as well as host nation decision/action cycles, when each has disparate vested interests and, at some point in time, the initiative.

Cognition Amplification

To bring the goals stated in this book into reality, technology needs to help bring forth use of the fundamentals of advanced analysis. As one technical solution, cognitive amplification software can help analysts decompose PIR/IR, wargaming hypotheses, hunches, expectations, and mysteries into the five types of observables this book advocates. Advanced analysts also need software tools to assist people in understanding *unexpected consequences of thought*. While our egos and self-perceptions often tell us our thinking is correct, we are sometimes wrong. Thus, we need unbiased help to assist in the difficult task of first examining potential problems with our thinking and subsequently examining the consequences of such thought.

Automated Thought Templates

Advanced analysis is too complex to remember all the details and connections. Thus, analysts need automated thought templates to help them organize their thoughts and remember the obscure parts of advanced analysis. Technology must develop automated thought templates that are really analytic decision aids complete with pick lists, artificial intelligence helpers that provide possible answers and approaches to problems, alternatives to prevalent ways of thinking, as well as reminders about errors of logic the analyst could be committing.

Three-Dimensional and GIS Models

Advanced analysts need the best possible three-dimensional/GIS models to help them think about what is, what might be, and constraints and limitations. This point is reinforced by author Robert R. Tomes in *Parameters*:

> Intelligence tools, furthermore, must be attuned to geographic conditions, which remain a factor in the ability of the regime to defeat the insurgent. This is an area where US forces should be seeking out and applying new capabilities. Geospatial intelligence capabilities, including integration of demographic information, play an overriding role in insurgency warfare. Insurgents tend to use geography against the new government, including the exploitation of active borders to receive outside support.[7]

This is particularly true when working with collection specialists to design collection to work against analyst-developed, specific observables. As the book discusses, the enemy will always have some kind of countersurveillance or early warning system comprised of both people and technology working. Thus, the analyst and the collection team need to work with three-dimensional/GIS visualization to identify sensor and HUMINT line of sight, fields of view, dead space, and the invisible occurrences of actions and electrical emanations, all of which contribute to making the countersurveillance viable.

Models

Modeling provides a way to think about complexity. Modeling helps the analyst engage in wargaming for the initiative. This feature of technology and wargaming came forth earlier in the discussion on four-pair wargaming. This type of wargaming needs intelligent software, programmed culturally, to think and act as the enemy in playing out act, react, and counteract cycles of wargaming. Synthetic environments are required for this human versus avatar competition to occur. This capability is not new—movies such as *Matrix, Lord of the Rings, Troy,* and *Alexander* use the kind of technology being recommended.

Pattern, Trend, and Link Decay Anticipatory Tools

Identifying patterns, trends, and links is a difficult endeavor for any analyst. This difficulty is largely due to the invisible nature of these three important aspects of any urban conflict. But, the problem is more than simply being able to see or touch the connections and relationships comprising patterns, trends, and links. That is, each will have a certain level of vibrancy, strength, and durability. As *Intelligence Analysis: How to Think in Complex Environments* discusses, patterns, links, and trends will each have a decay rate in which they can appear, be vibrant, emit energy, dissipate in strength, disappear, and possibly resurface again even when the analyst considers them dead. This disappearance can be attributed to a decay of the strength of that which holds the trend, pattern, or link together or with other things and could come from use or disuse, trust or mistrust, or purpose or no purpose. While highly abstract, this kind of mental work is important. Quite simply, if commanders and their intelligence analysts do not pay attention to the phenomenon of pattern, trend, and link decay, they could think their effects and actions work when they are really declining or dead. Thus, software and visualization to help in this process of understanding the decay of trends, patterns, and links is an important requirement for materiel developers.

Tools to Help with Decomposition

Advanced analysts need tools with which to help them in the complex work of decomposition. Decomposition tools will help the analyst break down requirements into their essential elements and identify possible observables in multiple domains. These tools will also help analysts visualize data and information pertinent to the resultant observables and what the outputs might appear as and be connected to when collected data returns to the analysts and they recomposes data into information and synthesizes information into actionable knowledge.

Tools to Help with Recomposition and Synthesis

Recomposition and synthesis are the two most important aspects of advanced analysis. They bring together and fuse data, turn data into information via recomposition, and synthesize information into knowledge. Machines can help with both recomposition and synthesis. While recomposition depends on machine work to turn data into information for sense making, synthesis can be a purely cerebral function. But, machines can certainly help with synthesis if analysts so choose. Materiel developers can develop software to scour incoming data, select what are pertinent to analytically defined data filters, and present them in ways that make sense to individual analysts' thought processes. Synthesis can use visualization software to pull seemingly disparate information and combine, expand, and interpret it for the purposes of developing knowledge.

Alarms for the Ascendancy of Sensitive Variables

Sensitive variables are enormously important to all sides in an urban conflict. They cause exponential change and growth that plague commanders as they attempt to accomplish their missions. An essential part of sensitive variables involves discerning what is important and sensitive to particular neighborhoods, groups of people, and politicians. When this importance is discerned, its elements needs to be reduced into essential observables and collected against. This entire process is something models and visualization can help with. Basically, technology needs to monitor the OE for the appearance of fragments of data that once woven into a tapestry could identify sensitive variables, provide alerts that sensitive variables are coming into being, identify windows of opportunity for use against the adversary and for protecting one's self, and identify possible courses of action the commander could take to preempt this potential eruption with effects and associated actions and, of course, more potential outcomes.

Software to Work with Uncertainty and Risk

Both uncertainty and risk are essential elements in any commander's decision cycle. Clearly, the military's materiel developers need to develop technology purposefully that helps commanders and their intelligence analysts reduce uncertainty to an acceptable level and to manage risk to allow freedom of action and not passively awaiting just the right data, information, or knowledge, which commanders fall victim to. Fundamental to this technology will be the range of what comprises uncertainty. As an example, commanders will always be worried about being surprised, the enemy's capabilities, the enemy's intent, and the enemy commander's views of the friendly force's capabilities, vulnerabilities, and strengths. Thus, it will take software and visualization to not only depict where enemy units or networks might be, but also to help describe what the enemy's intent, constraints, capabilities, and alternative choices might be.

Leadership

Leadership is at the center of advanced analysis. For advanced analysis to come into being, leaders must know it as well as traditional and conventional machines of war. Learning institutions and units must train and develop leaders to understand the cognitive processes inherent to advanced analysis. In this regard, leaders will come to view intelligence as a weapons system—key to struggles in the physical as well as the intangible environments of strife. The true brains behind this formidable ISR weapon system lie in intelligence analysis. It is through intelligence analysis that the commander understands his environment, its inhabitants, the enemy and other competitors in the OE, how the enemy thinks about him and his thought processes, the visible and invisible worlds comprising the OE, and how to compete for and attain the initiative. Thus, commanders need to know enough about advanced analysis to guide its efforts, focus attention, prioritize it efforts, and think like the enemy in wargaming and in anticipation of enemy activities, condition-setting, moves, and thought processes. It is through intelligence analysis that the commander purposefully seeks to reduce uncertainty, help manage risk, and anticipate the arousal of sensitive variables and windows of opportunity. As part of leader development, commanders will learn to provide early, specific, detailed guidance and intent to analysts who have to set conditions for analytic success, which in turn has a direct correlation with how well the commander plans and executes operations to accomplish his mission. Leaders will also learn to articulate dynamic information requirements (PIR and IR) to go with fast-paced and dynamic operations inherent to a large urban OE, but will also encourage and receive updates on the progress of analytic pursuit of hypotheses, expectations, hunches, and mysteries.

People

The military must compete for the best and brightest people to be advanced analysts. Advanced analysis is difficult to learn and use, but it is not impossibly difficult. The smarter people are, the easier they will learn the precepts of advanced analysis and learn to use it as a tool of great potential power. Recruited analysts must undergo constant intellectual development and stimulation throughout their careers. Leaders of all ranks must consciously and purposefully nurture and develop advanced analysts' intellects through individual, organizational, and institution learning. Along this line of thought, any organization that recruits and develops analysts must retain them, ensure they receive recognition and promotion, and constantly provide them with the wherewithal to improve their minds through formal and informal training and education. Advanced analysts' thinking abilities should be a factor of unit readiness and should be provided the same degree of supervision and stimulation as machines of war, organizations, and even linguists receive. Advanced analysts should continue to provide expertise even after retirement. This idea should become a permanent program that the Department of Defense manages. At a minimum, such a program should provide virtual mentors for younger advanced analysts striving to learn and also to work as subject matter experts in virtual knowledge environments.

CONCLUSION

This chapter provided the reader with a philosophy for advanced analysis. This philosophy has several important parts. It has basis *propositions*. The philosophy introduces its *essential elements*. It also identified *principles,* and it discussed *axioms*. This chapter also served a synthesis of the big ideas in *Intelligence Analysis: How to Think in Complex Environments*. The last part of the chapter presented the reader with an implication analysis including doctrine, organization, training and education, materiel, leadership, and people. The discussion purposefully omitted any discussion about facilities. This analysis provides a mental bridge between the foregoing discussions throughout the book and the recommendations that come forth in the final chapter—closing thoughts.

21

Closing Thoughts

Advanced analysis is a critically important aspect of winning engagements, battles, and campaigns against insurgents, irregulars, and terrorists. These adversaries are formidable, and they will purposefully engage U.S. forces from dense urban settings. They will hide in the noise and activities of the city and blend with the population and its normal activities, interactions, and transactions. The enemy the U.S. military faces will constantly become better, smarter, more adaptive, and they will learn to hide and blend with the populace better than they do today. This fact of life implies we must learn and adapt so as to be ahead of them. Both sides race to the future to outwit the other and to seek, find, and sustain the initiative and the advantages its possession enables. These urban OEs will always make it challenging to plan, conduct, and assess outcomes of intelligence operations. Regardless, the urban OE is what our military will face over the next 100 years; therefore, we must adapt and excel.

To win and keep winning in the battle of wits will take resources, time, and the will to persevere. The cost to broaden the cognitive capabilities and instill a "how to think" philosophy in the minds of intelligence analysts will be high, but the alternative is the status quo, which is unacceptable. While visiting Paris in 2007, I found a Goya etching in a museum entitled *The Sleep of Reason Produces Monsters*. It was one of those rare moments—an epiphany—in which I found the central theme of this book. That is to say, if we do not keep improving our reasoning capabilities, the "monsters" who constantly swim around our island of safety will surely breach our defenses and wreak havoc in our society. Concerned people must realize that the United States is in a desperate battle with the "monsters" to which Goya's work of art depicts as rising when reason sleeps. A way to ensure America always wins the battle of wits with a difficult enemy lies in providing advanced intelligence analysis training and education to all intelligence analysts that will help to keep the monsters, our implacable foes, at bay.

Admittedly, the task is vast—after all, this book advocates advanced analysis training, education, and operations for thousands of people and hundreds of organizations. As such, the field of analytic endeavor must include military intelligence analysts, civilian intelligence analysts, homeland security intelligence analysts, and commercial corporations that provide intelligence analysts to the Department of Defense, Department of Homeland Security, and elsewhere. Training and education must come through concentrated periods of intense learning, borrowing Hollywood technologies to develop sufficient M&S to provide realistic data environments and mission rehearsal capabilities, and advanced technology tool development for supporting intelligence analysts. While advanced analysis is complex and cerebrally intensive, America's bright people can learn not only to understand advanced analysis but also to use it to gain and sustain a constant intellectual advantage over the enemy. With the right training and education, advanced analysts will be confident and aggressive; they will drive collection and quickly make sense of the data collected to support rapid decision-making. With these cerebral enhancements, no enemy will be able to win in any war of wits against the United States, and there will be the highest probability of keeping the *monsters* at bay or shackled.

Through advanced analysis the U.S. intelligence analyst learns to know the enemy and his objectives, will, intent, and motives. Through advanced analysis the obscurity and invisibility of the OE become clear and visible. Through the aggressive employment of advanced analysis, analysts know where, how, and when to collect. Through advanced analysis, resultant collection-produced data become usable information, knowledge, and eventually understanding, in time to make a difference in decision-making. Through advanced analysis, U.S. commanders possess the constant wherewithal to win the struggle for the initiative across all domains—air, ground, sea, space, cyberspace, cognition, and information.

So, where does this leave us? Solutions do exist for improving our analysts' intellectual capabilities to meet the cognitive expectations *Intelligence Analysis: How to Think in Complex Environments* advocates. The following recommendations, if accepted and inculcated, will go far in helping raise the intellectual horizons of all intelligence analysts:

- Immediately implement extensive advanced analysis training programs. These programs range from a few hours for senior leaders, to two weeks, even to several months depending upon desired depths and cognitive skills. Such a broad, comprehensive program will be very detailed. It includes specific tasks, conditions, and standards. Such training programs include hands-on, performance-oriented training and many practical exercises led by experienced intelligence officers serving as mentors. The training occurs in seminars led by an experienced facilitator who uses screen captures, role players, and a Socratic dialogue. Such a course always uses a small VKE. This course must include intelligence analysts of all ranks, as well as combat-arms officers in the military and people in analytic positions, whether civilian or military.

- Supplemental mini–advanced analysis leadership seminars in the Department of Defense, the Department of Homeland Security, and state and local governments are imperative. Busy senior leaders will not have the time to attend a two- to four-week advanced analysis course. But they have time to attend a short introduction to advanced analysis within other professional development curricula (e.g., the Army's Pre-Command Course, the Joint Capstone Course, CIA's analytic courses, FBI's preparation of intelligence analysts, etc.). Through such short introductory seminars, senior Service and Joint leaders learn the power of advanced analysis. In these short seminars, senior leaders will quickly recognize the power of using advanced analysis as an influential twenty-first century weapon system. Advanced analysis is essential for successful shaping, condition-setting, actuating effects and actions, winning the fight for the initiative, gaining situational understanding of the OE and the enemy, as well as assessing outcomes of interactions. As a minimum requirement, senior leaders must know and understand how to use the basics of the 14 elements of advanced analysis and the five types of observables so as to provide specific guidance and intent to advanced analysts who set conditions for success well before the action or the demand for high-grade knowledge to make decisions and to assess outcomes occurs.
- The Department of Defense should develop and use a mandatory advanced analysis course for all Service and Joint command and staff colleges for majors.
- The Department of Defense should implement a mandatory advanced analysis course for all War College students.
- The Army and Marine Corps should develop an advanced analysis program for intelligence analyst mission rehearsal to prepare every deploying analyst to understand and use the basic precepts of advanced analysis.
- Advanced analysis should be incorporated into the military's combat training centers (CTCs), e.g., NTC, and 29 Palms. In this respect, the military needs a mission rehearsal process and system for its intelligence analysts. This mission rehearsal must help advanced analysts prepare for reality in a conflict deployment by presenting them with realistic problem sets and scenarios with a synthetic data environment

approximating what they will face in the impending deployment. They must be able to use a VKE, indigenous people, and red teams to help them think, plan, and provide the knowledge their commanders need. This mission rehearsal must be difficult and even overwhelming. As such, it should be more difficult than what the analysts will face as they implement the "how to think" precepts of advanced analysis. The ancient Romans had a system for training their soldiers, which the U.S. military should mimic. Flavius Vegetius Renatus, in *The Military Institutions of the Romans*, wrote long ago,

> The new levies also should be taught by the masters at arms the system of drill call armatura, as it is still partly kept up among us. . .And they afford certain proofs of the importance and effects of discipline in the difference we see between those properly trained in this branch of drill and the other troops. The old Romans were so conscious of its usefulness that they rewarded the masters at arms with a double allowance of provision. The soldiers who were backward in this drill were punished by having their allowance in barley. Nor did they receive it as usual, in wheat, until they had, in the presence of the prefect, tribunes, or other principal officers of the legion, showed sufficient proofs of their knowledge of every part of their study.[1]

- This is mission rehearsal for intelligence analysts. While this book certainly does not advocate withholding food from soldiers until they learn the basics of advanced analysis, it does suggest that the Romans had a good and usable point about the need for rigorous training, made more difficult than what reality was expected to bring forth, particularly for soldiers involved in the war of wits. Please permit me to explain just a little further about what I mean. The Romans made their training spears, swords, and shields heavier than their actual weight. Their soldiers had to practice with this weight and become proficient. Analysts should undergo "Armatura" for the intellect and analytic processes under the sage guidance of a mentor, such as Rackham was for Ender in *Ender's Game*, in a simulated environment against opponents who are much better and much faster in thought and deed than in real life. This type of mission rehearsal will prepare them to be fully operational and intellectually formidable when they arrive in the OE instead of becoming fully operational a few months later.

BREADTH OF KNOWLEDGE

All U.S. activities in urban OEs involve people. People are products of their culture. Thus, to understand the culture, analysts have to understand people and their institutions. But, any cultural intelligence aspect of advanced analysis involves a very wide diversity of subjects, causing operations in a strange culture to be difficult. Part of the difficulty lies in understanding different customs, mores, language, social patterns and inhibitions, education, religion, and beliefs. Part of the difficulty lies in language barriers and differences in how people process information, how they perceive, how they think, and how they make decisions. Part of the difficulty lies in trying to find insurgents embedded in a society and culture where they do not stand out, but instead blend. Lastly, part of the difficulty lies in the well-known fact that insurgents and terrorists are security conscious and paranoid about being discovered, so they are not easily observed.

As an insurgency matures and stretches out over a number of years, the process of natural selection creates perpetrators who are very smart and often uncannily wary. Conflict in an urban OE, then, becomes a battle of wits and learning. Each side strives to outthink the other, not only to stay alive, but also to win. Each side strives to learn and distribute that learning faster than the opponent to retain the initiative, which is so important for decision-making, positional advantage, and freedom of action. The side that learns and adjusts best will win.[2] Each side has to anticipate the other's moves and take the initiative by being in front of the enemy action and having a contingency plan in the event the enemy catches them by surprise, or vice versa. The only hope that a foreign power like the United States has when working in an urban OE against insurgents and terrorists is to gain a deep understanding of the culture in which the insurgency thrives or seek the help of SMEs to help them find valuable cultural knowledge and understanding sufficient to succeed.

When speaking of the essence of engaging the enemy in a war of wits, specifics matter. As U.S. forces and governmental agencies operate in urban environments, finding the adversaries' important nodes and cells depends on knowing specifics—in this case, cultural, technical, functional, situational, and biometric specifics. Being able to anticipate insurgent and terrorist attacks and predict their preparatory work (condition-setting) takes a painstaking devolution into specificity. To take the mental journey into specificity, advanced analysts must either have the necessary knowledge or have access to a cadre of SMEs that possess it. The help gained from SMEs contributes to developing specifics of sufficient depth and level of detail necessary for finding the hints, mistakes, subtleties, and anomalies leading to a person, link, or a cell or how the people are responding to U.S. attempts to disaggregate them from the insurgents. These specific, subtle relationships are important when perpetrators show only very subtle and nuanced signs, observables, or mistakes recognizable only to indigenous people.

STRENGTHS AND WEAKNESSES

Support from the populace can be a significant strength to a network. But people make mistakes. These mistakes become recognizable when collection people and sensors arm themselves with cultural observables projected to identify activities at a particular place, specific time, and with specific actions or behaviors. This recognition of cultural mistakes and anomalies, however, will need to occur speedily among masses of people. Once they occur, they may not occur again in exactly the same way. Thus, when cultural observables occur, for optimum exploitation, they must surface into a human watcher's consciousness immediately. If such observables appear in a flash, to notice them, analyst and collection teams must use one or more sensors in optimum combinations. In addition, the sensors need to couple with a computer programmed to watch for cultural signs or symbols (semiotics), inclinations to occur (tendencies), small changes or differences form the norm (anomalies), and additive activities (aggregation) to disambiguate the scene and allow cultural peculiarities or anomalies to come into a human being's awareness.

The rationale used by a populace to support an enemy network is the offspring of culture. If the culture is deprived or repressed and if it abides a deep historical, cynical, view of outsiders, indigenous law enforcement, or indigenous military, the people will undoubtedly provide more support to the insurgents or irregulars. Conversely, if the authorities understand the culture, they can design effects to cut across many domains, with the purpose of improving lifestyles and assuaging fears of the people in question. Knowledge of the culture helps people understand the temporal and emotional aspects of gaining trust and influencing people—this knowledge comes with cultural intelligence analysis.

Network Supporters

Intelligence analysts, with the help of U.S. and indigenous SMEs, work hard to notice and understand questionable actions, transactions, and interactions that occur in specific areas suspected to harbor the enemy's nodes, cells, and links. The military's ability to study these activities comes from the act of decomposition and using ISR to search for resultant observables. As subsequent data and human reports flow to operations centers, intelligence analysts and machines recompose data into knowledge. The analyst synthesizes the most important derived information into knowledge. Eventually the analyst is able to visualize and understand the enemy's networks even when the casual observer sees, hears, or senses nothing.

Actually, the culture can lend a helping hand in the advanced analyst's effort to see and understand the enemy's networks. The culture, for example, shapes how people support the insurgents' networks. The culture drives, shapes, and indeed wraps and heavily influences the activities, interactions, transactions, activities, and behaviors that occur. These hundreds and thousands of activities occur in a big city all day every day. Most often they are harmless and innocuous. Sometimes, however, activities supporting insurgent networks occur amidst the legitimate activities and thus U.S.

intelligence analysts will not see them because they are not looking for such activities or, if they are seen, they are not recognized as anything questionable or untoward.

The activities people perform while supporting the enemy's networks actually become the most important aspect of disrupting or finding and destroying the enemy's networks. These activities can lead U.S. analysts to enemy links and decisive nodes, cells, and connecting links, but only with extremely specific observables and responsive collection. Cultural observables team with functional, situational, biometric, and technical observables for gaining the best understanding of vague situations.

CONCLUSION

People responsible for developing the intellects of intelligence analysts can certainly choose to ignore advanced analysis and the effort it will take to help people to learn "how to think" as well as "what to think." With such a choice, America will miss out on its secret weapon—the minds of many smart people trained and educated to engage in " how to think" activities and cerebral machinations so as to seize the initiative, outthink the adversary, and disaggregate him from those who support him. America will be missing people who know and understand how to think, understand, and reduce the effectiveness of the enemy's networks, and most importantly, to learn how the enemy thinks and to exploit such knowledge to create advantages for U.S. decision makers.

I hope that people who read *Intelligence Analysis: How to Think in Complex Environments* will agree that America must accept the system of thought brought forth. After all, it is the higher level thought postulated in advanced analysis that will awaken reasoning, through constant improvement and learning to keep reason awake, and through an aggressive, anticipatory way of thinking, keep the monsters at bay. It is worthy of stating that we need to implement advanced analysis not only for ourselves, but for those who follow us.

Advanced analysis is neither too mentally challenging nor too difficult to implement. What it takes is the will to understand its fundamentals and implement its philosophy and precepts. Will in this sense, means being committed to pursue a goal and to sacrifice to accomplish it. In this case, the goal is the enlightenment of our very capable analysts and improvement of their cognition. We can and must win this war of wits; advanced analysis provides a way to accomplish this goal.

Like other enemies America has faced, our current enemy, comprised of irregular warriors, insurgents, and terrorists, has vowed to destroy America, its values, and way of life. We are in a long-term war to preserve our way of life against a global and very determined foe. While the United States has enormous conventional military capabilities, the upcoming battles will be, for the most part, mental. It is safe to conclude we are in a continuing war of wits that we cannot fail to win. To stay with the course with the status quo concerning the training and education of intelligence analysts is a gamble in the worst connotation of the word. To inculcate the precepts of advanced analysis is a cheap way to take advantage of not just one great mind, but thousands of great minds, bound by a common way of thinking and energized by a philosophy and system of thought. America needs advanced analysis to keep the monsters at bay and in shackles!

Notes

INTRODUCTION

1. Richards J. Heuer, Jr., *Psychology of Intelligence Analysis* (Washington DC: US Government Printing Office, 1999), 31.

2. Joint Publication 2.0, (Washington: Joint Chiefs of Staff, 2007), GL 5.

3. Joint Publication 2.0, GL 11.

4. US Joint Staff, *DoD Dictionary of Military and Associated Terms*, October 2007, http://www.dtic.mil/doctrine/jel/doddict/data/o/03921.html.

CHAPTER 1

1. T. E. Lawrence. *Seven Pillars of Wisdom*, (New York: Random House, 1926), 196.

2. Thomas L. Friedman. *The Lexus and the Olive Tree*, (New York: Anchor Books, 1999), 46–47.

3. Dictionary.com, Retrieved 24 August 2009, *The American Heritage® Dictionary of the English Language, Fourth Edition,* Copyright © 2009 by Houghton Mifflin Company. http://dictionary.reference.com/browse/nonlinear.

4. John Holland in M. Mitchell Waldrop, *Complexity,* (New York: Touchstone Books, 1992), http://en.wikipedia.org/wiki/Complex_adaptive_system.

5. Carl von Clausewitz. *On War*, (Princeton: Princeton University Press, 1977), 158.

6. WordNet® 3.0. Retrieved April 13, 2008, from Dictionary.com website: http://dictionary.reference.com/browse/xenophobic.

7. James Schneider, "T.E. Lawrence and the Mind of an Insurgent," *Army*, (July 2005): p.37.

8. Marc Sageman. *Understanding Terror Networks*, (Philadelphia: University of Pennsylvania Press, 2004), 165.

9. Lester W. Grau, "Guerrillas, Terrorists, and Intelligence Analysis," *Military Review*, July–August 2004, 44.

10. Schneider, 36.

CHAPTER 2

1. Dictionary.com. *WordNet® 3.0*. Princeton University; http://dictionary .reference.com/browse/symbiosis: the relation between two different species of organisms that are interdependent; each gains benefits from the other. *Author's note:* I am taking some liberty with the biological meaning of the word and veering into a relationship between man and machine that is not unlike the relationship between two sentient organisms. As machines become more human-like and man develops further dependencies and closeness of relationship and actual interdependencies, symbiosis will grow to conjoin man and machine even further.

2. David H. Petraeus, "Learning Counterinsurgency: Observations from Soldiering in Iraq," *Military Review*, January–February 2006, 8.

3. T. E. Lawrence, *Seven Pillars of Wisdom* (New York: Anchor Books, 1926), 196.

4. David Galula, *Counterinsurgency Warfare: Theory and Practice* (Westport, CT: Praeger Security International, 1964), xii–3.

5. Mao Tse-tung, *On Guerrilla Warfare*, trans. Samuel B. Griffith II, (Urbana, IL: University of Illinois Press, 1961), 98.

CHAPTER 3

1. Vojo Deretic and Daniel J. Klionsky, "How Cells Clean House." *Scientific American* (May 2008): 74.

2. David G. Myers. *Exploring Psychology*, 5th ed., (New York: Worth, 2003), xv.

3. Schneider, 34.

4. Clausewitz, 77.

5. Dictionary.com Unabridged (v 1.1). Retrieved April 20, 2008, from Dictionary.com website: http://dictionary.reference.com/browse/hypothesis.

6. Dictionary.com Unabridged (v 1.1). Retrieved April 20, 2008, from Dictionary.com website: http://dictionary.reference.com/browse/expectation.

7. Dictionary.com Unabridged (v 1.1). Retrieved April 20, 2008, from Dictionary.com website: http://dictionary.reference.com/browse/hunch.

8. Dictionary.com Unabridged (v 1.1). Retrieved April 20, 2008, from Dictionary.com website: http://dictionary.reference.com/browse/mystery.

9. The American Heritage® Dictionary of the English Language, Fourth Edition. Retrieved February 19, 2009, from Dictionary.com website: http:// dictionary.reference.com/browse/observable.

10. Joint Publication 2.0, 22 June 2007, I–17.

11. Joint Publication 2-0, Joint Intelligence, 22 June 2007, GL–08.

12. Stuart A. Herrington, *Stalking the VietCong* (New York: Ballantine Books, 1982), 25.

13. Heuer, 9.

14. The American Heritage® Dictionary of the English Language, Fourth Edition. Retrieved May 21, 2008, from Dictionary.com website: http://dictionary .reference.com/browse/context.

15. Dictionary.com Unabridged (v 1.1). Retrieved August 31, 2007, from Dictionary.com Web site: http://dictionary.reference.com/browse/contradiction.

16. Frederick Copleston, S.J. *A History of Philosophy, Volume VII*, (New York: Doubleday, 1963), 176.

CHAPTER 4

1. Alexander Bevin. *How Wars Are Won: 13 Rules of War From Ancient Greece to the War On Terror* (New York: Three Rivers Press, 2002), 261–269.

2. B. H. Liddell Hart. *Strategy*, (London: Faber & Faber Ltd, 1954), 326–327.

3. Wayne M. Hall. *Stray Voltage: War in the Information Age*, (Annapolis: Naval Institute Press, 2003) 60–61.

4. John Seely Brown and Paul Duguid. *The Social Life of Information*, (Harvard: Harvard Business School Press, 2002), 158.

5. Gary Klein. *Sources of Power: How People Make Decisions*, (Cambridge: MIT University Press, 1998), 116.

6. Orson Scott Card. *Ender's Game*, (New York: Tom Doherty Associates, 1977), 260.

7. Frank Kitson. *Low-Intensity Conflict: Subversion, Insurgency, and Peace-keeping*, (St. Petersburg: Hailer Publishing, 2007 reprint), 77.

8. Sun Tzu, 92.

9. M. Mitchell Waldrop. *Complexity: The Emerging Science at the Edge of Order and Chaos*, (New York: Touchstone, 1992), 12.

10. Clausewitz, 80.

11. T.E. Lawrence. *Seven Pillars of Wisdom*, (New York: Anchor Books, 1926), 195.

12. Clausewitz, 77.

13. Colonel John Boyd visited the School of Advanced Military Studies (SAMS) when I was a student there in the spring of 1985. His discussion of the OODA loop has influenced my thinking over the years.

14. Hall, 104–105.

15. Wargaming is about seeking insights related to the initiative. It seeks to anticipate either competitor actions (meaning they have the initiative) or competitor reactions (meaning we have the initiative) to our actions. In addition, the many competitors at work in the cauldron that is the urban OE will have their own goals, objectives, and strategies. As such, they will sometimes take actions antithetical to U.S. interests. If they catch our commanders by surprise, they will possess the initiative. Thus, although I have discussed four pairs, there certainly can be more. All can and often will influence the commander's decisions, actions, and desired outcomes.

16. Clausewitz, 102.

17. The American Heritage® Science Dictionary. Houghton Mifflin Company. 28 May, 2007.

18. This idea came from a discussion between the author and Colonel Scott Levin at Fort Huachuca, Arizona, on 25 April 2008. Colonel Levin explained that he had used an analytic strategy at JAC Molesworth and it was effective.

19. Dictionary.com Unabridged (v 1.1). Retrieved April 27, 2008, from Dictionary.com Web site: http://dictionary.reference.com/browse/strategy.

CHAPTER 5

1. David Bohm. *Wholeness and the Implicate Order*, (London: Routledge & Kegan Paul, 1980), 32.

2. Fritjof Capra. *The Tao of Physics*, (Toronto: Bantam Books, 1975), p.116–117.

3. Capra, 95.

4. DOD Dictionary of Military and Associated Terms, October 2007, http://www.dtic.mil/doctrine/jel/doddict.

5. Sun Tzu, 91.

6. Klein, 111, 147.

7. Dictionary.com Unabridged (v 1.1). Retrieved March 31, 2008, from Dictionary.com Web site: http://dictionary.reference.com/browse/expectation.

8. Dictionary.com Unabridged (v 1.1). Retrieved March 31, 2008, from Dictionary.com Web site: http://dictionary.reference.com/browse/hunch.

9. Dictionary.com Unabridged (v 1.1). Retrieved March 31, 2008, from Dictionary.com Web site: http://dictionary.reference.com/browse/mystery.

10. Dictionary.com Unabridged (v 1.1). Retrieved March 06, 2008, from Dictionary.com Web site: http://dictionary.reference.com/browse/disambiguate.

11. Dictionary.com Unabridged (v1.1). Retrieved March 31, 2008, from Dictionary.com Web site: http://dictionary.refrence.com/browse/baseline.

12. Hall. *Stray Voltage*, 199–200.

13. Wayne M. Hall, "Shaping the Future: A Holistic Approach to Planning, " unpublished paper, National War College, Washington DC, March 1992, 7.

14. David MacIssac, "Voices from the Central Blue: The Air Power Theorists," *Makers of Modern Strategy from Machiavelli to the Nuclear Age*, ed. Peter Paret (Princeton: Princeton University Press, 1986), 635.

CHAPTER 6

1. Myers, xv.

2. Heuer, 38–40.

3. Clausewitz, 156.

4. Clausewitz, 156.

5. Sun Tzu, 66–67.

6. Heuer, 70.

7. *DOD Dictionary of Military and Associated Terms*, October 17, 2007.

8. Heuer, 69.

9. Clausewitz, 177.

10. Fyodor Dostoevsky, "Notes from Underground," in *Existentialism from Dostoevsky to Sartre*, ed. Walter Kaufmann (New York: New American Library, 1975), 77.

11. Clausewitz, 158.

12. Clausewitz, 157.

13. Waldrop, 66.·

14. Waldrop, 252.

15. Sun Tzu, 92.

16. Dictionary.com, http://dictionary.reference.com/browse/ad hominem (accessed March 23, 2008).

17. *Webster's New Millennium Dictionary of English, Preview Edition* (v 0.9.7), Dictionary.com, http://dictionary.reference.com/browse/circular reasoning (accessed March 23, 2008).

18. Dictionary.com, http://dictionary.reference.com/browse/oversimplification (accessed March 23, 2008).

19. Wikipedia, "Post hoc, ergo propter hoc," http://en.wikipedia .org/wiki/Post_hoc_ergo_propter_hoc.

20. Wikipedia, "False dilemma," http://en.wikipedia.org/wiki/False_dilemma, (accessed March 23, 2008).

21. Heuer, 39.

22. Dictionary.com, http://dictionary.reference.com/browse/non sequitur (accessed March 23, 2008).

23. Dictionary.com, Unabridged (v1.1). Retrieved March 22, 2008, from Dictionary.com website: http://dictionary.reference.com/browse/data (accessed: March 22, 2008).

24. *Webster's II New Riverside University Dictionary* (Boston: Houghton Mifflin, 1984), 669.

25. *The American Heritage® Dictionary of the English Language*, 4th ed. (Houghton Mifflin Company, 2004),Retrieved from Dictionary.com website. http://dictionary.reference.com/browse/dialectic (accessed: March 23, 2008).

26. Frederick Copleston, S. J., *A History of Philosophy*, Volume VII, Book 3 (New York: Doubleday, 1985), 192.

27. Dictionary.com, Unabridged (v 1.1). Retrieved March 23, 2008, from Dictionary.com website: http://dictionary.reference.com/browse/synthesis (accessed March 23, 2008).

28. William James, *Psychology*, ed. G. Allport (New York: Harper & Brothers, 1961), 120.

CHAPTER 7

1. Clausewitz, 120.

2. Sun Tzu, 100.

3. Steven D. Levitt and Stephen J. Dubner, *Freakonomics* (New York: HarperCollins Books, 2005), 102.

4. I have taken the liberty to borrow a medical term to describe a perturbation of a link. When a link fibrillates, it twitches or pulses and thereby shows or acts differently than without the fibrillation. This is the desired state for U.S. advanced analysts—to cause the various kinds of links to fibrillate at the time, place, and circumstances of their choosing for creating various kinds of advantages for the U.S. commander.

5. Francis H. Cook, Hua-Yen Buddhism: The Jewel Net of Indra (College Station: Pennsylvania State Press, 1977), 2.

6. *The American Heritage Dictionary of the English Language*, 4th ed. (Houghton Mifflin Company, 2004), http://dictionary.reference.com/browse/periodicity (accessed February 17, 2008).

7. Dictionary.com, http://dictionary.reference.com/browse/link (accessed February 17, 2008).

8. Vojo Deretic and Daniel J. Klionsky, "How Cells Clean House," *Scientific American*, May 2008, 74.

9. Dictionary.com, http://dictionary.reference.com/browse/ignis fatuus (accessed February 17, 2008).

CHAPTER 8

1. Capra, 95.

2. Department of Defense, *DOD Dictionary of Military and Associated Terms*, Joint Publication 1-02 (Washington, DC: Joint Staff, Joint Doctrine Division, J7, April 12, 2001, as amended through October 17, 2007), 145.

3. Sun Tzu, *The Art of War*. Translated and edited by Samuel B. Griffith. (London: Oxford University Press, 1971.)

4. Hall, *Stray Voltage: War in the Information Age*. (Annapolis, MD: Naval Institute Press, 2003), 120.

5. Card, 268.

6. Dictionary.com, http://dictionary.reference.com/browse/aggregate (accessed February 16, 2008).

CHAPTER 9

1. U.S. Army, *FM 3-24* (Washington, DC: Headquarters, Department of the Army, December 2006), Glossary-8.

2. Clausewitz, 119–121.

3. Clausewitz, 158.

CHAPTER 10

1. Roger Trinquier, *Modern Warfare: A French View of Counterinsurgency* (Westport: Praeger Security International, 2006), 49.

2. Dictionary.com. *WordNet® 3.0*. Princeton University; http://dictionary.reference.com/browse/predict.

3. Department of Defense, Joint Staff, *Joint Publication 2.0, Joint Intelligence* (Washington, D.C.: U. S. Department of Defense, 2007), xiv.

4. Joint Publication 2.0, II–9.

5. Dictionary.com. *WordNet® 3.0*. Princeton University; http://dictionary.reference.com/browse/anticipate.

6. Wikipedia, "Complex Adaptive System," http://en.wikipedia.org/wiki/Complex_adaptive_system.

7. Mitchell M. Waldrop, *Complexity: The Emerging Science at the Edge of Order and Chaos* (New York: Touchstone Books, 1992), 11–12.

8. Field Manual 3.0, U.S. Army (Washington D.C.: U.S. Department of Defense, February 2008), p. Glossary-8.

9. Sun Tzu, 93.

10. Mao Tse-tung, *On Guerrilla Warfare*, trans. by Samuel B. Griffith II (Urbana: University of Illinois Press, 2000), 98.

11. William Slim, *Defeat into Victory* (New York: Cooper Square Press, 2000), 210.

12. Orson Scott Card, *Ender's Game* (New York: Tom Doherty Associates Book, 1977), 281–283.

13. George Friedman, Strategic Forecasting (STRATFOR), Geopolitical Intelligence Report 07.12.2007, *Week out of Focus: Washington, Iraq and Al Qaeda;* www.stratfor.com/reports.

14. Clausewitz, 102.

15. Dictionary.com. *WordNet® 3.0.* Princeton University; http://dictionary .reference.com/browse/proprioception.

16. Lawrence, 194-96.

17. Hall, *Stray Voltage: War in the Information Age*, 34.

CHAPTER 11

1. Ray Kurzweil, *The Age of Spiritual Machines* (New York: Viking, 1999), 16.

2. Kevin Kelly, *Out of Control* (Reading: Perseus Books, 1994), 21.

3. Schneider, 36.

CHAPTER 12

1. I am indebted to the following people for engaging with me in spirited conversations and thereby contributing to my thinking about the nascent idea of tendency analysis: Dr. Gary Citrenbaum, Michael Scheuer, Dr. Bill Anderson, MD, Gene Poteat, Frank Anderson, Colonel (Retired) Carol Stewart, Martha Kessler, Colonel (Retired) Pat Lang, Colonel (Retired) Harry Bakken, Ed Levitt, Mark Finkelstein, Dr. Pauletta Otis, Dr. Russ Glenn, Andre Kesteloot, Hayder Alhamdani, and Kadhim Al Waeli.

2. Fritjof Capra, *The Tao of Physics* (Toronto: Bantam Books, Revised Edition, 1984), 56.

3. Capra, 57.

4. Guy Claxton, *Hare Brain, Tortoise Mind* (New York: The Ecco Press, 1997), 72.

5. Charles W. Misner, Kip S. Thorne, and John Archibald Wheeler, *Gravitation* (San Francisco: W. H. Freeman, 1973), 1273.

6. Gary Zukav, *The Dancing Wu Li Maters* (Toronto: Bantam Books, 1979), 32–33.

7. Malcolm Gladwell, *Blink* (New York: Little, Brown and Company, 2005), 11.

CHAPTER 13

1. Kitson, 121.

2. Galula, 82.

3. Waldrop, 21.

4. Goetz, Thomas. "Finding Normal." *Wired* (May 2008): 023–024.

5. Dictionary.com. *WordNet® 3.0.* Princeton University; http://dictionary .reference.com/browse/disambiguation.

6. Clausewitz, 77.

CHAPTER 14

1. I am indebted to the following people for engaging with me in a spirited discussion about cultural analysis that helped me think about this complex subject: Dr. Gary Citrenbaum, Michael Scheuer, Dr. Bill Anderson, MD, Gene Poteat, Frank Anderson, Colonel (Retired) Carol Stewart, Martha Kessler, Colonel (Retired) Pat Lang, Colonel (Retired) Harry Bakken, Ed Levitt, Mark Finkelstein, Dr. Pauletta Otis, Dr. Russ Glenn, Andre Kesteloot, Hayder Alhamdani, and Kadhim Al Waeli.

2. Dictionary.com. *WordNet® 3.0.* Princeton University; http://dictionary.reference.com/browse/culture.

3. Grau, 44.

4. Thomas L. Friedman, *The World Is Flat* (New York: Farrar, Straus and Giroux, 2005), 8.

5. FM 3-24/MCWP 3-33.5, *Counterinsurgency* (Washington D.C.: Headquarters Department of the Army, December 2006), 3–1.

6. Galula, 4.

7. Petraeus, 8.

8. Michael Scheuer, *Through Our Enemies' Eyes* (Washington: Brassey's, Inc., 2002), 17.

9. Marc Sageman, *Understanding Terror Networks* (Philadelphia: University of Pennsylvania Press, 2004), 146.

10. Lee Harris, *The Suicide of Reason* (New York: Basic Books, 2007), xvii.

11. Dictionary.com. *WordNet® 3.0.* Princeton University; http://dictionary.reference.com/browse/interact.

12. Dictionary.com. *WordNet® 3.0.* Princeton University; http://dictionary.reference.com/browse/act (accessed: March 01, 2008).

13. Dictionary.com. *WordNet® 3.0.* Princeton University; http://dictionary.reference.com/browse/transact.

14. Dictionary.com. *WordNet® 3.0.* Princeton University; http://dictionary.reference.com/browse/behave.

15. Dictionary.com. *WordNet® 3.0.* Princeton University; http://dictionary.reference.com/browse/mores.

16. Heuer, 66–67.

CHAPTER 15

1. I am indebted to the following people for engaging with me in a spirited discussion about semiotics analysis that helped me think about this complex subject: Dr. Gary Citrenbaum, Michael Scheuer, Dr. Bill Anderson, MD, Gene Poteat, Frank Anderson, Colonel (Retired) Carol Stewart, Martha Kessler, Colonel (Retired) Pat Lang, Colonel (Retired) Harry Bakken, Ed Levitt, Mark Finkelstein, Dr. Pauletta Otis, Dr. Russ Glenn, Andre Kesteloot, Hayder Alhamdani, and Kadhim Al Waeli.

2. Bernard Lewis. *Islam and the West,* (Oxford: Oxford University Press, 1993), 135.

3. Ralph Patai. *The Arab Mind,* (New York: Hatherleigh Press, 2002), 56–57.

4. Hall. *Stray Voltage War In The Information Age,* 129.

5. Dictionary.com Unabridged (v 1.1). Retrieved March 09, 2008, from Dictionary.com website: http://dictionary.reference.com/browse/culture.

6. Galula, 52.
7. Lawrence, 196.
8. Sun Tzu, 100.
9. Waldrop, 12.

CHAPTER 16

1. Dictionary.com Unabridged (v 1.1). Retrieved February 27, 2008, from Dictionary.com Web site: http://dictionary.reference.com/browse/aggregate.

2. James Gleick. *Chaos: Making a New Science*, (New York: Penguin Books, 1987), 8, 23.

3. Ernest Hemmingway. *For Whom the Bell Tolls*, (New York: Scribner, 2003), 451.

4. William Shakespeare. *Macbeth*, (Danbury: Grolier Enterprises Corp, 1980), Act V, scene v, 388.

5. Dictionary.com Unabridged (v 1.1). Retrieved February 27, 2008, from Dictionary.com Web site: http://dictionary.reference.com/browse/synthesis.

6. WordNet® 3.0. Retrieved February 27, 2008, from Dictionary.com Web site: http://dictionary.reference.com/browse/holism.

7. John H. Holland in M. Mitchell Waldrop. *Complexity: The Emerging Science at the Edge of Order and Chaos*, (London: Penguin Books, 1994).

8. John Holland. *Hidden Order: How Adaptation Builds Complexity*, (New York: Basic Books, 1995), 10–11.

9. Waldrop, 11.

10. During a study I led for the Army in 1998 while on active duty in the military, I opined to a group of learned people that in the near future (then), criminal elements, terrorists, and insurgents would come together and cooperate via temporary partnerships. I went on to say these formations of aggregates would arise for self-interest and self-survival. One senior person in the group scoffed at the notion, saying there was no evidence of any group such as I mentioned ever coming together, and they would never do what I prognosticated because there was no evidence. Of course, we all now know that such groups have formed and disbanded, and their motives are always for self-interest.

11. Holland, 27.

12. Sun Tzu, 129.

13. Sun Tzu, 92.

14. Larry Downes and Chunka Mui. *Unleashing the Killer App*, (Boston: Harvard Business School Press, 1998), 11.

15. Downs and Mui, 13.

16. Waldrop, 12.

CHAPTER 17

1. Clausewitz, 96.
2. Klein, 147–149.
3. The American Heritage® Dictionary of the English Language, Fourth Edition copyright ©2000 by Houghton Mifflin Company. Updated in 2003. Published by Houghton Mifflin Company.

4. Hall. *Stray Voltage: War in the Information Age*, 92–93.

5. The American Heritage® Dictionary of the English Language, Fourth Edition. Retrieved March 03, 2008, from Dictionary.com Web site: http://dictionary.reference.com/browse/synthesis.

6. Dictionary.com Unabridged (v 1.1). Retrieved April 05, 2008, from Dictionary.com Web site: http://dictionary.reference.com/browse/information.

7. Sun Tzu, 96–97.

8. Hall, "Shaping the Future: A Holistic Approach to Planning," 10.

9. Clausewitz, 95.

CHAPTER 18

1. *Webster's II New Riverside University Dictionary* (Boston: Houghton Mifflin, 1984), 1175.

2. Capra, 116–117.

3. Hermann Hesse. *Siddhartha*, (New York: MJF Books, 1951), 26.

4. Sun Tzu, 92.

5. Clausewitz, 101–103.

6. Dictionary.com Unabridged (v 1.1). Retrieved February 20, 2008, from Dictionary.com Web site: http://dictionary.reference.com/browse/reductionism.

7. The American Heritage® Dictionary of the English Language, Fourth Edition. Retrieved February 20, 2008, from Dictionary.com Web site: http://dictionary.reference.com/browse/synergy.

8. Klein, 147–149.

9. Clausewitz, 240–250.

10. Thomas H. Brobjer, "Nietzsche's Affirmative Morality: An Ethics of Virtue," *The Journal of Nietzsche Studies*, 26 (Autumn 2003): 64–78.

11. Heuer, 15.

12. Mao Tse-tung, 98.

13. Sun Tzu, 91–92.

CHAPTER 19

1. Heuer, 3.

2. GENOA is not an acronym. It is simply a large triangular front sail on a sailboat.

CHAPTER 20

1. David Bohm, *Thought as a System* (London: Routledge, 1992), 19.

2. Michael Talbot, *The Holographic Universe* (New York: HarperPerennial, 1991), 49.

3. Dictionary.com. *WordNet® 3.0*. Princeton University; http://dictionary.reference.com/browse/philosophy.

4. Dictionary.com. *WordNet® 3.0*. Princeton University; http://dictionary.reference.com/browse/proposition.

5. Dictionary.com. *WordNet® 3.0*. Princeton University; http://dictionary.reference.com/browse/symbiosis:axiom.

6. Klein, 71.

7. Robert R. Tomes, "Relearning Counterinsurgency Warfare." *Parameters* (Spring 2004): 23.

CHAPTER 21

1. Flavius Vegetius Renatus, *The Military Institutions of the Romans*, ed. Wilhelm Lee, Thomas R. Phillips, Hugo Friedrich Philipp Johann Freytag-Loringhoven, Waldemar Erfurth, (Mechanicsburg: Stackpole Books, 1985), 84–87.

2. U.S. Army, *FM 3-24/MCWP 3-33.5*, Counterinsurgency. Washington, DC: Headquarters, Department of the Army, December 2006.

Select Bibliography

BOOKS

Alexander, Bevin. *How Wars Are Won: 13 Rules of War from Ancient Greece to the War on Terror*. New York: Three Rivers Press, 2002.

The American Heritage Dictionary of the English Language, Fourth Edition. Boston: Houghton Mifflin Company, 2003.

Bohm, David. *Thought as a System*. London: Routledge, 1992.

———. *Wholeness and the Implicate Order*. London: Routledge & Kegan Paul, 1980.

Brown, John Seely, and Paul Duguid. *The Social Life of Information*. Boston: Harvard Business School Press, 2002.

Capra, Fritjof. *The Tao of Physics*. New York: Bantam Books, 1984.

Card, Orson Scott. *Ender's Game*. New York: Tom Doherty Associates Books, 1977.

Clausewitz, Carl von. *On War*. ed. Michael Howard, Peter Paret, and Bernard Brodie. Princeton: Princeton University Press, 1976.

Claxton, Guy. *Hare Brain, Tortoise Mind: How Intelligence Increases When You Think Less*. New York: The Ecco Press, 1997.

Cook, Francis H. *Hua-Yen Buddhism: The Jewel Net of Indra*. College Station: Pennsylvania State Press, 1977.

Copleston, Frederick S.J., *A History of Philosophy*, Volume VII. New York: Doubleday, 1963.

Dostoevsky, Fyodor. "Notes from Underground." In *Existentialism from Dostoevsky to Sartre*. ed. Walter Kaufmann. New York: New American Library, 1975.

Downes, Larry, and Chunka Mui. *Unleashing the Killer App*. Boston: Harvard Business School Press, 1998.

Flavius Vegetius Renatus. *The Military Institutions of the Romans*, ed. by Wilhelm Leeb, Thomas R. Phillips, Hugo Friedrich Philipp Johann Freytag-Loringhoven, and Waldemar Erfurth. Mechanicsburg: Stackpole Books, 1985.

Friedman, Thomas L. *The Lexus and the Olive Tree*. New York: Anchor Books, 1999.

———. *The World Is Flat*. New York: Farrar, Straus and Giroux, 2005.

Galula, David. *Counterinsurgency Warfare: Theory and Practice*. Westport: Praeger Security International, 1964.

Gladwell, Malcolm. *Blink: The Power of Thinking Without Thinking*. New York: Little, Brown and Company, 2005.

———. *The Tipping Point: How Little Things Can Make a Big Difference*. New York: Little, Brown and Company, 2000.

Gleick, James. *Chaos: Making a New Science*. New York: Penguin Books, 1987.

Goya, Francisco. *The Sleep of Reason Produces Monsters*. Los Caprichos Plate 43, c. 1796–1797, Petit Palais, Paris, France. March 15, 2008.

Hall, Wayne M. *Stray Voltage: War in the Information Age*. Annapolis: Naval Institute Press, 2003.

Harris, Lee. *The Suicide of Reason*. New York: Basic Books, 2007.

Hart, B. H. Liddell. *Strategy*. New York: Henry Holt & Company Inc., 1954.

Hemingway, Ernest. *For Whom the Bell Tolls*. New York: Scribner, 2003.

Herrington, Stuart A. *Stalking the VietCong*. New York: Ballantine Books, 1982.

Hesse, Hermann. *Siddhartha*. New York: MJF Books, 1951.

Heuer, Richards J., Jr., *The Psychology of Intelligence Analysis*. Washington: US Government Printing Office, 1999.

Holland, John H. *Hidden Order*. New York: Helix Books, 1995.

James, William. *Psychology*. ed. G. Allport. New York: Harper & Brothers, 1961.

Kitson, Frank. *Low-Intensity Conflict: Subversion, Insurgency, and Peacekeeping*. St. Petersburg: Hailer Publishing, 2007 reprint.

Klein, Gary. *Sources of Power: How People Make Decisions*. Cambridge: The MIT Press, 1999.

Kelly, Kevin. *Out of Control*. Reading: Perseus Books, 1994.

Kurzweil, Ray. *The Age of Spiritual Machines*. New York: The Penguin Group, 1999.

Lawrence, T.E. *Seven Pillars of Wisdom*. New York: Anchor Books, 1991.

Levitt, Steven D., and Stephen J. Dubner. *Freakonomics*. New York: HarperCollins Books, 2005.

Lewin, Roger. *Complexity: Life at the Edge of Chaos*. New York: Collier Books, 1992.

Lewis, Bernard. *Islam and the West*. New York: Oxford University Press, 1999.

MacIssac, David. "Voices from the Central Blue: The Air Power Theorists." In *Makers of Modern Strategy from Machiavelli to the Nuclear Age*. ed. Peter Paret. Princeton: Princeton University Press, 1986.

Mao Tse-tung. *On Guerrilla Warfare*. Translated by Samuel B. Griffith II. Urbana: University of Illinois Press, 1961.

Misner, Charles W., Kip S. Thorne, and John Archibald Wheeler. *Gravitation*. San Francisco: W. H. Freeman, 1973.

Myers, David G. *Exploring Psychology*. 5th ed. New York: Worth, 2003.

Patai, Raphael. *The Arab Mind*. New York: Hatherleigh Press, 2002.

Sageman, Marc. *Understanding Terror Networks*. Philadelphia: University of Pennsylvania Press, 2004.

Shakespeare, William. *Macbeth*. Danbury: Grolier Enterprises Corp., 1980.

Slim, William. *Defeat into Victory*. New York: Cooper Square Press, 2000.

Sun Tzu. *The Art of War*. Translated and edited by Samuel B. Griffith. London: Oxford University Press, 1971.

Talbot, Michael. *The Holographic Universe*. New York: HarperPerennial, 1991.

Trinquier, Roger. *Modern Warfare: A French View of Counterinsurgency*. Westport: Praeger Security International, 2006.

Waldrop, M. Mitchell. *Complexity: The Emerging Science at the Edge of Order and Chaos*. New York: Touchstone Books, 1992.

Webster's II New Riverside University Dictionary. Boston: Houghton Mifflin, 1984.

Zukav, Gary. *The Dancing Wu Li Masters*. Toronto, Bantam Books, 1979.

GOVERNMENT DOCUMENTS AND WEB SITES

Department of Defense, *DoD Dictionary of Military and Associated Terms*, October 2007, www.dtic.mil/doctrine/jel/doddict/.

Department of Defense, Joint Staff, *Joint Publication 2.0, Joint Intelligence*. Washington, D.C.: U. S. Department of Defense, Joint Publication 2.0, 2007.

U.S. Army, *FM 3-24/MCWP 3-33.5*, Counterinsurgency. Washington, DC: Head-quarters, Department of the Army, December 2006.

———, *FM 3.0*, Operations. Washington, D.C.: Headquarters, Department of the Army, February 2008.

JOURNAL ARTICLES

Brobjer, Thomas H. "Nietzsche's Affirmative Morality: An Ethics of Virtue." *The Journal of Nietzsche Studies* (26; Autumn 2003): 64–78.

Deretic, Vojo, and Daniel J. Klionsky. "How Cells Clean House." *Scientific American* (May 2008): 74.

Goetz, Thomas. "Finding Normal." *Wired* (May 2008): 023–024.

Grau, Lester W. "Guerrillas, Terrorists, and Intelligence Analysis." *Military Review* (July–August 2004): 44.

Hall, Wayne M. "Shaping the Future: A Holistic Approach to Planning." unpub-lished paper, National War College, Washington DC, March 1992, 7.

Petraeus, David H. "Learning Counterinsurgency: Observations from Soldiering in Iraq." *Military Review* (January–February 2006): 8.

Schneider, James. "T. E. Lawrence and the Mind of an Insurgent." *Army* (July 2005): 31–37.

Tomes, Robert R. "Relearning Counterinsurgency Warfare" *Parameters* (Spring 2004): 23.

INTERNET SOURCES

The American Heritage Dictionary of the English Language, 4th Edition, 2006. "Context." dictionary.reference.com/browse/context.

———. "Dialectic." dictionary.reference.com/browse/dialectic.

———. "Mores." dictionary.reference.com/browse/mores.

———. "Periodicity." dictionary.reference.com/browse/periodicity.

———. "Philosophy." dictionary.reference.com/browse/philosophy.

———. "Proprioception." dictionary.reference.com/browse/proprioception.

———. "Synergy." dictionary.reference.com/browse/synergy.

The American Heritage Science Dictionary. Houghton Mifflin Company. 28 May. 2007.

Dictionary.com, v 1.1., 2008. "Act." dictionary.reference.com/browse/act.

———. "Ad hominem." dictionary.reference.com/browse/ad hominem.

———. "Aggregate." dictionary.reference.com/browse/aggregate.

———. "Anticipate." dictionary.reference.com/browse/anticipate.

———. "Baseline." dictionary.refrence.com/browse/baseline.

———. "Culture." dictionary.reference.com/browse/culture.

———. "Data." dictionary.reference.com/browse/data.

———. "Disambiguate." dictionary.reference.com/browse/disambiguate.

———. "Expectation." dictionary.reference.com/browse/expectation.

———. "Hunch." dictionary.reference.com/browse/hunch.

———. "Hypothesis." dictionary.reference.com/browse/hypothesis.

———. "Ignis fatuus." dictionary.reference.com/browse/ignis fatuus.

———. "Information." dictionary.reference.com/browse/information.

———. "Link." dictionary.reference.com/browse/link.

———. "Mystery." dictionary.reference.com/browse/mystery.

———. "Non sequitur." dictionary.reference.com/browse/non sequitur.

———. "Oversimplification." dictionary.reference.com/browse/oversimplification.

———. "Predict." dictionary.reference.com/browse/predict.

———. "Proposition." dictionary.reference.com/browse/proposition.

———. "Reductionism." http://dictionary.reference.com/browse/reductionism.

———. "Symbiosis." dictionary.reference.com/browse/symbiosis.

———. "Synthesis." dictionary.reference.com/browse/synthesis.

Webster's New Millennium Dictionary of English, Preview Edition (v0.9.7), 2008. "Circular reasoning." dictionary.reference.com/browse/circular reasoning.

Webster's Revised Unabridged Dictionary, 2007. "Axiom." dictionary.reference .com/browse/axiom.

Wikipedia, "Complex adaptive system." http://en.wikipedia.org/wiki/Complex _adaptive_system.

———. "False dilemma," http://en.wikipedia.org/wiki/False_dilemma.

———. "Nonlinearity." http://en.wikipedia.org/wiki/nonlinearity.

———. "Post_hoc_ergo_propter_hoc." en.wikipedia.org/wiki/Post_hoc_ergo_propter _hoc.

WordNet 3.0., 2008, "Disambiguation." dictionary.reference.com/browse/ disambiguation.

———. "Holism." dictionary.reference.com/browse/holism.

———. "Interact." dictionary.reference.com/browse/interact.

———. "Xenophobic." dictionary.reference.com/browse/xenophobic.

Index

About the Authors

WAYNE MICHAEL "MIKE" HALL, Brigadier General, U.S. Army, Retired, is a career intelligence officer. Currently president and CEO of Hall Consulting Services, Inc., he works with the military and private corporations providing consulting services in intelligence related matters. The author holds a BS from the University of Nebraska; a MS from Kansas State University; a MMAS from the U.S. Army CGSC; and a Doctorate from George Washington University. Brigadier General Hall attended Command and General Staff College (CGSC), School of Advanced Military Studies (SAMS), and the National War College. The author's first book, *Stray Voltage: War in the Information Age*, was published in April 2003. He is currently writing a book on advanced collection to support irregular warfare.

GARY CITRENBAUM, Ph.D., is President and Chief Scientist of System of Systems Analytics Inc., a small business that provides engineering and analytical services to DoD and the Intelligence Community. He has been conducting security-related analysis and designing analysis processes and tools for over 35 years.